A PLEA FOR LIBERTY

If every action which is good or evil in man at ripe years were to be under pittance, prescription, and compulsion, what were virtue but a name, what praise could be then due to well doing, what gramercy to be sober, just, or continent? . . .
They are not skilful considerers of human things who imagine to remove sin, by removing the matter of sin; . . . Suppose we could expel sin by this means; look how much we thus expel of sin, so much we expel of virtue: for the matter of them both is the same: remove that, and ye remove them both alike.

MILTON, *Areopagitica*: A Speech for the Liberty of Unlicensed Printing

A PLEA FOR LIBERTY

AN ARGUMENT AGAINST SOCIALISM AND SOCIALISTIC LEGISLATION

CONSISTING OF AN INTRODUCTION BY
HERBERT SPENCER
AND ESSAYS BY VARIOUS WRITERS

Edited by Thomas Mackay

LibertyClassics

INDIANAPOLIS

LibertyClassics is a publishing imprint of Liberty Fund, Inc., a foundation established to encourage study of the ideal of a society of free and responsible individuals.

The cuneiform inscription that serves as the design motif for our endpapers is the earliest known written appearance of the word "freedom" (ama-gi), or liberty. It is taken from a clay document written about 2300 B.C. in the Sumerian city-state of Lagash.

This LibertyClassics reprint is based on the one published in 1891 in New York by D. Appleton & Company.

Library of Congress Cataloging in Publication Data
Main entry under title:

A Plea for liberty.

   Reprint. Originally published: New York: D. Appleton, 1891.
With a new foreword by Jeffrey Paul and a new index.
   Includes index.
   Contents: The impracticability of socialism / by Edward Stanley Robertson—The limits of liberty / by Wordsworth Donisthorpe—Liberty for labour / by George Howell—[etc.]
   1. Socialism—Great Britain—Addresses, essays, lectures.   2. Socialism—Addresses, essays, lectures.   3. Liberty—Addresses, essays, lectures.
   I. Mackay, Thomas, 1849–1912.

HX246.P553   1981   335'.00941   81–80950
ISBN 0–913966–95–9   AACR2
ISBN 0–913966–96–7 (pbk.)

10 9 8 7 6 5 4 3 2 1

CONTENTS

FOREWORD

The latter third of the nineteenth century in England was a period of advancing government intervention. With growing alarm, Whigs and Tories observed the adoption of measures which served to circumscribe the rights of contract and property. Moreover, the extension of the franchise begun in 1867 slowly transferred effective control of the Parliament from aristocratic and commercial hands into those of the middle and working classes. The newly eclectic electorate could not be stimulated to express the kind of opposition to interventionist proposals which disposed of the Corn Laws in 1846.

If liberalism was to survive in this altered electoral environment it must persuade the masses of its benefactions and refute the claims of its enemies. In 1882 the Liberty and Property Defense League was formed to do just that. In 1891 it published the collection of essays which was to become its manifesto under the title, *A Plea for Liberty*.

1

The initial event that precipitated the League's founding was the passage of the Irish Land Act of 1881. Its provisions included the infamous "three F's"—fair rent, free sale, and fixed tenure. It provided for "fair" rents to be determined by specially established land courts. These rents were binding upon both parties for fifteen years. The Act additionally guaranteed fixed tenure for all who paid rents and most significantly, it permitted the unrestricted sale by the tenant of the remainder of his lease to a successor of his own choosing. Not surprisingly, the landed classes of England were appalled at this trampling of contractual freedoms and property rights. Furthermore, Radicals like Joseph Chamberlin seemed favorably disposed to a similar treatment of English landlords. Even Bright had criticized aristocratic land holdings. Feeling betrayed by Gladstone and his Liberal cohorts, the landowners had their insecurities instantly multiplied by the appearance in England of Mr. Henry George to preach his doctrine of land nationalization, and they began to cast about for a defender against possible further Parliamentary transgressions.

Industrialists were similarly distressed at the turn of events under Gladstone's administration. However, the particular object of their antipathy was the proposed Employers' Liability Act Amendment Bill.[1] This bill would have amended the Employers' Liability Act of 1880, which

---

[1] Norbert C. Soldon, *Laissez-Faire on the Defensive: The Story of the Liberty and Property Defence League, 1882–1914* (unpublished Ph.D. dissertation, 1969), p. 195.

provided for compensation to injured workmen when negligence on the part of their employer could be proven, by prohibiting persons from contracting out of the Act. Employers who had provided their workers with insurance against work accidents in exchange for their agreement to waive all claims against the employer were outraged by this prospective constriction of their contractual freedoms.

Philosophical individualists joined the commercial and landed interests in their repudiation of Gladstone's Liberal government. Herbert Spencer bemoaned the transformation of the Liberal Party into what he was disparagingly to call the "New Toryism," and Auberon Herbert was similarly critical. Even prior to Gladstone's second administration the individualists had begun to organize an opposition to state intervention. Wordsworth Donisthorpe had formed the State Resistance Union[2] to warn against the dangers of a variety of socialist palliatives and J. H. Levy had founded the anti-interventionist Personal Rights Defense Association in 1871 initially to oppose the Contagious Disease Acts.[3] In addition, Auberon Herbert had created the Personal Rights and Self-Help Association in 1877 in order "(1) to protect and enlarge personal liberty and personal rights, (2) to oppose the multiplication of laws and the tendency to control and direct, through Parliament, the affairs of the people."[4]

---

[2] Ibid., pp. 110–111.

[3] Ibid., p. 112.

[4] S. Hutchinson Harris, *Auberon Herbert: Crusader for Liberty* (London: Williams and Northgate, Ltd., 1943), p. 189.

In 1882 these three elements in the opposition to the new Liberal interventionism, the philosophical individualists, the landed interests and their commercial counterparts combined to launch what was to be the principal bulwark of economic liberalism for the next three decades, the Liberty and Property Defense League.

2

The founder of the League was the Earl of Wemyss, a self-described liberal conservative and landowner whose consternation over Gladstone's "betrayals" led him to combine with Wordsworth Donisthorpe to expand the scope and size of the State Resistance Union and to give it its new, less inflammatory name. Wemyss was to be its chairman until his death in 1914.

Francis Wemyss-Charteris-Douglas, tenth Earl of Wemyss, was a vigorous man whose life spanned almost an entire century, 1818 to 1914. Educated at Oxford, Wemyss entered the House of Commons as a Conservative in 1841. Except for a brief and involuntary respite in 1846–1847, he served there continuously until 1883 when he was called to the House of Lords. Originally a proponent of protectionism, he became a convert to free trade soon after taking his seat in the Commons and supported the repeal of the Corn Laws. His influence in the Commons reached its peak when he supported the Reform Act of 1867, believing that the limited suffrage provided for in that bill was preferable to the universal franchise demanded by the Reform League.[5] In 1867 he also carried

---

[5] Ibid., p. 68.

through Parliament a bill which ameliorated the effects of the Master and Servant Laws, changing the sanctions imposed upon workingmen for breaches of employment contracts from criminal to civil ones. In labor legislation, generally his views tended to be those of a classical liberal. He came to oppose laws restricting combination and preventing picketing, while resisting attempts to transform unions into coercive associations. Often he described himself as a liberal concerning civil and economic liberties and conservative on constitutional questions.

The accumulated Parliamentary intrusions on property rights during the 1870s led Wemyss to write two letters which inspired the actions leading to the constitution of the League. In 1880 Wemyss wrote a letter to the *St. James Gazette* which recommended the formation of a group that would transcend party affiliation and would forge a defense against governmental attacks upon contractual rights and personal liberties. Wordsworth Donisthorpe and William Carr Crofts were so moved by it that they formed the State Resistance Union to carry out its program.[6] Wemyss's second letter which was printed by the *Pall Mall Gazette*[7] impelled Donisthorpe and Crofts to expand the scope of the Union. A provisional committee was established to supervise this expansion, meeting at Wemyss's house on May 19, 1881. Wemyss explicitly identified its cause with the liberal tradition of Smith, Mill, Cobden, Spencer, Humboldt and Bastiat, and emphasizing the superiority of voluntary social arrangements to governmental regulation.

---

[6] Ibid., p. 107.

[7] Ibid., p. 114.

3

The League was a synthesis of two functions. It was at once a commercial lobby and a vehicle for expounding economic liberalism. Thus its membership included, on the one hand, commercial associations like the Iron Trades Employers' Association, the General Shipowner's Society, the Bradford Property Owners' Association, and the Licensed Victuallers' Protection Society. On the other hand, it included intellectuals and academics like social philosophers W. H. Mallock and Wordsworth Donisthorpe and, among its foreign affiliates, economists Vilfredo Pareto and Arthur Raffalovich.

Its dichotomous purpose led it to engage both in parliamentary lobbying and in educational pamphleteering and debating. Thus, it opposed a succession of bills which aimed at restricting the hours during which retail shops could conduct business, bills aimed at regulating unsanitary and overcrowded conditions in the cottages of Scottish farm servants, and bills which provided for public works during a depression. In the 1890s it directed its attention to the problems of "municipal socialism" and to an increasingly militant and coercive trade unionism. In all of these endeavors the League sustained some level of activity until the outbreak of World War I, slowly diminishing its efforts until its demise in 1933.

4

During its existence the League included a number of distinguished writers, businessmen, and legislators among its members. One of its most famous Parliamentarians was Lord Fortescue who served in both Houses and was a prolific writer, and a determined opponent of "free," i.e., tax defrayed, education. Sir William Lewis, the coal baron, was a particularly energetic member of the League. His mines were productive and famous for the machinery employed in them. Lewis, who had striven for labor-management harmony in the 1870s and 1880s, became a strident opponent of the New Unionism in the 1890s. The League member who attained the greatest success in his relations with labor was George Livesey, Chairman of the Board of the South Metropolitan Gas Company. Livesey inaugurated a profit sharing scheme which elicited the admiration and gratitude of his employees and achieved for his company the kind of congenial labor relations which were the envy of other businesses.

Of the League's intellectuals and publicists three stand clearly above the rest. Wordsworth Donisthorpe, cofounder of both the League and its predecessor, was brilliant, volatile and eccentric. Calling himself a philosophical anarchist, Donisthorpe repeatedly defended controversial positions which created friction between himself and other League members, leading to his resignation from its Council in 1887. As a legal positivist and follower of Hobbes he eschewed a natural rights defense of liberty, preferring to rest his case for it on evolutionary grounds. His works included *Overlegislation*, *Individualism*, and *Law in a Free State*.

Frederick Millar was the League's most prolific pamphleteer, and the editor of its unofficial journal, *Liberty Review*. In addition, he was Wemyss's "second-in-command," acting as the League's secretary until the former's death in 1914. He sustained the League thereafter until his own death in 1933.

Superior to either of these in intellect and ability was the author, William Hurrell Mallock. A graduate of Balliol College, Oxford where he was deeply affected by the thought of John Ruskin, Mallock acquired instant fame with the publication in 1877 of his *New Republic*, a book patterned after the Platonic dialogue. After the publication of several works on religious themes, Mallock became absorbed in questions of political economy and social philosophy. His interest derived from the increasing influence that egalitarian doctrines were having upon the educated classes and his concern that these were not being refuted. In 1882 he published *Social Equality*, a work in which he tried to demonstrate that inequality of circumstance is a *sine qua non* of the production of wealth. Later he published a more sophisticated version of the same doctrine, *Labour and the Popular Welfare*. His *Aristocracy and Evolution* defended the proposition that evolution tended to improve the elite stratas in society whose achievements are required to advance human welfare. In 1906 he toured the United States lecturing on the evils of socialism before university audiences at Columbia, Harvard, the Universities of Chicago and Pennsylvania, and Johns Hopkins. His addresses were later collected in a book called *A Critical Examination of Socialism*.

Mallock spoke for the League's Tory wing, preferring to think of himself always as an expositor of Conservative philosophy. His contribution to Conservative theory has been a major influence upon many twentieth century American Conservative intellectuals like Russell Kirk.

5

Unfortunately, Mallock was not a contributor to the volume which served as the League's manifesto, *A Plea for Liberty*, which was organized as the individualist response to the *Fabian Essays in Socialism* of 1889. The man nominated by the League to edit its manifesto was the prolific writer and staunch laissez-fairest Thomas Mackay.

Mackay was a successful wine merchant who had been educated at New College, Oxford and who retired from business in 1885 at the age of thirty-six in order to devote himself to the study of political and economic problems. He was an incisive critic of the English Poor Laws, seeing in them a subsidy for idleness and complacency. His *History of the English Poor Law from 1834 to the Present Time* details his attitudes on the subject. Mackay was especially concerned to find alternatives to the public dole for society's impoverished citizens.[8] One of his schemes was to have London subdivided into smaller units so as to simulate in each of these the ambience of a country village and thereby inculcate in their poor the rustic values of self-reliance and industry. His writings reflect the wide-ranging character of his economic and social interests and include: *Methods of Social Reform*, the *State and Charity*, *An Apology for Liberty*, and *Dangers of Democracy*.

---

[8] Ibid., p. 277.

Mackay followed *A Plea for Liberty* with a second collection of essays which he published in 1894 under the title *A Policy of Free Exchange.*

The first of the two volumes brought together a group of writers, several of whom had only informal connections with the League. Wemyss, who was not himself a contributor, prevailed upon one of these, Herbert Spencer, to write an introduction for the book. Perhaps the latter was moved to do so by the chiding given to him and the League by Sidney Webb:

> . . . No member of Parliament has so much as introduced a Bill to give effect to the anarchist principle of Mr. Herbert Spencer's *Man Versus The State.* The not disinterested efforts of the Liberty and Property Defense League fail to hinder even Conservative Parliaments from further socialist legislation.[9]

Spencer, of course, had supported the League both spiritually and financially since its inception but had refused formal membership in it because:

> I think it would be politic neither for the League nor for myself that I should join it. Rightly or wrongly it has acquired the repute of a Tory organization.[10]

The volume was concluded with an essay by Auberon Herbert, in many ways Spencer's intellectual heir, who also chose to forego any formal connection with the League. His refusal to do so is understandable in one so

---

[9] G. Bernard Shaw, ed., *Fabian Essays in Socialism* (Garden City, New York: Doubleday and Co., Inc., 1899), pp. 72–73.

[10] David Duncan, *Life and Letters of Herbert Spencer,* Vol. I (New York: D. Appleton and Co., 1908), p. 323.

doctrinaire. As the most uncompromising of the English individualists and libertarians, he felt that the League had been so zealous in its defense of property that it had given inadequate attention to questions of personal liberty.

6

The publication of *A Plea for Liberty* was the overture of the League's most frenzied decade during which it fought numerous Parliamentary battles frequently preventing the passage of interventionist bills. It effectively opposed the use of union violence to halt industrial production during strikes, by enlisting private police when municipal authorities were reticent to exercise their powers. It injected itself furiously into the Parliamentary campaign of 1895, warning the electorate against interventionist candidates from both parties.

By the turn of the century, however, its activity and influence began to wane; on the eve of the First World War it had become virtually moribund. And yet it lingered, finally dying a quiet death amidst the Great Depression.

Jeffrey Paul
Bowling Green State University

PREFACE

The essays contained in the present volume have a common purpose, which is sufficiently indicated on the title page. The various writers, however, approach the subject from different points of view, and are responsible for their own contributions and for nothing else.

As will be readily seen from a glance at the table of contents, no attempt has been made to present a complete survey of the controversy between Socialists and their opponents. To do this, many volumes would have been necessary. The vast extent of the questions involved in this controversy will explain the exclusion of some familiar subjects of importance, and the inclusion of others which, if less important, have still a bearing on the general argument. All discussion of the Poor Law, for instance, the most notable of our socialistic institutions, and its disastrous influence on the lives of the poor, has been omitted. The subject has often been dealt with, and the arguments are familiar to all educated readers. It seemed superfluous to include a reference to it in the present volume.

The introduction and the first and second articles deal with theoretical aspects of the question. The papers which follow may be described as illustrative. Mr. Howell traces the gradual advance of the working-class on the path of liberty. Mr. Fairfield and Mr. Vincent describe socialistic influences at work in an English colony and in the London streets. Mr. Mackay's paper is an endeavour to point out the disadvantage of monopoly, and the advantage of giving to free investment the largest possible sphere of action. The objections to 'Free' Education are very briefly set out by Mr. Alford, who takes a practical view of the subject, and declines to discuss the larger question of compulsory education as being for the moment at any rate beyond the range of practical politics. M. Arthur Raffalovich may be introduced to English readers as one of the secretaries of the *Société d'Études Économiques* recently founded in Paris, a frequent contributor to the *Journal des Économistes,* and author of an excellent work, *Le logement de l'ouvrier et du pauvre.* His article deals historically and from the cosmopolitan point of view with the question of the Housing of the Poor. The difficulty, he argues, is being overcome gradually, in the same way as other difficulties in the path of human progress have been overcome, by the solvent power of free human initiative. The Post Office is often quoted by persons of Socialist proclivities as an example of the successful organisation of labour by the State. Mr. Millar's paper points out that this department has not escaped from defects inherent in all State-trading enterprises. These are tolerable when they exist in a service comparatively simple and unimportant like the Post Office, but if Government monopoly were extended to more important and complicated industries, the inherent incapacity of compulsory collectivism would, it is argued, play havoc with human progress. The attempt of Free Liberty agitators to make their own favourite form of recreation a charge on the rates is criticised by Mr. O'Brien as unjust to those who love other forms of amusement and generally as contrary to public policy. Mr. Gordon, writing from the point of view of his profession, explains how the business of the electrical engineer has been let and hindered by the ill-considered, but no doubt well-intentioned, interference of the State. Mr. Auberon Herbert's paper contains a criticism on the present attitudes of Trade Unionism, and purposes for the consideration of working-class associations a new policy of usefulness.

It will be seen from the foregoing epitome of the volume that some of the illustrations chosen are in themselves of comparatively small importance. But the great danger in this matter lies in the fact that 'plain men' do not appreciate the enormous cumulative effects of these many small infractions of sound principle. They do not seem to realise that all this legislation means the gradual and insidious advance of a dull and enervating pauperism. The terrible tale of the degradation of manhood caused by the old poor law, was unfolded to the country in the judicial language of the Poor Law Commissioners. A similar burden of impotency is being day by day laid on all classes, but more especially on our poorer classes, by the perpetual forestalling of honest human endeavour in every conceivable relation of life. While this weakening of the fibre of character is going on, the burden of responsibility to be carried by

the State grows every day heavier. The difficulty of returning even a portion of this burden to the healthful influence
of private enterprise and initiative is always increasing.

If men will grant for a moment, and for the sake of argument, that, as some insist, our compulsory rate-supported
system of education is wrong; that it is injurious to the
domestic life of the poor; that it reduces the teacher to
the position of an automaton; that it provides a quality
of teaching utterly unsuited to the wants of a labouring
population which certainly requires some form of technical
training; that, here, it is brought face to face with its own
incompetence, for some of the highest practical authorities
declare that the technical education given in schools is a
farce; that therefore it bars the way to all free arrangements between parents and employers, and to the only system of technical education which deserves the name; if
this or even a part of it is true, if at best our educational
system is a make-shift not altogether intolerable, how terrible are the difficulties to be overcome before we can re-
trace our steps and foster into vigorous life a new system,
whose early beginnings have been repressed and strangled
by the overgrowth of Government monopoly.

Those who still have an open mind should consider carefully this aspect of the question. Each addition to the responsibility of the State adds to the list of ill-contrived
solutions of difficulty, and to the enlargement of the sphere
of a stereotyped regimentation of human life. Inseparable
from this obnoxious growth is the repression of private
experiment and of the energy and inventiveness of human
character. Instead thereof human character is degraded to

a parasitic dependence on the assistance of the State, which after all proves to be but a broken reed.

If the view set out in this volume is at all correct, it is very necessary that men should abandon the policy of indifference, and that they should do something to enlarge the atmosphere of Liberty. This is to be accomplished not by reckless and revolutionary methods, but rather by a resolute resistance to new encroachments and by patient and statesmanlike endeavour to remove wherever practicable the restraints of regulation, and to give full play over a larger area to the creative forces of Liberty, for Liberty is the condition precedent to all solution of human difficulty.

T. M.

SYNOPSIS OF CONTENTS

INTRODUCTION
FROM FREEDOM TO BONDAGE

1. THE IMPRACTICABILITY OF SOCIALISM

2. The Limits of Liberty

3. LIBERTY FOR LABOUR

4. State Socialism in the Antipodes

5. Working-Class Discontent

6. Investment

7. FREE EDUCATION

8. THE HOUSING OF THE WORKING-CLASSES AND THE POOR

9. The Evils of State Trading as illustrated by the Post Office

10. FREE LIBRARIES

11. THE STATE AND ELECTRICAL DISTRIBUTION

12. The True Line of Deliverance

INTRODUCTION

FROM FREEDOM TO BONDAGE

HERBERT SPENCER

INTRODUCTION

FROM FREEDOM TO BONDAGE

Of the many ways in which common sense inferences about social affairs are flatly contradicted by events (as when measures taken to suppress a book cause increased circulation of it, or as when attempts to prevent usurious rates of interest make the terms harder for the borrower, or as when there is greater difficulty in getting things at the places of production than elsewhere) one of the most curious is the way in which the more things improve the louder become the exclamations about their badness.

In days when the people were without any political power, their subjection was rarely complained of; but after free institutions had so far advanced in England that our political arrangements were envied by continental peoples, the denunciations of aristocratic rule grew gradually stronger, until there came a great widening of the franchise, soon followed by complaints that things were going wrong for want of still further widening. If we trace up the treatment of women from the days of savagedom, when they bore all the burdens and after the men had eaten received such food as remained, up through the middle ages when they served the men at their meals, to our own day when throughout our social arrangements the claims of women are always put first, we see that along with the worst treatment there went the least apparent consciousness that the treatment was bad; while now that they are better treated than ever before, the proclaiming of their grievances daily strengthens: the loudest outcries coming from 'the paradise of women,' America. A century ago, when scarcely a man could be found who was not occasionally intoxicated, and when inability to take one or two bottles of wine brought contempt, no agitation arose against the vice of drunkenness; but now that, in the course of fifty years, the voluntary efforts of temperance societies, joined with more general causes, have produced comparative sobriety, there are vociferous demands for laws to prevent the ruinous effects of the liquor traffic. Similarly again with education. A few generations back, ability to read and write was practically limited to the upper and middle classes, and the suggestion that the rudiments of culture should be given to labourers was never made, or, if made, ridiculed; but when, in the days of our grandfathers, the Sunday-school system, initiated by a few philanthropists, began to spread and was followed by the establishment of day-schools, with the result that among the masses those who could read and write were no longer the exceptions, and the demand for cheap literature rapidly increased, there began the cry that the people were perishing for lack of knowledge, and that the State must not simply educate them but must force education upon them.

And so it is, too with the general state of the population in respect of food, clothing, shelter, and the appliances of life. Leaving out of the comparison only barbaric states, there has been a conspicuous progress from the time when most rustics lived on barley bread, rye bread, and oatmeal, down to our own time when the consumption of white wheaten bread is universal—from the days when coarse jackets reaching to the knees left the legs bare, down to the present day when labouring people, like their employers, have the whole body covered, by two or more layers of clothing—from the old era of single-roomed huts without chimneys, or from the 15th century when even an ordinary gentleman's house was commonly without wainscot or plaster on its walls, down to the present century when every cottage has more rooms than one and the houses of artisans usually have several, while all have fireplaces, chimneys, and glazed windows, accompanied mostly by paper-hangings and painted doors; there has been, I say, a conspicuous progress in the condition of the people. And this progress has been still more marked within our own time. Any one who can look back sixty years, when the amount of pauperism was far greater than now and beggars abundant, is struck by the comparative size and finish of the new houses occupied by operatives— by the better dress of workmen, who wear broadcloth on Sundays, and that of servant girls, who vie with their mistresses—by the higher standard of living which leads to a great demand for the best qualities of food by working people: all results of the double change to higher wages

and cheaper commodities, and a distribution of taxes which
has relieved the lower classes at the expense of the upper
classes. He is struck, too, by the contrast between the small
space which popular welfare then occupied in public attention, and the large space it now occupies, with the result
that outside and inside Parliament, plans to benefit the
millions form the leading topics, and everyone having
means is expected to join in some philanthropic effort. Yet
while elevation, mental and physical, of the masses is going
on far more rapidly than ever before—while the lowering
of the death-rate proves that the average life is less trying,
there swells louder and louder the cry that the evils are so
great that nothing short of a social revolution can cure
them. In presence of obvious improvements, joined with
that increase of longevity which even alone yields conclusive proof of general amelioration, it is proclaimed, with
increasing vehemence, that things are so bad that society
must be pulled to pieces and re-organised on another plan,
In this case, then, as in the previous cases instanced, in
proportion as the evil decreases the denunciation of it increases; and as fast as natural causes are shown to be
powerful there grows up the belief that they are powerless.

Not that the evils to be remedied are small. Let no one
suppose that, by emphasizing the above paradox, I wish to
make light of the sufferings which most men have to bear.
The fates of the great majority have ever been, and doubtless still are, so sad that it is painful to think of them. Unquestionably the existing type of social organisation is one
which none who care for their kind can contemplate with
satisfaction; and unquestionably men's activities accompanying this type are far from being admirable. The strong

divisions of rank and the immense inequalities of means, are at variance with that ideal of human relations on which the sympathetic imagination likes to dwell; and the average conduct, under the pressure and excitement of social life as at present carried on, is in sundry respects repulsive. Though the many who revile competition strangely ignore the enormous benefits resulting from it—though they forget that most of all the appliances and products distinguishing civilisation from savagery, and making possible the maintenance of a large population on a small area, have been developed by the struggle for existence—though they disregard the fact that while every man, as producer, suffers from the under-bidding of competitors, yet, as consumer, he is immensely advantaged by the cheapening of all he has to buy—though they persist in dwelling on the evils of competition and saying nothing of its benefits; yet it is not to be denied that the evils are great, and form a large set-off from the benefits. The system under which we at present live fosters dishonesty and lying. It prompts adulterations of countless kinds; it is answerable for the cheap imitations which eventually in many cases thrust the genuine articles out of the market; it leads to the use of short weights and false measures; it introduces bribery, which vitiates most trading relations, from those of the manufacturer and buyer down to those of the shopkeeper and servant; it encourages deception to such an extent that an assistant who cannot tell a falsehood with a good face is blamed; and often it gives the conscientious trader a choice between adopting the malpractices of his competitors, or greatly injuring his creditors by bankruptcy. Moreover, the extensive frauds, common throughout the commercial

world and daily exposed in law-courts and newspapers, are
largely due to the pressure under which competition places
the higher industrial classes; and are otherwise due to that
lavish expenditure which, as implying success in the
commercial struggle, brings honour. With these minor
evils must be joined the major one, that the distribution
achieved by the system, gives to those who regulate and
superintend, a share of the total produce which bears too
large a ratio to the share it gives to the actual workers. Let
it not be thought, then, that in saying what I have said
above, that I under-estimate those vices of our competitive
systems which, thirty years ago, I described and denounced.[1] But it is not a question of absolute evils; it is a
question of relative evils—whether the evils at present suffered are or are not less than the evils which would be
suffered under another system—whether efforts for miti-
gation along the lines thus far followed are not more likely
to succeed than efforts along utterly different lines.

This is the question here to be considered. I must be ex-
cused for first of all setting forth sundry truths which are,
to some at any rate, tolerably familiar, before proceeding
to draw inferences which are not so familiar.

Speaking broadly, every man works that he may avoid
suffering. Here, remembrance of the pangs of hunger
prompts him; and there, he is prompted by the sight of the
slave-driver's lash. His immediate dread may be the punishment which physical circumstances will inflict, or may
be punishment inflicted by human agency. He must have

---

[1] See essay on 'The Morals of Trade.'

a master; but the master may be Nature or may be a fellow man. When he is under the impersonal coercion of Nature, we say that he is free; and when he is under the personal coercion of some one above him, we call him, according to the degree of his dependence, a slave, a serf, or a vassal. Of course I omit the small minority who inherit means: an incidental, and not a necessary, social element. I speak only of the vast majority, both cultured and uncultured, who maintain themselves by labour, bodily or mental, and must either exert themselves of their own unconstrained wills, prompted only by thoughts of naturally-resulting evils or benefits, or must exert themselves with constrained will, prompted by thoughts of evils and benefits artificially resulting.

Men may work together in a society under either of these two forms of control: forms which, though in many cases mingled, are essentially contrasted. Using the word co-operation in its wide sense, and not in that restricted sense now commonly given to it, we may say that social life must be carried on by either voluntary co-operation or compulsory co-operation; or, to use Sir Henry Maine's words, the system must be that of *contract* or that of *status*—that in which the individual is left to do the best he can by his spontaneous efforts and get success or failure according to his efficiency, and that in which he has his appointed place, works under coercive rule, and has his apportioned share of food, clothing, and shelter.

The system of voluntary co-operation is that by which, in civilized societies, industry is now everywhere carried on. Under a simple form we have it on every farm, where the labourers, paid by the farmer himself and taking orders directly from him, are free to stay or go as they please. And of its more complex form an example is yielded by every manufacturing concern, in which, under partners, come clerks and managers, and under these, time-keepers and over-lookers, and under these operatives of different grades. In each of these cases there is an obvious working together, or co-operation, of employer and employed, to obtain in one case a crop and in the other case a manufactured stock. And then, at the same time, there is a far more extensive, though unconscious, co-operation with other workers of all grades throughout the society. For while these particular employers and employed are severally occupied with their special kinds of work, other employers and employed are making other things needed for the carrying on of their lives as well as the lives of all others. This voluntary co-operation, from its simplest to its most complex forms, has the common trait that those concerned work together by consent. There is no one to force terms or to force acceptance. It is perfectly true that in many cases an employer may give, or an employee may accept, with reluctance: circumstances he says compel him. But what are the circumstances? In the one case there are goods ordered, or a contract entered into, which he cannot supply or execute without yielding; and in the other case he submits to a wage less than he likes because otherwise he will have no money wherewith to procure food and warmth. The general formula is not—'Do this, or I will make you'; but it is—'Do this, or leave your place and take the consequences.'

On the other hand compulsory co-operation is exemplified by an army—not so much by our own army, the service in which is under agreement for a specified period, but in a continental army, raised by conscription. Here, in time of peace the daily duties—cleaning, parade, drill, sentry work, and the rest—and in time of war the various actions of the camp and the battlefield, are done under command, without room for any exercise of choice. Up from the private soldier through the non-commissioned officers and the half-dozen or more grades of commissioned officers, the universal law is absolute obedience from the grade below to the grade above. The sphere of individual will is such only as is allowed by the will of the superior. Breaches of subordination are, according to their gravity, dealt with by deprivation of leave, extra drill, imprisonment, flogging, and, in the last resort, shooting. Instead of the understanding that there must be obedience in respect of specified duties under pain of dismissal; the understanding now is—'Obey in everything ordered under penalty of inflicted suffering and perhaps death.'

This form of co-operation, still exemplified in an army, has in days gone by been the form of co-operation throughout the civil population. Everywhere, and at all times, chronic war generates a militant type of structure, not in the body of soldiers only but throughout the community at large. Practically, while the conflict between societies is actively going on, and fighting is regarded as the only manly occupation, the society is the quiescent army and the army the mobilized society: that part which does not take part in battle, composed of slaves, serfs, women, etc., constituting the commissariat. Naturally, therefore, throughout the mass of inferior individuals constituting the commissariat, there is maintained a system of discipline identical in nature if less elaborate. The fighting body being, under such conditions, the ruling body, and the rest of the community being incapable of resistance, those who control the fighting body will, of course, impose their control upon the non-fighting body; and the *régime* of coercion will be applied to it with such modifications only as the different circumstances involve. Prisoners of war become slaves. Those who were free cultivators before the conquest of their country, become serfs attached to the soil. Petty chiefs become subject to superior chiefs; these smaller lords become vassals to over-lords; and so on up to the highest: the social ranks and powers being of like essential nature with the ranks and powers throughout the military organisation. And while for the slaves compulsory co-operation is the unqualified system, a co-operation which is in part compulsory is the system that pervades all grades above. Each man's oath of fealty to his suzerain takes the form—'I am your man.'

Throughout Europe, and especially in our own country, this system of compulsory co-operation gradually relaxed in rigour, while the system of voluntary co-operation step by step replaced it. As fast as war ceased to be the business of life, the social structure produced by war and appropriate to it, slowly became qualified by the social structure produced by industrial life and appropriate to it. In proportion as a decreasing part of the community was devoted to offensive and defensive activities, an increasing part became devoted to production and distribution. Growing more numerous, more powerful, and taking refuge in towns where it was less under the power of the militant class, this industrial population carried on its life under the system of voluntary co-operation. Though municipal governments and guild-regulations, partially pervaded by ideas and usages derived from the militant type of society, were in some degree coercive; yet production and distribution were in the main carried on under agreement—alike between buyers and sellers, and between masters and workmen. As fast as these social relations and forms of activity became dominant in urban populations, they influenced the whole community: compulsory co-operation lapsed more and more, through money commutation for services, military and civil; while divisions of rank became less rigid and class-power diminished. Until at length, restraints exercised by incorporated trades have fallen into desuetude, as well as the rule of rank over rank, voluntary co-operation became the universal principle. Purchase and sale became the law for all kinds of services as well as for all kinds of commodities.

The restlessness generated by pressure against the conditions of existence, perpetually prompts the desire to try a new position. Everyone knows how long-continued rest in one attitude becomes wearisome—everyone has found how even the best easy chair, at first rejoiced in, becomes after many hours intolerable; and change to a hard seat, previously occupied and rejected, seems for a time to be a great relief. It is the same with incorporated humanity. Having by long struggles emancipated itself from the hard discipline of the ancient *régime*, and having discovered that the new *régime* into which it has grown, though relatively easy, is not without stresses and pains, its impatience with these prompts the wish to try another system; which other system is, in principle if not in appearance, the same as that which during past generations was escaped from with much rejoicing.

For as fast as the *régime* of contract is discarded the *régime* of status is of necessity adopted. As fast as voluntary co-operation is abandoned compulsory co-operation must be substituted. Some kind of organization labour must have; and if it is not that which arises by agreement under free competition, it must be that which is imposed by authority. Unlike in appearance and names as it may be to the old order of slaves and serfs, working under masters, who were coerced by barons, who were themselves vassals of dukes or kings, the new order wished for, constituted by workers under foremen of small groups, overlooked by superintendents, who are subject to higher local managers, who are controlled by superiors of districts, themselves under a central government, must be essentially the same in principle. In the one case, as in the other, there must be established grades, and enforced subordination of each grade to the grades above. This is a truth which the communist or the socialist does not dwell upon. Angry with the existing system under which each of us takes care of himself, while all of us see that each has fair play, he thinks how much better it would be for all of us to take care of each of us; and he refrains from thinking of the machinery by which this is to be done. Inevitably, if each is to be cared for by all, then the embodied all must get the means—the necessaries of life. What it gives to each must be taken from the accumulated contributions; and it must therefore require from each his proportion—must tell him how much he has to give to the general stock in the shape of production, that he may have so much in the shape of sustentation. Hence, before he can be provided for, he must put himself under orders, and obey those who say what he shall do, and at what hours, and where; and who give him his share of food, clothing, and shelter. If competition is excluded, and with it buying and selling, there can be no voluntary exchange of so much labour for so much produce; but there must be apportionment of the one to the other by appointed officers. This apportionment must be enforced. Without alternative the work must be done, and without alternative the benefit, whatever it may be, must be accepted. For the worker may not leave his place at will and offer himself elsewhere. Under such a system he cannot be accepted elsewhere, save by order of the authorities. And it is manifest that a standing order would forbid employment in one place of an insubordinate member from another place: the system could not be worked if the workers were severally allowed to go or come as they pleased. With corporals and sergeants under them, the captains of industry must carry out the orders of their colonels, and these of their generals, up to the council of the commander-in-chief; and obedience must be required throughout the industrial army as throughout a fighting army. 'Do your prescribed duties, and take your apportioned rations,' must be the rule of the one as of the other.

'Well, be it so'; replies the socialist. 'The workers will appoint their own officers, and these will always be subject to criticisms of the mass they regulate. Being thus in fear of public opinion, they will be sure to act judiciously and fairly; or when they do not, will be deposed by the popular vote, local or general. Where will be the grievance of being under superiors, when the superiors themselves are under democratic control?' And in this attractive vision the socialist has full belief.

Iron and brass are simpler things than flesh and blood, and dead wood than living nerve; and a machine constructed of the one works in more definite ways than an organism constructed of the other—especially when the machine is worked by the inorganic forces of steam or water, while the organism is worked by the forces of living nerve-centres. Manifestly, then, the ways in which the machine will work are much more readily calculable than the ways in which the organism will work. Yet in how few cases does the inventor foresee rightly the actions of his new apparatus! Read the patent-list, and it will be found that not more than one device in fifty turns out to be of any service. Plausible as his scheme seemed to the inventor, one or other hitch prevents the intended operation, and brings out a widely different result from that which he wished.

What, then, shall we say of these schemes which have to do not with dead matters and forces, but with complex living organisms working in ways less readily foreseen, and which involve the co-operation of multitudes of such organisms? Even the units out of which this re-arranged body politic is to be formed are often incomprehensible. Everyone is from time to time surprised by others' behaviour, and even by the deeds of relatives who are best known to him. Seeing, then, how uncertainly anyone can foresee the actions of an individual, how can he with any certainty foresee the operation of a social structure? He proceeds on the assumption that all concerned will judge rightly and act fairly—will think as they ought to think, and act as they ought to act; and he assumes this regardless of the daily experiences which show him that men do neither the one nor the other, and forgetting that the complaints he makes against the existing system show his belief to be that men have neither the wisdom nor the rectitude which his plan requires them to have.

Paper constitutions raise smiles on the faces of those who have observed their results; and paper social systems similarly affect those who have contemplated the available evidence. How little the men who wrought the French revolution and were chiefly concerned in setting up the new governmental apparatus, dreamt that one of the early actions of this apparatus would be to behead them all! How little the men who drew up the American Declaration of Independence and framed the Republic, anticipated that after some generations the legislature would lapse into the hands of wire-pullers; that its doings would turn upon the contests of office-seekers; that political action would be everywhere vitiated by the intrusion of a foreign element holding the balance between parties; that electors, instead of judging for themselves, would habitually be led to the polls in thousands by their 'bosses'; and that respectable men would be driven out of public life by the insults and slanders of professional politicians. Nor were there better previsions in those who gave constitutions to the various other states of the New World, in which unnumbered revolutions have shown with wonderful persistence the contrasts between the expected results of political sys-

tems and the achieved results. It has been no less thus with
proposed systems of social re-organization, so far as they
have been tried. Save where celibacy has been insisted on,
their history has been everywhere one of disaster; ending
with the history of Cabet's Icarian colony lately given by
one of its members, Madame Fleury Robinson, in *The
Open Court*—a history of splittings, re-splittings, re-re-
splittings, accompanied by numerous individual secessions
and final dissolution. And for the failure of such social
schemes, as for the failure of the political schemes, there
has been one general cause.

Metamorphosis is the universal law, exemplified
throughout the Heavens and on the Earth: especially
throughout the organic world; and above all in the animal
division of it. No creature, save the simplest and most
minute, commences its existence in a form like that which
it eventually assumes; and in most cases the unlikeness is
great—so great that kinship between the first and the last
forms would be incredible were it not daily demonstrated
in every poultry-yard and every garden. More than this is
true. The changes of form are often several: each of them
being an apparently complete transformation—egg, larva,
pupa, imago, for example. And this universal metamorphosis, displayed alike in the development of a planet and
of every seed which germinates on its surface, holds also
of societies, whether taken as wholes or in their separate
institutions. No one of them ends as it begins; and the difference between its original structure and its ultimate
structure is such that, at the outset, change of the one into
the other would have seemed incredible. In the rudest tribe

the chief, obeyed as leader in war, loses his distinctive position when the fighting is over; and even when continued warfare has produced permanent chieftainship, the chief, building his own hut, getting his own food, making his own implements, differs from others only by his predominant influence. There is no sign that in course of time, by conquests and unions of tribes, and consolidations of clusters so formed with other such clusters, until a nation has been produced, there will originate from the primitive chief, one who, as czar or emperor, surrounded with pomp and ceremony, has despotic power over scores of millions, exercised through hundreds of thousands of soldiers and hundreds of thousands of officials. When the early Christian missionaries, having humble externals and passing self-denying lives, spread over pagan Europe, preaching forgiveness of injuries and the returning of good for evil, no one dreamt that in course of time their representatives would form a vast hierarchy, possessing everywhere a large part of the land, distinguished by the haughtiness of its members grade above grade, ruled by military bishops who led their retainers to battle, and headed by a pope exercising supreme power over kings. So, too, has it been with that very industrial system which many are now so eager to replace. In its original form there was no prophecy of the factory system or kindred organization of workers. Differing from them only as being the head of his house, the master worked along with his apprentices and a journeyman or two, sharing with them his table and accommodation, and himself selling their joint produce. Only with industrial growth did there come employment of a larger number of assistants and a relinquishment, on the part of the master, of all other business than that of superintendence. And only in the course of recent times did there evolve the organisations under which the labours of hundreds and thousands of men receiving wages, are regulated by various orders of paid officials under a single or multiple head. These originally small, semi-socialistic, groups of producers, like the compound families or house-communities of early ages, slowly dissolved because they could not hold their ground: the larger establishments, with better sub-division of labour, succeeded because they ministered to the wants of society more effectually. But we need not go back through the centuries to trace transformations sufficiently great and unexpected. On the day when £30,000 a year in aid of education was voted as an experiment, the name of idiot would have been given to an opponent who prophesied that in fifty years the sum spent through imperial taxes and local rates would amount to £10,000,000, or who said that the aid to education would be followed by aids to feeding and clothing, or who said that parents and children, alike deprived of all option, would, even if starving, be compelled by fine or imprisonment to conform, and receive that which, with papal assumption, the State calls education. No one, I say, would have dreamt that out of so innocent-looking a germ would have so quickly evolved this tyrannical system, tamely submitted to by people who fancy themselves free.

Thus in social arrangements, as in all other things, change is inevitable. It is foolish to suppose that new institutions set up, will long retain the character given them by those who set them up. Rapidly or slowly they will be transformed into institutions unlike those intended—so unlike as even to be unrecognizable by their devisers. And what, in the case before us, will be the metamorphosis? The answer pointed to by instances above given, and warranted by various analogies, is manifest.

A cardinal trait in all advancing organization is the development of the regulative apparatus. If the parts of a whole are to act together, there must be appliances by which their actions are directed; and in proportion as the whole is large and complex, and has many requirements to be met by many agencies, the directive apparatus must be extensive, elaborate, and powerful. That it is thus with individual organisms needs no saying; and that it must be thus with social organisms is obvious. Beyond the regulative apparatus such as in our own society is required for carrying on national defence and maintaining public order and personal safety, there must, under the *régime* of socialism, be a regulative apparatus everywhere controlling all kinds of production and distribution, and everywhere apportioning the shares of products of each kind required for each locality, each working establishment, each individual. Under our existing voluntary co-operation, with its free contracts and its competition, production and distribution need no official oversight. Demand and supply, and the desire of each man to gain a living by supplying the needs of his fellows, spontaneously evolve that wonderful system whereby a great city has its food daily brought round to all doors or stored at adjacent shops; has clothing for its citizens everywhere in multitudinous varieties; has its houses and furniture and fuel ready made or stocked in each locality; and has mental pabulum from halfpenny papers, hourly hawked round, to weekly shoals of novels, and less abundant books of instruction, furnished without stint for small payments. And throughout the kingdom, production! as well as distribution is similarly carried on with the smallest amount of superintendence which proves efficient; while the quantities of the numerous commodities required daily in each locality are adjusted without any other agency than the pursuit of profit. Suppose now that this industrial *régime* of willinghood, acting spontaneously, is replaced by a *régime* of industrial obedience, enforced by public officials. Imagine the vast administration required for that distribution of all commodities to all people in every city, town and village, which is now effected by traders! Imagine, again, the still more vast administration required for doing all that farmers, manufacturers, and merchants do; having not only its various orders of local superintendents, but its sub-centres and chief centres needed for apportioning the quantities of each thing everywhere needed, and the adjustment of them to the requisite times. Then add the staffs wanted for working mines, railways, roads, canals; the staffs required for conducting the importing and exporting businesses and the administration of mercantile shipping; the staffs required for supplying towns not only with water and gas but with locomotion by tramways, omnibuses, and other vehicles, and for the distribution of power, electric and other. Join with these the existing postal, telegraphic, and telephonic administrations; and finally those of the police and army, by which the dictates of this immense consolidated regulative system are to be everywhere enforced. Imagine all this and then ask what will be the position of the actual workers! Already on the continent, where governmental organizations are more elaborate and coercive than here, there are chronic complaints of the tyranny of bureaucracies—the *hauteur* and brutality of their members. What will these become when not only the more public actions of citizens are controlled, but there is added this far more extensive control of all their respective daily duties? What will happen when the various divisions of this army of officials, united by interests common to officialism—the interests of the regulators *versus* those of the regulated—have at their command whatever force is needful to suppress insubordination and act as 'saviours of society'? Where will be the actual diggers and miners and smelters and weavers, when those who order and superintend, everywhere arranged class above class, have come, after some generations, to inter-marry with those of kindred grades, under feelings such as are operative in existing classes; and when there have been so produced a series of castes rising in superiority; and when all these, having everything in their own power, have arranged modes of living for their own advantage: eventually forming a new aristocracy far more elaborate and better organized than the old? How will the individual worker fare if he is dissatisfied with his treatment—thinks that he has not an adequate share of the products, or has more to do than can rightly be demanded, or wishes to undertake a function for which he feels himself fitted but which is not thought proper for him by his superiors, or desires to make an independent career for himself? This dissatisfied unit in the immense machine will be told he must submit or go. The mildest penalty for disobedience will be industrial excommunication. And if an international organization of labour is formed as proposed, exclusion in one country will mean exclusion in all others—industrial excommunication will mean starvation.

That things must take this course is a conclusion reached not by deduction only, nor only by induction from those experiences of the past instanced above, nor only from consideration of the analogies furnished by organisms of all orders; but it is reached also by observation of cases daily under our eyes. The truth that the regulative structure always tends to increase in power, is illustrated by every established body of men. The history of each learned society, or society for other purpose, shows how the staff, permanent or partially permanent, sways the proceedings and determines the actions of the society with but little resistance, even when most members of the society disapprove: the repugnance to anything like a revolutionary step being ordinarily an efficient deterrent. So it is with joint-stock companies—those owning railways for example. The plans of a board of directors are usually authorized with little or no discussion; and if there is any considerable opposition, this is forthwith crushed by an overwhelming number of proxies sent by those who always support the existing administration. Only when the misconduct is extreme does the resistance of shareholders suffice to displace the ruling body. Nor is it otherwise with societies formed of working men and having the interests of labour especially at heart—the Trades Unions. In these, too, the regulative agency becomes all powerful. Their members, even when they dissent from the policy pursued, habitually yield to the authorities they have set up. As they cannot secede without making enemies of their fellow workmen, and often losing all chance of employment, they succumb. We are shown, too, by the late congress, that already, in the general organisation of Trades Unions so recently formed, there are complaints of 'wire-pullers' and 'bosses' and 'permanent officials.' If, then, this supremacy of the regulators is seen in bodies of quite modern origin, formed of men who have, in many of the cases instanced, unhindered powers of asserting their independence, what will the supremacy of the regulators become in long-established bodies, in bodies which have grown vast and highly organized, and in bodies which, instead of controlling only a small part of the unit's life, control the whole of his life?

Again there will come the rejoinder—'We shall guard against all that. Everybody will be educated; and all, with their eyes constantly open to the abuse of power, will be quick to prevent it.' The worth of these expectations would be small even could we not identify the causes which will bring disappointment; for in human affairs the most promising schemes go wrong in ways which no one anticipated. But in this case the going wrong will be necessitated by causes which are inconspicuous. The working of institutions is determined by men's characters; and the existing defects in their characters will inevitably bring about the results above indicated. There is no adequate endowment of those sentiments required to prevent the growth of a despotic bureaucracy.

Were it needful to dwell on indirect evidence, which might be made of that furnished by the behaviour of the so-called Liberal party—a party which, relinquishing the original conception of a leader as a mouthpiece for a known and accepted policy, thinks itself bound to accept a policy which its leader springs upon it without consent or warning—a party so utterly without the feeling and idea implied by liberalism, as not to resent this trampling on the right of private judgment which constitutes the root of liberalism—nay, a party which vilifies as renegade liberals, those of its members who refuse to surrender their independence! But without occupying space with indirect proofs that the mass of men have not the natures required to check the development of tyrannical officialdom, it will suffice to contemplate the direct proofs furnished by those classes among whom the socialistic idea most predominates, and who think themselves most interested in propagating it—the operative classes. These would constitute the great body of the socialistic organisation, and their characters would determine its nature. What, then, are their characters as displayed in such organisations as they have already formed?

Instead of the selfishness of the employing classes and the selfishness of competition, we are to have the unselfishness of a mutually-aiding system. How far is this unselfishness now shown in the behaviour of working men to one another? What shall we say to the rules limiting the numbers of new hands admitted into each trade, or to the rules which hinder ascent from inferior classes of workers to superior classes? One does not see in such regulations any of that altruism by which socialism is to be pervaded. Contrariwise, one sees a pursuit of private interests no less keen than among traders. Hence, unless we suppose that men's natures will be suddenly exalted, we must conclude that the pursuit of private interests will sway the doings of all the component classes in a socialistic society.

With passive disregard of others' claims goes active encroachment on them. 'Be one of us or we will cut off your means of living,' is the usual threat of each Trades Union to outsiders of the same trade. While their members insist on their own freedom to combine and fix the rates at which they will work (as they are perfectly justified in doing), the freedom of those who disagree with them is not only denied but the assertion of it is treated as a crime. Individuals who maintain their rights to make their own contracts are vilified as 'blacklegs' and 'traitors,' and meet with violence which would be merciless were there no legal penalties and no police. Along with this trampling on the liberties of men of their own class, there goes peremptory dictation to the employing class: not prescribed terms and working arrangements only shall be conformed to, but none save those belonging to their body shall be employed—nay, in some cases, there shall be a strike if the employer carries on transactions with trading bodies that give work to non-union men. Here, then, we are variously shown by Trades Unions, or at any rate by the newer Trades Unions, a determination to impose their regulations without regard to the rights of those who are to be coerced. So complete is the inversion of ideas and sentiments that maintenance of these rights is regarded as vicious and trespass upon them as virtuous.[2]

---

[2] Marvellous are the conclusions men reach when once they desert the simple principle, that each man should be allowed to pursue the objects of life, restrained only by the limits which the similar pursuits of their objects by other men impose. A generation ago we heard loud assertions of 'the

Along with this aggressiveness in one direction there
goes submissiveness in another direction. The coercion of
outsiders by unionists is paralleled only by the subjection
to their leaders. That they may conquer in the struggle they
surrender their individual liberties and individual judgments, and show no resentment however dictatorial may
be the rule exercised over them. Everywhere we see such
subordination that bodies of workmen unanimously leave
their work or return to it as their authorities order them.
Nor do they resist when taxed all round to support strikers
whose acts they may or may not approve, but instead, ill-
treat recalcitrant members of their body who do not
subscribe.

The traits thus shown must be operative in any new social organisation, and the question to be asked is—What
will result from their operation when they are relieved
from all restraints? At present the separate bodies of men
displaying them are in the midst of a society partially
passive, partially antagonistic; are subject to the criticisms
and reprobations of an independent press; and are under

---

right to labour,' that is, the right to have labour provided; and there are
still not a few who think the community bound to find work for each
person. Compare this with the doctrine current in France at the time when
the monarchical power culminated; namely, that 'the right of working is a
royal right which the prince can sell and the subjects must buy.' This contrast is startling enough; but a contrast still more startling is being provided for us. We now see a resuscitation of the despotic doctrine, differing
only by the substitution of Trades Unions for kings. For now that Trades
Unions are becoming universal, and each artisan has to pay prescribed
monies to one or another of them, with the alternative of being a non-
unionist to whom work is denied by force, it has come to this, that the
right to labour is a Trade Union right, which the Trade Union can sell and
the individual worker must buy!

the control of law, enforced by police. If in these circumstances these bodies habitually take courses which override individual freedom, what will happen when, instead of being only scattered parts of the community, governed by their separate sets of regulators, they constitute the whole community, governed by a consolidated system of such regulators; when functionaries of all orders, including those who officer the press, form parts of the regulative organization; and when the law is both enacted and administered by this regulative organisation? The fanatical adherents of a social theory are capable of taking any measures, no matter how extreme, for carrying out their views: holding, like the merciless priesthoods of past times, that the end justifies the means. And when a general socialistic organisation has been established, the vast, ramified, and consolidated body of those who direct its activities, using without check whatever coercion seems to them needful in the interests of the system (which will practically become their own interests) will have no hesitation in imposing their rigorous rule over the entire lives of the actual workers; until, eventually, there is developed an official oligarchy, with its various grades, exercising a tyranny more gigantic and more terrible than any which the world has seen.

Let me again repudiate any erroneous inference. Any one who supposes that the foregoing argument implies contentment with things as they are, makes a profound mistake. The present social state is transitional, as past social states have been transitional. There will, I hope and believe, come a future social state differing as much from the present as the present differs from the past with its mailed barons and defenceless serfs. In *Social Statics*, as well as in *The Study of Sociology* and in *Political Institutions*, is clearly shown the desire for an organisation more conducive to the happiness of men at large than that which exists. My opposition to socialism results from the belief that it would stop the progress to such a higher state and bring back a lower state. Nothing but the slow modification of human nature by the discipline of social life, can produce permanently advantageous changes.

A fundamental error pervading the thinking of nearly all parties, political and social, is that evils admit of immediate and radical remedies. 'If you will but do this, the mischief will be prevented.' 'Adopt my plan and the suffering will disappear.' 'The corruption will unquestionably be cured by enforcing this measure.' Everywhere one meets with beliefs, expressed or implied, of these kinds. They are all ill-founded. It is possible to remove causes which intensify the evils; it is possible to change the evils from one form into another; and it is possible, and very common, to exacerbate the evils by the efforts made to prevent them; but anything like immediate cure is impossible. In the course of thousands of years mankind have, by multiplication, been forced out of that original savage state in which small numbers supported themselves on wild food, into the civilised state in which the food required for supporting great numbers can be got only by continuous labour. The nature required for this last mode of life is widely different from the nature required for the first; and long-continued pains have to be passed through in remoulding the one into the other. Misery has necessarily to be borne by a constitution out of harmony with its conditions; and a constitution inherited from primitive men is out of harmony with the conditions imposed on existing men. Hence it is impossible to establish forthwith a satisfactory social state. No such nature as that which has filled Europe with millions of armed men, here eager for conquest and there for revenge—no such nature as that which prompts the nations called Christian to vie with one another in filibustering expeditions all over the world, regardless of the claims of aborigines, while their tens of thousands of priests of the religion of love look on approvingly —no such nature as that which, in dealing with weaker races, goes beyond the primitive rule of life for life, and for one life takes many lives—no such nature, I say, can, by any device, be framed into a harmonious community. The root of all well-ordered social action is a sentiment of justice, which at once insists on personal freedom and is solicitous for the like freedom of others; and there at present exists but a very inadequate amount of this sentiment.

Hence the need for further long continuance of a social discipline which requires each man to carry on his activities with due regard to the like claims of others to carry on their activities; and which, while it insists that he shall have all the benefits his conduct naturally brings, insists also that he shall not saddle on others the evils his conduct naturally brings: unless they freely undertake to bear them. And hence the belief that endeavours to elude this discipline, will not only fail, but will bring worse evils than those to be escaped.

It is not, then, chiefly in the interests of the employing

classes that socialism is to be resisted, but much more in
the interests of the employed classes. In one way or other
production must be regulated; and the regulators, in the
nature of things, must always be a small class as compared
with the actual producers. Under voluntary co-operation
as at present carried on, the regulators, pursuing their
personal interests, take as large a share of the produce as
they can get; but, as we are daily shown by Trades Union
successes, are restrained in the selfish pursuit of their ends.
Under that compulsory co-operation which socialism
would necessitate, the regulators, pursuing their personal
interests with no less selfishness, could not be met by the
combined resistance of free workers; and their power,
unchecked as now by refusals to work save on prescribed
terms, would grow and ramify and consolidate till it became irresistible. The ultimate result, as I have before
pointed out, must be a society like that of ancient Peru,
dreadful to contemplate, in which the mass of the people,
elaborately regimented in groups of 10, 50, 100, 500, and
1000, ruled by officers of corresponding grades, and tied
to their districts, were superintended in their private lives
as well as in their industries, and toiled hopelessly for the
support of the governmental organization.

HERBERT SPENCER

CHAPTER 1

THE IMPRACTICABILITY
OF SOCIALISM

EDWARD STANLEY ROBERTSON

CHAPTER 1

THE IMPRACTICABILITY OF SOCIALISM

I purpose, in this paper, to deal almost exclusively with the question whether Socialism is practicable. I shall confine myself, as much as I can, to the inquiry whether the means proposed are, or are not, likely to work out the end which is aimed at. I shall have to waive, in a very great degree, the previous essential questions whether the end is a desirable one in itself, and whether justice requires that it shall be held in view. For the purposes of the discussion I shall provisionally concede the affirmative to both; but in order to avoid all misunderstanding, I think it well to put on record here that I do so provisionally only. No such admission is hereafter to be quoted against me, as if I had accepted Socialist or Collectivist theories upon any moral, economical, or political question. Space does not admit of my making a detailed confession of faith upon these points; but it is open to me to state that I am not bound by any *à priori* theory. What is commonly called 'abstract justice' I confess I cannot discover in the history of any human institution. I cannot discover equality in the dispensations of nature itself.

This, I may be told, proves nothing. A great deal of our life consists of a conflict with nature; a continuous effort to redress inequalities in the course of nature, and to solve difficult problems which nature sets before us. True; and that is precisely part of my case. I affirm that social inequalities are inequalities which may be mitigated, but cannot be redressed wholly; that social problems are problems which, for the most part, only admit of a partial solution.

Such problems and such inequalities exist in material nature, and the difficulties they present are universally acknowledged. The day, in the tropics, is of about equal length with the night. So it is at the poles, with the difference that the tropical day and night are about twelve hours each, while at the poles each lasts somewhere about half the year. In the sub-tropical and temperate zones, the days in summer and in winter differ strikingly in length. In the latitude of London, the longest day is about a quarter of an hour shorter, and the shortest day about a quarter of an hour longer, than in the latitude of Edinburgh. Such is the inequality in a merely astronomical and geographical statement of fact; and when it comes to be applied to human affairs, its practical effect is more startling still. It means that a working day, if it were not for artificial light, may be twice as long in summer as in winter, and may vary in length for the difference in latitude between Southampton and Carlisle, and between Carlisle and Inverness. This difference in the length of the day does make a real difference in all the conditions of life, and most of all in the lives of what are usually called the working classes; but the difference is obscured by custom, and by the feeling that it cannot be helped. It is felt to be useless to agitate against 'the stars in their courses.' So again, in India and in many parts of the tropics the principal danger to agriculture is drought; in the British Islands the danger is excessive rainfall. If rain and sunshine could be distributed in exact proportion to the wants of each region, a far greater degree of prosperity would result. As it is, in the one class of countries it is necessary to have recourse to irrigation, and in the other to drainage, to correct, so far as is practicable, the inequalities of climate. One result of this is that the remedies not unfrequently turn out to contain the seeds of other diseases. In a drainage country, an unusually dry summer brings on a drought for which there is no preparation, and which may even be attended by pestilence. In a country of irrigation, an exceptional rainfall causes floods, which may destroy life both directly and indirectly. And even in ordinary seasons, there are difficulties and losses which are great hardships to individuals and classes, but which there is no way of obviating. All these things, and many others that could be added to the list, are accepted as part of the course of nature.[1] Nobody thinks of agitating against the weather, though we all grumble at it freely. We

---

[1] I will briefly refer to one other instance—I mean the influence of climate upon bodily condition. The human race can *exist* in almost any climate; but there is no climate in which the average human being can enjoy perfect health. Every region suffers from diseases peculiar to itself, and it may be doubted whether more human suffering is inflicted, e.g. by malarious fever in Africa or by lung disease in our own islands. Volumes have been written on nature's adaptation of means to ends, but I venture to think that volumes remain to be written on the imperfection of that adaptation.

know that there is no help for it, and there is an end of the matter. Now the human race, and human society, are just as much parts of nature as the heavenly bodies and the sunshine and rainfall. The organisation of society is just as much a matter of natural tendency (I purposely avoid the use of the phrase *natural law*) as the rising and setting of the sun, the rain in Devonshire or the hot wind of the Punjab. The difference is a difference of simple and complex phenomena. Every one can observe for himself or herself the discrepancy in the length of the days. It is not so easy to understand fully the dissimilarities of climate and their influence upon human affairs, but once the facts are grasped, there is no longer any room for speculation as to the possibility of things being otherwise. It is perceived at once that there is no use in attempting to fly in the face of nature. We can mitigate, but we cannot change. We can only mitigate, moreover, by playing off one tendency or set of tendencies against others. It is by obeying nature that we get the mastery of nature.

Now this brings us to the points at issue between Socialists and their opponents. Socialists would (I suppose) not deny that the human race and human society are part of nature. They would not deny that human communities are what they are, and have been what they have been, in virtue of streams of tendency, more difficult to observe and to co-ordinate than the observed antecedents and sequences of climatic tendencies, but not less real, and not less certain to work themselves out. If we only knew history as we know astronomy, sociology would be an exact science. If we even knew history as we know, or guess at, meteorology, many problems would be clear which are now obscure.

But although Socialists might not deny all this in terms, they seem habitually to think, and speak, and try to act and induce others to act, as if it were all untrue. They deal with human society as if it were that blank sheet of paper to which Locke incorrectly compared the childish intellect. They write and speak as if they thought that it only needed a conscious effort of the will on the part of any given human community to change all, or nearly all, the conditions in which it has hitherto subsisted. They seem to think that they can defeat nature by a front attack.

What, then, are the complaints of Socialists against the existing constitution of society, and how is it proposed to redress the alleged grievances?

In endeavouring to answer these questions, I take as my text-book Dr. Schäffle's *Quintessence of Socialism;*[2] the most businesslike account of the Socialist position which has yet appeared. Anyone who compares its calm and judicial statements with the violent, turgid, and heated rhetoric of the *Fabian Essays* will appreciate the reasons which guided me in choosing it.[3] I may go so far as to say that if Dr. Schäffle's style were a little more popular, the

---

[2] Eighth edition, translated by Bernard Bosanquet, M.A. Swan Sonnenschein & Co. 1889. When I quote other authorities I shall specify them, but most quotations will be from Schäffle.

[3] Socialism is very commonly called Utopian. But when one compares calm and temperate statements of Socialist projects, such as we find in Schäffle, with the wild rhodomontade of the Fabian Society, to say nothing of the still wilder oratory of Hyde Park meetings, it is not so much More's *Utopia* of which one is reminded, as Swift's *Laputa*.

substance of his work would render the writing of this
paper a superfluous effort. He evidently sympathises with
Socialism, and is resolved to make the best case he can for
its proposals. Yet every page displays the difficulties of
the scheme to the intelligent reader, even when the author
is not dwelling upon those difficulties. In his concluding
chapter he sums up calmly and judicially, but very
strongly, against the whole system of Democratic or Collective Socialism.

What then is the Socialist complaint against the existing
constitution of society? It may be summed up in the one
word, inequality. Quoting from Karl Marx, Schäffle speaks
of 'a growing mass of misery, oppression, slavery, degradation, exploitation.'[4] Schäffle himself speaks of 'the
plutocratic process of dividing the nation into an enormous proletariat on the one side and a few millionaires on
the other.'[5] If any one wants to be saturated with boiling
rhetoric on this topic, let him open the *Fabian Essays* at
random, or dip into the pages of Henry George's *Progress
and Poverty* and *Social Problems*.[6] Or, if the reader is in
search of quite as good rhetoric, but tempered by a good
deal more common sense, let him carefully read through
The Social Problem, by Professor William Graham,[7] especially chapter vi, 'The Social Residuum.' Mr. Graham does
not hold that what he calls the social residuum is an in-

---

[4] Schäffle, p. 15.

[5] Ibid. p. 12.

[6] I am bound to admit that Mr. George says he is not a Socialist. But on
the subject of the proletariat he writes as if he were one.

[7] Kegan Paul, Trench & Co. 1886.

creasing mass. The Fabian essayists and the Continental Socialists always affirm that it is, and Dr. Schäffle in the quotation already given appears to accept Marx's view.

Now this view is an untrue one. It is demonstrably untrue as regards the United Kingdom. It is demonstrably untrue as regards France. It is probably untrue of every other country in Europe, with the possible exception of Russia. Confining ourselves to the United Kingdom, I affirm that there exists, between the so-called 'millionaire' and the class described as the residuum, no gulf whatever, but an absolutely complete gradation. I need not load these pages with statistics in proof of what I say. The burden of proof is upon those who affirm the contrary. Socialist rhetoricians have no scruple in confusing their own and other people's ideas on this subject by their illogical use of the word 'proletariat.' At one time, it means people who have no land; at another, it seems to signify people who have no capital; in all cases it is used with a kind of tacit connotation of 'pauper.' We shall see presently that in a Socialist State the entire population would be one vast proletariat; but in the meantime it may be pointed out that to have no land and no capital is not necessarily to be a pauper. A professional man may be earning a very handsome and very secure income, and yet may, in that sense, belong to the proletariat. But Socialist declamation about millionaires and proletariat invariably covers the innuendo that the world actually contains a few thousand millionaires and thousands of millions of paupers. When this is stated, it is at once perceived to be untrue; and a very little inquiry confirms the inquirer in that conclusion. Socialist declamation, such as Schäffle quotes from Marx—

'misery, oppression, slavery, degradation, exploitation'—
is only true, if true at all, of the lowest residuum; and that
residuum is no more than a fringe on the border of society,
in any country where the capitalist is free. On the other
hand, this is true beyond all controversy of England and
of France—that between the millionaire and the worker
for daily or weekly wage there are stages innumerable,
which pass from higher to lower by a gradation that is
barely perceptible. If there is anything that can be called a
social gulf, it is the interval which separates the steady and
fairly well-paid workers from the loafers and the crim-
inals; and that gulf is quite as much moral as it is economic.

But even if all that is alleged were true, does Socialism
offer anything that can be called a remedy? In order to
answer this question, we must see what the Socialist
remedy is.

'The Alpha and Omega of Socialism is the transformation of private and competing capitals into a united collective capital.'[8] When, instead of the system of private and
competing capitals, which drive down wages by competition, we have a collective ownership of capital, *public*
organisation of labour, and of the distribution of the national income—then, and not till then, we shall have no
capitalists and no wage-earners, but all will be alike,
producers.'[9]

One more quotation. 'In their places' (i.e. in place of
private capital and competition) 'we should have a State-
regulated organisation of national labour into a social

---

[8] Schäffle, p. 20.

[9] Schäffle, pp. 28 and following. The whole passage will repay perusal, but
it is too long to quote *in extenso*.

labour system, equipped out of collective capital; the State would collect, warehouse, and transport all products, and finally would distribute them to individuals in proportion to their registered amount of social labour, and according to a valuation of commodities exactly corresponding to their average cost of production.'[10]

This, then, is the Quintessence of Socialism. This, and nothing more or less, is what is meant by the word, and is proposed by its advocates. Socialism does not mean that property is robbery, at least in the ordinary sense of the phrase.[11] Nor does it mean a periodical redistribution of private property.[12] Nor does it mean that private capital is to be confiscated, and no compensation made to owners, though it does mean that all such compensation must take the form of consumable goods, and must therefore be terminable.[13] Nor does Socialism, as understood by Dr. Schäffle, necessarily conflict with individual freedom. Upon this point, however, our author speaks but doubtfully, and his remarks require very careful perusal.[14] It does not even preclude the possession of a private income.[15] It has nothing to say to questions of marriage, 'free love,'[16] or religion.[17] In short, Socialism, or Collectivism, relates to the possession of land and capital—the totality of instru-

---

[10] Ibid. p. 45.

[11] Ibid. p. 23.

[12] Ibid. p. 30.

[13] Ibid. pp. 32, 33.

[14] Ibid. ch. iii. 39–45 inclusive.

[15] Ibid. ch. viii. pp. 97–110.

[16] Ibid. pp. 110, 111.

[17] Ibid. p. 116.

ments of production[18]—and not to anything else whatsoever, whether economic, political, or social.

Now, the first and most obvious criticism upon all this
is, that whereas Socialists denounce land-owning and
capital-owning, because they tend to the creation of a proletariat, their scheme, as announced by a benevolently-
neutral interpreter, proposes to turn all the world into one
vast proletariat. This is not mere juggling with words. It is
the Socialists who juggle with words, when they define a
proletarian as a person who does not own either land or
capital, and then proceed to talk of the proletariat as if the
word meant 'a mass of paupers.' If to be a proletarian is
to be a pauper, then Socialism undertakes to turn all the
world into a mass of paupers, including the very persons
who will be entrusted with the control of that monster
workhouse, the Socialist State. But I am willing to admit
that if all the world could be freed from the curse of poverty—if the social residuum could be done away with—
there would be a strong temptation to swallow the scheme
of Socialism, proletariat and all. Quitting verbal criticism,
let us try to think out how the suggestion would be likely
to work. Land and Capital are to be the property of the
whole community. They are to be managed by State officials. The produce is to be distributed in proportion to what
is described as the 'social labour-time' of every individual
worker; and this social labour-time is to be divided into
units of approximately equal value. In other words, every
Socialist community is to be one vast Joint Stock Company
for the manufacture and distribution of things in general!

---

[18] Ibid. p. 5.

Now, the moment this is stated, the first difficulty of Socialism is at once suggested. How do the directors of an ordinary manufacturing firm ascertain the conditions of their business? By a series of experiments, failure in which means the loss of their capital. How does Socialism solve the problem? 'The amount of supply necessary in each form of production would be fixed by continuous official returns furnished by the managers and overseers of the selling and producing departments.'[19] This is very well upon paper, and if we accept the hypothesis that the demand for any given object always remains nearly constant. But this is evidently not the case. There is no article of consumption, not even bread itself, for which the demand does not so vary from day to day that no official department could possibly provide for it in a 'budget of social production.' The existing order of things only provides such a 'budget' very roughly; and the bankruptcy court acts as a sort of steam-governor, when mistaken speculation sends a capitalist to waste. Even if it were admitted that the demand for food is virtually constant, which is manifestly untrue, there are many other things for which the demand could not be foreseen by any official department. Clothing is a very obvious case in point. It is a necessary of life, in a great part of the world, only second to food itself. Yet could any public department undertake to say how many suits of clothes a given population will wear out in a given season? Remember, it is of no use making calculations based upon decades, or even upon single years, and then striking averages. What is wanted

---

[19] Schäffle, p. 5.

is to know how many suits of clothes the department ought to have on hand, in order to meet the demand day by day. When clothing has to be served out to soldiers, the soldiers are put upon strict regulation as to its use. It is all the same pattern, and there is no personal choice about it. This is what makes the clothing of an army practicable; but in civil life the conditions are wholly different. When did women ever submit to a uniform, unless it were for religious reasons? I am prepared to be denounced, by Fabian essayists and other enthusiasts, as a cold-blooded and frivolous person, because I state such petty difficulties; but I affirm that it is very often trifles such as this which cause great projects to make shipwreck. A few ounces of iron in the wrong place in a ship will derange the compass and baffle the calculations of the most skilful navigator.

I do not know whether I am justified in surmising that the more extreme advocates of State Collectivism would cut this particular knot by decreeing that people should wear uniforms of some sort, and should be under quasi-military regulations in respect of the raiment served out to them. We may come to perceive, as we go on, that there is no real reason why this should not be done. The principles of collective production, and of distribution according to 'social labour-time,' involve infringements of personal freedom considerably more formidable than the compulsion to wear a uniform. It may suffice to say for the present that if Socialism does not cover this contingency, then collective production breaks down over the article of clothing. And, of course, to break down in one point is to break down in all. A chain is no stronger than its weakest link.

One of the most remarkable characteristics of Dr. Schäffle's work is the odd way in which he seems to ignore all particulars such as I have just now been calling attention to. After dwelling, as he does in chap. iii of the *Quintessence*, upon the vital importance of freedom of demand, which he declares to be a first essential of freedom in general, and the very material basis of freedom, he goes on to say that a complete and officially organised system of collective production could undoubtedly include at least as thorough a daily, weekly, monthly, quarterly, or yearly statistical registration of the free wants of individuals and families, as under the present system these effect each for themselves, by their demand upon the market.[20] But this is just what I deny, and I think I have given a good reason for my denial. An instance, such as that of the clothing question, is worth all the *à priori* assumptions that any one can make. The Socialist is bound to explain how he is going to organise his collection and registration of statistics in every single department of his State-controlled producing-agency. It will be noted that Schäffle declares Socialists not to contemplate an immediate conversion of all kinds of business into State departments.[21] But manifestly, until all capital is transformed into collective ownership, Socialism is incomplete. If the State took over the supply of food, but left clothing to private enterprise, all the vices now charged against private capitalism would continue to inhere in the clothing trade, until it too had been reduced into collective ownership.

---

[20] Schäffle, p. 43.

[21] Ibid. p. 48.

I now pass to another branch of the Socialist scheme; premising that the question just treated and that upon which I am now about to enter are so inextricably mixed up that I may have to recur now and then to topics which may seem to have been already discussed. And may I add another word of caution. If I seem to be almost exclusively answering Dr. Schäffle, it is simply because he is the most temperate as well as the clearest exponent of Socialism. If Socialism as expounded by him can be shown to be unworkable, much more will it be proved unworkable in the hands of its most extreme projectors.

To resume then. The Socialist State is not only to produce by means of land and capital owned in common and managed by public officials; it is also to distribute the wealth produced by this social co-operation according to the proportion of work performed by each individual.[22] Now here is one of the crucial difficulties of the entire Socialist scheme. It is not proposed to reward everybody alike. That would be a practical proposal, though not a very practicable one, because it would put an end at once and for ever to all spontaneity in the workers. But this is not what is contemplated. An attempt is to be made to equate the values of 'social labour-time' in different occupations, whether branches of production or services not directly productive. How this is to be done we are not very clearly told. It is intimated, indeed, that Marx has estimated the 'labour price' of a hectolitre of wheat at five days of 'socially determined labour,' supposing everybody to work eight

---

[22] Schäffle, p. 5.

hours a day.[23] One very striking feature of the scheme is
that there are to be no payments in metallic money or in
any equivalent for coin. We shall see presently that this
introduces a new and enhanced difficulty; but it is declared
to be an essential portion of the scheme, though there is
nothing even in the nature of Socialism itself to make it
so. Payments, under Socialism, however, are to be made
wholly in certificates of labour-time. Now it is abundantly
manifest that no such equation of labour-time could be
constructed as to bring out a unit of labour which should
be even approximately uniform. In the first place, it is totally impossible, as has been already shown, to fix the
demand for almost any given article of production at a
given time. The most that can be done is, in things for
which the demand is in some measure constant, such as
food, to produce a daily average; and the production of
such daily average may or may not require an average expenditure of labour. Indeed, in the case of agricultural
labour, no average day could be fixed at all. But it would
seem that Socialists think they can establish some such average, not for a single department of production, but for
the whole of what they call social labour. 'If we imagine'—
this is how Schäffle puts it—'all the species of products
which are being continually produced, valued by the expenditure of social labour as verified by experience, we
could find by addition the total of social labour-time which
is required for the social total production of the social total
of demand.'[24] It is difficult to strip this statement of its

---

[23] Ibid. pp. 82, 83.
[24] Schäffle, pp. 82, 83.

verbiage, but it seems to come to this; that it would be possible somehow to find out how many hours a day for how many days in a year every working member of a given community would have to work, in order that every man, woman, and child in such community should have exactly as much of everything as he, she, or it wanted, or perhaps more correctly, as the heads of the supply departments thought that he, she, or it ought to want. In order to achieve this it would be necessary to know the demand, which I have shown to be impracticable, in some departments at all events. It would be necessary to know what is the average number of hours' labour needed to produce a given quantity of a given commodity. Will anyone, I care not how skilled in agriculture, tell us how many days, of how many hours per day, it takes to produce a ton of wheat, or potatoes, or hay, or beans? How many hours per day of 'social labour' will prepare a bullock or a sheep for the market, or a milch cow to yield her daily supply of milk? Here, again, to ask these questions is to show that they are unanswerable. The fact is that Socialists invariably think of *factory* labour, when they are speculating about labour time. The labour spent in handling machinery can be timed; but there are other kinds of labour which cannot. How many hours a day ought a sailor to work, for example; and how is the value of an hour of his work to be ascertained in comparison with the value of an hour's work of a street lamplighter, or a letter-carrier?

Take another concrete example. How would Socialism regulate the hours, or estimate the value, of domestic service? I do not mean merely the menial service of the rich—

what Socialists call 'house slavery.'[25] The Socialist notion of domestic service, indeed, is as unpractical as the whole of the rest of their Laputa. I suppose they would class the services of a midwife under 'free professional services.' But what of the services of a nursemaid? How many hours a day ought such a person to be employed, and what is the value of her services, expressed in 'social labour-time?' What is the value of the 'social labour-time' of a working man's wife in childbirth, and during her subsequent withdrawal from the working strength of the community? Schäffle says 'the employment of women's labour, *now no longer needed in the family*, would find its fitting place without effort.'[26] This appears to me the strangest of all the strange utterances of Socialism. No longer needed in the family! If for 'family' we read 'factory,' there would be some sense in it, and perhaps, after all, the words may have been accidentally transposed. For my own part, I confess myself incapable of conceiving a state of things in which woman would not be absolutely essential to the 'family' as wife, mother, nurse, housekeeper, to say nothing of any other function. I can easily enough conceive the existence of factories without women workers; but that women should be set free from the family in order that they may enter the factory strikes me as being a complete inversion of the order of nature.

The question whether 'house slavery,' in the sense of purely menial service, could be abolished by Socialism,

---

[25] Schäffle, p. 112.
[26] Ibid. p. 113.

seems to depend upon considerations which cannot be discussed in this essay. It belongs to the topic of Classes under Socialism, a topic upon which Socialist literature affords the minimum of information. I pass on now to more general considerations on the valuation of labour.

The fallacy of Socialism in relation to labour appears to lie in the assumption that labour has a value of its own, in and for itself. It has no such value. No material thing is valuable because of the labour expended in producing it. No service is valuable because of the labour expended in rendering it. Material things are valuable because they satisfy wants, and therefore people will give material things which they possess in exchange for things they do not possess. If material things came into existence without labour, nobody would talk of the value of productive labour. If a thing is not wanted, there is no value attached to the labour of producing it. Who now would pay for the labour of producing candle-snuffers? The things have ceased to be useful; there is no demand for them; but it requires just as much labour to produce them now as it did a hundred years ago. But if any one possesses a useful article, he can always exchange it for another useful article, no matter whether one or both have been produced by labour or without labour. And what is true of productive labour is true of the labour expended in rendering services, when the necessary allowances are made. Services may be bartered for material objects of utility, or for other services. But in either case what is paid for is the service, not the labour expended in rendering the service; and when the service is rewarded with a material object, the service is rendered for the sake of getting that object, and not for the sake of the labour whereby the object was produced. Socialists would not, I think, deny all this in terms. Schäffle shows that he is acquainted with the truth, and admits it on the Socialist behalf, when he says that it is 'socially determined individual labour,' not actual labour expended by individuals, which is to be taken into account in estimating labour values.[27] But although the doctrine I have laid down might not be disputed in terms, it is consistently ignored in the entire Socialist scheme. The entire theory of surplus-value rests upon the assumption that labour employed in production has a sort of standard value of its own. The idea of regulating exchange by labour-time rests upon a similar fallacious assumption. Commodities are exchanged for other commodities because some people have what other people want, quite irrespective of how they got it. Commodities are exchanged for services, because he who can spare the commodity stands in need of the service, and *vice versa;* not because it required labour to produce the commodity, and will require labour to render the service.

In reply to all this I shall doubtless be reminded that although labour may have no intrinsic value, it has an inseparable value, because no commodity can be produced, nor can any service be rendered, without calling labour into requisition. That is quite true, but it does not affect the argument. The scheme of Socialism requires that some sort of equation should be established, whereby goods, and services, should be mutually interchangeable, and should possess values capable of being estimated in terms of labour. Under Capitalist Individualism, and under free Cap-

---

[27] Schäffle, p. 82.

italism in general, commodities and services are first of all values in terms of money, and then paid for in money which can be used to pay for other commodities and other services at the discretion of the recipient. In this way, a balance is established automatically. There is no need to construct elaborate calculations for the purpose of valuing one kind of labour in terms of another, or of establishing a common denominator for the value of all kinds of labour. The abolition of money is not necessarily part of the scheme of Collective Production. It is 'tacked on' to Collective Production because Socialists have taken up the idea that money is conducive to free Capitalism, as it undoubtedly is. But money could perfectly well co-exist with Collective Production, and that plan is not made in the least degree more practicable by being linked with a very clumsy form of inconvertible paper currency. The Socialists themselves admit that their State would want money, in so far as it had dealings with other States which had not yet adopted Socialism.[28] But even here there is a very important omission. It does not follow that even if all the world were to adopt Socialism, every State and every community would adopt it on precisely the same terms. For instance, one State may fix its labour day at ten hours, another at eight, another at six. Under such circumstances, how are social labour values to be computed and equated? Schäffle may ask 'whether the commonwealth of the Socialists would be able to cope with the enormous Socialistic bookkeeping, and to estimate heterogeneous labour correctly according to Socialistic units of

---

[28] Ibid. p. 70.

labour-time.'[29] It may here be noticed that Schäffle all through speaks of the Socialist State, as a 'close' economic community. To me this appears to imply, among other things, a protectionist community. It is not expressly laid down, I am aware, by the Socialists, that favour ought to be shown to home labour as against the labour of foreigners; but this does appear to follow from the general scheme. The entire basis of Socialist criticism on existing institutions is the assumption that labour does not get its due. It is not complained that production falls short, but only that the things produced are 'unjustly' distributed; and the 'injustice' is declared to lie in the fact that the surplus value of labour is appropriated by capitalists. Labour is assumed to have a value in and for itself. These things being so, I can well understand how the labourers in a Socialistic State might be induced to demand that nothing should be imported into the 'close community' from without which could possibly be produced within. Nay, I can conceive a veto being put upon labour-saving inventions, in order that 'the bread might not be taken out of the mouths of the people.' The attack upon invention in invariably proceeds from labour, or from persons posing as champions of labour, and as invariably takes the form of accusing capitalists of using inventions in order to secure an unfair advantage over labour. Some Socialists, indeed, such as the Fabian essayists, attack not only patents but literary copyright as the creation of a vicious capitalist and individualist system. One would have thought that if there was a moral basis for private property anywhere, it

---

[29] Ibid. p. 86.

would underlie that form of property which is described as 'property in ideas.' That an inventor should enjoy the profits of his invention—an artist, of his picture or statue —a musician, of his music—an author, of his literary ideas—all this seems almost self-evident, when we consider that these men have actually created the invention, the artistic work, the composition, and the literature. In their case, if anywhere, labour seems to have value in and for itself, and the fruit of labour to belong of right to its producer. Yet these are just the cases which the thoughtful Socialist ignores, and the rhetorical Socialist actually assails.[30] Under these circumstances, it would be futile to ask how the system of Collective Production and payment by social labour-time would equate the labour of an inventor with that of a ploughman, or the labour of a poet with that of a weaver. Still, one may suppose that mechanical invention at any rate would not be absolutely excluded. I will not ask what would have been the 'social labour value' of James Watt's time when he sat watching the lid of his mother's teakettle being lifted off by the steam. But it is fair to ask what Boulton would have done if, instead of being a private capitalist, he had been a Socialist industrial chief, when Watt proposed to him to make experiments on the condensing steam-engine. Would he have had resources at his disposal? It is very doubtful. If he were paid his salary as overseer in labour-certificates, we may say certainly not. Would he have felt justified in taking up the 'social labour-time' of the workmen under his supervision in making experiments of a costly nature, which,

---

[30] *Fabian Essays*, pp. 145, 146.

for all he could possibly foresee, might come to nothing?

And this raises another question. What machinery does Socialism provide for 'writing off' obsolete investments? Would a Socialist State ever have adopted the railway as its carrying machinery, and if so, how would it have disposed of the colective capital invested in canals and stagecoaches?

But we need not have the recourse to any conjectures or hypothetical cases. There are instances in abundance. I will mention one, which fortunately refers to a matter concerning which there need be no dispute as to either principle or method. No Individualist will deny that the maintenance of lighthouses is one of the proper functions of Government. Every Socialist would, I think, earnestly maintain that Government is bound to adopt every improvement which can be shown to increase the efficiency of lighthouses, and is bound also to investigate and test every alleged improvement, in favour of which a reasonable *prima facie* case can be made out. What has been the actual conduct of our own Board of Trade and Trinity House in regard to the improvement of lighthouse illuminants? I have before me a Blue Book of 143 pages, containing correspondence on the subject of the proposed supersession of oil by gas as a lighthouse illuminant.[31] On the part of the Board of Trade and Trinity House, the entire correspondence is one prolonged effort to evade and shelve the discussion. Toward the end we read: 'The Board of Trade were not without hope that a limit might now be reached in which the whole of the lighthouse authorities

---

[31] Parliamentary Papers, Lighthouse Illuminants, 27 Jan. 1887.

could agree, as being the limit of illumination beyond
which no practical advantage could result to navigation.'[32]
Well may Professor Tyndall remark upon this,[33] 'The
writer of this paragraph is obviously disappointed at finding himself unable to say to scientific invention, "Thus far
shalt thou go and no farther." It would, however, be easier
to reach the limit of illumination in the official mind than
to fix the limit possible to our lighthouses.' This is the way
in which the officials of our own day deal with a practical
problem which is undoubtedly within their province; concerning which they are undoubtedly bound to seek for the
most efficient appliances; and upon which they have the
evidence of a man of science of the very first rank. The
reason is not far to seek. Functionaries are under a chronic
temptation to keep on standing upon old paths. They habitually defend the machinery and the methods to which
they have got accustomed, and treat with coolness all proposals of reform or improvement. As I have already suggested, it seems very doubtful whether Socialist institutions could possibly admit of a Department for the
Investigation of Inventions. To draw a hard and fast rule
according to which all labour should be rewarded by a
share in the actual product of other labour would be to
negative every attempt at even mechanical improvement.
As to art and literature, the position seems to need no
comment. Experience teaches us that everything new in
art and literature requires, so to speak, to create its own
market for itself. Under Socialism, nothing could secure a

---

[32] Letter No. 111, page 139 of Report.
[33] Letter to *Times*, 7th April, 1888.

market which could not be put upon the market at once—for which, as it may be said, there was not a demand already, even before the process of production should have begun.

And this leads to a further consideration. Is a State department really a good machine for either production or distribution? The experience of State departments under existing conditions seems to answer this question in the negative. The departments of shipbuilding, of ordnance, of soldiers' clothing, and many others, seem to be open to the charge of inefficiency, at least as compared with private establishments for producing similar objects. It is remarkable that the producing departments are never referred to in this connexion by exponents of Socialism. The defence of the efficiency of State departments is always made to rest upon the distributing agencies, and chief among these is the Post Office. Schäffle mentions also the State railway, which we have not in England, the telegraph, and the municipal gas and water supplies.[34] Now the efficiency of the Post Office may be ungrudgingly admitted; but it must not be urged as proving more than it will bear.

In the first place, the Post Office has always been a monopoly. There never was a time when any private agency was permitted to compete with the State in the work of distributing letters. There has therefore been no opportunity of comparing State work in that department with private work. In the second place, the work of distributing letters is, after all, comparatively simple. We are accustomed, it is true, to hear and read of feats of great

---

[34] Schäffle, p. 53.

ingenuity in discovering obscure addresses; but these are
the exceptions. It is in the department of letter-carrying,
at all events, that the principal successes—it might almost
be said the only successes—have been achieved. The telegraphic department is not a success either financially or
administratively. The letter department largely supple-
ments the cost of the telegraph department. In other words,
people who write many letters, but send few telegrams,
are made to pay for the accommodation afforded to the
senders of many telegrams. Even in the letter-carrying department, there is plenty of room for improvement. It is
very well managed, on the whole, in country places; but in
London, and in large towns generally, the delivery of
letters within the town leaves much to be desired. In this
connexion I cannot refrain from noticing the breakdown
of letter-delivery arrangements which has taken place at
Christmas every year since the Christmas card came into
fashion. The breakdown under the weight of exceptional
complimentary correspondence is not even of our own day;
for Charles Lamb, in his essay on Valentine's Day, writes
of 'the weary and all-for-spent twopenny postman.' But,
of course, in the vast proportions of the Christmas crush,
it is necessarily modern, and the creation of the penny and
halfpenny postage. One would think that if, by the mere
fact of belonging to a department of Government, a preter-
natural faculty of dealing with statistics were conferred
upon officials, the officials of the Post Office ought, after
a brief experience, to have been able to foresee and provide
for this recurring difficulty. Yet no sooner does Christmas
come within measurable distance, than every Post Office
is placarded and every newspaper filled, with plaintive

appeals from the Postmaster-General to the Christmas-card despatching public, to 'post early, so as to ensure the punctual delivery of letters!'

It is worth noting, too, that the Post Office is not, strictly speaking, a working man's institution. It is the upper and middle classes who keep it going. The working class, or what is commonly so called, sends few letters and no telegrams. If what are usually called 'working' men and women corresponded by letter to anything like the extent to which correspondence is carried on by the commercial class alone, the revenue of the Post Office would be greatly enlarged. On the other hand, it is difficult to conceive how the telegraph system could possibly be administered, if that ever became a really popular institution. As it is, letters pay for telegrams, as already stated.

The arrangement whereby the surplus of receipts for letters is made to pay for the deficit in telegrams is the really Socialistic feature of the working of the Post Office. It may or may not be an advantage that the people who use the telegraph should do so at the expense of the larger public who write letters, but this proves nothing at all as to the probable success of the working of more complicated institutions by State machinery. As already pointed out, the delivery of letters is about as simple a work as any organisation could undertake, and next to it in simplicity is the transmission and delivery of telegrams. Nor should we omit to note to how great an extent the task of letter-delivery has been facilitated by railways and steam communication. It would be safe to say that but for these aids the penny post would at best have barely paid its way, if indeed it had not proved a total failure. Briefly it may be said that the success of the Post Office, such as it is, depends upon the circumstances which assimilate it to a private undertaking, and which at the same time cause it to differ from other Governmental institutions.

But it is not altogether fair to blame Governmental institutions, merely as such, for the shortcomings which they undoubtedly exhibit. The truth is that they share these shortcomings with all institutions in which industrial operations are conducted upon a large scale. Every large joint stock company, and especially every company whose business is of the nature of a monopoly, displays tendencies which are, after all, only carried out to an extreme in Government monopolies and in Government manufacturing establishments. Every great railway company is apt to be slow at adopting improvements and new or untried methods of business. That is because, in the first place, every such undertaking is upon a very large scale, and requires the co-operation of a great many heads and hands. Things must be done very much by fixed rule. There is less scope for personal initiative than in smaller and more elastic businesses. But in addition, the business is more or less of a monopoly. The public must use the railway in question, or go without the carrying facilities of which it stands in need. The only check upon the arbitrary power of the directors and other officials is the necessity of finding a dividend for the shareholders, and that check once taken away there is nothing to hinder the management from becoming despotic. Where there is less monopoly, the management is under greater inducements to strive after making the business popular. But it is not until we come to individual enterprise, where the merchant or shopkeeper or other head of the establishment is brought into direct personal relation with his customers, that the conduct of business becomes really elastic and automatic. It is because their personal gain or loss is not directly dependent upon the working of the institution that Government officials are less efficient than those of joint-stock companies, and the latter than those of private firms; these last themselves being inferior to the partners or proprietors, when they are brought into personal relations with the customers of the house.

I may be told that this is all speculation. As a matter of fact, I may be reminded, small traders are even more behind-hand than any big monopoly. If it were not so, how is it that so many private businesses are now being turned into joint-stock companies? My reply is that in all these cases the business began with private enterprise, and that not until private enterprise had pretty fully done its work did it become practicable to apply the joint-stock principle. I would add that this very principle is itself on its trial just now, and that it is premature to pronounce any judgment until we shall have had much larger experience. The analogous principle of co-operation would seem to be working fairly well as regards distribution, but not so well in production. We must remember also that the possession of large capital confers upon joint-stock enterprises an advantage which in some measure counterbalances, though it does not wholly neutralise, the special advantages attaching to private management. Nor should it be forgotten that this capital itself has been accumulated under private enterprise. The private businesses turned into limited companies are survivals; those that fall behind in the race are

the failures of individualism, and no one affirms that individualism makes no failures. I for my part am disposed
to think that the circumstances which cause large joint-
stock companies to resemble Government undertakings
are drawbacks and not advantages. It appears to me that if
railways could compete as omnibuses do, they would perform the carrying work of the country as cheaply and as
efficiently as, on the whole, the omnibus services of London and other great cities perform the services which they
render. Owing to exceptional circumstances, railway companies have to place themselves under State patronage, and
therefore to submit to State control; and in so far as this is
the case, it detracts from their efficiency. Owing, moreover, to the scale on which work has to be carried on, these
large enterprises are all more or less tainted with the vice
of departmentalism. To use a colloquial phrase, they are
tied up with red tape. The terrible railway accident in June,
1889, in the north of Ireland, was largely due to the want
of a proper system of brakes, and this want was itself due
to slovenly management and a blind trust in old methods.
There are plenty of railways still unprovided with fit appliances, despite Board of Trade inspection. I know of one
line in the vicinity of a great seaport, two of whose suburban stations have no telegraph wire between them, and
the railroad consists of a single line running along the face
of a crag overhanging the sea. A postal telegraph line
passes both stations, and a very trifling expenditure would
connect it with both, but the directors 'do not see their
way'!

I need not go on multiplying instances. The burden of
proof lies upon those who assert that departmentalised

management is superior to private enterprise. Their crucial instance, the Post Office, breaks down when it is tested. I think I have shown sufficient cause for my belief that private enterprise does not gain, but loses, by assimilation to State departmentalism. I may however be pardoned if I refer briefly to contemporary events. The strikes of policemen and postmen (June and July, 1890) seem to prove that a Government department is not necessarily more successful than a private firm or a joint-stock company in securing the contentment of the people who are in its employ.

On the whole, it seems that we should be warranted in drawing the conclusion that State departments are neither good producers, good distributors, nor good employers of labour, as compared with private producers, distributors, and employers.

I now come to a part of my task which I approach with some reluctance. There are certain social and economic matters which it is impossible to discuss without running a risk of offending certain perfectly legitimate susceptibilities, yet which must be discussed if a judgment of any value is to be formed on the social problem. I have elsewhere pointed out that the Collectivist community is always spoken of as a 'closed economic unit.' It is not easy to discover in the works of Schäffle or of any other exponent of Socialism whether they contemplate the exclusion of imported labour. If they do not, it only remains to be said that they are not honestly facing the consequences of their own system. If a collective production and distribution of wealth is to be carried on at all, it must be on the condition that the producers know exactly how much to produce, and that the distributors know exactly how much, and to whom, to distribute. This, as I have already shown, is a task beyond human power, even if the fluctuation of numbers could be to some extent foreseen. But we know that the fluctuation can by no means be foreseen, and we know the reason why. I have endeavoured to lead up to my main question by referring in the first instance to the importation of foreign labour; but that in reality is only a very minor matter. In spite of the silence of Schäffle and other recognised exponents of the system, I suspect that no thoroughgoing Socialist would shrink from prohibiting foreign immigration. But there is an immigration which goes on day after day—an immigration of mouths to be fed, without, for the time being, hands to labour for food. Every child that is born is for years a helpless being, dependent upon others for its support, and incapable of rendering anything in return. Nay, more, every child renders its mother incapable of contributing to the support of the community for weeks, if not for months.[35] The disablement of the mother may be considered a matter of no very great consequence, but it is certainly a serious matter to the community to be compelled to maintain an entirely unproductive consumer for a period of some fourteen years. It may fairly be taken for granted that a Socialist community would not exact less in the way of education than is demanded by the community as at present existing. The present school age does not end until

---

[35] I am here speaking of civilised communities. I am quite aware that savage women are fit to work in a very short time after child-bearing; but Socialism contemplates a state of civilisation not inferior to what now prevails, with, it may be presumed, a civilised and not a savage *physique*.

thirteen. We may be pretty sure that under Socialism the period would not be shorter, and might be longer. Even this is not all. The young person of thirteen or fourteen would then have to be provided with a vocation. How far any liberty of choice would or could be left is a difficult question, but fortunately it does not require a detailed answer. The liberty of choice must under any circumstances be limited by the number of vocations open to the candidate; and we may safely assume that this number would itself depend upon the judgment of the collective authorities. So, then, these authorities would have not only to provide for all the mothers who from time to time bore children, and for all the children from birth till about fourteen years old, but also to find employment for all the boys and girls who lived to the age of fourteen. Nor is even that all. They would be bound, in offering employment to each candidate, to hold out some reasonable expectation that such employment should be a provision for life. At present, under the ordinary *régime* of individualism and competition, the father of a family is as a general rule responsible for the careers of his children. The children themselves have some kind of a voice in choosing a trade or a profession. If a mistake is made, the consequences may, no doubt, be very disastrous; but as a rule, he who commits the error suffers the consequences. Every now and then it happens that a particular vocation is, so to speak, superseded and rendered obsolete. Still more often it happens that a candidate for employment adopts the wrong vocation, or that work drifts away to other quarters, so that although the employment itself may be prosperous enough, particular workers or classes of workers are thrown out. Under individualism,

there takes place a survival of the fittest, which may be
very cruel to individuals and to classes. One of the aims
of collective production and distribution is to eliminate
this survival, with its attendant cruelty. Can it be done?

We have seen that the more sober exponents of Socialism declare that there is no intention of interfering with
family life. Even the extreme fanatics avoid the question,
and seem to assume that it may somehow or other be expected to solve itself. But there are indications, underlying
all the more outspoken utterances on the subject, that
attempts would be made to limit the increase of the population. Curiously enough, the most earnest advocacy of
artificial restraints on multiplication is to be found in John
Stuart Mill's *Political Economy*; and Mill was not a Socialist or Collectivist. Mill, indeed, advocated a voluntary
restriction which to most readers has seemed a quite unpractical and impracticable proposal. When we consider
how other habits—that of drinking, for instance—which
are admitted to be immoral and disgraceful, are nevertheless far too frequently and freely indulged, it is difficult
to read Mill's speculations on this subject without a smile.
But Mill, in spite of his enthusiasms, was a clear-headed
man. He saw what the puzzle-headed latter-day fanatic
does not see, that unless multiplication is to be somehow
restrained, no artificial devices for promoting social prosperity have any chance of success. Whether, under a Collectivist *régime*, restraints on multiplication would in the
long run succeed in promoting social prosperity is another
question. My belief is that they would not. We have seen
already that the scheme of Collectivism implies the regulation of employment. Every child must be maintained

until his or her schooldays are over. Every youth and maiden, on leaving school, must be provided with some kind of employment. How is this to be done? What government, central or local, is wise enough and strong enough to perform such a task? If we suppose it placed in the hands of a very widely ramified local organisation—parish councils for example—is there not as much danger of their entering upon a course of competition as if they were private families?

We have seen that Schäffle explicitly disclaims any project of restrictions upon population, and that the fanatical Socialists, such as the Fabian essayists, are completely silent upon the subject. It may, nevertheless, be worthwhile to refer to the only country where such restrictions are actually in force under the influence of a public opinion such as Mill hoped might come into existence. France, which Mill held up as an example, is now beginning to complain that her population is becoming actually scanty. French statesmen are seriously talking of offering rewards to the parents of large families. The remedies for overpopulation, so eloquently advocated by Mill, have done their work rather too well. But is France free from complaints of the existence of a 'proletariat?' By no means. Is France free from Socialist agitation? By no means. Germany, it is true, is just at present the headquarters of the movement, and it is also true that France is more free than most other European countries from the evils brought about by the presence of what Socialists call a proletariat. But France has by no means laid aside Socialism. There are, it is true, no Saint Simons, no Fouriers, no Louis Blancs; but French workmen are as fond of the phrases of

Socialistic agitation as ever they were. French men of letters, too, have by no means left off playing the role of
eloquent Aaron to the inarticulate but suggestive Moses
of German thought.

In spite of all this—in spite, especially, of the extremely
meddlesome character of public authority—France is, in
two respects, extremely far from being a Socialistic nation.
Nowhere is private property so jealously guarded. Nowhere is what we may call the individualism of the family
held so sacred. However willing he may be to observe self-
imposed restraints, no Frenchman would tolerate for a
moment a law prescribing a limitation on the number of
his children. But the more clear-headed of the English
philanthropists are beginning to see that some such law
there must be if Socialism, or anything akin to Socialism,
is to have effect. Schäffle, it is true, says the German Socialists do not demand any such law. The Fabian rhetoricians give the subject the go-by. But there are others who
see clearly enough that it must come to such a law sooner
or later. A writer in the daily press recently proposed
that the clergy and the civil registrars should have a dis-
cretionary power to refuse marriage under certain circumstances to couples applying for their services. We know
very well that the clergy would never exercise any such
discretion. We may be pretty sure that the civil registrars
would not do so, any more than the clergy. But suppose
they did, every one knows what the consequence would
be. Restraints on marriage always result in an increase of
illicit unions and of illegitimate births. Are we prepared to
make cohabitation out of wedlock a crime? The mediaeval
Church tried to do that, and conspicuously failed. Indeed,

it is wonderful in how many instances modern Socialism is compelled, as it were, to hark back to the methods of mediaeval despotism, civil and ecclesiastical.

The situation may be summed up in a sentence: Socialism, without restraints on the increase of population, would be utterly inefficient. With such restraints, it would be slavery.

In a word, Socialism—the scheme of collective capital and collective production and distribution—breaks down the moment it is subjected to any practical test. Considered merely as a scheme for supplying the material wants of the community, it is seen at a glance to be totally incapable of adjusting the relation between supply and demand. I have suggested the practical test. If any Socialist were asked, 'Suppose Socialism established now, how many suits of clothes, and of what qualities, will have to be in stock for the township of Little Pedlington on the first of next June?' either he could not answer the question at all, or he would be compelled to fall back upon the device of a uniform. Still more difficult would it be to answer the question, 'Of the children born this year, how many boys do you propose to apprentice as tailors, and how many girls as dressmakers, in 1904?' Until Socialists can answer these questions, and others of like nature, Socialism has simply no *locus standi* as a practical scheme for the supply of material wants. That being so, *à fortiori* it is valueless as a scheme for the supply of wants which are not material. To do the enthusiasts of Socialism justice, none of them even pretend to include art and literature in their projects. This is all the more curious, because the present is a time when art and literature are being cultivated for the sake of profit more, apparently, than at any previous period of history.[36] But inasmuch as the Socialist exponents, sober or enthusiastic, shirk the topic, I am entitled to say that they do not expect the Socialist community to cultivate art or literature.

In addition to all this, it seems to me a very open question (to say the least) whether Socialism would really promote the comfort of the entire working class, supposing that it could be worked without the difficulties I have noted. The energetic workman, it may be conceded, would be successful under Socialism; but then, he is already successful under Individualism. All workmen, however, are not energetic. What of the man who is below the average, or barely up to it, in energy, honesty, and sobriety? What of the man who has no vices, but whose character is shiftless, irresolute, wanting in 'backbone'? Such a man, under Individualism, becomes a failure; what would be his fate under Socialism? I know of no infallible prescription whereby an idle man can be rendered industrious, or an irresolute one steady of purpose, except one—the sharp spur of want! Are Socialists prepared to suggest any other? If they are not, wherein is their system better than Individualism? If they are, what is it? The prison, perhaps, or the scourge? If so, some one may be tempted to say concerning the ten-

---

[36] Some very striking remarks on the rewards given by society to men of letters will be found in Professor Graham's work, cited above (*The Social Problem*, ch. v. p 167 et seq., 'Spiritual Producers and their Work'). Professor Graham is not a Socialist, though his opinions have some bias in that direction. But the interest of the reference lies in this; that Professor Graham emphasises very strongly, though quite unconsciously, the fact that literature is a profession, and is subject in the long run to commercial influences like other professions.

der mercies of the philanthropist what the inspired writer said concerning those of the wicked.

It remains only to sum up what I have attempted to prove, and I think succeeded in proving.

Socialism would be totally inefficient as a producing and distributing scheme. Society is not an army, which can be fed on rations, clothed in a uniform, and lodged in barracks. Even if it were, the task would be too much for Government departments, which habitually fail, or commit shortcomings, in dealing with the special classes which they do undertake to feed, clothe, and lodge. The army and navy are composed of young men, and picked men, who are, or ought to be, in good average health and vigour. Yet the supply departments of both services, it is acknowledged on all hands, leave much to be desired. How much more difficult would the task be of maintaining women, children, the aged and the sick!

I have dealt pretty fully with the one department of Government which is always called successful, and I have shown that the success which is claimed for it must, to say the least, be conceded subject to large qualifications. I have shown that Government departments are not more meritorious as employers of labour than they are as producers and distributors.

I have suggested that the scheme of Socialism is wholly incomplete unless it includes a power of restraining the increase of population, which power is so unwelcome to Englishmen that the very mention of it seems to require an apology. I have showed that in France, where restraints on multiplication have been adopted into the popular code of morals, there is discontent on the one hand at the slow

rate of increase, while on the other, there is still a 'proletariat,' and Socialism is still a power in politics.

I have put the question, how Socialism would treat the
residuum of the working class and of all classes—the class,
not specially vicious, nor even necessarily idle, but below
the average in power of will and in steadiness of purpose.
I have intimated that such persons, if they belong to the
upper or middle classes, are kept straight by the fear of
falling out of class, and in the working class by positive
fear of want. But since Socialism purposes to eliminate the
fear of want, and since under Socialism the hierarchy of
classes will either not exist at all or be wholly transformed,
there remains for such persons no motive at all except
physical coercion. Are we to imprison or flog all the 'ne'er-
do-weels'?

I began this paper by pointing out that there are inequalities and anomalies in the material world, some of
which, like the obliquity of the ecliptic and the consequent
inequality of the day's length, cannot be redressed at all.
Others, like the caprices of sunshine and rainfall in different climates, can be mitigated, but must on the whole
be endured. I am very far from asserting that the inequalities and anomalies of human society are strictly parallel
with those of material nature. I fully admit that we are
under an obligation to control nature so far as we can.
But I think I have shown that the Socialist scheme cannot
be relied upon to control nature, because it refuses to obey
her. Socialism attempts to vanquish nature by a front attack. Individualism, on the contrary, is the recognition, in
social politics, that nature has a beneficent as well as a
malignant side. The struggle for life provides for the various wants of the human race, in somewhat the same way

as the climatic struggle of the elements provides for vegetable and animal life—imperfectly, that is, and in a manner strongly marked by inequalities and anomalies. By taking advantage of prevalent tendencies, it is possible to mitigate these anomalies and inequalities, but all experience shows that it is impossible to do away with them. All history, moreover, is the record of the triumph of Individualism over something which was virtually Socialism or Collectivism, though not called by that name. In early days, and even at this day under archaic civilisations, the note of social life is the absence of freedom. But under every progressive civilisation, freedom has made decisive strides—broadened down, as the poet says, from precedent to precedent. And it has been rightly and naturally so.

Freedom is the most valuable of all human possessions, next after life itself. It is more valuable, in a manner, than even health. No human agency can secure health; but good laws, justly administered, can and do secure freedom. Freedom, indeed, is almost the only thing that law can secure. Law cannot secure equality, nor can it secure prosperity. In the direction of equality, all that law can do is to secure fair play, which is equality of rights but is not equality of conditions. In the direction of prosperity, all that law can do is to keep the road open. That is the Quintessence of Individualism, and it may fairly challenge comparison with that Quintessence of Socialism we have been discussing. Socialism, disguise it how we may, is the negation of Freedom. That it is so, and that it is also a scheme not capable of producing even material comfort in exchange for the abnegation of Freedom, I think the foregoing considerations amply prove.

EDWARD STANLEY ROBERTSON

CHAPTER 2

THE LIMITS OF LIBERTY

WORDSWORTH DONISTHORPE

CHAPTER 2

THE LIMITS OF LIBERTY

The power of the State may be defined as the resultant of all the social forces operating within a definite area. 'It follows,' says Professor Huxley, with characteristic logical thoroughness, 'that no limit is, or can be, theoretically set to State interference.'

Ab extra—this is so. I have always endeavoured to show that the effective majority has a right (a legal right) to do just what it pleases. How can the weak set a limit to the will of the strong? Of course, if the State is rotten, if it does not actually represent the effective majority of the country, then it is a mere sham, like some little old patriarch who rules his brawny sons by the prestige of ancient thrashings.

The time comes in the life of every government when it becomes effete, when it rules the stronger by sheer force of prestige, when the bubble waits to be pricked, and when the first-determined act of resistance brings the whole card-castle down with a crash. The *bouleversement* is

79

usually called a revolution. On the contrary, it is merely
the outward and visible expression of a death which may
have taken place years before. In such cases a limit can
be set to State interference by the simple process of explod-
ing the State. But when a State *is* (as Hobbes assumes) the
embodiment of the will of the effective majority—*force
majeure*—of the country, then clearly no limit can be set
to its interference—*ab extra*. And this is why Hobbes (who
always built on fact) describes the power of the State as
absolute. This is why he says that each citizen has conveyed all his strength and power to the State.

I fail to see any *à priori* assumption here. It is the plain
truth of his time and of our own. We may agree with John
Locke that there ought to be some limit to despotism, and
we may keep on shifting the concentrated force from the
hands of the One to those of the Few; from the hands of
the Few to those of the Many; and from the hands of the
Many to those of the Most—the numerical majority. But
this handing about of the power cannot alter its nature; it
still remains unlimited despotism, as Hobbes rightly assumes. Locke's pretence that the individual citizens reserved certain liberties when the State was formed is of
course the merest allegory, without any more foundation
in fact than Rousseau's *Contrat Social*. It is on a par with
the 'natural right' of every citizen born into the world to
an acre of land and a good education. We may consider
that nation wise which should guarantee these advantages
to all its children, or we may not; but we must never forget
that the rights, when created, are created by the will of the
strong for its own good pleasure, and not carved out of the
absolute domain of despotism by any High Court of
Eternal Justice.

Surely it is the absence of all these *à priori* vapourings, common to Locke, Rousseau, and Henry George, which renders the writings of Hobbes so fascinating and so instructive.

Shall we then sit down like blind fatalists in presence of the doctrine 'no limit can be set to State-interference'? Certainly not. I have admitted that no limit can be set *from without*. But just as we can influence the actions of a man by appeals to his understanding, so that it may be fairly said of such an one, 'he cannot lie,' and of another that it is easier to turn the sun from its course than Fabricius from the path of duty: so we may imbue the hearts of our own countrymen with the doctrine of individualism in suchwise that it may sometime be said of England, 'Behold a free country.' It is to this end that individualists are working. Just as a virtuous man imposes restrictions on the gratification of his own appetites, *apparently* setting a limit to his present will, and compelling a body to move in a direction other than that of least resistance, so, it is hoped, will the wise State of the future lay down a general principle of State-action for its own voluntary guidance, which principle is briefly expressed in the words *Let be*.[1]

In his effort to supply destructive criticism of *à priori* political philosophy, which is the task Professor Huxley

---

[1] Is it not a pity to go to France for a term to denote a political idea so peculiarly English? The correct and idiomatic English for *laissez-faire* is *let-be*. 'Let me be,' says the boy in the street, protesting against interference. Moreover, it is not only colloquial but classical. 'The rest said, Let be, let us see whether Elias will come to save him' (Matt. xxvii. 49). There is a barbarous ring about *Let act*, which is calculated to reflect on the doctrine conveyed. For the last seventeen years I have always found it convenient to speak of the Let-be School.

set before him, it seems to me he has been a little unjust to Individualism. He has taken for granted that it is based on *à priori* assumptions and arguments which are as foreign to the reasoning of some of its supporters as to his own. The individualist claims that under a system of increasing political liberty, many evils, of which all alike complain, would disappear more rapidly and more surely before the forces of co-operation than they will ever do before the distracted efforts of democratic 'regimentation.'

Of course there are individualists as there are socialists, and, we may add, artists and moralists and most other -ists who hang most of their conclusions on capital letters. We have Liberty and Justice and Beauty and Virtue and all the rest of the family; but it is not fair to assert or even to insinuate that Individualism as a practical working doctrine in this country and in the United States is based on reasoning from abstractions. Professor Huxley refers to 'moderns who make to themselves metaphysical teraphim out of the Absolute, the Unknowable, the Unconscious, and the other verbal abstractions whose apotheosis is indicated by initial capitals.' And he adds, 'So far as this method of establishing their claims is concerned, socialism and individualism are alike out of court.' Granted—but so is morality. Honesty, Truth, Justice, Liberty, and Right are teraphim when treated as such, every whit as ridiculous as the Unknowable or the Unconditioned. Nevertheless it is surely possible to label general ideas with general names, after the discovery of their connotation, without being charged with the worship of abstractions. And unless Professor Huxley is prepared to dispense with such general ideas as Right and Wrong, True, Beautiful and Free, I fail to see what objection he can have to the Unknowable when employed to denote what has been so carefully and clearly defined under that term by Mr. Spencer.

At the same time I admit that we have reason to thank Professor Huxley for his onslaught on Absolutism in politics, whereby he has done more good to the cause of progress than he could ever hope to do by merely dubbing himself either individualist or socialist. When the Majority learns that its acts can be criticised, just as other people's acts are criticised; that it can behave in an 'ungentlemanly' manner, as well as in a wrongful manner; that it should be guided in its treatment of the minority by its *conscience*, and not solely by laws of its own making; then there will be no scope for any other form of government than that which is based on individualism; and the Rights of Man will exist as realities, and not as a mere expression denoting each man's private notions of what his rights *ought* to be.

No one with the smallest claim to attention has been known to affirm that this or any other nation is yet ripe for the abolition of the State. Some of the more advanced individualists and philosophical anarchists express the view that absolute freedom from State-interference is the goal towards which civilisation is making, and, as is usual in the ranks of all political parties, there are not wanting impatient persons who contend that *now* is the time for every great reform.

Such are the people who would grant representative institutions to the Fijians, and who would model the Government of India on that of the United States of America. They may safely be left out of account. I suppose no one

acquainted with his political writings will accuse Victor
Yarros of backwardness or even of opportunism. Yet, says
he:

> The abolition of the external State must be preceded by the
> decay of the notions which breathe life and vigour into that
> clumsy monster: in other words, it is only when the people learn
> to value liberty, and to understand the truths of the anarchistic
> philosophy, that the question of practically abolishing the State
> looms up and acquires significance.

Again, Mr. Benjamin Tucker, the high priest of anarchy in
America, claims that it is precisely what is known in
England as individualism. So far is he from claiming any
natural right to liberty, that he expressly repudiates all
such *à priori* postulates, and bases his political doctrine on
the evidence (of which there is abundance) that liberty
would be the mother of order. Referring to Professor
Huxley's attack on anarchists as persons who build on
baseless assumptions and fanciful suppositions, he says:

> If all anarchists were guilty of such folly, scientific men like
> Professor Huxley could never be expected to have respect for
> them: but the professor has yet to learn that there are anarchists
> who proceed in a way that he himself would enthusiastically
> approve; who take nothing for granted; who vitiate their argu-
> ments by no assumptions; but who study the facts of social life,
> and from them derive the lesson that liberty would be the
> mother of order.

The truth is that the science of society has met with
general acceptance of late years, and (thanks chiefly to Mr.
Spencer) even the most impatient reformers now recognise
the fact that a State is an organism and not an artificial

structure to be pulled to pieces and put together on a new model whenever it pleases the effective majority to do so. Advice which is good to a philosopher may be bad to a savage and worse to an ape. Similarly institutions which are well suited to one people may be altogether unsuited to another, and the best institutions conceivable for a perfect people would probably turn out utterly unworkable even in the most civilised country of this age. The most ardent constitution-framer now sees that the chances are very many against the Anglo-Saxon people having reached the zenith of progress exactly at the moment when Nature has been pleased to evolve *him* as its guide. And if it must be admitted that we are not yet ripe for that unconditioned individual liberty which may be the type of the society of the future, it follows that *for the present* we must recognise some form of State-interference as necessary and beneficent. The problem is, What are the proper limits of liberty? and if these cannot be theoretically defined, what rules should be adopted for our practical guidance? With those who answer No limits, I will not quarrel. Such answer implies the belief that we have as a nation already reached the top rung of the ladder—that we are ripe for perfect anarchy. This is a question of fact which each can answer for himself. I myself do not believe that we have attained to this degree of perfection, and furthermore those who do believe it cannot evade the task of fixing the limits of liberty in a lower plane of social development. We can force them to co-operate with us by admitting their contention for the sake of argument, and then asking whether the Russians are ready for absolute freedom, and if so, whether the Hindoos are ready, or the Chinese, or the Arabs, or the

Hottentots, or the tree-dwarfs? The absolutist is compelled to draw the line sooner or later, and then he is likewise compelled to admit that the State has legitimate functions on the other side of that line.

And he must also admit that in practice people have to settle where private freedom and State-action shall mutually limit each other. Benjamin Tucker's last word still leaves us in perplexity as to the practical rule to be adopted *now*. Let me quote his words and readily endorse them—as far as they go:

> Then liberty always, say the anarchists. No use of force, except against the invader; and in those cases where it is difficult to tell whether the alleged offender is an invader or not, still no use of force except where the necessity of immediate solution is so imperative that we must use it to save ourselves. And in these few cases where we must use it, let us do so frankly and squarely, acknowledging it as a matter of necessity, without seeking to harmonise our action with any political ideal or constructing any far-fetched theory of a State or collectivity having prerogatives and rights superior to those of individuals and aggregations of individuals and exempted from the operation of the ethical principles which individuals are expected to observe. This is the best rule that I can frame as a guide to voluntary co-operators. To apply to it only one case, I think that under a system of anarchy, even if it were admitted that there was some ground for considering an unvaccinated person an invader, it would be generally recognised that such invasion was not of a character to require treatment by force, and that any attempt to treat it by force would be regarded as itself an invasion of a less doubtful and more immediate nature, requiring as such to be resisted.

But how far does this 'best rule' carry us? Let us test it by the case selected. Mr. Tucker thinks that under a *régime* of liberty it would be generally recognised that such an invasion of the individual's freedom of action as is implied by compulsory vaccination is a greater and a worse invasion than the converse invasion of the general freedom by walking about in public 'a focus of infection.' Perhaps it would be so recognised in some future state of anarchy, but is it so recognised *now*? I think not. The majority of persons, in this country at least, treat it, and consider that it ought to be treated, as an offense; just as travelling in a public conveyance with the scarletina-rash is treated. And the question is, What, in face of actual public opinion, ought we to do today? The rule gives us no help. Even the most avowed State-socialist is ready to say that compulsion in such matters is justifiable only when it is 'so imperative that we *must* use it to save ourselves.' He is ready to do so, if need be, 'fairly and squarely, acknowledging it as a matter of necessity.' But so is the protectionist; so is the religious persecutor. Mr. Tucker continues:

> The question before us is not what measures and means of interference we are justified in instituting, but which of those already existing we should first lop off. And to this the anarchists answer that unquestionably the first to go should be those that interfere most fundamentally with a free market, and that the economic and moral changes that would result from this would act as a solvent upon all the remaining forms of interference.

Good again, but why? There must be some middle principle upon which this conclusion is based. And it is for this middle principle, this practical rule for the guidance of those who must act at once, that a search must be made. To restate the question:

Can any guiding principle be formulated whereby we

may know where the State should interfere with the liberties of its citizens and where it should not? Can any definite limits be assigned to State action? Where in theory shall we draw the line, which in practice we *have to draw somewhere?*

Surely an unprincipled State is as bad as an unprincipled man. Yet what should we think of a man who, in moral questions, decided each case on its merits as a question of immediate expediency? Who admitted that he told the truth or told lies just as it suited the object he had presently in view? We should say he was an unprincipled man, and we should rightly distrust him. An appeal to Liberty is as futile as an appeal to Justice, until we have defined Liberty.

Various suggestions have been made in order to get over this difficulty. Some people say, Let every man do what is right in his own eyes, provided he does not thereby injure others. To quote Mill:

> The principle is that the sole end for which mankind are warranted, individually or collectively, in interfering with the liberty of action of any of their number, is self-protection: that the only purpose for which power can be rightfully exercised over any member of a civilised community against his will is to prevent harm to others.

To this Lord Pembroke shrewdly replies:

> But how far does this take us? The very kernel of our difficulty is the fact that hardly any actions are purely self-regarding. The greater part of them bear a double aspect—one which concerns self, another which concerns others.

We might even go further; we might plausibly maintain that every act performed by a citizen from his birth to his death injures his neighbours more or less indirectly. If he eats his dinner he diminishes the supply of food and raises the price. His very existence causes an enhanced demand for the necessaries of life; hence the cry against over-population. One who votes on the wrong side of a Parliamentary election injures all his fellow-countrymen. One who marries a girl loved by another injures that other. One who preaches Christianity or Agnosticism (if untrue) injures his hearers and their relatives and posterity. One who wins a game pains the loser. One who sells a horse for more than it is worth injures the purchaser, and one who sells it for less than it is worth injures his own family.

Taking practical questions concerning which there is much dispute; there are advocates of State-interference with the citizen's freedom to drink what he likes, who base their action not on the ground that the State should protect a fool against the effects of his folly, but on the ground that drink fills the workhouses and the prisons, which have to be maintained out of the earnings of the sober; and, furthermore, that drink leaves legacies of disease and immorality to the third and the fourth generation. Advocates of compulsory vaccination have been heard to say that they would willingly leave those who refuse the boon to perish of small-pox, but that unvaccinated persons are foci of infection, and must be suppressed in the common interest. Many people defend the Factory Acts, not for the sake of the apathetic workers who will not take the trouble to organise and to defend themselves, but for the sake of the physique of the next generation. The suppression of gambling-hells is favoured by many, not on account of the green-horns who lose their money, but because they are schools of cheating and fraud, and turn loose upon society a number of highly-trained swindlers. On the whole, Mill's test will not do.

Some say, 'We must fall back on the consensus of the people; there is nothing else for it; we must accept the arbitrary will—the caprice—of the governing class, be they the many or be they the few.' Others, again, qualify that contention. These say, let us loyally accept the verdict of the majority. This is democracy. I have nothing to urge against it. But, unfortunately, it only shoves the question a step further back. How are the many to decide for themselves when they ought to interfere with the minority and when they ought not? This is just the guiding principle of which we are in search; and it is no answer to tell us that certain persons must decide it for themselves. We are amongst the number; what is our vote going to be? Of course the stronger can do what they choose; but what ought they to choose? What is the wisest course for their own welfare, leaving the minority out of the reckoning?

Socialists say, treat all alike, and all will be well. But equality in slavery is not liberty. Even the fox in the fable would not have had his own tail cut off for the fun of seeing the other foxes in like plight. After the event, it was quite another matter; and one can forgive those who are worked to death for demanding that the leisured classes shall be forced to earn their living. Lock us all up in jail, and we shall all be equally moral and equally happy.

Nor is it any solution of this particular problem to abolish the State, however prudent that course might or might not be: the answer to the present question is not 'No Government!' For this again merely throws the difficulty a step further back. We may put the State on one side and imagine a purely anarchic form of society, and the same question still arises. That is to say, philosophical anarchists do not pretend that the anarchy of the wild beasts is conceivable among sane men, still less desirable, —though they are usually credited with this imbecile notion. They believe that all necessary restrictions on absolute liberty can be brought about by voluntary combination. Let us admit that this may be so. The question then arises, for what purposes are people to combine? Thus the majority in a club can, if they choose, forbid billiard-playing on Sundays. Ought they to do so? Of course the majority may disapprove of and refrain from it, but ought they to permit the minority to play? If not, on what grounds? The Christians in certain parts of Russia have an idea that they are outwitted and injured by their Jew fellow-citizens. If unrestrained by the stronger majority outside—the State—they persecute and drive off the Jews. Ought they to do this? If you reply, 'Leave it to the sense of the people,' the answer is settled, they ought. It is, therefore, no answer to our question to say, 'Away with the State.' It may be a good cry, but it is no solution to our problem. Because you cannot do away with the effective majority.

To reply that out of one hundred persons, the seventy-five weak and therefore orderly persons can combine against the twenty-five advocates of brute-force, is merely to beg the whole question. Ought they to combine for this purpose? And if so, why not for various other purposes? Why not for the very purposes for which they are now banded together in an association called the State?

You rejoin, 'True, but it would be a voluntary State, and that makes all the difference; no one need join it against his will.' My answer is, he need not join it now. The existence of the burglar in our midst is sufficient evidence of this. But since the anarchy of the wild beasts is out of the question, it is clear that certain arbitrary and aggressive acts on the part of individuals must be met and resisted by voluntary combination—by the voluntary combination of a sufficient number of others to overpower them by fear, or, if necessary, by brute force. Again I ask, for what purposes are these combinations to be made?

Whether we adopt despotism or democracy, socialism or anarchy, we are always brought back to this unanswered question, What are the limits of group-action in relation to its units? Shall we say that the State should never interfere with the mutual acts of willing parties? (And by the State I wish to be understood as here meaning the effective majority of a group, be it a club or be it a nation.) This looks plausible, but alas! who are the parties? The parties acting, or the parties affected? Clearly the latter, for otherwise, two persons could agree to kill a third. But who then are the persons affected? Suppose a print-seller, with a view to business, exposes in his shop-window a number of objectionable pictures, for the attraction of those only who choose to look at them and possibly to buy them. I have occasion to walk through that street; am I a party? How am I injured? Is my sense of decency shocked and hurt? But if this is sufficient ground for public interference, then I have a right to call for its assistance when my taste is hurt and shocked by a piece of architecture which violates the laws of high art. I have similar ground of complaint when a speaker gets up in a public place and preaches doctrines which are positively loathsome to me. I have a right of action against a man clothed in dirty rags, or with pomaded hair or a scented pocket-handerchief.

If you reply that in these cases my hurt is not painful enough to justify any interference with another's freedom, I have only to cite the old and almost forgotten arguments for the inquisition. The possible eternal damnation of my children, who are exposed to heretical teaching, is surely a sufficiently painful invasion of my happiness to warrant the most strenuous resistance. And even to modern ears, it will seem reasonable that I should have grounds of action against a music-hall proprietor who should offend the moral sense of my children with songs of a pernicious character. This test then will not do.

It has been suggested that the State should not meddle except on the motion of an individual alleging injury to himself. In other words, that the State must never act as prosecutor, but leave all such matters entirely to private initiative; and that no person should be permitted to complain that some *other* person is injured or likely to be injured by the act complained of. But there are two valid objections to this rule: firstly, it provides no test of injury or hurt; secondly, it would not meet the case of cruelty to animals or young children, or imbeciles or persons too poor or too ill to take action. It would permit of the murder of a friendless man. This will not do.

May I now venture to present my own view? I feel convinced that there is no *à priori* solution of the problem. We cannot draw a hard and fast line between the proper field of State-interference and the field sacred to individual freedom. There is no general principle whereby the effective majority can decide whether to interfere or not. And yet we are by no means left without guidance. Take the parallel region of morals: no man has ever yet succeeded in defining virtue *à priori*. All we can say is that those acts which eventually conduce to the permanent welfare of the agent are moral acts, and those which lead in the opposite direction are immoral. But if any one asks for guidance beforehand, he has to go away empty. It is true, certain preachers tell him to stick to the path of virtue, but when it comes to casuistry they no more know which *is* the path of virtue than he does himself. 'Which is the way to York?' asks a traveller. 'Oh, stick to the York Road, and you can't go wrong.' That is the sum and substance of what the moralists have to tell us. And yet we do not consider that we are altogether without guidance in these matters. Middle principles, reached by induction from the experience of countless generations, have been formulated, which cannot be shown to be true by any process of deduction from higher truths, but which we trust, simply because we have found them trustworthy a thousand times, and our parents and friends have safely trusted them too. Do not lie. Do not steal. Do not hurt your neighbour's feelings without cause. And why not? Because, as a general rule, it will not pay.

Where is the harm in saying two and two make five? Either you are believed or you are disbelieved. If disbelieved, you are a failure. One does not talk for the music of the thing, but to convey a belief. If you are believed, you have given away false coin or a sham article. The recipient thinks he can buy with it or work with it, and lo! it breaks in his hand. He hates the cause of his disappointment. 'Well, what of that?' you say; 'if I had been strong enough or plucky enough I would have broken his head and he would have hated me for that. Then why should I be ashamed to tell a lie to a man whom I deliberately wish to hurt?' Here we come nearly to the end of our tether. Experience tells us that it is mean and *self-wounding* to lie, and we believe it. Those who try find it out in the end.

And if this is the true view of individual morals, it should also be found true of what may be called Group-morals or State-laws. We must give up all hope of deducing good laws from high general principles and rest content with those middle principles which originate in experience and are verified by experience. And we must search for these middle principles by observing the tendency of civilisation. In morals they have long been stated with more or less precision but in politics they are still unformulated. By induction from the cases presented to us in the long history of mankind we can, I believe, find a sound working answer to the question we set out with. All history teaches us that there has been an increasing tendency to remove the restrictions placed by the State on the absolute liberty of its citizens. That is an observed fact which brooks no contradiction. In the dawn of civilisation, we find the bulk of the people in a state of absolute bondage, and even those who supposed themselves to be the independent classes, subject to a most rigorous despotism. Every act from the cradle to the grave must conform to the most savage and exacting laws. Nothing was too sacred or too private for the eye of the State. Take the Egyptians, the Assyrians, the

Babylonians, the Persians; we find them all in a state of the most complete subjection to central authority. Probably the code of law best known to us, owing to its adoption as the canvas on which European religion is painted, is the code of the Jewish theocracy. Most of us know something of the drastic and searching rules laid down in the books of Moses. Therein we find every concern of daily life ruled and regulated by the legislature; how and when people shall wash themselves, what they may eat and what they must avoid, how the food is to be cooked, what clothes may be worn, whom they may marry, and with what rites; while, in addition to this, their religious views are carefully provided for them and also their morals, and in case of transgression, intentional or accidental, the form of expiation to be made. Nor were these laws at all peculiar to the Jews. On the contrary, the laws of some of the contemporary civilisations seem to have been, if possible, even more exacting and frivolously meddlesome. The Greek and Roman laws were nothing like the Oriental codes, but still they were far more meddlesome and despotic than anything we have known in our day. And even in free and merry England we have in the older times put up with an amount of fussy State-interference which would not be tolerated for a week now-a-days. One or two specimens of early law in this country may be cited in order to recall the extent and severity of this kind of legislation.

> They shall have bows and arrows, and use the same of Sundays and holidays; and leave all playing at tennis or football and other games called quoits, dice, casting of the stone, kailes, and other such importune games.
>
> Forasmuch as labourers and grooms keep greyhounds and

other dogs, and on the holidays when good Christians be at church hearing divine service, they go hunting in parks, warrens, and connigries, it is ordained that no manner of layman which hath not lands to the value of forty shillings a year shall from henceforth keep any greyhound or other dog to hunt, nor shall he use ferrets, nets, heys, harepipes nor cords, nor other engines for to take or destroy deer, hares, nor conies, nor other *gentlemen's game,* under pain of twelve months' imprisonment.

For the great dearth that is in many places of the realm of poultry, it is ordained that the price of a young capon shall not pass threepence, and of an old fourpence, of a hen twopence, of a pullet a penny, of a goose fourpence.

Esquires and gentlemen under the estate of a knight shall not wear cloth of a higher price than four and a-half marks, they shall wear no cloth of gold nor silk nor silver, nor no manner of clothing embroidered, ring, button, nor brooch of gold nor of silver, nor nothing of stone, nor no manner of fur; and their wives and daughters shall be of the same condition as to their vesture and apparel, without any turning-up or purfle or apparel of gold, silver nor of stone.

Because that servants and labourers will not, nor by a long season would, serve and labour without outrageous and excessive hire, and much more than hath been given to such servants and labourers in any time past, so that for scarcity of the said servants and labourers the husbands and land-tenants may not pay their rents nor live upon their lands, to the great damage and loss as well of the Lords as of the Commons, it is accorded and assented that the bailiff for husbandry shall take by the year 13s. 3d. and his clothing once by the year at most; the master hind 10s., the carter 10s., the shepherd 10s., the oxherd 6s. 8d., the swineherd 6s., a woman labourer 6s., a dey 6s., a driver of the plough 7s. at the most, and every other labourer and servant according to his degree; and less in the country where less was wont to be given, without clothing, courtesy or other reward by covenant. And if any give or take by covenant more than is above specified, at the first that they shall be thereof attainted, as well the givers as the takers, shall pay the value of the excess so taken, and at the second time of their attainder the double value of such excess, and at the third time the treble value of such excess, and if the taker so attainted have nothing whereof to pay the said excess, he shall have forty days' imprisonment.

One can cite these extraordinary enactments by the score, with the satisfactory result of raising a laugh at the expense of our ancestors; but before making too merry, let us examine the beam in our own eye. Some of the provisions of our modern Acts of Parliament, when looked at from a proper distance, are quite as ludicrous as any of the little tyrannies of our ancestors. I do not wish to tread on delicate ground, or to raise party bias, and therefore I will resist the temptation of citing modern instances of legislative drollery.[2] Doubtless the permanent tendency in this country, as all through history, is in a direction opposed to this sort of grandmotherly government; but the reason is not, I fear, our superior wisdom; it is the increasing number of conflicting interests, all armed with democratic power, which renders it difficult. The spirit is willing, but the flesh is weak.

I can imagine no healthier task for our new school of social reformers than a careful enquiry into the effects of all State attempts to improve humanity. It would take too long to go through even a few of them now. There are all the statutes of Plantagenet days against forestalling and regrating and usury; there are the old sumptuary laws, the fish laws, the cloth laws, the Tippling Acts, the Lord's

---

[2] I may, however, refer to a quaint tract entitled 'Municipal Socialism,' published by the Liberty and Property Defence League. This capital satire on modern local legislation I take up in the name of our forefathers and fling at the heads of those pharisaical reformers of today who never weary of tittering at 'the wisdom of our ancestors.'

Day Observance Act, the Act against making cloth by machinery, which, by its prohibition of the 'divers devilish contrivances,' drove trade to Holland and to Ireland, and thus made it needful to suppress the Irish woollen trade. Still, on the whole, as I have said, State interference shows signs of becoming weaker and weaker as civilisation progresses. And this brings us back to our original question, What is the rule whereby the majority is to guide itself as to where it should interfere with the freedom of individuals and where it should not? It is this: while according the same worship to Liberty in politics that we accord to Honesty in private dealings, hardly permitting ourselves to believe that its violation can in any case be wise or permanently expedient—while leaning to Liberty as we lean to Truth, and deviating from it only when the arguments in favour of despotism are absolutely overwhelming, our aim should be to find out by study of history what those classes of acts are, in which State interference shows signs of becoming weakened, and as far as possible to hasten on the day of complete freedom in such matters.

When the student of history sees how the Statute of Labourers broke down in its effort to regulate freedom of contract between employer and employed, in the interest of the employer, he will admit the futility of renewing the attempt, this time in the interest of the employed. When he reads the preamble[3] (or pre-ramble as it is aptly styled in working-men's clubs) to James's seventh Tippling Act,

---

[3] 'Whereas, notwithstanding all former laws and provisions already made, the inordinate and extreme vice of excessive drinking and drunkenness doth more and more abound, to the great offence of Almighty God and the wasteful destruction of God's good creatures . . .'

he will be less sanguine in embarking on modern temperance legislation.

We find the same record of failure and accompanying
mischiefs all along the line, and it is mainly our ignorance
of history that blinds us to the truth. By this process of
induction, the earnest and honest reformer is led to discover what those individual acts are which are really compatible with social cohesion. He finds that while the State
tends to suppress violence and fraud and stealth with ever-
increasing severity, it is at the same time more and more
tolerant, not from sympathy, but from necessity, of the
results, good, bad, and indifferent, of free contract between
full-grown sane men and women.

And when a well-wisher to mankind has once thoroughly appreciated and digested this general principle,
based as it is on a survey of facts and history, and not
woven out of the dream-stuff of *à priori* philosophy, he
will be content to remove all artificial hindrances to progress, and to watch the evolution of society, instead of trying to model it according to his own vague ideas of the
Just, and the Good, and the Beautiful.

I wish to show that the only available method of discovering the true limits of liberty at any given period is the
historic. History teaches us that there has been a marked
tendency (in the main continuous) to reduce the number of
State-restrictions on the absolute freedom of the citizens.
State-prohibitions are becoming fewer and more definite,
while, on the other hand, some of them are at the same time
more rigorously enforced. Freedom to murder and rob is
more firmly denied to the individual, while in the meantime
he has won the liberty to think as he pleases, to say a good

deal more of what he pleases, to dress in accordance with his own taste, to eat when and what he likes, and to do, without let or hindrance, a thousand things which, in the olden times, he was not allowed to do without State-supervision. The proper aim of the reformer, therefore, is to find out, by a study of history, exactly what those classes of acts are in which State-interference shows signs of becoming weaker and weaker, and what those other classes of acts are in which such interference tends to be more rigorous and regular. He will find that these two classes are becoming more and more differentiated. And he will then, to the utmost of his ability, hasten on the day of absolute freedom in the former class of cases, and insist on the most determined enforcement of the law in the latter class. Whether this duty will in time pass into other hands, that is to say, whether private enterprise will ever supplant the State in the performance of this function, and whether that time is near or remote, are questions of the greatest interest. What we are mainly concerned to note is that the organisation or department upon which this duty rests incurs a responsibility which must, if society is to maintain its vitality, be faithfully borne. The business of carrying out the fundamental laws directed against the lower forms of competition—murder, robbery, fraud, etc.—must, by whomsoever undertaken, be unflinchingly performed, or the entire edifice of modern civilisation will fall to pieces.

It is enough to make a rough survey of the acts of citizens in which the State claims, or has at one time claimed, to exercise control; to track those claims through the ages; and to note the changes which have taken place in those claims. It remains to follow up the tendency into the future.

Anyone undertaking this task will, I repeat, find himself in the presence of two large and fairly well-defined classes of State-restrictions on private liberty; those which tend to become more thorough and invariable, and those which tend to become weaker, more spasmodic and variable. And he will try to abolish these *unprincipled* interferences altogether, in the belief, based on history, that, though some harm will result from the change, a far more than compensating advantage will accrue to the race. In short, what we have to do is to find the Least Common Pond in politics, as a mathematician finds the Least Common Multiple in the field of numbers.

Take these two joint-stock companies, and consider their prospects. The first is formed for the purpose of purchasing a square mile of land, for getting the coal from under the surface, for erecting furnaces on the land, for making pig-iron and converting it into wrought iron and steel, for building houses, churches, and schools for the workpeople, and for converting them and their neighbours to the Catholic faith, and for doing all such other matters and things as shall from time to time appear good to the Board of Directors. The second company is formed for the purpose of leasing a square mile of land, for getting the coal from under the surface, and selling it to the coal-merchants. Now that is just the difference between the State of the past and the State of the future. The shareholders in the second company are not banded together or mutually pledged and bound by a multitude of obligations, but by the *fewest compatible with the joint aim*. The company with the Least Common Bond is usually the most prosperous. A State held together by too many compacts will perform all or most of its functions ill. What we have to find is this Least Common Bond. Surely it would be absurd to argue that because the shareholders should not be bound by too many compacts, therefore they should not be bound by any. It is folly to pretend that each should be free to withdraw when and how he chooses; that he should be free to go down into the pits, and help himself to the common coal, in any fashion agreeable to himself, so long as he takes no more than his own portion. By taking shares in the Midland Railway Company, I have not bought the right to grow primroses on the line, or to camp out on the St. Pancras Station platform. My liberty to do what I choose with my share of the joint-stock is suspended. I am to that extent in subjection. My fellow-shareholders, or the majority of them, are my masters. They can compel me to spend my own money in making a line of rails which I am sure will never pay. Yet I do not grumble. But if they had the power (by our compact) to declare war on the Great Northern, or to import Dutch cheeses and Indian carpets, I should not care to be a citizen or shareholder of that particular company or state.

What we have got to do, then, is to purge the great company which has long ago been formed for the purpose of utilising the soil of this country to the best effect, from the multifarious functions with which it has overburdened itself. We, the shareholders, have agreed that the Red-Indian system is not suited to this end; and we have therefore agreed to forego our rights (otherwise admitted) of taking what we want from each other by force or fraud. This seems to be a necessary article of association. There is nothing to prevent us from agreeing to forego other rights and liberties if we choose; and possibly there may be some other restraints on our individual liberty which can be shown to be desirable, if not essential, to the success of the undertaking. If so, let them be stated, and the reason for their adoption given. If, on the other hand, it can be shown that a large and happy population can be supported on this soil without any other mutual restriction on personal freedom than that which is involved in the main article of association, would it not be as well for all if each kept charge of his own conscience and his own actions?

And here I should like to guard myself against misapprehension. Individualists are usually supposed to regard the State as a kind of malevolent ogre. Maleficent it is; but by no means malevolent. The State never intervenes without a reason, whether we deem that reason valid or invalid. The reasons alleged are very numerous and detailed, but they all fall under one of two heads. The State interferes either to defend some of the parties concerned against the others, or to defend itself against all the parties concerned. This has nothing to do with the distinction between crimes and civil injuries; it is more in line with the ethical distinction between self-regarding and other-regarding vices. Thus when a State punishes prize-fighters, it is not because one of them injures the other, but because the sport is demoralising: the State is itself injured, and not any determinate person. Similarly, there are many laws punishing drunkenness, quite apart from the violence and nuisance due to it. In these cases the State alleges that, though no determinate citizen is injured, yet the race suffers, and rightly punishes the offence with a view to eliminating the habit.

Putting on one side all those acts which injure determinate persons, whether crimes or civil injuries, let us see what the State has done and is doing in this country with regard to acts against which no particular citizen has any good ground of complaint. We may classify the subjects of these laws either according to the object affected, or according to the vice aimed at.

Taking some of the minor objects of the State's solicitude by way of illustration, we find that at one time or another it has interfered more or less with nearly all popular games, many sports, nearly the whole of the fine arts, and many harmless and harmful pleasures which cannot be brought under any of those three heads.

In looking for the motive which prompted the State to meddle with these matters, let us give our fathers credit for the best motive, and not, as is usually done, the worst. Football, tennis, nine-pins, and quoits were forbidden, as I have pointed out, because the State thought that the time wasted over them might more advantageously be spent in archery, which was quite as entertaining and far more useful. That was a good reason, but it was not a sufficient reason to modern mind; and moreover the law failed in its object. Some other games, such as baccarat, dice, trump, and primero, were put down because they led to gambling. And gambling was objected to for the good and ample reason that those who indulge in it are morally incapacitated for steady work. Lotteries and betting come under this censure. One who thinks he sees his way to make a thousand per cent. on his capital in a single evening without hard work cannot be expected to devote himself with zeal to the minute economics of his trade, for the purpose of

making six per cent. instead of five on the capital invested.
Wealth-production is on the average a slow process, and
all attempts to hurry up nature and take short cuts to opu-
lence are intoxicating, enervating, disappointing, and injurious, not only to those who make them, but to all those
who witness the triumph of the lucky, without fixing their
attention on the unsuccessful. Gambling, in short, is
wrong; but this does not necessarily warrant the State in
forbidding it. Another reason alleged on behalf of the interference was, and still is, that the simple are outwitted by
the cunning. But as this is true of all competition, even the
healthiest, it does not seem to be a valid reason for State-
action. It is also said that games of chance lead to cheating
and fraud. But this is by no means a necessary consequence. Indeed, some of the most inveterate gamblers are
the most honourable of men. Again, the State refuses to
sanction betting contracts for the same reason that under
the Statute of Frauds it requires certain agreements to be in
writing; namely, to ensure deliberateness and sufficient
evidence of the transaction. I think Barbeyrac overlooks
this aspect of the case in his *Traité de Jeu,* in which he de-
fends the lawfulness of chance-games. He says:

> If I am at liberty to promise and give my property, absolutely
> and unconditionally, to whomsoever I please, why may I not
> promise and give a certain sum, in the event of a person proving
> more fortunate or more skilful than I, with respect to the result
> of certain contingencies, movements, or combinations, on which
> we had previously agreed? . . . Gaming is a contract, and in
> every contract the mutual consent of the parties is the supreme
> law; this is an incontestable maxim of natural equity.

But, as a matter of fact, the State does not prohibit, or

even refuse to sanction, all contracts based on chance. It merely requires all or some of the usual guarantees against impulse, together with sufficient evidence and notification. It is true, you are not allowed to bet sixpence with a friend in a public-house that one horse will beat another in a race; you are allowed to bet a thousand pounds on the same event in your own house or at Tattersall's; but if you win and do not get paid you have no redress in a Court of law. But if you bet that your baby will die within twelve months, you are not only permitted to make the bet, but, in case the contingency arises, you can recover the stakes in a Court, provided always the gentlemen you bet with have taken the precaution to dub themselves Life Assurance Society. You may also send a ship to sea, and bet that it will go to the bottom before it reaches its destination. You will recover your odds in a Court, provided the other parties are called underwriters, or some other suitable name. You may bet that some one will set fire to your house before next Christmas, and, if this happens, the Court will compel the other party to pay, though the odds are about 1000 to 1—provided such other party is called a Fire Insurance Office. Again, if twenty men put a shilling each into a pool, buy a goose, a surloin of beef, and a plum-pudding, and then spin a teetotum to see who shall take the lot, that is a lottery, and the twenty men are all punished for the sin by the State. But if a lady buys a fire-screen for £3, and the same twenty men put a sovereign each into the pool, and spin the teetotum to see who shall have the screen, and the £20 goes to the Missionary Society, this is called a bazaar raffle, and no one is punished by the State. If a dozen men put a hundred pounds apiece into a pool, to be the property of him who outlives the rest, that is called tontine, and is not only permitted but guaranteed by the State. If you bet with another man that the Eureka Mine Stocks will be dearer in three months than they are now, that is called speculation on the Stock Exchange, and the State will enforce the payment of the bet. But if you bet that the next throw of the dice will be higher than the last, that is called gambling, and the State will not enforce the payment of the bet. If you sell boxes of toffee for a penny each, on the understanding that one box out of every twenty contains a bright new threepenny-bit, that again is called a lottery, and you go to prison for the crime. But if you sell newspapers for a penny each, on the understanding that in a certain contingency the buyer may net £100, that is called advertisement, and you go *not* to prison, but possibly (if you sell plenty) to Parliament. If you bet that somebody will redeem his written promise to pay a certain sum of money at a certain date, that is called bill-discounting, and the State sanctions the transaction; but if you bet that the same person will defeat his opponent in a chess-match (though similarly based on a calculation of probabilities and knowledge of his character and record), it is a transaction which the State frowns at, and certainly will not sanction. Who now will say that the State refuses to sanction bets? Gambling, speculation, raffles, lotteries, bill-discounting, life-assurance, fire-insurance, underwriting, tontine, sweepstakes—what are these but different names for the same kind of bargain— a contract based on an unforeseen contingency—a bet? And yet how differently they are treated by the State! Neither is it fair to charge the State with a puritanical bias against gambling. Religion had nothing to do with anti-gambling legislation; for the State both tolerates and enforces wage-contracts, when they are the result of mature deliberation, sufficiently evidenced, and, as in the case of life-assurance, insurance against fire, and shipwreck, etc., free from the suspicion of wild intoxication.

The State has prohibited certain sports because they are demoralising, e.g. prize-fighting; and others because they are cruel without being useful, e.g. cock-fighting, bear-baiting, bull-fighting, etc. Angling it regards as useful, and therefore does not condemn it, although it combines cruelty with the lowest form of lying. Agitations are from time to time set on foot for the purpose of putting down fox-hunting on similar grounds. But, fortunately, the magnificent effects of this manly sport on the physique of the race are too palpable to admit of its suppression. Pigeon-shooting is a very different matter. Chess never seems to have fallen under the ban of the law; but billiards, for some reason which I cannot discover, has always been carefully supervised by the State.

Coming to the fine arts, they all of them seem to be regarded by the legislature as probable incentives to low sensuality. Architecture is the solitary exception. Even music, which would seem to approach nearer to divine perfection and purity than any other earthly thing, is carefully hedged about by law; possibly, however, this is on account of its dangerous relation to poetry, when the two are wedded in song. When we come to the arts of sculpture, of painting (and its allies, printing, drawing, photography, etc.), of literature (poetry and prose), of the drama, and of dancing, we are bound to admit that in the absence of

State-control they *are* apt to run to licentiousness. But whether it is wise of society, which has been compelled to abstain from interference with sexual irregularity, to penalise that which is suspected of leading to it, is an interesting point. Fornication in itself is no longer even a misdemeanour in this country. The Act 23 & 24 Vict. c. 32 applies only to conspiracy to induce a woman to commit fornication; 'provided,' as Mr. Justice Stephen surmises, 'that an agreement between a man and a woman to commit fornication is not a conspiracy.' At the same time, whatever we may think of these State efforts to encourage and bolster up chastity by legislation, it is not quite honest to ignore or misrepresent the State motive. Monogamy is not the outcome of religious asceticism. We have only to read the Koran or the Old Testament to see that polygamy and religion can be on very good terms. The highest civilisations yet known are based on the monogamic principle; and anyone who realises the effect of the system on the children of the community must admit that it is a most beneficial one, quite apart from the religious aspect. Whether the action of the State conduces to this result is quite another question. All I assert is that the State is actuated by a most excellent motive.

The first observation on the whole history of this kind of legislation is that it has been a gigantic failure. That is to say, it has not diminished the evils aimed at in the smallest degree. It has rather increased them. It has crabbed and stunted the fine arts, and then vulgarised them. By its rough and clumsy classifications it has crushed out the appeals of Art to the best feelings of human nature, and it has diverted what would have been pure and wholesome into other channels. The man who does not see every emotion of the human soul reflected and glorified in nature's drama around him must be a poor prosaic thing indeed. But we need not go to nature for what has lately been termed suggestiveness. We need not stray beyond the decorative art of dress, which seems to have exercised a special fascination over the sentimental Herrick. The logical outcome of systematic repression of sensual suggestiveness is State-regulated dress. Something like this has often been attempted. In England, during the thirteenth and two following centuries, dress was both regulated by Act of Parliament and cursed from the pulpit. Eccleston mentions how Sero d'Abon, after preaching before Henry I on the sinfulness of beards and long hair, coolly drew a huge pair of scissors from his pocket after the sermon, and, taking advantage of the effect he had produced, went from seat to seat, mercilessly cropping the king himself and the whole congregation. The same writer, speaking of the Early English period, tells us that 'long toes were not entirely abandoned till Henry VII, notwithstanding many a cursing by the clergy, as well as severe legal penalties upon their makers.' I am afraid neither the cursing of the clergy nor the penalties of the law have had the desired effect, for we must remember that it was not the gold nets and curled ringlets and gauze wings worn at each side of the female head, nor the jewelled stomachers, which were the peculiar objects of the aversion of State and Church, but the sensualising effect of all over-refinement in the decoration of the body.

If there is one thing more difficult than another, it is to say where the line should be drawn between legitimate body-decoration and meretricious adornment. When art-critics like Schlegel are of opinion that the nude figure is far less allective than carefully arranged drapery, it is surely the height of blind faith to entrust the State and its blundering machinery to lay down the laws of propriety in the matter of dress. What we should think indecent in this country is not thought indecent among the Zulus, and since the whole question is as to the effect of certain costumes on certain persons, and since those persons are the general public in any particular country, one would imagine that the proper course to adopt would be to leave the decision upon particular cases, as they crop up, to that public. The public may be a bad judge or a biassed judge, but at least it is a more suitable judge than a lumbering State, working on general principles vaguer than a London fog.

Again, recent modern attempts to 'purify' literature have brought the whole crusade into derision, and made us the laughing-stock of Europe. Yet all has been done with the best intentions—even the prosecution of the sellers of Boccaccio's *Decameron*.

But there are moral questions in which the State concerns itself, which do not fall under the heads of games, sports, nor fine arts, such as drinking, opium-eating, tobacco-smoking, and the use of other stimulants. These indulgences and artificial aids to sensual gratification have been and still are regulated and harassed by the State. Nor is it so long ago that the memory of man runneth not, since our own Government made stringent rules as to the number of meals to be eaten by the several grades of society. The Roman law actually specified the number of courses at each meal. An ancient English writer refers with disgust to the then new-fangled cookery which was coming into vogue in his day, 'all breening like wild-fire.' But I have yet to learn that gluttony is on the decrease. And we have it on the highest medical authority that more deaths and more diseases can be traced to over-eating than to over-drinking, even in this tippling country. Nor have the laws enacted against sexual irregularities from time immemorial up to this day diminished, much less stamped out, the evil. We empty the casinos only to fill the streets, and we clear the streets only to increase the number and deteriorate the quality of houses of ill-fame. And during both processes we open the door to official black-mailing. The good old saying that you cannot make people moral by Act of Parliament has been, and still is, disregarded, but not with impunity. Surely the State, which has conspicuously failed in every single department of moralisation by force, may be wisely asked in future to mind its own business.

But is it not possible to fix our eyes too persistently and fanatically on the State? Do we not suffer from other interferences quite as odious as the tyrannies of the Effective Majority? Here is what Mr. Pickard said on the Eight-hours question at the Miners' Conference at Birmingham some months since. Somebody had pointed out that the Union could themselves force short hours upon the employers, if need be, without calling upon the legislature. 'If,' he replied, 'no bad result is to follow trade-union effort, how is it possible for a bad result to follow the same arrangement brought about by legislation?' Commenting on this with approval, *Justice*, the organ of the Social Democratic Federation, says:

> This is a question which Mr. John Morley and the rest of the politicians who prate about the need for shorter working hours, while opposing the penalising of over-work, should set themselves to answer. Obviously there is no answer that will justify their position. If the limitation of the hours of labour is wrong in principle, and mischievous, harmful, and destructive of our national prosperity, it is just as much so whether effected by trade-union effort or by legislation.

There is a soul of truth in this. Of course we may point out firstly that the passing of a Bill for the purpose is no proof that the majority of the persons primarily affected really desire it, whereas the enforcement of the system by trade-unionism is strong evidence that they do: and secondly, that the legislature cannot effect these objects without simultaneously creating greater evils owing to the necessary operation of State machinery. But I venture to say that the central truth of Mr. Pickard's remark lies a good deal deeper than this. I think we individualists are apt to fix our eyes too exclusively upon the State. Doubtless it is the greatest transgressor. But after all, when analysed, it is only a combination of numerous persons in a certain area claiming to dictate to others in the same area what they shall do, and what they shall not do. These numerous persons we call the effective majority. It is precisely in the position of a cricket-club, or a religious corporation, or any other combination of men bound together by rules. At the present moment in this country a bishop is being persecuted by the majority of his co-religionists because he performs certain trifling rites. I would ask the Church of England whether, in *its own interest*—in the interest of the majority of its own members—would not be wiser to repeal these socialistic rules against practices perfectly harmless in themselves. Last year there was a *cause célèbre* tried before the Jockey Club. Quite apart from the outside interference of the State, this club can and does sanction its own laws most effectively. It can ruin any trainer or jockey whenever it chooses, that is to say, whenever he violates the laws it has made. These laws, fortunately, are about as good as human nature is capable of, and those who suffer under them richly deserve their fate. But it might be otherwise. And even in this exemplary code there is an element of despotism which might be dispensed with. A jockey must not be an owner. Very good: the object is clear, and the intention is excellent. Of course a jockey ought not to expose himself to the temptation of riding another man's horse so as to conduce to the success of his own. No honourable man would yield to the temptation. On the other hand, few owners would trust a jockey whose own horse was entered for the same race. Now I venture to submit that it would be better to leave the matter entirely to the jockey's own choice, and to reserve the penalty for the occasion where there is convincing evidence that the jockey has abused his trust. A jockey charged with pulling, and afterwards found interested as owner or part-owner or backer of another horse in the same race, would then be dealt with under the Jockey Club law, not before. I would strongly advise a jockey to keep clear of ownership, and even of betting (on any race in which his services are engaged), but I would not make an offence out of that which in itself is not an offence, but which merely opens the door to temptation. This has nothing whatever to do with the State or with State law. It is entirely a question of what may, broadly speaking, be called Lynch law. I have recently examined the rules of some of the principal London clubs, and I find that they are, many of them, largely socialistic. Unless I am a member, I do not complain. I merely ask whether the members themselves would not do wisely to widen their liberties. The committee of a certain club had recently a long and stormy discussion as to whether billiards should be permitted on Sundays. In nineteen out of twenty clubs the game is disallowed. The individualists predominated, and the result is that those who do not want to play can refrain: they are not compelled to play. Those who wish to play are not compelled to refrain.

I can imagine a people with the State reduced to a shadow—a government attenuated to the administration of a very tolerant criminal code—and yet so deeply imbued with socialism in all their minor combinations as to be a nation of petty despots: a country where every social clique enforces its own notions of Mrs. Grundy's laws, and where every club tyrannises over its own members, fixing their politics and religion, the limits of stakes, the hours of closing, and a countless variety of other matters. There is or was a club in London where no meat is served on Fridays. There are several in which card-players are limited to half-crown points. There are many more where one card game is permitted and another prohibited. Whist is allowed at the Carlton, but not poker. Then again the etiquette of the professions is in many cases more irksome and despotic than the law of the land. Medical men have been boycotted for accepting small fees from impecunious patients. A barrister who should accept a brief from a client without the intermediary expense of a solicitor would sink to swim no more: although the solicitor's services might be absolutely worthless. Consider also the rules of the new Trade-unionism. I need not go into these. The freedom, not only of voluntary members, but of citizens outside the ring, is utterly trampled under foot. And this brings us back to Mr. Pickard and the soul of truth in his argument. I affirm that a people might utterly abolish and extirpate the State, and yet remain steeped to the lips in socialism of the most revolting type. And I think, as I have said, it is time for those of us who value freedom and detest despotism, from whatever quarter it emanates, to ask ourselves what are the true principles of Lynch law. Suppose, for example, there was no State to appeal to for protection against a powerful ruffian, what should I do? Most certainly I should combine with others no stronger than myself, and overpower the ruffian by superior brute-force. Ought I to do this? Ought I not rather to allow the survival of the fittest to improve the physique of the race—even at my expense? If not, then ought I to combine with others against the freedom of the sly pick-pocket, who through his superior dexterity and agility and cool courage prevails over me, and appropriates my watch, without any exercise of brute force? Are not these qualities useful to the race? Then why should I conspire with others against the harmless sneak who puts chicory in his coffee? If I do not like his coffee, I can go and buy somebody else's? If he chooses to offer me stone for bread at fourpence a pound, and if I am foolish enough to take it at the price, I shall learn to be wiser in future, or else perish of starvation and rid the race of a fool. Then again why should I *not* conspire? Or are there some sorts of combination which are good, and properly called co-operation, while others are bad, and properly called conspiracy? Let us look a little into this matter of combination, —this arraying of Quantity against Quality.

Hooks and eyes are very useful. Hooks are useless; eyes are useless. Yet in combination they are useful. This is co-operation. Where you have division of labour, and consequent differentiation of function, and eventually of structure, there is co-operation. Certain tribes of ants have working members and fighting members. The military caste are unable to collect food, which is provided for them by the other members of the community, in return for which they devote themselves to the defence of the whole society. But for these soldiers the society would perish. If either class perished, the other class would perish with it. It is the old fable of the belly and the limbs.

Division of labour does not always result in differentiation of structure. In the case of bees and many other insects we know that it does. Among mammals beyond the well-marked structural division into male and female, the tendency to fixed structural changes is very slight. In races where caste prevails, the tendency is more marked. Even in England, where caste is extinct, it has been observed among the mining population of Northumbria. And the notorious short-sightedness of Germans has been set down to compulsory book-study. As a general rule, we may neglect this effect of co-operation among human beings. The fact remains that the organised effort of 100 individuals is a very great deal more effective than the sum of the efforts of 100 unorganised individuals. Co-operation is an unmixed good. And the Ishmaelitic anarchy of the bumble-bee is uneconomic. Hostility to the principle of co-opera-tion (upon which society is founded) is usually attributed by the ignorant to philosophical anarchists, while socialists never weary of pointing to the glorious triumphs of co-operation, and claiming them for socialism. Whenever a number of persons join hands with the object of effecting a purpose otherwise unattainable, we have what is tanta-mount to a new force—the force of combination; and the persons so combining, regarded as a single body, may be called by a name—any name: a Union, an Association, a Club, a Company, a Corporation, a State. I do not say all these terms denote precisely the same thing, but they all connote co-operation.

Let the State be now abolished for the purposes of this discussion. How do we stand? We have by no means abolished all the clubs and companies in which citizens find themselves grouped and interbanded. There they all are, just as before—nay, there are a number of new ones, sud-denly sprung up out of the debris of the old State. Here are some eighty men organised in the form of a cricket-club. They may not pitch the ball as they like, but only in accordance with rigid laws. They elect a king or captain, and they bind themselves to obey him in the field. A mem-ber is told off to field at long-on, although he may wish to field at point. He must obey the despot.

Here is a ring of horsemen. They ride races. They back their own horses. Disputes arise about fouling, or perhaps the course is a curve and some rider takes a short cut; or the weights of the riders are unequal, and the heavier rider claims to equalise the weights. All such matters are laid before a committee, and rules are drawn up by which all the members of the little racing club pledge themselves to be bound. The club grows: other riding or racing men join it or adopt its rules. At last, so good are its laws that they are accepted by all the racing fraternity in the island, and all racing disputes are settled by the rules of the Jockey Club. And even the judges of the land defer to them, and refer points of racing law to the club.

Here again is a knot of whalers on the beach of a stormy sea. Each trembles for the safety of his own vessel. He would give something to be rid of his own uneasiness. All his eggs are in one basket. He would willingly distribute them over many baskets. He offers to take long odds that his own vessel is lost. He repeats the offer till the long odds cover the value of his ship and cargo, and perhaps profits and time. 'Now,' says he, 'I am comfortable: it is true, I forfeit a small percentage; but if my whole craft goes to the bottom I lose nothing.' He laughs and sings, while the others go croaking about the sands, shaking their heads and looking fearfully at the breakers. At last they all follow his example, and the net result is a Mutual Marine Insurance Society. After a while they lay the odds, not with their own members only, but with others; and the risk being over-estimated (naturally at first), they make large dividends. But now difficulties arise. The captain of a whaler has thrown cargo overboard in a heavy sea. The owner claims for the loss. The company declines to pay, on the ground that the loss was voluntarily caused by the captain and not by the hand of God or the king's enemies; and that there would be no limit to jettison if the claim were allowed. Other members meet with similar difficulties, and finally rules are made which provide for all known contingencies. And when any dispute arises, the chosen umpire (whether it be a mutual friend, or an agora-full of citizens, or a department of State, or any other person or body of persons) refers to the common practice and precedents so far as they apply. In other words, the rules of the Insurance Society *are* the law of the land. In spite of the State, this is so to-day to a considerable extent; I may say, in all matters which have not been botched and cobbled by statute.

There is another class of club springing out of the altruistic sentiment. An old lady takes compassion on a starving cat (no uncommon sight in the West End of London after the Season). She puts a saucer of milk and some liver on the door-step. She is soon recognised as a benefactress, and the cats for a mile round swarm to her threshold. The saucers increase and multiply, and the liver is an item in her butcher's bill. The strain is too great to be borne single-handed. She issues a circular appeal, and she is surprised to find how many are willing to contribute a fair share, although their sympathy shrivels up before an unfair demand. They are willing to be taxed *pro rata*, but they will not bear the burden of other people's stinginess. 'Let the poor cats bear it rather,' they say; 'what is everybody's business is nobody's business. It is very sad, but it cannot be helped. If we keep one cat, hundreds will starve; so what is the use?' But when once the club is started, nobody feels the burden; the Cats' Home is built and endowed, and all goes well. Hospitals, infirmaries, alms-houses, orphanages, spring up all round. At first they are reckless and indiscriminate, and become the prey of impostors and able-bodied vagrants. Then rules are framed; the Charity Organisation Society co-ordinates and directs public benevolence. And these rules of prudence and economy are copied and adopted, in many respects, by those who administer the State Poor Law.

Then we have associations of persons who agree on important points of science or politics. They wish to make others think with them, in order that society may be pleasanter and more congenial for themselves. They would button-hole every man in the street and argue the question out with him, but the process is too lengthy and wearisome. They club together, and form such institutions as the British and Foreign Bible Society, which has spent £7,000,000 in disseminating its literature all over the world. We have the Cobden Club, which is slowly and sadly dying of inconsistency after a career of merited success. We have scientific societies of all descriptions that never ask or expect a penny reward for all their outlay, beyond making other people wiser and pleasanter neighbours.

Finally, we have societies banded together to do battle against rivals on the principle of 'Union is strength.' These clubs are defensive or aggressive. The latter class includes all trading associations, the object of which is to make profits by out-manoeuvering competitors. The former or defensive class includes all the political societies formed for the purpose of resisting the State—the most aggressive club in existence. Over one hundred of these 'protection societies' of one sort and another are now federated under the hegemony of the Liberty and Property Defence League.

Now we have agreed, for the sake of argument, that the State is to be abolished. What is the result? Here are Watch Committees formed in the great towns to prevent and to ensure against burglars, thieves, and like marauders. How they are to be constituted I do not clearly know; neither do I know the limits of their functions. Here, again, is a Mutual Inquest Society to provide for the examination of dead persons before burial or cremation, in order to make murder as unprofitable a business as possible. Here is a Vigilance Association sending out detectives for the purpose of discovering and lynching the unsocial wretches who knowingly travel in public conveyances with infectious diseases on them. Here is a journal supported by consumers for the advertisement of adulterating dealers. And here again is a filibustering company got up by adventurous traders, of the old East India Company stamp, for the purpose of carrying trade into foreign countries with or without the consent of the invaded parties. Here is a Statistical Society devising rules to make it unpleasant for those who evade registration and the census, and offering inducement to all who furnish the required information. What sort of organisation (if any) will be formed for the enforcement (not necessarily by brute force) of contract? Or will there be many such organisations dealing with different classes of contract? Will there be a Woman's League to boycott any man who has abused the confidence of a woman and violated his pledges? How will it try and sanction cases of breach of promise?

Above all, how is this powerful company for the defence of the country against foreign invaders to be constituted? And what safeguards will its members provide against the tyranny of the officials? When a Senator proposed to limit the standing army of the United States to three thousand, George Washington agreed, on condition that the honourable member would arrange that the country should never be invaded by more than two thousand. Frankenstein created a monster he could not lay. This will be a nut for anarchists of the future to crack.

And now, to revert to the Vigilance Society formed for lynching persons who travel about in public places with small-pox and scarlatina, what rules will they make for their guidance? Suppose they dub every unvaccinated person a 'focus of infection,' shall we witness the establishment of a Vigilance Society to punch the heads of the detectives who punch the heads of the 'foci of infection'? Remember we have both those societies in full working order today. One is called the State, and the other is the Anti-Vaccination Society.

The questions which I should wish to ask are chiefly these two: (1) How far may voluntary co-operators invade the liberty of others? And what is to prevent such invasion under a system of anarchy? (2) Is compulsory co-operation ever desirable? And what form (if any) should such compulsion take?

The existing State is obviously only a conglomeration of several large societies which would exist separately or collectively in its absence; if the State were abolished, these associations would necessarily spring up out of its ruins, just as the nations of Europe sprang out of the ruins of the Roman Empire. They would apparently lack the power of compulsion. No one would be compelled to join against his will. Take the ordinary case of a gas-lit street. Would a voluntary gas-committee be willing to light the street without somehow taxing all the dwellers in the street? If yes, then there is inequity. The generous and public-spirited pay for the stingy and mean. But if no, then how is the taxing to be accomplished? And where is the line to be drawn? If you compel a man to pay for lighting the street, when he swears he prefers it dark (a householder may really prefer a dark street to a light one, if he goes to bed at sunset, and wants the traffic to be diverted into other streets to ensure his peace); then you will compel him to subscribe to the Watch fund, though his house is burglar-proof; and to the fire-brigade, though his house is fire-proof; and to the prisons as part of the plant and tools of the Watch Committee; and, it may logically be urged, to the churches and schools as part also of such plant and tools for the prevention of certain crimes.

Moreover, if you compel him to subscribe for the gas in the street, you must make him pay his share of the street itself—paving, repairing, and cleansing, and if the street, then the highway; and if the highway, then the railway, and the canal, and the bridges, and even the harbours and lighthouses, and other common apparatus of transport and locomotion.

If we are not going to compel a citizen to subscribe to *common* benefits, even though he necessarily shares them, how are we to remove the injustice of allowing one man to enjoy what another has earned? Some writers are of opinion that this and all similar questions can be settled by an appeal to Justice, and that the justice of any particular case can be extracted by a dozen jurymen.[4] Now, in all sincerity, I have no conception of what is comonly meant by Justice. Happiness I know; welfare I know; expediency I know. They all mean the same thing. We can call it pleasure, or felicity, or by any other name. We never ask why it is better to be happy than unhappy. We understand pleasure and pain by faculties which underlie reason itself. A child knows the meaning of stomach-ache long before it knows the meaning of stomach. And no philosopher knows it better. Expediency, in the sense in which I use the term, has a meaning. Justice has no meaning at all: that is to say, it conveys no definite meaning to the general understanding. Here is a flat-race about to be run between a strong, healthy boy of sixteen and a delicate lad of twelve? What says Justice? Are we to handicap them; or are we not? It is a very simple question, and the absolutist ought to furnish us with a simple answer. If he says Yes, he will have half the world down upon him as a socialist leveller. If he says No, he will have the other half down upon him as a selfish brute. But he must choose. Lower yet; even supposing that Justice has a distinct connotation, and furthermore that it connotes something sublime, even then, why should I conform to its dictates? Because it is a virtue? Nonsense: *because it is expedient*. Why should I tell the truth? There is no reason why, except that it is expedient for me, as I know from experience. There is no baser form of lying than fly-fishing. Is it wrong? No. Why not? Because I do not ask the fishes to trust me in the future. That is why.

---

[4] See Mr. Spence's contribution to the *Symposium on the Land Question*, p. 42, 1890 (T. Fisher Unwin).

I have said that Justice is too vague a guide to the solution of political questions. We are told that, when the question is asked, What is fair and just between man and man? 'you can get a jury of twelve men to give a unanimous verdict.' And 'that by reasoning from what is fair between man and man we can pass to what is fair between one man and several, and from several, to all: and that this method, which is the method of all science, of reasoning from the particular to the general, from the simple to the complex, does give us reliable information as to what should be law.'[5]

The flaw in this chain of reasoning is in the assumption that, because you can get a *unanimous* verdict in the majority of cases as to what is fair between man and man, therefore you can get a *true* verdict. Twelve sheep will unanimously jump through a gap in the hedge round an old quarry, if one of them will but give the lead. I do not believe that a jury of twelve philosophers, or of twelve members of Parliament, or of twelve judges of the realm, or of twelve anybodies, could decide correctly what is just and right between man and man in any one of a thousand cases which could be stated without deviating from the path of everyday life. And the more they knew, the less likely they would be to agree.

The same writer thinks the intelligence of the 'ordinary elector' quite sufficient to tell him that 'it would be unjust to take from a man by force and without compensation a farm which he had legally and honestly bought.' Well, this is not a very complex case: and yet I doubt whether 'the

---

[5] *Symposium on the Land Question.*

ordinary elector' could be trusted even here to see justice, and to do it. This recipe for making good laws forcibly reminds me of an old recipe for catching a bird: 'Put a pinch of salt on its tail.' I remember trying it—but that is some years ago. I grant that, having once got at a sound method of deciding what is fair and right between man and man, you can easily proceed from the particular to the general, and so learn how to make good laws. Yes, but first catch your hare. First show us what is fair between man and man. That is the whole problem. That is my difficulty, and it is not removed by telling me you can get a dozen fellows together who will agree about the answer.

Take a very simple case. X and Y appoint me arbitrator in their dispute. There is no allegation of malfeasance on either side. Both ask for justice, and are ready to accord it, but they cannot agree as to what is justice in the case. It appears that X bought a pony *bona fide* and paid for it. That is admitted. It further appears that the pony was stolen the night before out of Y's paddock. It is hard on Y to lose his pony—it is hard on X to lose his money. To divide the loss is hard on both. Now how can Justice tell me the true solution? I must fall back on expediency. As a rule, I argue, the title to goods should be valid only when derived from the owner. But surely an exception should be made in the case of a *bona fide* purchaser: 'for it is expedient that the buyer, by taking proper precautions, may at all events be secure of his purchase: otherwise all commerce between man and man would soon be at an end.' These are the words of Sir William Blackstone, but they are good enough for me. Therefore (and not for any reason based on justice) I should feel disposed to decide that the pony should remain the property of the purchaser. But on further reflection, I should bethink me how extremely easy it would be for two men to conspire together to steal a pony under such a law. One of them leads the pony out of the field by night, sells it to his colleague, gives him a receipt for the money, and disappears. Is this farce to destroy the owner's title? What am I to do? Justice entirely deserts me. I reflect again. There seems to be something 'fishy' about a night sale in a lane. Now had the purchaser bought the pony at some public place at a reasonable hour when people are about, there would have been less ground for suspicion of foul play. How would it be then, I ask myself, to lay down the general rule that, when the deal takes place at any regular public place and during specified hours, the purchaser's title should hold good: but when the deal takes place under other circumstances, the original owner's title should stand? This would probably be something like the outcome of the reflections of a simple untutored mind actuated by common sense. But it is also very like the law of England.

If I appeal for guidance to the wise, the best they can do is to refer me to the writings of the lawyers, where I shall find out all about market overt and a good many other 'wise regulations by which the law hath secured the right of the proprietor of personal chattels from being divested, so far as is consistent with that other necessary policy that *bona fide* purchasers in a fair, open, and regular manner should not be afterwards put to difficulties by reason of the previous knavery of the seller.'[6] But we have not got to

---

[6] Blackstone.

the bottom of the problem yet. There are chattels *and* chattels. Tables have legs, but cannot walk: horses can. Thereby hangs a tale. Consequently when I think I have mastered all these 'wise regulations,' I am suddenly knocked off my stool of superior knowledge by a couple of elderly statutes—2 P. & M. c. 7 and 31 Eliz. c. 12— whereby special provision is made for horse-dealing. It is enacted that—

> The horses shall be openly exposed in the time of such fair or market for one whole hour together, between ten in the morn- ing and sunset, in the public place used for such sales, and not in any private yard or stable; and shall afterwards be brought by both the vendor and vendee to the bookkeeper of such fair or market, who shall enter down the price, colour, and marks of such horse, with the name, additions, and abode of such vendee and vendor, the latter being properly attested. And even such sale shall not take away the property of the owner, if within six months after the horse is stolen, he put in his claim before some magistrate where the horse shall be found; and within forty days more prove such his property, by the oath of two witnesses, and tender to the person in possession such price as he *bona fide* paid for the horse in market overt. And in case any of the points before mentioned be not ob- served, such sale is to be utterly void, and the owner shall not lose his property; and at any distance of time may seize or bring an action for his horse, wherever he happens to find him.

And further refinements on these precautions have since been made.

I do not say that we need approve of all these safeguards and rules, but I do say that they testify to a perception by the legislature of the complexity and difficulty of the question. And furthermore, if anybody offers to decide such cases off-hand on general principles, and at the same time to do justice, he must be a bold man. For my part, the more I look into the law as it is, the more do I see in it of wisdom (not unadulterated of course) drawn from experience. The little obstacles which have from time to time shadowed themselves upon my mind as difficulties in the way of applying clear and unqualified general rules to the solution of all social disputes, are brought into fuller light, and I perceive more and more clearly how hopeless, nay, how impossible it is to deduce the laws of social morality from broad general principles; and how absolutely necessary it is to obtain them by induction from the myriads of actual cases which the race has had to solve somehow or other during the last half-dozen millenniums.

I regard law-making as by no means an easy task when based on expediency. On the contrary, I think it difficult, but practicable: whereas to deduce good laws from the principle of Justice is impossible.

One word more about Justice. I have said that to most people the term is absolutely meaningless. To those who have occasional glimmerings, it conveys two distinct and even opposed meanings—sometimes one, sometimes the other. And it has a third meaning, which is definite enough, but merely negative; in which sense it connotes the elimination of partiality. I fail to see how any political question can be settled by that. That the State should be no respecter of persons, that it should decide any given case in precisely the same way, whether the litigants happen to be *A* and *B* or *C* and *D*, may be a valuable truth, without casting a ray of light on the right and wrong of the question.

In this negative sense of the term I will venture to define Justice as the Algebra of Judgments. It deals in terms not of Dick, Tom, and Harry, but of X, Y, and Z. Regarded in this light, Justice may properly be described as blind, a quality which certainly cannot be predicated of that Justice which carefully examines the competitors in life's arena and handicaps them accordingly. Consider the countless questions which Impartiality is incompetent to answer. Ought a father to be compelled to contribute to the maintenance of his natural children? The only answer we can get from Impartiality is that, if one man is forced, all men should be forced. Should a man be permitted to sell himself into slavery for life? Should the creditors of an insolvent rank in order of priority, or *pro rata*? Suppose a notorious card-sharper and a gentleman of unblemished character are publicly accused, untruly accused, of conspiring together to cheat, should they obtain equal damages for the libel?

To all these questions Impartiality is dumb, or replies oracularly, 'What is right for one is right for all.' And that throws no light on the subject.

In short, it is easy to underrate the difficulty of finding out what is fair and right between man and man. To me it seems that this is the whole of the difficulty. And although I think that this can best be overcome by an appeal to expediency, I must not be understood as contending that each particular case must be decided on its merits. We must be guided, as we are guided in our own personal conduct, by middle principles which have stood the test of time and experience. Do not steal. Do not lie. It is by the gradual discovery of similar middle principles by induction from the disputes of everyday life that we shall some day find ourselves in possession of true and useful guides through labyrinth of legislation and politics.

To sum up; I have tried to show that the right course for the State to adopt towards its own citizens—Group-morals —cannot be discovered by deduction from any abstract principles, such as Justice or Liberty; any more than individual morals can be deduced from some underlying law of Virtue. The rules of conduct by which States should be guided are intelligible canons based on centuries of experience, very much like the rules by which our own private lives are guided; not absolutely trustworthy, but better than no general rules at all. They are usually described as the laws of the land, and in so far as the expressed laws really do reflect the nomological laws actually at work, these laws stand in the same relation to the State as private resolutions stand to the individual citizen. In law, as in all other inductive sciences, we proceed from the particular to the general. The judge decides a new case on its merits, the decision serves as a guide when a similar case arises; the *ratio decidendi* is extracted, and we have a general statement; these generalisations are themselves brought under higher generalisations by jurists and judges, and perhaps Parliament; and finally we find ourselves in the presence of laws or State-morals as general as those cardinal virtues by which most of us try to arrange our lives. That the generalisations made by the legislature are usually false generalisations is a proposition which, I submit, is capable of proof and of explanation. It is wise to obey the laws, firstly, because otherwise we come into conflict with a stronger power than ourselves; secondly, because in the great majority of cases, it is our enlightened interest to do so; the welfare of individual citizens coinciding *as a rule* with the welfare of the race, and tending to do so more and more. History shows that (probably as a means to that end; though of this we cannot speak positively) the State's sphere of action is a diminishing one—that as it moves forward, it tends to shed function after function, until only a few are left. Whether these duties will pass into the hands of voluntary corporations at any time is a question of the greatest interest; but it is observable that the latest functions remaining to the State are those which are most rigorously performed. And this seems to point to the future identity of the State (in the sense of the sovereign power) with the widest voluntary association of citizens—an association based on some common interest of the widest extent. Thus it is probable that even now an enormous majority of persons in this country would voluntarily forego the right of killing or robbing their neighbours on condition of being guaranteed against similar treatment by others. If so, the voluntary society which Anarchy would evolve and the State which ancient Socialism has evolved, tend in the long run to be one and the same thing. The State will cease to coerce, because coercion will no longer be required.

WORDSWORTH DONISTHORPE

CHAPTER 3

LIBERTY FOR LABOUR

GEORGE HOWELL

CHAPTER 3

LIBERTY FOR LABOUR

Few subjects have more profoundly exercised the minds of philosophic thinkers than the question as to the rightful sphere of law, in its application to daily life and labour. It is, indeed, an old, old tale, the threads of which are to be found running through all the centuries of British history, from Saxon times to our own days, in this year of grace, 1890. The warp of legal enactment was laid in the Ordinances of the Guilds, the weft being skilfully woven in by the shuttle of legislation in various reigns, until it produced the fabric known as 'Statute Law.' The earlier conception of the sphere of law was the restraint of lawlessness and brute force. Its second development was the limitation of power and authority, which had been used to limit liberty, and restrain individual freedom. It has taken long ages to repeal the Acts passed for the suppression of personal liberty, and to restrict within reasonable limits the exercise of authority created by statute. But liberty and lawlessness should not be confounded, one with the other; they are

separate and distinct, legally and morally. Individual liberty is consistent with law and order, and the ideal of a
State is reached in proportion to the individual liberty
attained, and the order which is maintained, in the commonwealth of a free people. State regulation was the third
step in legislative achievement, but it developed early, and
ran concurrently with the attempts to restrain individual
liberty; with this difference, however, that the conception
of regulation originated with the governed rather than
with the governors, as the Ordinances of the Guilds testify.
The work of succeeding generations has been to undo the
mischief of State regulation; but the present century has
been distinguished also by the substitution of other kinds
of regulation in the place of that repealed.

It cannot be denied that individual liberty necessitates
regulation, which, after all, means restraint. Each person in
the State must be restrained from infringing upon, or interfering with, the liberty of another, all being equally protected in the exercise of their undoubted rights, constitutional and moral. But State Law, or legislation, cannot
reach, nor should it reach, all the details, trivialities, or
incidents of private life. Above and beyond law, there exist
mutual restraints, for mutual protection, developed by civilised communities, and embodied in what may be called a
code of Social Laws, all the more powerful and exacting,
perhaps, by reason of the fact that they are unwritten
laws, similar in one respect to what is termed the Common
Law. 'Society' is a law unto itself, as the 'family' is a law
unto itself. There are, however, breaches of the law which
neither the family nor society can reach and adequately
punish. The Common Law, and the Statute Law, are de-

signed to reach and punish offences not effectually dealt with in any other way. How far these should operate and extend, is a matter of opinion, upon which there is great divergence among all classes. There is, however, a general consensus of opinion that law, properly so called, should enter as little as possible into the domain of every-day life. In the privacies of ordinary life there is a limit which instinct seems to indicate as a kind of boundary line, beyond which legislation should not extend. The tendency has hitherto been to stop short at such point, or to deal cautiously with any and every proposal to go beyond it. Recently, the tendency to extend the boundary has developed enormously, to such a degree, in fact, that it is doubtful whether, in the opinion of many, there should be any boundary line at all. The effacement of the individual seems to be their aim, the merging of the *man* into the *mass;* the fusion of atoms into a solid concrete body, moved and movable only by the State.

The principal object of the following pages is to deal with law as applied to labour, or the interference by the State with the individual man in the exercise of his skill, intelligence, faculties, and strength, for the purpose of getting his living, increasing his store, and promoting his own and his family's prosperity and happiness in his own way, so long as he does not interfere, *de facto*, with his neighbour. To the latter, as a matter of fact and of argument, reference will be more specifically made further on. In order to understand the question in all its bearings, it is essential to trace the origin and growth of legislative interference, the roots of which lie deeply buried in the past. The tree has been lopped here and there, but while its branches have been cut, the roots have expanded, and these have sprung up, with even greater luxuriance, bearing fruit after its kind, and sometimes of a kind which seemed foreign to its nature and the character of the soil out of which it grew.

I. The earlier interference with labour was by mutual consent and arrangement in the old guilds, for the mutual protection of its members, each being responsible for each, and all for all, as regards conduct, support, protection, and advancement. The guild was also responsible to the State, the frank-pledge being accepted in all cases. As society expanded, and newer developments arose which could not be dealt with by the associated members in the guild, ordinances were enacted, by which the members were bound to abide, whether or not they were within the district in which the guild existed and exercised jurisdiction. Those earlier guilds subsequently expanded into fraternities, generally composed of similar classes, each class or fraternity having objects in common, for the benefit of all. These again extended in their turn, until we find associated guilds, or fraternities of the same class or classes, with ramifications in various parts of the country, and sometimes even in other countries, in different parts of the world. As time wore on there arose separate guilds of distinctive classes, the political element finding a place in their deliberations and determinations. The earlier social guild was not restricted to a class, or to a section. The Merchants' Guild was an off-shoot, sectional and restrictive. The Burghers' Guild contested for political rights; they sought for equal privileges with the feudal barons in the government of the townships. From these sprang into existence the Craft-Guilds, in which the workmen sought equal rights with the merchants and burghers of the towns.

Those guilds were essentially protective. They sought the welfare of the particular individuals of which the guild was composed, or of the section or class to which they belonged; and they sought to perpetuate their advantages, their craft-rights, and their privileges as distinctively as the peerage does by descent of title, of lands, and of other entailed or devised property incident thereto. The guilds were a law unto themselves, but they enforced their ordinances and guild statutes upon others not in their own circle. Many of their objects were good, and were excellently administered; but they had in them the seeds of decay, even at their birth. The very life-germ of their existence was exclusion; and they grew more and more exclusive as time went on, until they became little less than mere corporate trading associations, whose object was the monopoly of power and authority over all the crafts of the time, and the enjoyment of all the privileges and immunities which that power and authority gave, quite irrespective of all and sundry outside the guild. Socialistic in their origin and birth, these fraternities degenerated into intolerable monopolies, cliques, and factions, even to the defiance of law, order, and custom, being often their own avengers in case of wrong, or supposed wrong, wresting privileges where they could, and purchasing them when they could not, until their final suppression in the reign of the Tudors.

By such institutions, under what may be described as primeval conditions, in the very infancy of society and of industry in this country, the ordinances and statutes re-

specting labour were first formulated and promulgated. As
time wore on, and the conditions of society and of life
changed, those ordinances did not fit the circumstances of
the times. They were not expansive enough; there was no
elasticity in them. It is, indeed, extremely doubtful whether
the industry of modern England could have developed to
any large extent under the guild system. The guilds were
too clannish to be national, and too limited in their scope
to be cosmopolitan. When they were instituted they doubtless fulfilled their mission. They enlarged the family and its
responsibilities to groups of families, then to a class. But
diversified interests arose as soon as the expansion began;
and those diversified interests became more and more distinctive and accentuated with each inclusion, until the
original guild split into fragments, which fragments established their own guild. The formulas and regulations which
were accepted by the initial guilds did not completely satisfy the needs and aspirations of the coteries which the
extended family embraced, and they became irksome
whenever they were applied to, and were enforced upon,
persons and families beyond the range of the exclusive
circle by which they were instituted and promulgated.
Secession followed; new combinations arose; other guilds
were established, and contentions were rife, as to the incidence of power and authority, in a variety of forms. The
battles of the guilds form an instructive chapter in the history of association, and especially as identified with labour,
compared with which the contentions of trade-unions sink
into insignificance, bitter as some of the feuds have been
among the unions of modern times.

II. The ordinances of the guilds ultimately gave birth to statute laws pertaining to labour. The earlier Labour Laws, such as the Statutes of Labourers, directly resulted from their action. It was but the natural outcome of regulation, the fruit after its kind. Figs do not grow on thorns, nor grapes on thistles—thorns grow thorns, and thistles, thistles. The attempts to fix the price of labour, to limit the number of labourers in a particular industry, to regulate by ordinance or official sanction the hours of work, and to restrict the individual rights of the labourers, produced a reaction, which reaction found vent in counter-statutory enactment, the results of which continued to operate for centuries. For a long period, the ordinances of the guilds and legal statutory enactments ran side by side. Sometimes they had the same objects, and operated concurrently; at other times they were opposed to each other, the one being a check upon the other. One effect of their operation was to establish customs which had the force of law. Those dual forms of regulation continued in various, and often diversified forms, until the 'dissolution of the monasteries,' and the final suppression of the guilds. It was not until after that date that legislative enactment supplanted the ordinances of the guilds, and usurped their functions. If the legislature of that period had resisted the prompted inducements to an interference with labour, and had restricted its actions to such provisions as would have ensured freedom to all, and protection to each, in the exercise of that freedom, many of the evils of what is termed grandmotherly legislation would have been averted. The modern forms of interference are the direct result, the natural and inevitable result, of conditions which were created by State regulation, following upon the failure of corporate regulation as imposed by the craft-guilds of the middle ages.

Legal enactment took two distinct forms; there were (1) the Statute Law, as embodied in the Statutes of Labourers, commencing with the 23 Edw. III, and continued throughout the thirteenth century by various statutes, and in the fourteenth century by further regulations, as to wages and prices and hours of labour. Those enactments reached their fullest development in the reign of Queen Elizabeth, when the laws were consolidated into what might be termed a code, and were made binding upon all the trades and industries of that time. And (2) charters, which were granted in some of the early reigns, and were continued down to very recent times, many of which were obtained by purchase, as is the case of the companies of the city of London, and some other corporate towns. The rage for legislative regulation is an outgrowth of those earlier conditions, a reverting back to the infancy of civilised society. This tendency is always strong in proportion to the lack of intelligence among the masses to perceive the true relation between cause and effect, and the inevitable results of a given policy, whatever that policy may be. The history of that interference seems to be but a hazy dream to most men, even to those tolerably educated, or we should find greater hesitancy to embark on the same treacherous stream.

Legislation was inaugurated by two distinct parties: (a) By that portion of the community opposed to the restrictive action of the guilds; and (b) by the guild fraternities, in order to maintain their power, privileges, and immunities. The former contended that guild law, by ordinance or statute, was opposed to public policy, and they sought to suppress all kinds of associative effort, as mischievous and dangerous to the State. The latter desired to perpetuate monopoly by law. As the Israelites sighed for the flesh-pots of Egypt, during their journey through the wilderness, so the guild-brothers sighed for the continuance and maintenance of their power and authority over the trades and industries represented by their crafts. The demand for protective law by the guild marks the period of their decay. They had recourse to legislation by statute, or regulation by charter, because they had failed, or were failing, to enforce their ordinances as theretofore. But this very failure of mutual control, by guild-law, is proof positive that it was bad law in actual practice, either because it was ill-timed and unsuited to circumstances, not embodying enactments such as those for whose special benefit they were framed desired, or because the provisions were in themselves vicious. In either case the law was ineffective, and in the end it was disabling in its operation and results.

With the suppression of the guilds, legislation took the place of guild ordinances and regulations. As the legislature at that period was non-representative, the legislation initiated was prompted by a class, for a class, as it was natural that it should be under the circumstances. Act was piled upon Act. One trade after another was brought within the sphere of the statute law, until all handicrafts, and nearly all kinds of labour, were subject either to statute or to ordinances under charter. As population increased, as society progressed, and as industries grew and expanded, there arose a revolt against those statutes and charters. The misfortune was, however, that instead of merely repealing restrictive laws, the employers, then all-powerful in Parliament, sought to substitute, and did substitute very often, other restrictive laws generally adverse to labour. The masters desired, by law, to inflict disabilities upon workmen, and the workmen similarly desired to impose conditions upon masters which were intolerable. This contest was continued for centuries, sometimes one and sometimes the other gaining ascendancy.

The victory ultimately remained with the masters. Statute after statute was repealed, in so far as they were favourable to the workman, with the result that the latter were left wholly unprotected by law, and were unable to protect themselves by mutual association, because of the Combination Laws and other statutes. On the other hand, most of the laws which were in the interest of the masters remained unrepealed, thus leaving the workman in a hopeless state of dependence and disability. A period of transition is nearly always a desperate time for the weak and unprotected. So it was under the repealed laws referred to, ere association by the workman was possible, to mitigate the evils consequent upon the industrial changes then taking place in this country. For a long time the workpeople tried to defend the law and the institution, as their sole means of protection. The masters wanted freedom from the law—for themselves, but with the power to prevent combinations among the men. This unequal struggle continued up to the end of the first quarter of the present century, when, in 1825, the Combination Laws were repealed. Even then, however, the Master and Servant Acts were still in force and were administered with unwonted severity. These were not finally dealt with, in any liberal spirit, until 1867.

The movement amongst the workpeople for freedom to combine began after all efforts to keep in force the old protective law had failed, which was towards the close of the last century. At first, and for a very long period, the tendency was to repeal disabling laws. The Statutes of Apprentices, the particular Acts relating to special trades, the old Combination Laws, Acts relating to Corresponding Societies, and subsequently the Master and Servant Acts, were either partially, some wholly, others temporarily repealed, until, in 1875, after persistent efforts for nearly one hundred years, the remnant of the old Labour Laws, together with the Master and Servant Acts, till that date suspended, were wholly repealed. At the same date the Conspiracy Laws were abolished, in so far as they applied to labour disputes. Ere this had been accomplished, trade-unions were accorded the protection of the law by the Trade Union Act, 1871, and further, as regards their funds, by the Amending Act of 1876. Some other obsolete statutes were repealed last session, by the Master and Servant Act, 1890. All through this long struggle one sentiment was predominant; the healthy sentiment of freedom was paramount. The workmen in effect said: We want no favour; we only want fair play; and by their attitude they declared —we will have it. The demand was simply for the repeal of restraining and disabling laws, with liberty to act, either individually or collectively, for their mutual advantage, whichever was deemed to be best.

III. But long ere the freedom to combine was granted

there arose a demand for protective law. And protective
law, as then conceded, appears to have been an absolute
necessity, remembering the state in which industry was
left by the action of the legislature, as before recorded.
The system of domestic manufacture, which had been the
universal practice for centuries, under the guild system,
and under legislation by statute and charter, had almost
suddenly changed to a form of factory life, in which
women and young children were largely employed in several important industries. These changes were due mainly
to the discoveries and inventions, and the application of
mechanical powers and means to productive labour in the
eighteenth century, whereby motive power, first by water,
and subsequently by steam, was utilised to extend and increase production. The newer processes had the effect of
bringing together young and old, of both sexes, to work
under the new industrial system. These were aggregated
together in out-of-the-way places, where they were often
brutally treated, worse frequently than slaves in American
plantations, and were absolutely without power of redress.
The vivid pictures of that period, as portrayed in the pages
of Michael Armstrong, tell the tale of their woes; it is further told in the Reports of the Royal Commissions and of
Select Committees, appointed by Parliament to inquire
into these matters, not in the glowing language and glaring
colours of Mrs. Trollope, but in the sober blue-book language and truth, usual in such publications of the Government. The scenes there depicted were common in many
industries nearly to the middle of the present century.

With the dawn of the nineteenth century came the first
Factory Act, 'for the Preservation of the Health and Morals

of Apprentices and others employed in Cotton and other Industries.' The necessity for this Act had deeply impressed Sir Robert Peel, himself a manufacturer, who had made a careful study of the subject. From that date, 1801–2 to 1878, when the long series of Acts were consolidated and amended, the provisions of the earlier Act were extended and amended until they embraced all factories and workshops in which women, young persons of both sexes, and children were employed. They are no longer confined to the textile trades, but extend to all classes and kinds of manufacture. The Mines Regulation Acts, in their earlier conception and application, were similar in character, and had almost precisely the same objects. For a period of ninety years there have been three concurrent movements—one for the protection of women and children; another for the protection of life and limb, and health of all engaged in industry; and the other for the repeal of old restrictive laws, in so far as they pertained to adult males in their daily avocations in life. These have progressed side by side, all through the present century, and are still operating without cessation in nearly all trades.

Those movements were not and are not inconsistent or incompatible one with the other. A politician or statesman might support each without violating his principles or endangering his reputation for consistency. But two opposing forces have arisen in this connection; the one would undo the legislation of the past, as vicious and mischievous, the other would so extend it as to embrace within the sphere of its influence not only women and children but adult males, in substitution for, or as going back to, the ordinances and statutes of earlier times. The action of both parties is provocative of diversified antagonism. In the struggle for ascendancy, the chances are either that the good accomplished will be rendered nugatory by repeals of useful statutes, or that the principles underlying them will be so enlarged and applied as to become harmful to the mass of the people. This is the danger to be apprehended, and to be guarded against.

IV. The principles which underlie the Factory and Workshop Acts, and all similar Acts, are clear, definite, and distinct. Generally, they have for their object the *protection* of women and children, who were, and still are, to a great extent, the latter wholly, and the former partially, unable to protect themselves. If the Acts, instead of protecting, disable, or if they are no longer needed for protection, then they become vicious and mischievous. But it must be remembered that the whole tenor of public law has been adverse, in several important respects, to women. The conditions under which they laboured were altogether different to those of men. Combination by women was almost totally unattainable. Isolation and weakness were their lot, until marriage gave them a 'protector.' Even then the protection was nearly nil, especially when engaged in any occupation. Often indeed they supplanted their husbands, and became the bread-winners for the family. The extent to which this operated is now scarcely conceivable, certainly it is not realised or appreciated by those who oppose all such legislation. The Reports of the Royal Commission, 1840–43, give an inkling of the extent, baneful influences and effect, of child labour and women labour, in various industries of that time, in so far as the conditions of employment were concerned, while the reports on the sanitary condition of the labouring population, at the same date, show the direful results in the home-life of the people. These reports are seldom perused now, but no one can understand to what fearful depths of degradation, greed and need pressed down the workers in factories and workshops, in collieries and mines, and in other occupations in the industrial centres of Great Britain. Health and morals were the chief objects of the series of statutes to which reference is made, including sanitation, meal times, separation of the sexes, number of hours worked, night work, overcrowding, etc.

V. The other object sought by protective law was the safety of the workers. Sometimes health, morals, and safety were sought in one and the same measure; as, for example, when fencing of machinery and ventilation of mines were provided for in the same Act which prohibited the employment of women and children in mines; or where regulations were enforced as to the employment of men and women, boys and girls in the mine or factory, under conditions provocative of immorality, and where common decency could scarcely be said to possibly exist. In addition to personal safety of life and limb, responsibility in cases of injury while engaged in the ordinary occupation for which the workers were hired, was added. This, however, was not a new law; it was rather statutory limitation and application of the principles of Common Law, derived from the Roman Law, which were general throughout Europe and America. Thus protective law, in this instance, was designed to prevent fatal accidents or injury, or to punish under civil process those who were responsible,

but who neglected proper safeguards for the employees'
safety.

VI. The Public Health Acts are of a different class, but
their aim was in the same direction, their provisions being
on the general lines. Instead, however, of being solely, or
even mainly, instituted for the protection of workers engaged in a particular employment, they were designed for
the benefit of the whole community, of which the work-
people form but a section. Nevertheless, under the Public
Health Acts, the Nuisances Removal Acts, and numerous
other general Acts, all classes of workers are directly, as
well as indirectly, benefited, in addition to the special
protection given to them under the Factory and Workshop
Acts, and other specific Acts. To this category might be
added many groups of Acts of a general character, such as
the Railway Acts, Building Acts, Drainage Acts, Housing
of the Working Classes Acts, and others, all of which extend protection to workers, as part of the whole community, while some contain clauses for their especial benefit.

VII. The motives which actuated those by whom all
such legislation was inaugurated and extended in various
directions, were good, and the objects sought were definite
and generally commendable. The promoters assumed, as a
matter of course, that the individual could not protect
himself in such cases; that many of the circumstances
which had arisen, necessitating interference by law, had
been created by law, or were the direct or indirect results
of law. The argument was, and is, that inasmuch as the
conditions of modern society are mainly the outcome of
legislation, in one form or another, those least benefited by
such legislation should be protected against encroachments

on their liberty of action, and of mutual association, by those who had reaped the greatest advantages from enactments by positive law. How far, and to what extent, the position thus taken up is a right one may be open to argument; and some of the facts alleged in support of either side or view may be challenged. In any case no one will contend that all such interference by statutory enactment is vicious. The questions in dispute mainly are: when, where, and how the interference shall take place; and under conditions and to what extent? The general view is that, in matters relating to labour, the line shall be drawn at adult males; that legislation for the protection of women and children is justifiable, and quite within the sphere of legitimate and positive law; but that interference with the rights and liberties of grown men is an impertinence and a danger which ought to be resented and resisted. Such legislation is undoubtedly an innovation in the strict sense of the term. Indirectly adult males have been protected by Factory and Workshop Acts, and by Mines Regulation Acts, Truck Acts, and similar Acts. For the most part such Acts were not passed ostensibly for the protection of men, except in so far as health and safety are concerned, the one exception being the Truck Acts. In all such legislation the whole community is concerned, as well as the workers. In this respect it was not class law for a section, but general law for the mass. The Truck Acts are of a different class, but they really aimed a blow at a system of fraud, perpetrated by those who had supreme control over the labour market, and against whom the workers were powerless to compete. Many of these conditions were manifestly created by, or were the outcome of law, by

which masters were free to combine, and under which
workmen were refused the right of combination, and consequently of resistance.

VIII. The demand for an extension of the provisions of
positive law to cases not heretofore within its pale, or
domain, is, it is to be feared, as much due to unwise attempts in the direction of limitation as to unwise attempts
to run in advance of public opinion by its extension. For
instance, there was an outcry against what is called 'grandmotherly legislation' by the *Laissez-faire* school of political
economists, as they are termed, with the object of restricting such legislation. The Liberty and Property Defence
League of to-day is regarded by many as carrying to the
very extreme the principle of non-interference by law in
matters of 'contracts of service' in the realm of labour. The
adherents of this school appear to be inclined to appeal to
philosophical principles only in so far as they are protective
of their own interests. This is not perhaps intentional, but
proceeds from forgetfulness of what they owe to earlier
legislation and regulation. They protest, and in many cases
rightly, against the enactment of fresh restraints on individual liberty, but they are not enthusiastically eager to
part with advantages which earlier legislation has conferred upon the class from which the members of that
school are drawn. For example, the State undertakes to
maintain entails and settlements, and provides facilities
for the collection of debts, therein conferring advantages
on the landowning, trading, and capitalist class. If progress
is to bring with it a gradual diminution in the use of legal
machinery in the affairs of every-day life, it is obvious that
these and similar agencies provided by the State must be

modified, as being harmful to the development of human character, and be excluded just as much as enactments which seek to confer advantages upon, and to protect and advance the interests and status of, the labourer. There should be some reciprocity among all classes, thus showing confidence in the expanding tree of liberty as a refuge for the protection of all. Such dogged resistance to any extension of the domain of law leads the advocates of extension to discard all notions of limit, and in reality it reacts in favour of the wildest conceivable schemes of Municipal and General Law, for all kinds of purposes, and for all sections of the people. Both parties seem to have a very confused notion as to the true basis of law, and of the issues involved therein. They are divided into two armies, for attack and defence; they aim wildly at each other, neither having a very clear idea where the other is in the fray. They have no conception of a golden mean in matters of State policy, or that there is a plateau of debatable land on either side of the imaginary boundary line of legislative interference, which may still be open for demarcation and delimitation. The political philosopher, and the social statist or political economist, must attempt to trace the exact line, if an exact line can be traced, where the State shall act or interfere, and where it shall be neutral, resisting alike those who seek to pass the boundary in whatever direction, whether by further extension of legislation, or by the repeal of legislation in force. This is now all the more necessary, seeing that 'statesmen' and those who seek 'parliamentary honours' are subject to continuous external pressure for new legislation, on old or new lines, as the case may be. Every member of the popular branch of the legislature is being forced, almost against his will, to support this or that measure, the exact bearing of which, beyond its more immediate objects, he does not see, or in the least degree perceive. Such pressure is exercised quite irrespective of other pressure in a contrary direction, by another set of enthusiasts.

The requisition for legislation during the last six years has been enormous, it is becoming more and more irresistible and dictatorial each year, and it will be perpetual and growing, until some principle of policy is formulated by which thoughtful men can stand. Whether or not this be possible is a question for debate; but the absence of a policy is dangerous to all concerned—to the State, as a living organism, and to the various sections of the community of which it is made up.

IX. The sphere of legislation is now sought to be extended in various directions, covering a wide field. Some of the measures demanded belong to a class which has had the sanction of all parties in the State, and also of the majority of economists, to whichever school they may belong. There have been differences of opinion as to the degree and exact extent of the legislative interference to be conceded; and some few have protested against the kinds, and the methods adopted; but actual resistance to its principles has been small. The particular branches of subjects embraced in the new demands may be classified and summarised as follows:

(*a*) Acts for extending existing provisions relating to the safety of persons engaged in more or less dangerous occupations. This series of enactments is based upon principles which are not generally called in question, as being in any sense an infringement of legitimate law. It is universally admitted that no man has a right to contribute to the injury of another, whether the person injured is in the employ of such other person, or is a 'stranger,' not in his employ. This personal protection is indeed the essence of all law. The State exists for no other rightful purpose; all else is usurpation, no matter what euphonious name may be applied to the condition of things in which such protection is denied.

(*b*) Compensation for injury is of the same class, and is the natural sequence of the foregoing. The Common Law has always held the person causing the injury responsible, and liable to pay compensation. The Employers' Liability Act does not extend the responsibility; on the contrary, it rather limits its application, and also the amount of compensation to be awarded. As a set-off to this limitation, it gives an easy remedy by summary process for the amount claimed. Instead of expensive litigation in the Superior Courts, the County Court may assess damages up to a certain restricted amount. Against measures of this sort there can be no legitimate objection, provided they are framed and administered with equity. The limitation of responsibility and liability only dates back some five and forty years, and was not even then the subject of positive law, but of interpretation by the highest legal tribunal, the House of Lords.

(*c*) The Public Health Acts endeavour to ensure, as far as practicable, immunity from dangerous conditions arising from unhealthy occupations, carried on in unsanitary dwellings, or premises, where the work has to be performed; and also protection to the inhabitants from the

effects of unhealthy areas, bad drainage, or other defects
dangerous or injurious to health. When a person undertakes to do certain work he runs the risks usually incidental
to such employment. But it is always understood that such
risks are limited to those that are not preventible. To
endanger a man's life needlessly is upon a par with man-
slaughter. The worker has a right to expect that all reasonable care shall be taken to lessen the danger, and prevent
accidents wherever possible. In accepting a tenancy, the
tenant has the same rights as against his landlord. All this
is old law, and is good law; nor can it be abrogated without
danger to the community, and to the State.

(*d*) The Factory and Workshop Acts constitute the special group to which exception is mainly taken. In this class
of legislation there is a growing tendency towards expansion and extension, and of including objects and purposes
not within the purview of existing law. Many regard this
tendency with strong disfavour; even those most favourable see in it a great danger. Demands are being daily made
for the extension of these Acts. The advocates thereof urge
that such legislation shall be logical, and face the full consequences of recognised principles, in enactments already
in force. It is not always clear that the proposals made are
the logical outcome of legislation now in force. And even
were it so, there may be, and often are modifying circumstances or conditions that prevent the application of the
specific 'principle' alluded to; while there are many cases
to which such principle does not logically apply. Each case
must be taken on its merits, and no man need feel any
obligation, moral or otherwise, to support new proposals
because he has felt it incumbent upon him to support

similar legislation in other cases to which such Acts apply. Circumstances alter cases in numberless instances and ways, certainly not less in matters of legislation than in affairs relating to conduct, and of every-day life. Those who urge legislation on the ground of logic, must be prepared to face the logical sequence of their own proposals, both in life and conduct, and in Statute Law. We shall presently see where such proposals will land us, and shall ask those who seek to discredit the action of reformers who do not see eye to eye with them, whether they are prepared to accept the full consequences of the legislation demanded, not only in the realm of labour, but in the domain of social and private life. The question must be faced, for the nation is verging to the point of danger in this connection.

X. The recent inquiry by the Lords' Committee into the Sweating System, as it is called, has opened up a wider field. Not that there is anything absolutely new in connection with it, except perhaps that it has developed more widely, and evoked a deeper interest on the part of the public. Those who will turn to the pages of *Alton Locke*, published forty years ago, will find that the Rev. Charles Kingsley laid bare the chief features of the Sweating System. Mr. Henry Mayhew also, in his 'London Labour and London Poor,' showed to what extent it had crept into the furnishing trades, especially in all that pertained to cabinet-making and fancy work connected therewith; and also into the tailoring trades and some other industries. Those men preached to deaf ears. The public conscience was not touched. There was no response to the earnest appeals then made, which were treated either as the appeals of fanatics, or were regarded as of so sentimental a char-

acter as not to come within the pale of practical politics.
The 'Sweating System' in itself is hard to define; even the
Select Committee of the Lords hesitated to commit themselves to any definition. Mr. Arnold White gave the highly
philosophical description of 'grinding the faces of the
poor'; but the Committee felt that this definition was not
sufficiently precise for legislative purposes. All the witnesses were able to adduce evidence as to the evils of the
system. The Lords' Committee were deeply impressed by
the voluminous evidence given before them, as to the extent of the evils, and the baneful effects, in various ways.
But they were not able to formulate any plan for dealing
with them by enactment. They advised combination, co-
operative production, and sanitary inspection, the latter
only being in the direction of positive law. But to be able
to deal with any subject of statutory enactment, the promoters thereof should be in a position to define the objects
aimed at, and the precise extent of the contemplated interference. It is not sufficient to state the evils to be remedied,
because these may arise from various causes, some of
which are scarcely within the sphere of practical legislation and some remedies might intensify rather than cure
the disease.

XI. The Sweating System is mainly the outgrowth of a
domestic system of industry, but apparently not wholly
so. At any rate, it attains its highest development in those
trades in which the family can perform the work independently at home. This is seen in the tailoring trades, the
boot and shoe trades; and in the cabinet-making trades;
and also in the chain-making, nut and bolt-making industries, in Staffordshire and parts of Worcestershire. It is

almost universal in connection with women's work, of all kinds, especially so where they are able to do the work at home. The 'sweater' is the outcome of many elements, the result of many causes; some of these might come within the domain of legitimate law, but many are beyond the province of positive enactment. The head of the family, the responsible bread-winner, has been the chief promoter of sweating. He has preferred independence and isolation as a home worker, where he has the freedom to work when he likes, and to idle when he pleases. He has utilised the skill of his wife, and then of his children, to enable him to produce quickly, while the competition of other men, similarly placed, has compelled him to produce cheaply— too cheaply perhaps to enable him to live decently, as a skilled workman should live. This system of domestic manufacture, has in recent times been carried on under such conditions as to become a positive danger to health, not only to those who live immediately under such conditions, but to the locality in which they dwell, and often to the whole surrounding district. This has led to the demand for sanitary inspection, with power to 'invade the sanctuary of the home,' even when the family only are employed. Workers, in very despair, invoke this power, and sanitary reformers seek it as a means, in their opinion the only means, of abating a widespread evil, the consequences of which might become dangerous, or at least very injurious to the whole community.

XII. The desire for legislative interference has of late been growing to such a degree that it has become a passion, in many breasts an all-pervading passion, which is apparently insatiable. It is with many a mere dilettante longing for some change, which shall bridge the gulf of classes, now separated by an almost impassable chasm. With others it is the cry of despair. They feel the terrible struggle for existence so acutely, and see no possible means of escape from the intensified and continuous strain, mentally and physically, that they look to the State to interfere, for protection and support. If it be not despair, it is decadence, true manhood being crushed out, in so far as its higher attributes are concerned. Others, again, seek the aid of the State out of utter idleness, and ingrained laziness; their idea of life seems to be not to do anything for themselves, except that which they are compelled to do from sheer necessity. The most serious proposal in recent times, is the application of the principle of State interference with the labour of adult males, and the fixing of their hours of labour by law. The proposals at present before the country are various; some propose to go only a little way, others go the 'whole hog.' Of the two the whole hog people are the most logical and consistent. They seek a universal law of Eight Hours, for all sections of the people, without distinction of class or industry. The possibility of its application is quite another matter. The advocates of this 'principle' do not trouble themselves with such trifling questions as possibilities; what they demand is the principle of a uniform day of Eight Hours; it is for the legislature to find out the way, and the methods of its application. If, they say, the thing is right, Parliament can formulate the provisions and the means. It is the duty of Parliament to put into language, and give expression to the aspirations of the people. The conclusion is simple, and, may we say, profound.

XIII. The definite formulated proposals now before the

country are limited to certain employments; but the advocates, for the most part, regard those as only initial steps towards the grand consummation, by them devoutly wished for. The first measures suggested are:

(*a*) An Eight-Hour day for all Government employees. It is not quite clear whether the advocates of this policy seek to enforce eight hours' continuous work upon all Government employees, or whether they only desire that those who work longer than eight hours shall be brought within that limit, leaving those who work less than eight hours, the full enjoyment of present privileges. This is a point upon which they are discreetly silent.

(*b*) There is a further demand that all persons employed by Municipal Corporations, and all Local bodies and Authorities, shall be employed for eight hours only. Here, again, it is not quite clear whether the rule shall be universal, or only partial, in its application. The demand is general, the advocates disdaining to descend to particulars, either as to the application of the regulations, or the limitation (if any) of their operation.

With regard to these two classes of employees, there is no kind of pretension that they are over-worked, or that their labour is exhausting or dangerous. The contention merely is that the State, or the Municipal Institution or Local Body, should show an example to other employers, by working the men fewer hours, and paying them at the highest rates of remuneration. No one will contend that the State should under-pay, or over-work, its employees. But, on the other hand, few will assert that the State should so deal with labour, as practically to regulate the hours of labour, and fix its price. Yet the contention of those who

seek such interference involves these conditions, in its
operation and results. Custom has the force of law; and a
State-regulated day, and a fixed rate of wages for such
working day, would in effect govern the labour market
generally, certainly for the same kind of labour, in all parts
of the country.

(c) A section, and it must be admitted that they constitute a very considerable section, of the miners, seek for
a State-regulated day of Eight Hours. Their various Associations have prepared a Bill for that purpose, which Bill
has been introduced into Parliament. The representatives
of the counties of Durham and Northumberland have,
with the general assent of their mining constituents, with-
held their sanction to the measure; but the representatives
of other mining districts support it, and they denounce all
those who withhold their support. The supporters of the
Bill contend that the mining industry is a dangerous occupation, and that labour in the mine is exhaustive, and,
therefore, that the hours of work in the mine should be
limited. With regard to the question of danger, the law is
pretty severe at present, and any plea on the score of
danger will command attention and respect. But legislation in this direction comes under a totally different head,
and ought not to be pleaded on behalf of State regulation
of the hours of labour. The exhaustive nature of the work
is admitted, but the plea holds good in other industries.
Yet the supporters of the Bill declare that the measure is
limited to mining, and is not intended to apply to other
trades. Leaving the question of danger out of the calculation, it might be asked whether iron-workers and steel-
workers, blast-furnacemen, and some others, could not put

in as reasonable a plea on the score of exhaustion, and the laboriousness of their occupation. Some of those employed on railways could also plead both danger and exhaustion, and therefore the limitation proposed, for miners only, will scarcely hold good. Besides, no class of men in this country have done so much for themselves, by themselves, as the miners. To their credit be it said, they have shown an example, worthy of all praise, of self-help, and mutual help by associative effort, such as might be advantageously followed by the workmen of all classes in the country.

(*d*) The Shop Assistants of the country, especially those in the metropolis, have formulated demands for the early closing of shops, either generally, on all days of the week, or specifically, on certain days, with half-holidays, because, as they assert, they have found it impossible to adequately curtail their hours of labour otherwise. The fact is that the pressure of long hours has not been felt sufficiently to induce them to combine for shorter hours, or they would ere this have gained their ends. In many houses the hours of labour have been reduced considerably, without State interference, and the tendency is still further to reduce the working hours of this class of employees. Where women and young persons are employed, the law operates as it stands, under existing legislation.

(*e*) But the most curious requisition of all is the demand, by a large number of Shopkeepers, that shops shall be closed at a certain hour by Act of Parliament, under Municipal or Local regulation, by the majority of the votes of those engaged in the particular business to be regulated. Sir John Lubbock's measure admits the difficulty by omitting certain establishments, and shops, from its operation.

Those omitted are, in point of fact, the very places in which the hours are the longest, such as public-houses, hotels, restaurants, eating-houses of all sorts, tobacconists, news-agents, and some others. The exceptions prove that State regulation is difficult and dangerous. Many of those who clamour for the interference would resent any attempt to put in force a law prohibiting Sunday trading, yet this would give one whole day's rest in seven. All these pro-posals practically admit that voluntary regulation is not possible to the extent demanded. Does not this imply that State regulation is impracticable? Is it not an admission that statutory enactment is not required by those for whose benefit it is ostensibly intended? The power to close at a given hour exists in all places.

(*f*) Another of the proposals made is to insist that in all Railway Bills and Tramway Bills, and of course, naturally, in all Bills involving the employment of labour, and re-quiring Parliamentary sanction, provisions shall be in-serted fixing the hours of labour at eight per day, as a condition precedent to the passing of such measures. No-tice to that effect was given in the session of 1890, but the question was not the subject of debate upon any Bill, nor was any attempt made to raise it. This mode of Parlia-mentary interference and regulation is perhaps the most extraordinary ever submitted to the House of Commons. The proposal bears no resemblance to the provisions in-serted in Railway and Street Improvement Bills relating to the housing of the working-classes, as powers are given in such Bills to compel the vacating of dwellings within the area taken compulsorily, and that too without any com-pensation or consideration to the poor families evicted under the Acts. By the Housing of the Working Classes Act, 1890, some provision is made for the costs of removal, when the dwellings are required for demolition, in order to clear the area; but even this proviso does not really amount to compensation. There is, however, no analogy whatever between the two sets of cases; nor can that enactment be quoted in support of the former demand, upon any logical or reasonable grounds. If Parliament is to be called upon to interfere in matters relating to labour in all Bills brought before the Legislature for Parliamentary sanction, there is an end to the respective 'rights,' whatever these may be, of capital and labour. It would be better at once to fix the hours of labour, and its wages or price, by legal provisions which shall be binding upon all classes, employers and workmen alike, in all departments of industry, all over the kingdom.

XIV. There are four very serious objections to this kind of legislation, all of which must be removed before it can be initiated and carried into effect. These are:

(1) The impracticability, nay impossibility, of its universal adoption and application. All laws which are partial in operation are made by a class, for a class; and class legislation is generally condemned, most of all by the working-classes, and rightly so. For more than a century we have been busily engaged in undoing the class legislation of previous centuries—in repealing the statutes, and in removing the obstacles they had created. The work is not yet completed, for the effects remain long after the statutes are repealed. Everybody who may be at all acquainted with the history of past legislation, admits that the earlier legislation in this direction hampered trade,

hindered the advancement of the people, and operated adversely to labour. It took an entire century to repeal the Labour Laws, and some of them are not even now repealed. We are asked to revert back to similar legislation; to fix the number of hours of the working-day, and to practically set up a standard of wages. Can this be done effectually for all trades? One would like to see the draft of a measure, setting forth in detail, in a schedule, all the industries of the country, with the number of hours to be worked as the normal working day for each trade, and the minimum rates of wages to be paid. In such schedule, what should govern the length of the day, or the rate of wages? Should it be skill, the exhaustive character of the labour, the cleanliness or dirtiness of the occupation, the insanitary conditions under which it is carried on, or what? It would be an interesting session in which all these questions were discussed and settled, if settled they ever could be. Each class and section would have its accredited experts, whose duty it would be to show that his clients deserved to be put in this or that class, or to be exempt from this or that regulation. That time is not yet come.

(2) The inelasticity of positive law is adverse to the development of human intelligence and skill. An Act of Parliament is necessarily directed more to the restraint of liberty than to its expansion. Hence the principle upon which it is, or ought to be, conceived, is that caution is better than recklessness, and that it is above all things advisable to hasten slowly in matters of legislation. The great majority of people do not at all understand the nature and character of an Act of Parliament. Working-men especially seem to regard it merely as an ordinary resolution,

registered by both Houses of Parliament, and capable of being as easily and readily rescinded or amended as any resolution passed at a public meeting, or by the committee or council of the body with which they are associated, and with whose acts and resolves they are more or less familiar. An Act of Parliament is certainly not like a law of the Medes and Persians; it is not an enactment which cannot be abrogated or set aside. But it frequently takes a longer time, and involves more agitation and expense, to repeal an Act, even when its effects have admittedly been pernicious, than it did to place it on the statute book originally. It is no light matter either to enact or repeal a statute; even to amend it often requires years of earnest and persistent effort. Of legislation generally it might with truth be said that fools rush in where angels fear to tread. The House of Commons is slow, frequently very slow, to embark on new experimental legislation; and when such is initiated the expedient of 'temporary law' is often resorted to, requiring that its assent shall be renewed year after year, in order to see how it works before it is made a permanent statute. Many such laws are renewed session after session by an Expiring Laws Continuance Bill, at the close of each session; an indication of the extreme caution of the Legislature in any new departure in positive enactment.

(3) Supposing there was no question as to the 'principle' of such legislation, the administration of the law would frequently involve hardships more intolerable than the evils they were meant to cure. The inspection required, to see that the laws were enforced, would necessitate an army of inspectors, all of whom would, in the very nature of

things, become more and more dictatorial, inasmuch as they would be the masters of employers and employed alike. Labour would have to cease at the sound of the State gong, and any work performed beyond the legislative limit would be an infraction of the statute. If the necessities of the hour required that work should be continued after the fixed point of time, a permit would have to be granted by the inspector, magistrate, town council, or some other recognised authority constituted for the purpose. Over-time would have to be abolished in all cases, except in instances of great emergency. Overtime, with a fixed legal day, would be impossible, or the legislation itself would be a farce. Those workmen who chuckle in their sleeve at the prospect of putting in more overtime, at higher rates of pay, would find that an Eight Hour Law was a law to be administered and enforced; not an elastic regulation, capable of indefinite interpretation and modified application. Besides which, an Eight Hour Law would be a hollow sham which permitted working beyond the normal fixed day. Eight hours, and no more, must be the motto of those who seek it, if they are honest in their contention that such an enactment is needed as a means of providing work for the workless. This aspect of the case is kept back by the advo-cates of the 'legal day' of eight hours, but it must be insisted on, as part of the bargain. One month's experience of the administration of such a law would cure many of its advocates of their phrensy for State regulation, by a State official, in the ordinary affairs and conduct of every-day working life.

(4) Such legislation would fail, as all similar legislation has failed in the past. It is useless to say that the conditions

are changed—human nature is not changed—certainly not for the better in these respects. The greed of gain is as rife today as when Christ drove the money-changers out of the Temple, or as it was in the Middle Ages, when the Guilds regulated, or sought to regulate, labour and wages. The history of the Guilds discloses the fact that for centuries there was an intensely bitter contest between the Guild members of the various fraternities for the supreme control and for ascendancy. The feuds only ended with their suppression. The contests did not subside, but were continued under the enactments which were substituted for the earlier ordinances, until those were, in their turn, repealed. The charters from time to time granted were but abuses of power, by the creation of monopolies and privileges, and these for the most part had either to be abrogated, or so abridged as to be incapable of doing much mischief. Where they still partially exist the abuses linger and continue; and even the advocates of legislative interference apparently desire the final extinction of chartered monopolies and of power. In what way have the conditions of labour changed, or the character of workmen, to lead us to believe that legal enactment will be more fruitful of benefits now than of yore? Even the conduct of many of the advocates of such legislation belie the contention, for they are more bitter in their attacks, more unscrupulous in their action, and more offensive in their conduct, than were the antagonists of a bygone age, when such labour legislation was in force, and in the struggles when it was sought to be abrogated. Fitness for restraint is a condition precedent to legal enactment; that fitness is not discoverable in the language and conduct of the chief advocates of

Acts of Parliament for the regulation of labour, and for determining how long a man, in the plenitude of his strength, shall work at his trade, or what he shall earn by his industry.

XV. The advocates of further legislative interference in labour questions urge, above all things, as previously indicated, that we shall be logical in the matter of positive law. They quote Acts, and parts of Acts, in order to show that the 'principle' of interference has been adopted and applied; and they accuse all who hesitate to extend the 'principle,' on the lines they indicate, of cowardice in withholding assent to the newer forms of legislative action which they suggest. 'We are all socialists now,' said an eminent Parliamentary hand. Yes; in a sense that is so. Some are socialists by conviction, no matter upon what inadequate grounds; others may be regarded as socialists by their silence, and an attitude of noncommittal, because they shrink from combating socialistic views and tendencies; and many are socialists from lack of knowledge, lack of energy, and the absence of self-sustaining power. The growth of socialism is due to the enormous expansion of our wealth resources, the advantages and benefits of which are only shared by the comparatively few, instead of the many and by the consequent contrast of poverty and riches, which may be seen on every hand. This state of things is to be deplored, and as far as practicable to be remedied; the only question is—how? The two distinctive proposals put forward by the Fabians and the Socialists are, firstly, the extension of the provisions of the Factory and Workshop Acts to all the trades of the country, where only adult males are employed, as well as where women and children are employed; and they seek to apply the provisions of those Acts to domestic manufacture of all kinds, where the family only are engaged in productive labour, as well as to industry where persons are hired by an employer. And, secondly, they seek the regulation of the hours of labour by statute-law, generally and uniformly, or partially, as the case may be, as before stated. Those two points may be said to cover the present demands relating to labour.

XVI. The extension of the provisions of the Factory and Workshop Acts to domestic industries, where the members of the family only are employed, will inevitably destroy domestic manufacture in all trades. Some affect to deny this, but all the better informed advocates of such extension acknowledge that such will be its effects and results; and they even rejoice at the prospect. It is not necessary for present purposes either to attack or defend the system of domestic industry. Great evils are connected with the system, many are the natural outcome of it. It is, however, essential that all classes and sections of the community should know what is sought, and what is inevitable, if the legislation proposed is carried into effect. If all places and premises where work is carried on are to be inspected; if a certain cubical space is to be insisted upon in all such rooms; if the hours of labour, of meal-times, and the provision especially that meals are not to be taken in the same room, are enforced, how is it possible for any kind of work to be done at home? The thing is impossible. This fact must be clearly understood by all who are likely to be affected by such legislation. The sleeping room of the family will have to be as open to the inspector as an ordinary workshop, for it is well known that in numberless instances one room serves for all the purposes of living, working, cooking, and sleeping. Are the mass of the people prepared for so drastic a measure—will they submit to it? And not only will the domestic 'workshop' be absolutely abolished, but the small masters will have to go, just as the small private schools practically ceased to exist with the institution of School Boards. The effect will be that industry of all sorts will be concentrated, centered in fewer hands; huge establishments will monopolise trade, and the workers will, in consequence of their own action, be at the mercy of a few large firms, or great trading companies, with the result that in the event of being discharged, for certain reasons, no other establishment will be open to them.

XVII. It might be thought that the demands of the new school of labour advocates have been exaggerated, and that the possible evils resulting from such demands have been maximised. One fact alone will disabuse either notion, if it exists. Recently, as late as August, 1890, the newly formed Dockers' Union, led by the men who claim to be the originators of what they are pleased to describe as the 'New Trade Unionism,' decreed that their books should be closed; that no new members were to be enrolled; that they were now sufficient in numbers to perform the work at the docks, and that any addition would but impede their progress, by being brought into competition with the accredited members of the Union. Any departure from this decree was to be left in the hands of the Executive of the Union. This autocratic ukase is worthy of the most unscrupulous despotic tyrant that ever disgraced the pages of history; no parallel for it can be found in the annals of labour, except, perhaps, in the more degenerate days of the trading corporations of the Middle Ages, or possibly in some of the commercial 'rings' of modern times. It says, in effect: We, the members of the Dockers' Union, are quite sufficient in numbers to do all the dock-work of the port of London, or other ports; we only are to be employed; no other men shall come into competition with our labour, and we will dictate the terms and conditions upon which we shall be employed. If you don't like it, we will stop all industry until you cave in. Supposing all other Unions adopted the same policy, and shut out all labour except that which had been enrolled in the books of the Union—what is to become of the unemployed? Beggary, or the workhouse, is to be the lot of all new comers into the field of industry, unless they can be banished into other lands. If any doctrine so abominable had been propounded by employers the world of labour would have been up in arms. The monopoly of the land, or of the Upper Chamber of the Legislature, sinks into insignificance by the side of this unexampled piece of wicked stupidity on the part of the new leaders, the apostles of the new trade unionism.

The mere fact that such a piece of stupendous folly could be seriously entertained by any body of sane persons is bad enough; but that it should be promulgated, and be treated by any portion of the press otherwise than as the ravings of fanatics, shows to what depths of utter imbecility, ignorance, and presumption men can be found to descend when blinded by passion, led by bigotry, and actuated by mere selfishness in the attainment of their objects. Men of this stamp, if once they had supreme control over the legislative machine, would annihilate individual liberty, and reduce

God's image to a mere photograph of one human pattern, as lifeless as clay, to be reproduced mechanically, as the sole type of manhood in the world. They seem not to know that the Great Creator has impressed upon the human soul an individuality as complete, and as multifarious, as is to be found in the forms and features of the myriads of men and women which constitute the mass of humanity; and they appear not to be aware of the fact that it is as impossible to mould the human mind to one stereotyped pattern, as it would be to shape the form and features in one iron mould, to the same model. It is not only impossible; it is undesirable, even were it possible. In all nature variety is charming; certainly it is not less so in human character than in other animate, and in all inanimate objects. Dull uniformity realises the highest conception of life, conduct, and character in the breasts of those who have no distinct individuality of their own. When Pope said of the female sex, 'Most women have no character at all,' he was regarded as having libelled the sex; but absence of character would seem to be the acme of perfection, according to the new gospel of socialism, in which manhood is to be crushed out of humanity, and the State is to regulate the desires, attainments, and needs of all, individually and in the concrete. To rise at morn to the sound of a State gong, breakfast off State viands, labour by time, according to a State clock, dine at a State table, supplied at the State's expense, and to be regulated as to rest and recreation, do not realise a very high conception either of life or conduct. Yet this is the dream of the new social innovators, whose aim is to suppress individuality, and substitute therefor State control and Municipal regulation in all that concerns private life.

XVIII. Lest it should be thought that the foregoing remarks are somewhat strong, as regards the leaders of the new labour movement, it is only necessary to refer to the action of the Unionists towards those who abstain from joining the Union, or refuse to be bound by its rules and regulations. The claim of the pioneers in the cause of labour hitherto has been that no man shall be tabooed socially, or be placed under the ban of the law, because of his belonging to a trade union. This was always the plea of those who sought the repeal of the Combination Laws. That plea was for liberty to act, not for the power to coerce. Unionism is being used for the latter purpose of late, to a degree which is dangerous and wicked. To what extent it might be used if the unions, controlled by such men, were powerful enough to exercise their authority, especially if they had behind them the sanction of statute law, which the new leaders invoke, it is not possible to conjecture, but we can have some faint idea from what has taken place, and is taking place, in various parts of the country. Law and liberty ought to exist side by side, the former protecting and guaranteeing the latter. When the two are divorced, law degenerates into tyranny, and liberty into license. Progress without order is impossible, and law is simply regulation, order being its essence. The endeavour should therefore be so to regulate, that the highest and noblest instincts and aspirations of man shall have full scope for their development and exercise, in every department and condition of life. This is always difficult enough, for society is in con-

spiracy against non-conformity; how much more difficult
then will it be when positive law is invoked to enforce and
maintain uniformity in the domain of labour, and in the
affairs of social life? It might be urged that the regulation
of the hours of labour will not necessarily involve the
abnegation of individual rights in the manner described.
But we reply that as the logical outcome of the regulation
sought it would be inevitable.

XIX. The domain of law as applied to labour may be
generally described under two heads: (1) Protective law,
the object and purposes of which are to protect the weak
against the strong, as exemplified in the Factory and Workshop Acts, for the protection of women and children; and
all extensions of such law to cases where life and limb
are concerned. (2) Enabling law, the aim and purposes of
which are to remove obstacles to, and provide facilities for,
the promotion of the well-being and happiness of the individual and of the mass of the people. To these might be
added preventive law, whose province it is to interpose
when any citizen, or any number of citizens, attempt to
interfere with the legitimate rights of others. Herein is
the rightful province of law; beyond is always doubtful,
mostly dangerous. The multiplication of laws is perilous;
each new Act, almost of necessity, creates the need for further legislation; it propagates itself, until newer circumstances arise to render it obsolete or useless. We have too
much law, and too little justice. Additional law will scarcely
tend to augment equity, in the true sense of the term.
Therefore, instead of increasing the bulk of statute law, or
extending it in newer directions, of bringing it to bear upon
labour, in the manner proposed by its recent advocates, the

object rather should be to curtail it, to simplify it; to codify that which is useful and approved; to repeal what is bad and mischievous, and to give a fuller freedom to the faculties of man in all that is noble and good. The demand for more law indicates a decadence of manhood, an absence of self-reliant, self-sustaining power. It marks an epoch of dependence, the sure precursor of decay in men and in nations. Labour has been strong under persecution, has won great victories in the conflict of industrial war. Its successes seem to have bewildered many, and they seek repose under the baneful fungi of legislative protection and regulation.

GEORGE HOWELL

CHAPTER 4

STATE SOCIALISM IN THE ANTIPODES

CHARLES FAIRFIELD

CHAPTER 4

STATE SOCIALISM IN THE ANTIPODES

Knowledge, most serviceable to students and investiga-
tors of political, social, and economical growth, change,
and decay, as well as to all those who practise the art or science of government, is to be gathered from our great self-
governing colonies. In Australasia and in Canada alone
have democracies already given several years' fair trial to
certain measures, of a socialistic character, recommended
in these days to our legislators at home, but, up to the
present, almost solely on theoretical or abstract grounds.
Although much laborious, minute, honest, and ingenious
consideration has recently been given by thinkers in Great
Britain, for example, to such 'socialistic' remedies as a compulsory Eight Hours Law for all industries (or for government and municipal undertakings only), Free State Education (at the expense of the general tax-payer), Early
Closing of Shops, and Local Option, the most convinced
advocates of those experiments cannot do more than guess
how they would work in the United Kingdom. It is to be

regretted that the public in this country have as yet no
complete, careful, and unbiassed account of important
legislative acts adopted by the colonies, which are in advance—or perhaps rather in excess—of correlated Imperial
Acts and of the results, already manifest in *corpore vili*
beyond sea.[1] For purposes of enquiry and comparison men
and women in Australia are still very like Britons at home.
Special forces there are, slowly fashioning out of populations of British origin a new and distinct type of citizen,
with special ideas. But deep speculations on the future evolution of races and nationalities are not requisite in order
to understand the effect either of specific laws or of State
Socialism grafted on to a community, transplanted it is
true, yet bearing with it institutions copied closely from
our own and based upon ideas and traditions with respect
to civil and religious liberty, property, order, law, commerce, and economic conditions generally which have been
the common property of all liberal thinkers and legislators
in this country for the last fifty or sixty years.

What Australasian colonists have done is especially instructive, because they have been specially privileged—

---

[1] Returns relating to colonial legislation—Canadian liquor legislation
chiefly—have been occasionally presented to Parliament. In 1889 Mr.
Bradlaugh obtained one return showing the limitation of hours of labour
'in Canada and the United States'; but as Acts of Congress are often
loosely carried out, or allowed to remain dormant, American 'results' are
not very instructive. When Sir John Lubbock's Early Closing of Shops Bill
was discussed, in 1888, some reference was made to the Victorian Factory
Act of 1885. In 1890, when Mr. Goschen's Local Taxation Bill was re-
viewed, it was not noticed at all that the whole question of 'compensation'
to owners and lessees of licensed premises had been fully thrashed out and
dealt with in Victoria in 1884, under conditions almost exactly similar to
our own. A Glasgow newspaper (Aug. 1890) stated that Mr. Bradlaugh

enjoying indeed from the start a free hand. Their reforms or experiments have not been thwarted by the lack of money wherewith to give beneficence a fair trial. So vast has been the extension of credit to the Australasian colonies during the last thirty years, that private investors in Europe now enable Australasian governments, financial institutions, and private firms to dispose of some £300,000,000 sterling of foreign capital. Colonial statesmen have indeed been as happy as the heir to a great fortune in a novel, who is able to indulge the author's brightest dreams of how to better things in general. Money borrowed in Europe has been, as a rule, laid out by colonial governments honestly, even if recklessly or unwisely. The honourable traditions of modern official administration in the United Kingdom have been transplanted in principle to the Antipodes, and no prominent public man there has enriched himself by the shameful means common in the American Republics. Opportunist statesmen, willing to go great lengths in order to retain power and salary and to win the favour of the ruling classes, have held office, and now hold office, in Australia; but as far as corruption or

---

next session might raise the question of obtaining—either through colonial governors, or by small commissions sitting in the colonies—independent evidence as to the scope and results of certain State Socialistic enactments in Australia; and added, rightly enough, that the British public, through 'Consular Reports,' knew a good deal more about American, or Portuguese, legislation than about colonial. Of course the official etiquette in such matters is to refer to the Agents General for the Colonies. But although these gentlemen are always most willing to give information, the majority of them have now been absent from their own colonies for years; they may also, while members of Colonial Parliaments, have been zealous partisans—or opponents—of the very legislation on which an unbiased opinion is required.

official peculation is concerned, ministers, legislators, and government servants have stood the rough assay of criticism and publicity well. Beneficent legislation has had a fair trial in the colonies, for the additional reasons that there is much less of that tangled undergrowth of private interests and acquired rights which confronts reformers and legislators in this country to clear away, while colonial democracies have no real knowledge of those historical, religious, or class grievances and animosities which warp and distort questions here. Except during an era of artificial and grotesque political rancour, subsequent to the 11th May, 1877, party bitterness has never flourished. It has no tap-root in the colonies, and quickly withers under the sun-rays of material prosperity. Nobody, it has been asserted, is ever really very angry with anybody else for more than a week together in the Australasian colonies.

The public in this country could have obtained fuller evidence with respect to the success or failure of legislation based on State Socialism, in the only part of the world where it has really had an extensive trial, were it not that, in the first place, colonists dare not now do much to dissipate the haze which discreetly veils their affairs.[2] Year by

---

[2] A then member of the opposition in one of the colonial legislatures—himself an acute observer, able thinker, and scathing critic in the Local Assembly of the financial, economical, and moral results of State Socialism—visited London early in 1890. On his return to Australia he assured a newspaper interviewer that he had been careful, in conversation with public men in London, to refrain from mentioning any awkward facts which might tend to alarm investors in the United Kingdom. This reticence is significant. Yet, it is not the business of Australian colonists to warn investors here against lending them that money without which State Socialism—including protected industries, fancy wages, short hours, extravagant educational privileges, and other 'collective' luxuries—would

year the private and personal interests of classes and masses alike are becoming more and more bound up with the borrowing policy of their governments, and with the enormous extension of commercial credit and nominal transfer of investment money from this country to the banks and financial institutions in the large colonial cities. The success of the periodical and now absolutely indispensable loans floated on the London market being at present the first and most vital of Australian interests, it is considered unpatriotic as well as suicidal to circulate widely any statements prejudicial to governmental or joint-stock credit.[3]

Many returned colonists residing in this country might furnish independent and valuable testimony on the new experiments and their results; but, by a curious natural coincidence, the man who is capable of making and keeping a fortune can seldom describe instructively, in print or in speech, the country, the people, or the institutions which have contributed to his success. There is, for instance, the typical returned colonist, possibly a wool-grower, professional man, or employer of labour on a large scale, and

---

long since have collapsed. *Caveat emptor* is a principle discreetly inculcated by colonists of all classes.

[3] Although there is not, and never has been, any speculation—in the gambler's sense—in colonial securities on the London Stock Exchange, and although no large account in them is ever open 'for the fall' there, an uneasy superstition prevails in the colonies that 'the Stock Exchange bears' are, somehow, habitually interested in depressing those securities. As far as that institution is concerned, colonial bonds are taken up and held in large blocks, by a few very rich 'jobbers,' who try to retail them gradually to the investing public. Practically the Stock Exchange must always be a 'bull' of colonial securities.

possibly a man of standing, experience, and powers of observation. When he first settles in South Kensington he
may patriotically resolve to give the British public his particular views about protective tariffs, political financing, or
the latest vagaries of Trade Union absolutism, in his particular colony, through the medium of the London Press.
But, even supposing that he is neither a bore, a crotchet-
monger, nor a mere partisan, when he settles in South
Kensington our typical squatter, merchant, or man of culture is apt to become so delighted with the ways of the
up-to-date Londoner, the cheapness of art-furniture, over-
coats, stationery and umbrellas in the shops, and the sol-
emn luxury of West-end clubs, that he grows pleasantly
confused and ultimately dumb, as far as Britons anxious
for information about State Socialism in the Antipodes
are concerned. We have heard of late years something
about the evils of Free Trade in New South Wales from
furious protectionist partisans, hitherto in a minority in
that colony; we have had some notes from gentlemen with
a tiny Home Rule axe to grind. In the year 1886 the Sydney
Protectionists, Trade Unionists, and Socialists paid the
expenses of a special envoy to London, partly accredited
by the Melbourne Trades' Hall Council, whose business it
was to enlighten the British public, and to dissuade British
wage-earners from emigrating to the Aptipodes or spoiling
the labour-market there. The British public learns something, but not much, from the third-rate literary man who
occasionally voyages as far as New Zealand and back, then
determines to make a book. The few journalists of ability
who have made flying visits to the colonies of recent years
refrain from saying much about graver colonial questions,

chiefly because they recognise that it is extremely difficult to obtain trustworthy information, off-hand, on political, economic, industrial, or financial matters even on the spot. Australians are not demonstrative nor communicative to strangers, while local discussion of the serious and sinister problems accumulating behind the dominant policy of State Socialism is for various good reasons economised as much as possible at present. There is practically no magazine or review literature in Australasia. Two or three of the great newspapers published in Melbourne or Sydney contain of course a mine of undigested facts and information about State Socialism in the colonies, but they are virtually unread in this country.

The notes collected by Mr. Froude during his trip to the Antipodes in the early part of 1885 contain, like all his work, profound, brilliant, and suggestive passages. But 'Oceana' does not profess to be more than a sketch. Baron von Hubner's 'Voyage through the British Empire' is a shrewd and sympathetic survey, by an historical friend of England, of the self-sown Englands beyond the sea. He does not offer to draw broad deductions for us. Lately some clerical tourists of more or less eminence have described for home readers what they saw in the colonies. It is well to remember that the various unestablished religious bodies there have from time to time received valuable grants of land from the State; the Scots Church in Melbourne, and the First Presbyterian Church in Dunedin, for example, possess real estate of enormous value at current rates. The principal ministers of religion are therefore well paid, prosperous, and enabled to maintain an informal standing reception committee, which takes traveling clerical celeb-

rities from this country in hand, and, in the true spirit of
Oriental hospitality supplies them with that kind of information as to Free State Education and crypto-socialism
which is likely to gratify them. Persons with mines to sell,
bi-metalists, and imperial federationists from beyond sea
merely darken counsel.

This year Sir Charles Dilke has caused to be published a
handsome book, in two volumes, wherein some of the
problems confronting rudderless democracy in the great
self-governing colonies are noticed. The opinions on such
matters of one of the most industrious and conspicuous of
our political recluses were awaited with curiosity. Some
persons even hoped that Sir Charles Dilke might, after
many years of intermittent interest in the affairs of the
colonies, make democracy in Australia as instructive a
text for, at all events, a brief homily, as De Toqueville made
of democracy in America. But his new book leaves the impression that Sir Charles Dilke lacks, among other things,
the critical insight, as well as the mental equipment generally, required in order to examine and explain for English
readers those profoundly interesting problems of which he
has heard. He has perhaps no political philosophy of his
own, or if he has he economises it. Possibly the domination
of a political philosophy, which adds so much to the sym-
metry and penetrating effect of French criticism, would
have been inconvenient in this case. Its absence in an ambitious writer, proposing to deal instructively with problems which take us down to the very bed-rock of civil
society, is in these days a defect. Sir Charles Dilke, it appears, has not visited the Australasian colonies for over
twenty years. That is another defect. He rightly pays most

attention to the colony of Victoria, but has virtually made himself the conduit-pipe through which to distribute the views of a group of cultured and interested Victorian protectionists and half-fledged socialists to the British public. A thriving and contented political party, generally describing themselves as Radicals, exists in Victoria. The impression remains that Sir Charles Dilke pined to call the radicalism of the New World into existence to redress the balance of the Old. Accordingly he wrote for information about problems to some worthy Radical gentlemen in Victoria. And they wrote back to him in a cordial spirit, being delighted to find that a politician who was very much thought about in England, and had once been a minister of the Crown, was prepared to accept a brief from them.

Yet a man will hardly travel right round the world without learning that there is something to learn, and Sir Charles Dilke has done one service to the reading and thinking public here by discovering, and then frankly and clearly pointing out that State Socialism entirely permeates the ruling classes in Australia, and inspires the policy of ministries and legislatures there. 'In Victoria,' he says (i. 185), 'State Socialism has completely triumphed.' Nearly all previous writers on Australasia have failed to see that, and have discussed colonial borrowing. Protective Tariffs, hindrances to immigration and to the growth of population, the Labour question, Free State Education, etc., as though they were so many isolated or detachable phenomena. They are not isolated or accidental, but have all the same origin, being in their later phases merely the necessary product of half-digested socialistic ideas and theories. Sir Charles Dilke makes Victoria his principal text, no

doubt because it is easier to get information, good or bad,
about the finances, administration and general condition
of that colony than of the others. Such facilities are mainly
due to what might be called accident, that is to say, to the
superior status and activity of the newspaper Press, in a
country where newspapers may exercise immense influence. In New South Wales the daily Press is virtually represented by one enormously wealthy journal, 'The Sydney
Morning Herald,' which now prudently expounds a dull
opportunism, as far as colonial problems are concerned.
It would be harsh and almost inhuman to criticise seriously
the Adelaide (South Australian) newspapers. There is a
true saying in the antipodes that 'nothing ever happens in
South Australia,' although Mr. Henry George announces
frequently that his views are making great progress there.
The Brisbane newspapers perhaps cannot—they certainly
do not—lead or direct public opinion intelligently. In New
Zealand there is no single town population wealthy enough
to support a really great newspaper, and the Press is pov-
erty-stricken and uninfluential. In contrast to all this, during the last twenty years the people of Victoria have
chanced to be served by two daily newspapers, as ably conducted, wealthy, and powerful as any printed in the English language. Englishmen are beginning to forget that it
was once asserted, with some truth, that the London newspapers 'governed England.' While our innumerable London newspapers are, perhaps, wisely abandoning the attempt to steer English opinion, the Melbourne 'Argus' and
the Melbourne 'Age' still conscientiously keep up the old
fiction, and between them do govern and misgovern the
colony. Their rivalry has been in many ways profitable to

the colony. They make certain blunders and abuses—allowed to pass in the neighbouring colonies—impossible, and try to keep a search-light turned on to the administration. They do not quite succeed. Sir Charles Dilke, adopting views put forward by masters of 'bounce' and *réclame* here, who have done so much to finance colonial State Socialism, asserts (i. 243) that we in England 'understand the way in which they float their loans' (in Victoria), 'and their system of bookkeeping; . . . and we are well informed as to the objects on which their debts (*sic*) are spent'; adding (ii. 230), 'that no one who knows the public offices of South Australia, Victoria, or Tasmania can accuse them of more laxity in the management of public business than is to be found in Downing Street itself.'

I fear that our author has here yielded to the temptation to 'sit down quickly and write fifty,' in order to make unto himself friends, at any rate among our socialistic kin beyond sea. The truth is that nothing definite can be known about the finances of the Australasian colonies. State Socialism there dares not present a genuine balance sheet. As may also be said of the French Republic at this day, there is in Australasia no system of public accounts similar to that which prevails in Downing Street. In Victoria, New South Wales, Queensland, South Australia, and New Zealand, the control of expenditure by local Parliaments is really very weak. No attempt has been made to introduce the imperial system of simple, methodical, and exact account keeping. Audit or check upon public expenditure is loose and ineffective in all the colonies. If we in England really understand 'the system of bookkeeping, and the object on which debts are spent' in Victoria, we know more than colonists themselves know. Meanwhile, for years past reports of imaginary surpluses, as well as misleading and worthless 'official' statistics, have been circulated in the Australasian colonies, and have been carelessly reproduced here.[4] The statement is constantly put forward, for example, that the Victorian State railways, which are supposed to represent an expenditure on productive public works of the bulk of the money borrowed by that colony since 1865, honestly earn a surplus in excess of the interest on their cost. That statement is not, and never has been, true. The memorandum from the Railway Commissioners, read with the budget statement in the Victorian Assembly on the 31st July, 1890, at last frankly admits that the earnings of the State Railways fell short of the accruing interest for the year by more than £220,000.

Yet religions, or dogmas, which nobody can possibly

---

[4] A Colonial Office Return, 81 of 1890, 'Statistics of the Colony of Victoria,' gives (p. 50) the 'net earnings' of the State Railways since 1884 at a fraction over four per cent. The reality of these 'net earnings' is extremely doubtful. The 'Finance Account' on p. 32 will not bear examination. A note on the same page gives the 'statement' (really an official *précis* of that year's budget) 'distributed to members of the Legislative Assembly in July, 1889,' which showed a credit balance, or surplus, of £1,607,559. These figures, it is cautiously added, were 'not final.' They certainly were not; for by the close of the Parliamentary session, on the 21st November, 1889, it was discovered that the huge surplus—which the hon. the treasurer in August had generously distributed in doles, such as £60,000 a year extra, to railway labourers; £140,000 a year to municipalities; £250,000 bounties on exports, to already 'protected' industries, cottage asylums, wire netting for the State rabbits, public buildings, etc.— had no existence.

The whole story of this bogus surplus had already been told in the Melbourne Press two months before the Colonial Office Return in question (which reproduces it as genuine with the endorsement of the then governor of the colony, Sir Henry Loch), was 'presented to both Houses

comprehend do frequently make converts; perhaps because of the haze obscuring the financial basis of Colonial
State Socialism, Sir Charles Dilke (i. 195) judges that 'Lord
Bramwell himself would' find salvation, and 'become a
state socialist if he inhabited Victoria.' Here we have the
testimony of an absentee 'inhabitant,' who has not set
foot in the colony for more than twenty years. Sir Charles
Dilke, while vaguely civil to socialists in general, hardly
understands that socialism is always a most logical, consistent and imperative creed. He has indeed a hazy notion
that there are 'moderate European Socialists' with 'practical programmes'—set to stop as soon as mischief threatens. Although he finds that New South Wales has built and
managed her railways in accordance with socialistic teaching, he seems to look forward (i. 274) to their being worked
'upon strictly commercial principles' some day. In that

---

of Parliament, by command of her Majesty.' In the last hours of the
session of 1889, the hon. the treasurer announced that the government
balance in the hands of the associated banks had fallen to £142,000, that
he had been compelled like all his predecessors to borrow from 'Trust
Funds,' but to the extent of £1,230,000, and that he would require to float
at once on the London market a loan for £1,600,000 (formally devoted by
Parliament to railway construction in 1885) as well as a further loan of
£4,000,000 to square his accounts. It was subsequently admitted by ministers that the surpluses of that and previous years had been mainly
arrived at by the strange but, it appears, time-honoured bookkeeping
expedient of crediting the revenue with all money received during the
financial year and 'carrying forward' certain expenditures, or debits, to
futurity. A memorandum to the Premier from Mr. Edward Langton (an
old Victorian public servant and financier of ability, who is banished
from political life because he is a free trader) was published in the principal Melbourne newspaper, Dec. 4, 1889, and showed that, according to
the Victorian audit commissioners, for years past, large sums had been
expended without the sanction of Parliament, improperly withdrawn
from the debit side of the public accounts and carried forward for sub-

case, he thinks, they could pay interest on their cost. He apparently does not understand how State Socialism works, why it is popular, seductive, and under favourable financial conditions, cumulative in its action, nor why it is combated and denounced by Lord Bramwell and other people. I take it the rough objections to State Socialism everywhere are, that it does not profess to 'pay,' in the business or commercial sense; that, as regards Great Britain, therefore, funds to meet deficits and to keep the system going could only be obtained by levying novel and penal taxes upon industrious and thrifty people, and by plundering owners of fixed capital, either by sheer violence or by violence cloaked in hypocrisy; that even if placed, somehow, on a paying basis State Socialism weakens and demoralizes the national character, by striking at the whole conception of patient, courageous and orderly toil, strug-

---

sequent adjustment. Since 1885–6 this 'charging forward' amounted to £3,500,000. The audit commissioners, it further appeared, are powerless to interfere with this 'system of bookkeeping.' It transpired at the same time that no separate or distinct Railway departmental account or budget existed; the audit commissioners and the railway department did not even agree as to the real amount of the railway capital account; no railway 'sinking fund,' or reserve, to meet losses, such as compensation to passengers for railway accidents, existed; while expenditure which, by the General Post Office, or by any solvent railway, in this country, would be charged to revenue, was habitually charged to a floating capital account, to be recouped out of future loans. The fiction of 'non-political control' of the Victorian railways is reproduced by Sir Charles Dilke. It is true that (chiefly owing to the efforts of the 'Argus') since 1884, Mr. Speight, a railway authority of great experience from the Midland Company, a born judge of work and possessed of singular energy, ability and tact, has been 'at the head' of the Victorian Railway department. But in matters of high State Socialistic finance the 'Minister of Railways' was, until the attempt to create a new Parliamentary Committee *ad hoc* in 1890, supreme. Mr. Speight has been constantly attacked and thwarted by the

gle and endeavour—the most wholesome and ennobling conception human beings have as yet thought out for themselves.

With a splendid subject and a splendid opportunity before him Sir Charles Dilke might have told us by what agencies the primary financial difficulty has been got over in Australia. He shirks all that, but says there is now 'no objection or resistance to state ownership of railways' or to 'state interference' generally; that 'state socialistic movements render Australia a pioneer for England's good,' and hints that 'the Australian colonies as regards State Socialism present us with a picture of what England will become.' He is not able to tell us how State Socialism is affecting the national character, whether it is producing a nobler or baser type of man and woman in Australia. Our author has not however emancipated himself from the old-fash-

---

labour party and their political satellites, but now shows some signs of having become a convert to their ideas. Chaotic as is the condition of Victorian 'bookkeeping,' matters are still more confused in New South Wales. From February, 1886, to January, 1887, an Irish gentleman, who in the romantic garb of a disguised troubadour had won the heart of a charming colonial heiress, and thus laid the foundation of political eminence, was premier of the colony. He managed, before stumbling out of office, to associate himself with a deficit of £1,000,000, which has since been stated in the local Parliament, Feb. 1889, to have grown to £4,064,844. The truth is that no one in the colony knows how the matter stands. In South Australia and Queensland the 'system of bookkeeping' and 'the objects on which their debts are spent,' are, as Mr. Herbert Spencer would say, 'unthinkable.' New Zealand, the colony whose credit has stood lowest of recent years, alone has what may perhaps be called a sinking fund, and managed, at least on paper, to reduce her debt by £1,383,432 in 1889–90. Irregularities and bad management in the public accounts of Victoria and New South Wales might no doubt be remedied in time, were it not that the prosperity of the dominant class and their dependents is now inextricably bound up with the continuance and extension of

ioned prejudice that triumphant socialism implies, sooner
or later, the proclamation of the *commune*, the burning
of public buildings and the shooting of hostages; he is delighted to be able to report that the sky has not fallen, that
hens still lay, and that tradesmen still come round regularly
with provisions in the morning, in a country where State
Socialism is supreme. To him it is 'an amazing fact' that
Socialism 'in the French or English sense,' and 'Revolutionary, European or Democratic' Socialism absolutely do not
exist among the all-powerful working class in the colonies;
he is so pleased with this aphorism that he repeats it in at
least eleven different places.[5] But whether State Socialism
be installed by a revolutionary mob, by a dictator or by a
Parliament, is not the main point. The real questions are:
can the thing itself be honestly made to pay, and will it give
to a nation healthier, wealthier, and wiser men and
women? In Europe and the United States socialism does
usually suggest the idea of revolutionary, violent or terrorist methods, simply because state treasuries are not easily
lootable and because tax-payers and owners of fixed capital
there still resolutely offer all the resistance in their power
to the very practical, and almost the first, demand made by
modern socialists, for money to carry out beneficent plans

---

reckless financing. In order to appreciate the State Socialistic 'system
of bookkeeping' in Victoria, we ought to imagine Mr. Goschen dimly
suspecting a deficit, drawing freely on funds in the hands of the Receiver
General of the Court of Chancery in order to pay off incoherent issues
of Exchequer bills; and squaring one year's public accounts by council
drafts on India—in the following year. Meantime distributing 'surpluses'
thus obtained in bribes to various political groups, suggested by the Social
Democratic Federation.

[5] Pp. i. 185, ii. 264, 265, 267, 268, 269, 272, 279, 288, 296, 357.

which cannot possibly pay on their merits. Probably nobody is a Revolutionary Socialist 'in the French or English sense' from choice.

Victorian Trade Unionists concentrated in one or two large towns have of late years been allowed by the cowardice or apathy of all other classes in the colony to monopolize political power. Although Trade Unionists still jealously dislike to see men belonging to their special class in Parliament they have long 'owned' ministers and legislators, and thus obtained peaceable but complete control over the public purse.[6] They can pledge the credit of the colony in order to finance railways and public works which provide them, on their own terms, with 'State' employment and set the market rate of wages. In the course of a debate on Protection versus Free Trade held in the Concert Hall of the Melbourne Exhibition building before

---

[6] Mr. Mathew Macfie, in a paper read before the Colonial Institute, Dec. 10, 1889, designed to show that the Australian colonies were crippled and restricted by lack of population, and efficient labour, says, 'The operatives in Victoria are organized into a compact phalanx under leaders who have succeeded by dogged persistence in imbuing the colony with the notion that they constitute the party which controls voting power at elections. So widely is this assumption believed that candidates at a Parliamentary Election, to whom salary or political influence is a consideration, defer with real or affected humility to the wishes of the Trades Hall Council in Melbourne. The inevitable outcome of this state of political subjection on the part of the members of the House, and in many cases of the Government also, is the injustice of class legislation.' Sir Charles Dilke, writing perhaps from the point of view of an 'inhabitant' of a quarter of a century ago, describes (ii. 316), the great respect felt for the Trades Councils, and their almost invariable wisdom, moderation, sense of responsibility, and marked spirit of justice.

Mr. Macfie, who spent several years in Victoria, and only returned in 1889, is however a specially valuable witness, because he lived right in the centre of the Protectionist and State Socialist camp, having been

2,000 people on the 8th April, 1890, between Mr. Henry
George and Mr. Trenwith, the latter—a member of the
Legislative Assembly for one of the Melbourne divisions
and President of the Trades Hall Council—boasted, with
truth, that 'The Trade Unionists, wanting respectable
houses, with a carpet on the floor and a piano, as well as
good clothes and education for their children, told the legislators—their servants: "Put a duty on such and such goods
for us." ' Sir Charles Dilke notices (ii. 275), that 'there is
no timidity in the South Sea Colonies with regard to taxation upon land,' and intimates (i. 193), that the Victorian
land tax—turned into a penal enactment by the radical
party after their triumph in 1877 as an act of vengeance on
their opponents—'is certain to be extended whenever the
colony is in want of money.' This tax, our author truly says
(ii. 275), has caused 'a certain depression'—subjective timidity perhaps. Colonial ministries now find easier ways
of raising money than by a land tax; but as long as the
power remains of imposing taxes on large landowners, in
order to pay off loans contracted and expended without the
latter's consent or approval, the setting up of barricades,

---

editor of a powerful weekly journal, mainly owned by the same gentleman whom Sir Charles Dilke styles (ii. 272) 'the Founder of Australian
Protection,' adding that 'he might easily, had chance so willed it, have
made in the world the same name that has been made in later days by
Mr. Henry George, having put forward in most eloquent and powerful
language the same principles at a much earlier date.' In the Antipodes
Evolution, of course, proceeds *à rebours*, and the Founder of Protection
in question, who might, had chance so willed it, have become the rival of
Mr. Henry George, although he still diverts his admirers, whose pennies
and patronage are making him a millionaire, with cheap denunciation of
capitalism and landlordism, is today the wealthiest landowner in the
colony.

burning cities, and shooting hostages will always be, for Australian State Socialists, works of supererogation.

If our domestic socialists 'in the French and English sense,' effectually controlled the Imperial Treasury, they might renounce felonious talk, cease to foment mutiny in the British Army and become Conservatives—in the best sense of the term. Sir Charles Dilke seems at one moment to realise how thoroughly practical are the aims and aspirations of the ruling class in Victoria, for he says (ii. 303), 'The Christianity that they understand is an assertion of the claim of the masses to rise in the scale of humanity.' This kind of Christianity has been understood in the same sense by the dominant classes in all ages and countries— from landowners, lay and clerical, in mediaeval times, down to British middle-class employers and capitalists of a couple of generations ago—who controlled the national purse strings. All those people honestly believed in turn that they were 'the masses'—in the best sense of the term —and they raised themselves in the scale of humanity, at the public expense, accordingly. Meanwhile our author fails to see that Colonial Federated Labour or Trade Unionism cares little for abstract ideas. It is doubtful whether British artisans anywhere have hitherto cared much about them; the founders of the International and the leaders of the Comteist movement in this country at all events considered it doubtful after years of experiment. Australian Trade Unionists—if occasionally given to violence and prone to break their engagements—are as good-natured, friendly, affable and well-conducted as the representatives of any dominant class of Britons that history tells of. They are fond of amusement, manly sports, and betting on horse

races. The same might have been said of that large class
who at the end of the last century lived and thrived on the
Irish Pension List. Sir Charles Dilke seems further to have
imagined that even if Australian working-class democrats
abjured 'Revolutionary' Socialism 'in the French and English sense,' they must at least hanker after land nationalization. He is pleased to find that they do not. Yet why
should they? Unless the Australian Trade Unionist sees
30s. a week extra for himself in any State Socialistic movement he takes no interest whatsoever in it. There is no
profit, direct or indirect, for any human being in nationalization of the land, hence in Australasia land nationalizers,
or single tax leaguers, are, politically, about as influential
and important a body as, let us say, the Swedenborgians in
this country.[7] In March 1890, Mr. Henry George visited
Australasia. He became an object of curiosity and attention there, partly because of recent years many colonial
politicians, especially in Queensland and New Zealand,
have suffered from a chronic indigestion of his theories.
Sir Robert Stout, Mr. Ballance, Mr. Dutton and Sir S. Grif-
fith have each tinkered, in fragmentary, mischievous and

---

[7] Mr. William Webster of Aberdeen once described to me, as evidence
of the spread of the light in the colonies, an ardent land nationalizer
from the Colonial Little Peddlington, South Australia, who owned much
land himself. It was, I gathered, mortgaged, beyond its then value to
local banks. Now there are two sections of land nationalizers, confisca-
tionists and anti-confiscationists, the former being, of course, mere brig-
ands, the latter honest, but ignorant folk, who imagine that the mystic
'State' can, somehow, invent money wherewith honestly to buy up all
the freehold land in the world before nationalizing it. The Little Peddlington landowner, it seems, had joined the anti-confiscationist section, and
as his land was quite unsaleable and a burthen to him, I was not surprised
to hear that he had high hopes from 'the State,' and was very enthusiastic.

futile fashion, with the Land Legislation of their colonies on Mr. George's lines. Colonists however insisted, in 1890, on studying Mr. George as a Free Trader, and the local socialists, who are perhaps more logical than Mr. George is, refused to believe that Free Trade—which is so wrapped up with equal liberty to make contracts, unrestricted competition, self-help, cheap necessaries and other 'individualist' delusions—could work in with Nationalization of the Land, one of the most extreme developments of State Interference and State Socialism. Mr. Henry George, as an incoherent Free Trader, managed to puzzle and offend, instead of converting, Australian socialists who, quite logically, are Protectionists also. The fact, noticed by Sir Charles Dilke, that masses and classes in the colonies are now alike deeply interested in land 'booms' and in keeping up the value of freeholds, further explains Mr. Henry George's recent decisive rebuff there.

High wages, in exchange for short hours of labour, do not come under the heading of *idées*, but are practical things. The prevalence of the eight hours' rule in so many colonial industries is indirect, but strong, proof of the irresistible power conceded to Federated Labour. Although political dependents of the dominant class in Victoria at one time thought it worth their while to embody 'the eight hours' in one or two Mining and Tramway Acts,[8]

---

[8] *The Melbourne Tramway and Omnibus Act* (765) of 1883, Sect. 62 says: 'The days of labour (*sic*) of any person employed by the Company . . . shall be eight hours,' but permits overtime, 'for special payment,' to the amount of sixty hours' work per week. 'The Company shall be liable to a penalty not exceeding £5 for every breach of this section.' It has never been necessary to enforce this penalty. *The Regulation of Mines Act* (783) of 1883, Sec. 5. says: 'No person shall be employed . . . for more than eight hours in

Trade Unionists have been of late years strong enough to get what they want without help of the law.[9] Indeed owing to the non-repeal of the old British Statutes against 'combination,' Trade Unions were technically illegal in Victoria as late as 1885. Sir Charles Dilke says little about the Australian 'eight hours' system. He seems puzzled (i. 250) to understand how Victorian manufacturers manage to compete with foreign rivals, although 'paying double wages for 20 per cent less time than at home.' But he entirely underestimates the 'protection' of the tariff, as well as the other advantages enjoyed by the local manufacturer, and increases his confusion by taking 'an average duty of 11 per cent' on the total Victorian imports.[10] He says (ii. 286) that the eight hours' day 'according to general admis-

---

any day, except in case of emergency.' The penalty for a breach of this section by a 'mine owner' is £50 fine; by 'any other person' a fine of £10, recoverable by summary process before two justices. Although I can find no cases of prosecutions under this section, it seems to have been evaded, for an Amending Act *ad hoc* (883) of 1886 enacts, solely, that: 'no person shall be employed below the ground in any mine for more than eight consecutive hours . . . from the time he commences to descend the mine until he is relieved of his work.' . . . The burthen of proving innocence of charges under these sections is thrown upon the mine owner or 'other person.'

[9] A familiar argument for an eight hours' statute in Great Britain is that Trade Unions cannot enforce the rule themselves. Legal agencies are sometimes superfluous. In the grim days when landlords were absolute in Ireland the legal machinery for collecting rents was very imperfect, actually far behind that existing in England; the Act of 1860 first gave large powers in that respect to Irish landowners. Aware of this, I once asked a venerable Irish farmer how landlords managed to collect rent in his youth? 'Well, you see,' he said, 'landlords didn't want much lawyer's law in thim times. The mashther's rint-warner just wint round wid' a big cart-whip, and he found no pettyfoggin' impidimints at all.'

[10] The bare, or 'face,' duty on the principal imported articles, which really

sion has been found as satisfactory throughout Australia as in Victoria,' a generalization which omits much one would like to know. 'We might gradually,' he thinks, 'introduce it into the contracts of the State and the municipalities in this country, and give it the force of a general law in the case of those trades to which it would be most easily applied,' but does not tell us by what devices the inconveniences of diminished 'supply' or production—as well as the waste and loss due to reduced efficiency of labour—are met and counterbalanced; nor whether the conditions which make the eight hours' rule possible in Australia are to be found in Great Britain.

Short hours of labour and high wages seem to me largely convertible terms. Both are good things. The leisure enjoyed by colonial workmen, their brisk, cheerful and robust appearance, and the activity and 'go' displayed by one or two out-door trades (such as masons and house carpenters) who work under the eight hours' system, are pleasant to

---

compete with local manufactures, will be found over a course of years to average from 30 to 50 per cent *ad valorem*. On some kinds of paper, matches, earthenware porcelain, china and glass and on wearing apparel, it has worked out of recent years at some 75 to 150 per cent *ad valorem*. In order to arrive at the total advantage or 'pull' which the Victorian manufacturer enjoys, we may safely treble the nominal or 'face' amount given in the tariff list. Thus, a nominal duty of 25 per cent *ad valorem* means that at least 75 per cent protection is enjoyed by the local manufacturer. Victorian importers must provide two separate capitals, and pay an average of 6 per cent interest on at least one of them; one is locked up, perhaps for many months, in the Custom House; the other is required partly in Europe to pay for goods and partly to work with in Melbourne. We must add freight, insurance, and heavy port and landing charges, at a port where wharf labourers get 1s. 3d. per hour for seven and a-half hours of work, and difficulty, loss of time and interest involved in executing orders in a market 13,000 miles distant.

behold. A very high 'standard of comfort' prevails amongst Australian workers, and no doubt, as Fleeming Jenkin argued,[11] the standard or expectation of comfort, and the ideal scale of living for the family maintained by wage-earners, do determine the amount of effort which they will put forth to raise wages or reduce hours of labour. It is well to remember that the success of such efforts depends upon very variable conditions, political, social, etc. The 'standard of comfort' firmly believed in by Australian alluvial gold diggers in 1851–3 'embraced' champagne at five guineas a bottle for themselves, gold horse-shoes, now and then, for their horses, and silk dresses at five guineas a yard, for the partners of their joys. What made that lofty standard of comfort possible in 1851–3 was the easily won gold on Bendigo flats and other alluvial diggings. What are the conditions which have enabled Australian Trade Unionists of late years to maintain a particular standard of comfort, wages, and hours? Sir Charles Dilke does not tell us. I believe they are entirely exceptional and artificial.

The first local circumstance, or condition, favourable to the success and permanence of 'The Eight Hours' rule in Victoria is the protective tariff. The second condition is the absence of keen competition among workers of all grades themselves. The third is the settled policy which regularly provides *ateliers nationaux*, or employment for that class which is supposed to be all-powerful at election time on state railways and so-called productive public works, thus 'keeping a market' for labour and creating a

---

[11] *Recess Studies*, Edinb., Edmonstons, 1870.

standard of hours and wages which private employers cannot compete against or vary. The fourth, correlated of course to the last, is the now inevitable, financial, or borrowing, policy of the various colonial governments; which reacts upon local banks and credit institutions. Colonial land legislation and the concentration of population in large cities are also favourable conditions. How many of these, it may be asked, exist in Great Britain?

With slight exceptions the above conditions are in Australia all within the control of the very class which benefits directly by the eight hours' rule. The absence of competition is indeed mainly due to the fact that Australia is remote from the European labour market. A voyage thither means, for an artisan or labourer in search of work, £18 at least, if he be a single man, and far more of course if he be married and have a family. These are, to millions of European workers, prohibitive rates, and constitute a natural or geographical protective duty upon human beings, i.e. upon competing 'labour.' We have only to compare steerage fares from Europe to United States ports—as well as from Continental ports to the United Kingdom—with passage rates to Australia to understand, firstly, why the eight hours' movement has failed hitherto in America and, next, how necessary it will be to stave off, somehow, the competition of Continental labour in many of our home industries if one of the principal elements of the success of the Australian 'eight hours' is to be secured here. Except in Queensland, colonial labour leaders have compelled their political dependents to do away with that really socialistic measure, State-aided immigration. The various colonial governments have been similarly compelled to protest against any large immigration schemes, promoted from this side, even to remote West Australia. Every now and then Trade and Labour Councils urge governments to represent through the Agents General at home that there is really no field for labour in the colonies, and they take the most elaborate means to circulate the same fable in this country. Where land is abundant and nature propitious workmen make work for workmen. There is an absolutely illimitable field for free labour as applied to the resources of nature in the Australasian colonies. The development of that field would of course benefit every man, woman and child now living in Australia. But the arguments used by the old school of American Protectionists (who were individualists, perhaps without knowing it) that growing population and immigration make the surest market for native industries, or home manufactures, cannot be used by State Socialists in Australia. The horrors of competition and the necessity for quelling it are their main texts. This was the lesson which Mr. Benjamin Douglas, President of the Trades Hall Council, inculcated upon Lord Rosebery in Melbourne in 1884, and the virtual teaching of Australian labour leaders today is that every additional worker who lands, or is born and reared, in the colony is an additional competitor and therefore an enemy. While the 'goal' or 'ideal' of the economist and Free Trader, who finds before him boundless natural resources, may be roughly described as an 'infinite' increase in the number of workers—never quite overtaking 'infinite' increases in the demand for labour, production of exchangeable utilities and rise in wages —the goal or ideal of State Socialists and Protectionists, so far as it can be ascertained from the speeches, writings, and actions of such persons in Australia, is one single worker[12] earning all the wages paid in his own, rigidly protected and stationary, trade and producing an infinitesimal amount of exchangeable utilities.[13] This astounding but of course unacknowledged 'principle' underlies the whole policy of the dominant labour party and their political satellites in Victoria. They therefore remain consistently indifferent to the slow growth of population and its actual decline in the mining and agricultural districts, to steadily diminishing exports and the neglect or decay of innumerable profitable employments for labour, such as the production of frozen salted and tinned meat, fresh and preserved fruit, wine, oil, tobacco, dried fish, hides, pelts, butter, cheese, condensed milk, etc., for export. As long as their political dependents will borrow money incessantly in London, spend it on so-called useful public works in and around Melbourne and increase the tariff at regular intervals, the labour party are well satisfied. Deputations representing various trades have constantly and successfully urged government to increase the duty on the article they

---

[12] The Victorian Tariff Commission of 1883–4 elicited the curious fact that one lonely human being earned his living by cutting corks in the colony. Thus, for the benefit of this cherished unit, a duty of 4*d.* per lb. on cut corks had been maintained, which was extremely irksome and injurious to the Colonial wine industry generally.

[13] The Victorian Commissioners to the last Calcutta Exhibition were denounced at the succeeding Annual Trade Union Congress in 1884 for having suggested that a market might be found in British India for some Victorian manufactures. They were accused of a design to reduce Victorian wages to the Indian level. Representative Trade Unionists have recently protested against the State Technical Colleges because young Victorians learn to become 'fitters,' lathe hands, etc., there, and thus compete with 'Labour.'

were interested in, on the general ground that unless it
were raised above 25 per cent *ad valorem* they would have
to sacrifice the eight hours' principle and reduce wages.[14]

Colonial State Socialism revolves in a sort of circle, and
the same sequence appears to present itself at whatever
point we inspect it. Politicians sanction and float loans, to
provide employment for their patrons on pleasant terms;
local banks and credit institutions make use of the proceeds
of State borrowing to 'finance' building societies, importers, manufacturers, tradesmen and private speculators,
who in turn give credit to working men for goods, or for
land and houses bought by them at inflation prices out of
their savings. Neither shop debts, interest, nor instalments
on purchases of land and houses, can be paid unless wages
are good, and work on political railways and 'useful public
works' plenty. These pleasant practices grow upon the

---

[14] Victorian Free Traders have come to use arguments really borrowed
from American Free Traders, from a country where 'Protection' is merely
a patch of a strange colour on a garment woven throughout of 'individual-
istic' materials; contending, for example, that Protection in *no way* benefits the material interests and pocket of the Victorian working-man. Mr.
E. Jowett, of the newly-formed Democratic Free Trade League, in a public
debate with Mr. Hancock of the Trades Hall Council, on June 11, 1890,
took this ground. In the United States Mr. Jowett's contention is a truism,
and, if we consider wage-earners as a class, and connote free trade in
labour, no doubt it is equally true everywhere. But if we consider merely
those Trade Unionists now alive in Victoria, and the circumstances determining 'competition' among them, I think it will be found that the high
tariff, by increasing enormously the cost of living, has frightened away
transient or casual workers, has deterred others from marrying early or
rearing large families, and has thus diminished 'competition' generally.
Except among Jews and Roman Catholics, the birth and marriage rates in
the colony are ominously low. Married women born there are living under
artificial, and in many respects unhealthy social conditions, shirk more
and more of recent years the duties and exertions of maternity and rearing

community like opium eating. Ministers therefore dare not now hold their hand, calculate ways and means closely, or stop borrowing, lest the whole top-heavy fabric of State Socialism should come toppling down about their ears. The expenditure for all purposes by the Victorian government for the last two or three years has been at the rate of about £14,000,000 per annum.[15] Part of this sum has been obtained by issuing bonds on the London Market, part from revenue. Under the existing hand-to-mouth financial policy it looks very much as though recent loans have been regularly floated to meet accruing interest on old loans; that is, on the total bonded debt of the colony. When those Melbourne banks, which keep the government account, require to remit money to London to cash half-yearly coupons coming off the Bonds, they can draw upon London against the proceeds of each fresh loan, instead of having to buy wool or wheat drafts in the local market, and remit them. This agreeable system appears to be never ending; as the local phrase goes, it 'relieves the banks,' and largely enables them to use their deposits to 'carry' land speculators, and to expand local credit generally. The other half of the State expenditure in Victoria is derived from revenue, i.e. from Customs duties mainly. Neither coin nor

---

children. Already the most lucrative branch of medical practice in the colony depends on this sinister fact. The enervating effect of the climate upon women and young children, cost of house-rent, necessaries of life, servants, and even milk, in Melbourne, explain if they do not excuse 'civic cowardice' of this type.

[15] During the last seven years Government expenditure has increased by 41 per cent, while population has increased by 15 per cent only. Public and corporate debts have increased by £22,000,000, and annual exports of 'produce and manufactures' fallen from twelve to nine millions.

bullion are in these days sent to Australia. Transfers of 'money' from Europe to the colony therefore invariably take the shape of bankers' drafts, against goods exported to the colonies; a fact which explains the abnormally large imports into Victoria of recent years. Government, through the Custom House, thus takes a heavy toll upon all foreign 'money' sent on private account for employment in Victoria. In addition, it levies a second toll upon any balance of new loans—left over after paying half-yearly coupons, or interest charges in London—which ultimately finds its way (in the shape of goods) to the colony. Thus the very same 'money' may figure twice over in the public accounts; once as the proceeds of Railway or Irrigation loans sanctioned by Parliament, a second time as 'revenue' intercepted in the Custom House.

This methodical system of inflation, this recurring *Milion Segen* from Lombard St., is locally so convenient and popular, that no class frets itself over such minutiae as the effect of the eight hours' rule in diminishing the efficiency of labour and restricting production. There is great latitude in regard to public works. The generous policy of government is contagious. If the estimated cost of a new railway or public building be exceeded, in practice, a supplementary vote is hustled through Parliament late in the session; the whole thing is finally shaken up, shuffled, and discrepancies righted out of the next loan. No doubt the net effect of short hours, high wages and dishonest or slovenly 'labour' in Victoria is represented ultimately in diminished production of utilities for export.[16]

---

[16] Anyone who attempts to estimate the economic effect of the reduced

But the Trade Unionist who has just wrung from his employer a good rise in wages, or the average citizen, the 'consumer,' who has just been told by a kite-flying land syndicate that his back yard is worth £30,000, does not fret himself about dwindling production or exports. In Australasia there have been no means either of judging whether successive reductions in the hours of labour have created employment for 'the unemployed,' because in the first place no efficient workers are 'unemployed,' in the sense sometimes legitimately used here, in any of the colonies; and in the second place the Federated Trade Unions prevent 'outsiders' from obtaining employment, or even appearing in the labour market at all. Nor is any light thrown upon the argument that reducing the hours of labour in this country alone to eight would 'kill' certain trades. What is meant by the latter phrase in Great Britain,

---

hours and fancy wages enjoyed by Labour in Victoria, is at once confronted by the fact that the whole industrial or manufacturing system there is very much a system *pour rire*. While economists in Europe dispute the existence of a 'wage fund,' one becomes aware in Victoria of three such 'funds,' a fictitious 'wage fund,' an equally fictitious 'capital fund,' and finally a 'consumers' fund,' all miraculously supplied by the State and the foreign investor. The 'efficiency of labour' means something definite in the United Kingdom, where labour and capital jointly compete in 'market overt' for the world's custom, where withdrawal of capital or diminished efficiency of labour would at once tell upon the nation's home trade, exports and imports. But in Victoria, where every £1 worth of local manufactures which figures in official returns has cost at least £1 10s. to produce, and is nevertheless ensured a forced consumption in the colony by the protective tariff, close calculations as to the effect of reduced hours of labour, wages, etc., are almost impossible.

The population of Victoria in 1883, when resistance to State Socialism virtually ceased, was 921,743, and the exports of home produce were £13,300,000. In 1887 the population was 1,036,119 (estimated), and the exports (which have since risen and then declined again) £8,502,979. Thus,

of course, is that our manufacturers could not compete either in the Home, or in neutral markets, with foreign manufacturers. Victorian manufacturers do not care about the great neutral markets; they export goods (in steadily diminishing quantities, by the way) to the adjacent colonies, but manage to do that partly because of the subsidiary advantages mentioned above, and partly by selling goods there at a reduction—as compared with prices charged to Victorian consumers—equal to the amount of the Victorian duty on such goods. The tariff, of course, protects the flank of capital and labour alike against the competition of foreign goods in the home market.

Australian State Socialists have for many years past opposed and thwarted sales of the freehold of 'Crown' land —'the national patrimony' they call it—and shilly-shallying attempts have been made to force the State 'leasehold system'[17] upon farmers and settlers. They have failed disastrously; but one indirect result has been curious. The land already 'alienated,' or granted in freehold, in the col-

---

while population had increased some 27 per cent, exports had decreased nearly 40 per cent. All the while the class (farmers, graziers, etc.) who do produce utilities for export, actually work far more than eight hours per diem. The diminution in the yield of gold appears however to be largely due to the action of 'the amalgamated miner' who has long enforced 'the eight hours.' Indirectly, too, short hours and high wages in Melbourne affect the supply as well as the efficiency of labour and production generally in the colony, workers being tempted to despise the slow process of developing the natural resources of the colony by hard toil.

[17] An unfortunate expression of the late Professor Fawcett's to the effect that he 'viewed with alarm the rapid alienation of the public domain in Australasia,' is constantly quoted by the advocates of 'bottling up' the nation's patrimony. The net result is that while the land's departments may not sell freeholds to willing purchasers, the 'nation's patrimony' is a huge breeding ground for rabbits, costing thousands of pounds annually for wire fencing, etc., and, as far as production of utilities is concerned, useless.

onies, is now the only land which can be freely dealt in. There has been, in fact, an artificial scarcity, or official land 'corner' in Victoria, South Australia, and New South Wales. The quantity in the market being thus artificially limited, and land speculation being, with the exception of the turf, the only one not liable to be suddenly upset by strikes and legislation 'in the interests of labour,' the most reckless real estate gambling goes on from time to time in Melbourne, Adelaide, and Sydney. A dangerously large proportion of the investment money remitted from this country of recent years, for employment in Melbourne, has gone to sustain land 'booms,' and is now represented by the 'paper' of land gamblers, held at fabulously inflated prices, by banks, building societies, mortgage, finance, and trust companies. Meantime enormous profits have been made by those persons who 'got out at the top' of the rise in land and house values in and near Melbourne. The phenomenal and ever-increasing concentration of population in a few large towns such as Melbourne, Sydney, Adelaide, Brisbane, and Newcastle of course stimulates the building and allied trades. It also swells the earnings of suburban railways and tramway companies, which depend for revenue on pleasure traffic. In Melbourne the heavy suburban railways traffic partly obscures the deficit which has to be faced on the interest account of the railway loans.[18] The concentration of population also gives to the

---

[18] Mr. Andrew Harper, M.L.A., estimates the loss—after deducting net earnings from interest payable—on the State railways (excluding the Hobson Bay system, the most remunerative of the suburban lines) at £258,000 for 1888–9, and the *Melbourne Argus*, in July, 1890, estimated this loss, for 1889–90, at £500,000. 'Working expenses' alone, it seems, having risen from 52½ per cent in 1879 to 68 per cent in 1889–90.

Federated Trade Unions immense strategical advantages. Nevertheless peaceable combination among wage-earners, even when reinforced by perhaps the most efficient, rapacious, and unscrupulous organization now existing anywhere, does not seem to diminish the profits of the large capitalist—or, in other words, the market rate of earnings —apportioned to capital in Australia by economic circumstances, which in the long run are really more powerful than socialistic legislators and labour organizations combined.[19]

Possibly Mill's earlier opinions on that matter were shaken by a succession of notable Trade Union victories about twenty years ago. The mountebank economists of our own day assert that as State Socialism progresses, even unskilled labour in this country will henceforward secure an ever-increasing and permanent benefit, at the expense of capital. We have had, among other events, the London Dock Strike of 1889, in which the police observed an attitude of neutrality; also the triumph of a riotous and violent mob of municipal gas workers at Leeds. No doubt Irish farmers have in recent years secured for themselves a vastly increased share of the profits derived from Irish land; but that latter triumph, especially, was brought about

---

[19] I saw nothing in Victoria to justify the opinion expressed by J. S. Mill in his latter years (*Fortnightly Review*, May, 1869) that 'There is absolutely available for the payment of wages, before an absolute limit is reached, not only the employer's capital but the whole of what can possibly be retrenched from his personal expenditure . . . there is no law of nature making it inherently impossible for wages to rise to the point of absorbing not only the funds which the capitalist has intended to devote to carrying on his business, but the whole of what he allows for his private expenses beyond the necessaries of life.'

by extra-legal, barbarous, or terrorist methods. To such methods any conceivable re-adjustment of proportionate profits, at the cost of the weakest class, is possible. As long however as the struggle between capital and labour proceeds peaceably according to the recognised 'rules of the ring'; in other words, wherever civil order and civil rights are upheld by the executive, as they have been, with few exceptions in the colonies, combination, Trade Unionism, and incessant strikes do not seem to alter permanently the value of what might, at any given epoch, be called the normal fraction representing the proportionate shares of capital and labour. What we shall probably see from time to time, and under exceptional conditions of the market, will be merely numerator and denominator multiplied by a higher figure, the value of the fraction remaining unchanged. Employers and industrial firms in the colonies have been now and then crippled, impoverished, and driven from business by sudden and vigorously conducted strikes. Frequently Trade Unions in Melbourne and Sydney have without any warning 'gone for' an employer, tied by the terms of a large contract, and, as in the case of the original contractor for the Melbourne Parliament buildings, ruined him completely. In order to remedy such wrongs, the Melbourne Harbour Trust in 1886 proposed to insert a 'strike clause' in future contracts. The Trades Hall Council thereupon appealed to Government to withdraw the contributions from the Treasury to the Trust as a punishment. As far back as 1885 an Australian Steam Navigation Company was driven out of business by the action of the Federated Seamen's, Firemen's, Cooks' and Stewards' Union, and this latter, helped by allied bodies, has effectually strangled the development of the coasting trade, or anything like an Australian 'merchant navy.' The result is that the monopoly of a few old-established firms in the steam coasting trade is not challenged; they charge high freight and passenger rates; life is extremely insecure on these routes, and sea-borne trade is crippled and paralyzed. It is clearly seen in the United States that a high protective tariff alone will not keep up the prices of certain staple articles of manufacture, in face of keen local competition among capitalists themselves. Cutting rates, discounts, etc., help considerably by reducing from time to time the prices of manufactured goods in Europe and the United States. But in the United States, Factory Acts are not enforced, while 'labour,' although restless and irreconcilable, is utterly disorganized, and, as compared with labour in Australasia, impotent. The latter country, under State Socialism, seems to me to present the 'ideal' conditions for very rich capitalists: (1) a protective tariff; (2) vexatious and inquisitorial Factory Acts, based on the principle that the first duty of the State and the Legislature is to favour the Trade Unionist; (3) an all-powerful Trade Union organization, manipulated by unscrupulous, narrow-minded, selfish, and ignorant men. The irresponsible despotism of the latter implies perhaps even more than the tariff, for it reduces competition among capitalists themselves to a minimum. The dread of facing the insatiable demands and exactions of Federated Labour, and the costly and harassing provisions of Colonial Factory Acts, more and more deter small capitalists, beginners, or 'small masters' as they would be called here, from rivalling old-established firms and starting new competitive enterprises;

while co-operative manufacturing does not of course com-
mend itself to the thriftless and light-hearted Australian
working-man.[20]

'Free, Secular and Compulsory' State Education in Victoria is noticed by Sir Charles Dilke among his problems.
The Victorian system is described in the 'Official Year
Books' as 'secular instruction without payment for all
children whose parents are willing to accept it.' It is compulsory and truancy is punishable by fine. Sir Charles
Dilke (pp. 366–383 of his second volume) does no more
than translate the opinions of two of the best-known Melbourne partisans of the Act into guarded language, yet
the history of this experiment in State Socialism and the
result after eighteen years' trial, ought to be carefully
studied by legislators and by educators in Great Britain,
seeing that it is now proposed, by various groups of poli-

---

[20] A partner in one of the two great Melbourne newspapers mentioned to a
friend one day that the Union to which his compositors belonged was about
to decree some increase of wages or fresh advantages for its members.
The friend replied that he was not surprised to hear it; and further coun-
selled the employer to receive a deputation from the Unionists in question;
to grant their demands gracefully; in addition, to present each of them with
a gold watch. 'But,' objected the first speaker, 'why the gold watch?' 'Because,' said the other, 'the consistent tyranny and the never-ending exactions of this same Union, which is ever with you, are rapidly making
your fortune, by effectually keeping out of the business every man with
capital enough to think of starting a newspaper in this city. If you go into
your composing-room you will see a strange thing; your type-setters,
instead of being mostly young men, as in London, New York, or San Fran-
cisco, are mostly grey-haired men. Were Melbourne in "the States" the
most intelligent and ambitious of your "hands" would long since have
got credit and help somewhere and started newspapers for themselves;
there would have been at least six Melbourne daily morning papers—
four of them making money, and thereby reducing your profits. As it
is you have one serious rival, if you have even that. Certainly as long as

ticians here, either to copy the main principles of the
Victorian Education Act, No. 447 of 1873, or to embark on
the very policy which made that Act logically inevitable.
Sir Charles Dilke truly says that 'Victorians are strongly
attached to their free sytsem'; that it has 'a marvellously
strong hold upon their affections'; that 'centralization is
not unpopular,' and that Dr. Pearson, the Minister for
Education, seems to be well content with the education
policy of his colony as compared to other colonies. Of all
State Socialistic measures Free Education seems to be the
most enticing. A political party could hardly choose a more
attractive dole or bribe for the electorate. Its success, however, is cumulative, and it is only after some years' experience that parents appreciate thoroughly what it does for
them. Cash outlay to pay for the feeding, clothing, and
education of children is, to selfish and self-indulgent parents, a constant source of irritation. The small sums which
should go to buy bread and butter, boots or bonnets, for
youngsters, or to pay for their schooling, may be much
needed by the male parent for tobacco, drink, and perhaps
'backing horses,' while the mother constantly needs new
articles of dress and amusements. Free Education, at the
expense of that pillageable abstraction 'the general tax-
payer,' thus appeals to some of the strongest of modern
instincts. In Victoria it would now be absolutely impossible
for any Ministry, or political party, to withdraw or curtail
the privileges and advantages given under the Education

---

the Compositors' Union absolutely holds the field here, you will never
have another. Meanwhile your type-setters expect to die type-setters, while
you and your partners will die millionaires.'

Act. The tendency is to increase them and to add to the cost of the system year by year.[21] No candidate for Parliament in Victoria now ventures even to criticise the system lest the cry of the 'Education Act in danger' should be raised against him. In Victoria, as in England, and more often in Scotland, rich parents do not scruple to throw the burthen of the primary education of their children upon their less prosperous neighbours.[22] The excuse sometimes offered in the Colonies is that amalgamation of all classes of society in the State Schools is a democratic idea. The actual result, however, is that, where classes and masses do live in juxtaposition, many State School teachers try to make their schools select and quasi-aristocratic. In Melbourne gutter-children are edged out on any pretext, and a special school had to be set apart there for this class—the very class on whose behalf the 'free' element in the system was orig-

---

[21] During the debates on the present Act the late Mr. J. W. Stephen, Attorney-General in the Francis Ministry, in charge of the Bill, declared that the cost per scholar in average attendance would never exceed £2 per head. It is now close upon £5. The Elementary education vote has grown from £217,704 in 1872–3 to over £600,000 in 1887–8. One official excuse for lavish expenditure is that in rural or remote districts the cost of giving education of a high quality to all children must be far greater than in the towns. All the time the rural population steadily decreases, while the town, i.e. the Melbourne, population is now over 40 per cent of the total for the colony. In 1861 it was 25.89, in 1871 28.87, and in 1881 32.81. The school attendance has only grown from 184,000 in 1874 to 192,000 in 1887. Apparently interest on some £1,120,000, cost of State school buildings, wear and tear, depreciation, etc., do not figure in the education vote, and seem to be paid out of the imaginary net surplus from the State railways.

[22] In 1888 a Board School teacher in Glasgow puzzled me not a little by complaining bitterly of some charge of trifling misbehaviour against his pupils (out of school hours), which had appeared in a newspaper for which

inally advocated. Popular as the Act is with Victorian town populations, it is in the remote and sparsely-settled agricultural and mining districts W. of long. 143, E. of long. 146, and, excluding Bendigo, N. of lat. 37, that the Act has the strongest hold. Farmers and 'selectors' who have little money to spare, amalgamated miners, who have killed 'the golden goose' of investment in mining properties by their organized idleness and short-sighted rapacity, are conscious that they could not possibly provide by co-operation, or local rating, anything approaching the educational privileges and luxuries bestowed by the central department in Melbourne. Meantime, 'the general taxpayer' has indeed become a mere mathematical, or algebraic, expression in Victoria; he has apparently neither body, parts, nor passions, does not cry out when he is squeezed, and is not represented in the Legislature. Sir Charles Dilke is right in saying that educational State Socialism is popular in Victoria and that the Minister for Education is well content.[23]

I was at the moment responsible. He feared, I discovered, that his school might lose the genteel *cachet* which it enjoyed. Some of the best people in Buchanan Street, he said, sent their children to him. There is, however, historical excuse for this trait among the best people, seeing that the Scottish Board School system is in some way 'sib' to the noble old parochial, burgh, and grammar school system, which for nigh two centuries did so much, in the Scottish Lowlands, to keep alive the true spirit of local self-government, and to develop, brace, and stimulate the best points in the national character.

[23] This philanthropic and cultured gentleman, formerly a Fellow of Oriel College, Oxford, and, according to the testimony of Mr. David Gaunson, ex-M.L.A., one of the greatest living authorities on the history of the middle ages, may be regarded as the Prosper Mérimée of the State Socialistic Empire in Victoria. He entered politics as a Free Trader, but was speedily reconciled and received into the Protectionist and State Socialistic fold. In the latter interest he stood unsuccessfully for a constituency in

On the other hand, it is alleged that the Victorian Act has produced the evils of centralization in their worst form; that as soon as the State took over the entire cost of the system local control and responsibility at once became illogical and have now completely disappeared; that the cost of the system tends to increase indefinitely, owing largely to the fact that the State School teachers are banded together in a powerful Trade Union, the avowed object of which is to increase their salaries and privileges by political pressure; finally, that a distinct religious grievance, or disability, has been created by the Act of 1873. Protests against some or all of these evils and abuses have been made by colonists of high character and ability—all of them, except Mr. Archer, Protestants—in recent years; by the late Dr. Hearn, LL.D., Chancellor of Melbourne University, Mr. Andrew Harper, M.L.A., Judge Warrington Rogers, the present Bishop of Manchester, the Rev. W. H. Fitchett, Professor McCoy; and by critics as far apart in their Educational views as Sir Archibald Michie, Mr. W. H. Archer, and the present Bishop of Melbourne. No reply is made to these gentlemen by the apostles of Victorian

---

1877. On the accession of the Protectionist party to power in that year the Ministry declared a Royal Commission on the Education Act to be urgently required, and Professor Pearson (anticipating the Duke in *The Gondoliers*) became a Royal Commission (limited). He however contented himself with writing a thin but interesting Essay on the education question in the colony, in which, with rare prescience, he condemned the evils of 'payment by results.' His suggestions were entirely ignored by his political patrons, but a fee of £1000 was paid to him for his literary labours upon the thin Essay. Afterwards he was provided with a seat in the Legislative Assembly, a gentleman, whose original avocation was that of a brewer's traveller, having resigned his seat in order to become Librarian to Parliament.

State Socialism, because, from the point of view of practical politics, none is needed.

The whole patronage, finance, and administration of the State schools, down to the most minute details, are centered in one large department in Melbourne. The promoters of the present Act did their work thoroughly in 1872.[24] The late Mr. Stephen and Mr. Francis sincerely believed that it was their mission to create a benevolent Educational despotism, a Ministerial department which would mould the youth of the colony into one admirable form, and, among other things, 'control the evil of denominationalism which had raised its head there to such a fearful extent.' Accordingly, when during the discussion of the Bill the principle of 'free' schooling—at the expense of the State alone—was accepted, the majority in Parliament, logically enough, rejected Local Option, or any claim by districts and localities to interfere with Elementary school patronage, finance, or administration. Boards of Advice were created, feeble parodies of the School Boards in this country; but they represent no fee or ratepayers, were given no power in 1872, and exercise none now. The only basis of local responsibility and control, as well as of authority, which can be claimed by local boards over the elementary education of the people, is local contributions, either in rates or school fees. On the other hand, if the State Treasurer be sole paymaster, Parliament insists, sooner or later, that the State shall be 'master' in every

---

[24] The educational policy of 1872 received an impetus from the Franco-German war! The classic fiction, that the German forces owed their victories over the French to superior 'book-learning,' did duty in Australia at the time, and is repeated there to this day.

sense. Had the original promoters of the Victorian Act realised how completely it involved centralization, they might have shrunk from the prospect of responsibility for details since forced upon the Minister in Melbourne. The action, the inevitable action, of members of the Legislature has gradually brought about this latter state of things. Questions are asked in the Legislative Assembly, almost daily, as to the salaries of teachers, perhaps in remote districts, price of school books, supply of drinking water to children, repair of school buildings, etc. There is no one else in the colony—save the Minister of Education, who pays for all these things—to ask. It is quite useless for either Minister or Members of Parliament to refer back to local bodies; the latter pay nothing and manifestly have no status, and no right whatsoever to interfere. Naturally, therefore, the living interest and the stimulus given to education by the School Board system in Great Britain (outside the metropolis) are wanting in Australia. Victorian children are passed through the State machine, that is all the parents know. The majority of the latter may not approve of State school influences upon the morals, character, and behaviour of their children, but the whole thing, school books and materials included, costs nothing. Evils, abuses, and blunders, similar to those which have grown up under the London School Board, abound, but in aggravated form, under the Central Educational Department in Melbourne —official supervision, discipline, and methods being of course defective in a colony where the supply of first-class civil servants is limited, where petty office-seeking is a growing vice, where the schools to be looked after are, in many cases, practically as remote from Melbourne as London is from the Shetland Isles. The tangle of red tape, the unmanageable accumulation of returns, correspondence, and official documents, the delay, waste, and paralysis at the centralized Melbourne office, have been often described by responsible colonists.[25] The Ministry, however, do not require to make any reply to such charges as these. They can always borrow their way out of such difficulties, and they know that as long as electors do not pay, electors do not care.

In a limited electorate such as that of Victoria, the State school teachers' vote is a serious consideration. Although they have been, since 1885, under the Public Service Act, which was supposed to do away with political patronage, they have formed a powerful Trade Union, which meets regularly in conference, like the railway servants or any other labour Junta in the Colony, and threatens ministers and legislators. The principle that political influence should be used to extort money and other benefits for themselves from the Treasury is as frankly accepted and acted upon by these Victorian public servants as it was by Irish borough-mongers and Scottish 'controulers' at the close of the last century. It is said that in London the teachers' vote and influence are potent at School Board elections, and fatal to the chances of candidates suspected of a desire to check extravagance and waste. In the United

---

[25] After eleven years' working of the Act it was admitted before the Royal Commission of 1882–4, by officials of the department, that they had never yet been able to compile a trustworthy school census, and the number of children in average attendance was still a matter of guesswork. Professor Pearson, in 1882, described the whole school census system as 'confused and disorderly.'

Kingdom, however, it may be anticipated that under Free State Education the teachers' political vote and influence would be swamped by other, and far more numerous, political groups who have miscellaneous designs upon the Imperial Treasury. Theoretically such defects as exaggerated centralization at headquarters, decay of local interest and of 'local' control over extravagant expenditure, are not incurable. They might disappear in time were it not that any reformers are at once met by the money barrier. Reform would mean increase to local burthens, and Victorian colonists, used to having their children educated 'for nothing' or rather, at the cost of some person or persons unknown, by means of a financial legerdemain which has enabled the State Treasurer to borow surpluses regularly in London, are less disposed every year to relieve the State Treasury of its tribute. Even the perpetuation of the religious grievance, which Roman Catholics complain of so bitterly, seems to me mainly due to financial considerations. I came to the conclusion in Victoria that Roman Catholics are subjected to a wrong more galling, but not unlike that which compulsory payment of church rates inflicted upon Dissenters in this country. A strange state of things in a self-governing community, the vast majority of whom are of English, Scotch, or Welsh birth or parentage. I found a partial explanation in the action and language of certain Victorian politicians who supported the Roman Catholic educational claims in the past. The late Sir John O'Shanassy, one of the Conscript Fathers of the colony, and a splendid specimen of the old Tipperary yeoman stock, managed this delicate matter, and managed it badly, for years. Sir C. G. Duffy managed it so much

worse that colonists finally refused doggedly to even discuss the Roman Catholic grievance. Verily much can be
forgiven to a colony which has reckoned Sir Charles Gavan
Duffy among its leading politicians, which has learnt to
know him, which indeed can never forget him.[26] But unless
the action, language, and opinions of those who complain
of wrong and ask for concessions afford clear proof that
granting their demands would imperil the lives, liberty,
and property of their fellow-subjects, no enlightened community should be influenced by the blunders, follies, and
excesses of the spokesmen. In Victoria it seemed to me the
noxious virus secreted by State Socialism, State bribes, and
State doles has already penetrated so far that colonists
deliberately inflict a wrong in educational matters mainly
because they have been persuaded that justice would cost
a great deal of money.

Roman Catholic ecclesiastics and laymen in Victoria
submit that although the State professes to provide money
out of the taxes for the elementary education of all Vic-

---

[26] Mr. W. H. Archer, the gentlest of men and the most earnest advocate
of the Roman Catholic claims in Victoria, in a memoir of his friend, Sir
John O'Shanassy (*Melb. Rev.* xxxi. 243), mildly, but firmly, repudiates
the insinuation that he himself was responsible for bringing Sir C. G.
Duffy to the colony. It appears that Mr. Archer wrote to the late Frederick Lucas, editor of *The Tablet*, asking him to come out to Australia to
champion the Roman Catholic cause. When the letter reached England
Lucas was dead, but it was published in the London press. By the next
mail, oddly enough, Mr. C. G. Duffy arrived in Melbourne. Then he was
presented with £5000. Afterwards, according to Mr. Archer, Mr. Duffy
'used an unlucky expression as to his being "an Irish rebel to the backbone
and spinal marrow;" ' this, it seems, made the English, Scotch, and Welsh
colonists angry. They did not then comprehend their Mr. C. G. Duffy,
nor foresee that he would continue for many years to draw the only
pension accepted by an ex-minister in the colony, quite in a loyal manner.

torian children this money is now so distributed that they, as conscientious Catholics, cannot possibly benefit by it in any way. As proof of their earnestness they have since 1872 expended nearly £300,000 in providing school buildings in which the children of conscientious Roman Catholic parents are now instructed in religious as well as secular subjects. Some twenty or thirty thousand children are thus provided for at no expense whatsoever to the colony, the secular education given being quite equal to that in the State schools. The Roman Catholic party now propose to continue to build their own schools, to appoint their own teachers, subject to Government examination as to efficiency in secular subjects, and ask for a *per capita* grant or share of the free education vote, based, as far as I understand, not on the departmental rate, but rather on the actual cost per child under their system of instruction (about one-half the departmental rate) for all children who pass the Government Inspectors' examination in secular, or nonreligious subjects, according to the official standard for age, etc. This demand is refused. The replies vouchsafed to calm and moderate protests from both Protestant and Catholic colonists differ in no way from the stock apologies put forward for the religious disabilities of Protestants, Roman Catholics, Quakers, and other dissenters elsewhere in the past. The 'thin edge of the wedge' argument is used. It is said that if Victorian Roman Catholics were given a *per capita* grant for each child duly educated in secular subjects they would soon demand a grant for new school buildings also. It is said that the Roman Catholic religion is a bad religion and inimical to civil and religious freedom; indeed, Sir Archibald Michie, whose sensitive conscience prompted him to write one of the few existing pamphlets on this question, mentions the massacre of St. Bartholomew and the horrors of the Inquisition, and also quotes largely from Macaulay to prove this latter statement. What Macaulay says, and what all history teaches, about the effect of Roman Catholic ascendency upon human societies would be much to the point if it were proposed to give the hierarchy of that religion virtual control over the civil and religious liberties of citizens anywhere, but hardly answers the complaint that conscientious Victorian Catholics cannot possibly benefit from the annual education grant. It is said further that Roman Catholic Governments do not give money to Protestant schools; also that a portion of any grant given to Catholics in Victoria might be sent as a present to the Pope, instead of being used for education; also, that the alleged 'Catholic conscience' in this matter is really a 'breeches-pocket conscience'; also, as has been said to Protestants who sought to establish schools of their own in Roman Catholic countries, that the teaching sanctioned by the State is very good teaching—if the dissatisfied ones would only think so. It is also alleged that the majority of Victorian Catholic parents now cheerfully send their children to the State schools. But that to my mind merely proved, in some instances, that such parents are lukewarm Catholics. The fact remains that a certain percentage of Victorian parents, rightly or wrongly, consider the anti-Christian education given in the State schools pernicious. If there were only fifty such parents in the colony a grievance would still exist under the Act. Apparently, also, Roman Catholic priests sometimes sanction the sending of children to the State schools, if no Roman Catholic school exists in the neigh-bourhood, possibly as a general indulgence to eat meat on Fridays is extended to sick or shipwrecked people, the inhabitants of beleagured cities, etc., but those, I think, are matters for Catholics to settle among themselves. Mr. Sutherland, a cultured member of the Unitarian body in Melbourne, has disclosed what seems to me the most effective argument against the Catholic claims. In a long letter to the Melbourne *Argus*, of April, 1885, he states that among sensible men and women in the colony there is a strong but vague hostility to the Catholic claim. 'The object of my letter,' he says, 'is to give that consciousness a basis of figures and more definite form, so that the nation at large may be fortified in its refusal to entertain the Catholic claim.' He then declares that 'if the Catholics ever succeed in obtaining a separate grant it would imply the closing of several hundreds of the smaller State schools.' I do not think Mr. Sutherland proved his case at all, but the vague impression that he might be correct in his view had a great influence with the colonists at the time, and has still.

I followed this controversy closely when in the colony, because I marvelled to see a so-called free, enlightened, and progressive democracy sheepishly furbishing up at the end of the nineteenth century rusty weapons and rusty argu-ments of religious intolerance. After a while it seemed to me still more significant and instructive that the desire of the majority to grab all the State money going should be the chief reason for this rare intolerance. Shabby selfish-ness and chronic mendicancy are imperceptibly, but surely, developed by State Socialism. Later, there follows in-

capacity to do a single just or liberal act. It is not denied by
the partisans of the Victorian Education Act that if Roman
Catholics should ever 'pocket their conscience,' as they are
invited to do, and abandon their separate schools, an enormous sum would have to be at once spent on school-
buildings for the children thus thrown upon the State,
while the educational vote would be at least £100,000 a
year higher. Roman Catholics thus virtually take a large
amount of expenditure on their own shoulders, and colonists accept an alms from the denomination whose conscientious scruples they deride. I judged that men and
women, degraded by State and Municipal borrowing
and begging, lose national self-respect altogether after a
while.[27]

The complaints of Roman Catholic Educators in Victoria
are worth noting, because the Education Act of 1873 placed
them under much the same disabilities as Church of England, Wesleyan and other Protestant Nonconformist
Educators in the United Kingdom would endure if Mr.

---

[27] The Report and evidence furnished by the Royal Commission on Education which sat in Victoria from early in 1882 to the middle of 1884, are a
mine of information on the working of free, secular, and compulsory State
education. I do not suppose that so much could be learnt on this important subject from any other source. It is unpleasant reading for Victorian
State Socialists, and after adopting a few trifling recommendations contained in the report they have quietly ignored it. A *précis* or synopsis of
the minute and exhaustive evidence procured by the Commissioners as
well as the final 'majority' and 'minority' reports, which are not very
lengthy, ought to be available for members of the Imperial Parliament
before 'Free Education' is seriously debated in this country. The Commissioners by a majority of one, out of eleven, decided against the Catholic
claims on the general grounds that a grant to Roman Catholic schools
would amount to endowment of one particular form of religion.

Morley's declaration of the 21st of February, 1890,[28] were embodied in an Imperial Education Act. But while Mr. Morley offered, 'on behalf of the Liberal party,' special privileges to Roman Catholics and Jews in the United Kingdom, the Victorian Act imposes equal disabilities upon all citizens who believe that the teaching of the Christian religion ought to be encouraged in elementary schools.

That which some regarded as merely a graceful philopena-present from Mr. Morley to Mr. Sexton raised certain hopes and gave a certain amount of satisfaction in other directions. Possibly the Roman Catholic hierarchy, who are well informed on these matters, did see the pitfall lying behind the offer from the so-called 'Liberal party,' but some of the Roman Catholic clergy and laity in the United Kingdom must have been pleased at the recognition by so distinguished a catechumen as Mr. Morley of the claim of 'one of the great hierarchies of obscurantism'[29] to dispose of an educational grant from the Consolidated Fund as they pleased. Mr. John Morley has declared, too, that the educational claims of the Roman Catholic bishops and priests represent 'the black and anti-social aggression of the syllabus and the encyclical,'[30] and that 'the supposed

---

[28] Mr. Morley, speaking to Mr. Acland's amendment in favour of free education, said: 'Our position I think is this, that when a school is intended for all it should be managed by the representatives of the whole community. When on the other hand the school claims to be for the use of a section of the community, as for example the Catholics or the Jews, it may continue to receive public support as long as it is under the management of that sect.'

[29] 'The Struggle for National Education,' reprinted from the 'Fortnightly Review,' 1872–73, second edition, p. 97.

[30] Ibid. p. 63.

eagerness of the parent to send his child to a school of a special denomination is a mere invention . . . of the priests.'[31] Some Nonconformists, as well as the whole of the secularist or anti-Christian body in the United Kingdom, may also have rejoiced at the prospect of financial vengeance upon the Church of England held out by an ex-Minister.

What has happened in Victoria shows how many of these hopes and anticipations are likely to be realised. I think there is conclusive proof that a free grant from the Consolidated Fund, or from 'the State,' implies secular or anti-Christian teaching, and no other kind, in 'State' schools; that it would be impossible permanently to single out one or two denominations and give to them a portion of such grant to dispose of as they please; finally, that the secularist or anti-Christian party, although actually in a minority—as they always have been and still are in Victoria—will manage, sooner or later, to drive a wedge between the rival Christian denominations and to impose their own educational, or may we say atheological, ideas upon the State.

Up to the 11th July, 1851, 'the Port Philip District,' now the colony of Victoria, was a portion of New South Wales. For eleven years after 'separation' or the grant of Autonomy, the educational system inherited from the parent colony was administered fairly well by a National Board and a Denominational Board, disposing between them of the Government grant.[32] In August 1862 the Common

---

[31] Ibid. p. 87.

[32] In 1851 the grant for denominational schools was, according to Mr.

Schools Act, promoted by Mr. Richard Heales, came into operation. It was administered by five quasi-independent Commissioners of Education. The Principle of the Act is alleged to have been secular education, pure and simple, but the Commissioners at first made regulations which sanctioned the blending of religious with secular instruction in voluntary or denominational schools. The latter increased slowly under the Common Schools Act. In 1872, when it was repealed, there were 408 of them in the Colony altogether, which had cost some £185,000 to erect. Of this sum the State had contributed £104,000. From the first there were conflicts and jealousies between the Ministry of the day and the Educational Commissioners, who insisted on exercising independent patronage and control. Among the community generally the discussion of educational problems between 1862 and 1872, as well as the investigations by the Royal Commission on Public Education in 1866, brought out like views to those common in this country at the time. There was the same jealousy of the ascendancy of 'the creeds' and 'the parsons' on the part of the Victorian average ratepayer, and the same want of cohesion and unanimity—or positive antagonism—among 'the creeds' themselves who were expected to champion the cause of religious instruction in Elementary State schools. The existing Act, No. 447, of 1873, is chiefly due to Mr. (afterwards Mr. Justice) Wilberforce Stephen, a doctrinaire liberal, possessed of much industry, sincerity, and

---

W. H. Archer, thus divided. Church of England, 48 per cent; Presbyterians, 22 per cent; Wesleyans, 6 per cent; Roman Catholics, 22 per cent. In the following year he says, the latter 'obtained a grant in proportion to their real numerical strength.'

erudition, now deceased. When Mr. J. G. Francis formed a Liberal-Conservative Ministry on the 10th June, 1872, in succession to Mr. C. G. Duffy, Mr. Stephen became his Attorney-General, and an Education Bill, reforming the abuses alleged to have sprung up under the Common Schools Act of 1862, was part of the Ministerial programme. The Protestant clergy of all denominations thereupon held a series of conferences, beginning in July, 1872, under the presidency of the late Bishop Perry, to discuss the situation. The partisans of secular instruction, pure and simple, consisting mainly of free-thinkers but reinforced by a few clergymen and sincerely religious laymen, had formed a Victorian Education League. It cannot be said that colonists generally were seriously discontented with the Common Schools Act; but they shared the educational enthusiasm among Britons generally at that epoch, and hoped also to get from a department of State a better and a cheaper system than 'the parsons' had given them. The Roman Catholic body in Victoria, who had even hesitated to accept State aid under the limitations embodied in the Common Schools Act, at once suspected serious mischief from Mr. Stephen's policy, and prepared, in secret as their way is, to offer what resistance they could to the forthcoming Bill. As happened in this country when Free State Education was mentioned at the beginning of 1890, the Protestant denominations, clergy and laymen, were by no means irreconcilable towards what they believed to be the Free State Educational ideas of Government. In 1872 it was not understood how thoroughly Mr. Stephen intended to secularize Victorian education. Actuated by that spirit of futile opportunism, which to this day inspires the high strategy of so many Anglican Churchmen in the United Kingdom, the members of the conference of 1872 contented themselves with a series of moderate, neutral, and, as it looks now, entirely reasonable resolutions. They were unanimously in favour of what Mr. Morley has called 'the organic principle of our constitution,' local control of some sort over elementary education. Parents they thought should have something to say in the choice of teachers; the latter being permitted also to give religious instruction in State school buildings out of school hours; while Government would perhaps be able to draw up a Scripture lectionary, containing selected passages agreeable to all Protestant denominations. They were willing that henceforth no new 'voluntary' schools should be established in the colony, a self-denying ordinance which, by the way, struck directly at the Roman Catholics. Two or three members of the Protestant Conference declared for free, secular, and compulsory State education in principle, arguing that religious teaching could, and ought to be, carried on quite apart from secular teaching, by the clergy or by lay helpers, instead of by State school teachers. The late Professor Hearn, the most profound and brilliant thinker who has served the colony, appears to have foreseen most clearly the economical objections to Free State Education, and he indeed predicted, in a pamphlet issued at the time, the very evils of over-centralization, extravagance, and abuse of patronage at the Central Department which the Royal Commissioners unearthed ten or twelve years afterwards. The Education Bill was introduced into the Legislative Assembly by Mr. Stephen on the 12th September, 1872, in a speech of mammoth dimensions, yet not uninteresting

reading even now, for it sets forth most of the sophistries
and illusions which charmed educational enthusiasts
twenty years ago. In those days Buckle was not yet regarded by advanced Liberals as a fossilized thinker, and
traces of his influence crop up in Mr. Stephen's interesting comparisons between enlightened and well-educated
French youth, since the Revolution, and British youth, still
in the trammels of 'the creeds.' Mr. Hepworth Dixon's and
Mr. Matthew Arnold's *rococo* opinions about Swiss and
Prussian education all figured at immense length in this
speech and helped to benumb the intellects of worthy colonists, at that period hovering at the summit of the well-
greased slide which was to carry them towards complete
State Socialism. Mr. Stephen convinced the Legislative Assembly that elementary education directed by a central
State authority would effectually purge the colony of
clericalism and religious animosities. It was his belief that
in a couple of generations, through the missionary influence of the State schools, a new body of State doctrine and
theology would grow up, and that the cultured and intellectual Victorians of the future would discreetly worship
in common at the shrine of one neutral-tinted deity, sanctioned by the State department. Noticing the objection that
patronage would be abused under his Bill, Mr. Stephen
declared that no minister would ever 'dare' to appoint
teachers from political motives. A few years later, when
Victorian protectionists and State socialists had made an
end of Conservative ministries, this Conservative Education Act was used by Mr. Stephen's opponents to pension
and reward their followers, and teachers of the worst char-

acter and antecedents were pitch-forked wholesale into the State schools.

The opposition to the Educational Bill in the Assembly was half-hearted and feeble. Indeed, its various 'principles' proved themselves and each other as the discussion went on. The 'compulsory' principle was almost unanimously accepted from the first, probably because of the Prussian and alleged American examples. The old quibble, that education if 'compulsory' must be 'free,' next did service. Then, it having been assumed that the State must be teacher, it became manifest that the different groups who opposed the Bill, not being agreed among themselves, were utterly unprepared to answer the question 'what particular religion is to be taught?' The only logical solution was, 'no religious teaching at all.' The Bill passed triumphantly through committee on the 19th October, and came into force on the 1st January, 1873. Zealous Roman Catholics at once rejected the new Act. They refused to accept State aid on the official terms, and 'went out into the wilderness.' And there they are still. But they set to work to build new schools and to provide for the schooling of as many children as possible.[33] The Church of England, Presbyterians,

---

[33] Mr. J. F. Hogan, late of Melbourne, writes to me, 'In a few of the Roman Catholic primary schools in Melbourne fees are charged, but in the vast majority throughout the colony expenses are paid by collections and donations . . . So that practically the system is as "free" as that of the State. The religious orders are now largely employed as teachers, and expenses are thereby reduced to a minimum. Recently new scholarships, new Inspectors and a new curriculum have been introduced. . . . In country districts a few Protestant children used formerly to attend Roman Catholic schools, retiring during the religious instruction half-hour. But this is becoming rare.'

Wesleyans, and other Protestants determined, on the contrary, to give the Act a fair trial; as some put it, they walked straight into the trap. They gave up control of their schools and surrendered the buildings to Government, receiving compensation for valid interests, and have made no attempt to carry on 'voluntary' elementary schools since 1873. Mr. Morley, writing on the Victorian experiment at the time, gracefully describes what was done by Mr. Stephen in 1872 as 'throwing a handful of dust over the raging insects,' i.e. the Christian denominations. In the same work he quotes the saying of an opponent: 'religion can only be taught in elementary schools by the lay master. If taught by the clergyman it would only be regarded as an insupportable bore.' This certainly has been the experience in Victoria. State school teachers are heavily fined if they give religious instructions 'at any time.' During the last ten years earnest efforts have been made by Protestant ministers of religion and laymen to get together classes of State school children for religious instruction after school hours, the buildings being always at their disposal then. These efforts have completely failed. Secularism, or what some call free-thought, is the one creed virtually established and endowed by the Victorian Education Act. It may be questioned whether neutrality is possible in this matter; children either learn some form of belief or of disbelief. In the State schools, we are told officially, 'lessons on morals and manners are given fortnightly; for the treatment of those apparently drowned and of those bitten by snakes, periodically.' Eclectic heathenism is the note of State school morality in Victoria. The children are however taught English Grammar, Arithmetic, and Geography very well indeed;

and the way in which they will repeat the names of all mountains, capes, bays, lakes—as well as of the two rivers —in Australia, perhaps suggests that, after all, *fin de siècle* heathenism may be 'much misunderstood.' Meanwhile the system must continue to be extravagantly costly: it is swathed in and strangled by red tape; it inflicts injustice upon conscientious religious bodies; it deposes parents from responsibility and the teacher from the free exercise of his noble craft; it prescribes a stereotyped form of procedure on a track where constant progress and free experiment are most essential.

In his survey of the colony of Victoria, Sir Charles Dilke (i. 248–52) mentions the Early Closing of Shops—under the 45th clause of the amended Factory Act (862) of 1885 —among 'experiments tried' not among 'problems' of Greater Britain. But it is perhaps entitled to rank among the rapidly accumulating problems of Sillier Britain, seeing that Sir John Lubbock's Bill still loiters with intent round the door of the House of Commons. The readers of Sir Charles Dilke's book are led to understand that in Victoria the experiment is a success, and that since 1886 retail shops have been compulsorily closed at the statutory hours of 7 P.M. on weekdays and 10 P.M. on Saturdays, without injury to business, without protest from tradesmen or customers.

The 45th clause of the Act in question gave a species of local option to municipal bodies, and, *inter alia*, the power to fix the fines for selling goods after 7 P.M.[34] Certain mu-

---

[34] The 45th clause permitted 'shops of any particular class' (not scheduled as exempted), 'on obtaining a license,' to keep open after 7 P.M. '. . . on a petition certified by the municipal clerk as being signed by a ma-

nicipalities at once exercised all the powers available to mitigate the impending nuisance, thereby exciting the wrath of the Socialist party, who promptly threw over the principle of local option and complained that a beneficent measure was being defeated by a base conspiracy. Sir Charles Dilke seems to sympathise with these complaints. He mentions the unfriendliness of the municipalities and the lowness of the fines, and adds somewhat inconsequently, 'the light fines have been a success, for the publication of the names of the offenders has been sufficient.' It was sufficient in one notable instance[35] to get the fines paid for the offender by public subscription; but that of course is not what Sir Charles Dilke means.

The story of the Victoria Early Closing law is worth recalling. It has long been practically obsolete in the colony, and when it was (on that very ground) proposed in 1890 to

---

jority of the shopkeepers keeping such shops, within . . . district.' It also gave municipalities power to fix fines. This power was taken away by an amending Act, *ad hoc*, 961 of 1887, which imposed fines, for a minimum of 10s. to a maximum of £5.

[35] A Shop Assistants' League, patronized by a few political hacks, socialists, and idle apprentices, finding that government did not care to enforce the Act, employed *agents provocateurs* to 'spot' tradespeople selling goods after 7 P.M. in the outlying suburbs, wherever the municipalities had lacked courage to follow the example of the Melbourne Town Council, and exercise the powers of local option under the 45th clause. On the 23rd of August following, a grocer named John Peregrine, in the suburb of Prahran, was spotted and fined £2 7s. for selling 'small quantities of tea and soap' after 7 P.M. The *Argus* next day commenting, in a leader, on Peregrine's conviction, said, 'this we believe, is the first instance of a crime of this particular sort having met with retribution in any civilized community. A medal of some inexpensive substance might be struck to commemorate this epoch-making event.' The article wound up by asking, 'Are there any public-spirited people who will subscribe to a fund for the payment of

enact a similar, but far more drastic, measure, the public appeared to have forgotten not only the details but even the date of the first experiment.

Colonial Factory Acts profess to be modelled on Imperial Acts, but contain important variations and 'extras.' Labour being well able to take care of itself is, generally speaking, indifferent to that legislative protection which has been thought necessary for European workers under their entirely different conditions. Yet for years prior to 1885, the Trades Hall leaders, anxious to have all operatives well in hand and under discipline, had demanded, on behalf of the bootmaking and clothing trades chiefly, legislation which would drive all outside piece-workers into factories. Female hands work at these 'light' trades, and girls of some refinement, aged or sick people, cripples, women with babies to look after, etc., who dislike factory life, take work home. Male Trade Unionists in the Antipodes have always objected to female labour, being anxious to get all the wages paid in all trades into their own pockets. Accordingly a bogus outcry was raised that 'the sweating system' prevailed in Melbourne boot and clothing factories, and the politicians in 1882 packed a Royal Commission to solemnly enquire into the evils of the sweating system in a country where the supply of well-paid labour never approaches the demand. A Report containing various foolish and futile suggestions duly appeared; some of these were embodied in a Ministerial Factory Bill introduced, but dropped, in 1884. In the middle of February, 1885, a dispute was

---

these abominable fines?' In a day or two this appeal was successful, a list of subscribers appeared in the paper, and Peregrine's fine was repaid to him.

worked up by the Trades Hall Leaders in the boot trade on this very question of 'giving out' piece-work. It lasted for fourteen weeks and was settled by arbitration and compromise, largely in favour of the Trade Union. In the following session the Chief Secretary, yearning to do something for 'the paper-collar-proletariat,' introduced a modified Factory Bill which, in addition to sops thrown to the Trades Hall Council, contained the Early Closing provision for the benefit of shop assistants, who also considered that they ought to be raised in the scale of humanity by the State. Hardly any attention was paid by the outside public or the shop-keeping class to the Early Closing proposal while it was before Parliament. Victorian citizens, modest as M. Jourdain, are not generally aware that they have developed such a grand institution as State Socialism. They leave such matters to politicians and geniuses. Business was not very flourishing at the end of 1885, and small tradesmen in Melbourne, trying their best to make a living, and taking for granted that the Members of the Legislative Assembly were absorbed in their normal avocations of drawing their salaries, squabbling over obscure personal matters (absolutely uninteresting to outsiders), and fetching and carrying for the Trades Hall Council—paid little attention to the Factory Bill, while the one Melbourne newspaper which saw what was going to happen failed to rouse the interest of shop-keepers on the subject. Members of the Legislative Council (who are elected under a more restricted franchise than Members of the Assembly and get no salaries) insisted on tacking the principle of local control on to Early Closing when it came up to them and would probably have rejected the clause altogether if tradesmen outside had known at first what they found out subsequently and had made some vigorous protest. The Bill quietly slipped through both Houses in December and came into operation—after the triennial elections for the Assembly were over—in March, 1886. Early Closing of shops got a fair trial—for a week. That was quite sufficient. The powerful City Council which rules in Central or 'Greater' Melbourne as it is called, worthily represents many of the noble and ancient traditions of self-government. It is independent of the politicians and the dominant class, too wealthy to require to sponge upon the Treasury and strong enough to do its duty. A few days after the 'Silly Shops Act, 1885,' came into operation the Melbourne Town Council called upon tradesmen aggrieved under its provisions to petition. They were all aggrieved and they nearly all petitioned. The hours of closing were at once extended, and to show their appreciation of this piece of legislative folly the Town Council fixed the fines at a nominal sum. One or two of the suburban Councils quickly plucked up courage to follow the example. Meanwhile the Early Closing Law remained in force in many districts. The results gradually developed were most remarkable and, as there was no precedent in any civilised country for a similar absurdity, unexpected. It was found that Early Closing did not operate alike in any two districts; even at different ends of the same street it produced quite different results. It would, indeed, have been as reasonable to prescribe one uniform class, style and quality of goods for shops in all quarters of the city as to prescribe a uniform hour for ceasing to buy goods. In the fashionable parts of Melbourne, for example, the Act had no direct effect whatever,

for the large shops there always closed at 5 o'clock; the
class of customers who dealt with them, living in the
suburbs, all went home about that hour. It was discovered
that many of the assistants in fashionable shops kept small
shops themselves in the suburbs, which practically did no
business before 7 P.M. It was discovered that closing at 7
in some of the suburbs really meant, to large retail drapers
and grocers, closing at 6, because all their assistants went
to tea in relays at the latter hour; six to seven was in short
the 'off' hour. Female servants, who in Melbourne patron-
ise the shops extensively, began to find that they could not
get out in the evening to make their purchases; by the time
they had cleared away and washed up the dinner or tea
things the shops were closed. A large number of small
retail tradesmen of course kept no assistants, doing the
whole work themselves. 'Friends of Man' and Socialists
had defended the Early Closing law on the plea that the
downtrodden assistant wanted to improve his mind at
night and to attend lectures and classes; but if there were
no assistant at all in the shop, his or her mind could hardly
be improved; still the shop had to close. Business men,
clerks, artisans, etc., at work all day in Melbourne, began
to find out that by the time they got to their homes or
lodgings in the suburbs, had their dinner or tea and strolled
out to make purchases, or even to get their hair cut, the
shops were all closed. This class was obliged to lose half an
hour from their work in the middle of the day to do their
shopping in Central Melbourne. A vast amount of trade
was therefore at once transferred from the suburbs to the
shops in the centre of the town. It was discovered that a
number of poor people—washerwomen, dressmakers,

casual workers—as a rule did not bring back work, or get paid for it, till late in the evening; when they had money wherewith to do their small shopping, they found shops closed. As the Australian winter drew in, the streets, unlit by the lamps in shop windows, were dismal and deserted. The 'exempted' tradesmen[36] began to find to their surprise that customers would not even deal with them when the streets were half dark; one shop, it appears, in some way brings business to another. It had been necessary expressly to prohibit exempted tobacconists, chemists, etc., from selling stationery, cutlery or groceries at night, after the stationers', cutlers', and grocers' shops were shut. Mr. E. G. Fitz-Gibbon, the Town Clerk of Melbourne, stated, a few months after the Act came into operation, that he had received hundreds of letters from small suburban trades-people complaining that they were being utterly ruined by it, and similar results were described in the Legislative Assembly, without contradiction, in July 1890. Meanwhile the local municipal bodies one after another put the various powers given to them by the 45th clause into effect. A Shopkeepers' Union (after the mischief was done) commenced a vigorous agitation. This was met by a counter-agitation, comprising mass-meetings, processions, rioting, breaking the windows of large shops, and cowardly violence on the part of young loafers belonging to the Political Early Closing League and the Shop Assistants' League. A great meeting of the latter had been held in the Town Hall just before the Act came into operation, at which one of

---

[36] Chemists, coffee-houses, confectioners, eating-houses, restaurants, greengrocers, tobacconists, booksellers and news agents, were exempted under schedule 3.

the least 'serious' members of the discredited Government
of May, 1877, as well as the notorious Dr. Rose, M.L.A.,
and a popularity-hunting gentleman, who was just then
weaning a new religion, made soulful orations. Nevertheless Government hesitated to enforce the Early Closing
law, almost from the first. It gradually dropped into disuse,
and has long remained a dead letter in the colony. It was
remarkable that some few tradesmen approved of and supported it all through.[37] They devoutly held the socialistic
doctrine that the public might be, and ought to be, dra-
gooned, by a paternal Government, into shopping at certain hours; not at the hours which suited customers but at
the hours which suited indolent shopkeepers. The majority
of Melbourne shop assistants, mostly young fellows born
in the colony, seemed to have grasped the root principle of
State Socialism thoroughly, namely that the Legislature
ought to provide what Sir Charles Dilke calls a 'beautiful
national existence' for them, and that it was to the State,
rather than to their own exertions, that tradesmen's assistants ought to look for success, wealth, and comfort in life.

During the last twenty years professional office holders,
paid legislators, half-educated dreamers and enthusiasts in
Australasia, have attempted to satisfy these new and vague
longings; to enact the part of a State socialistic 'stage uncle'
towards the democracy there; but have never had sufficient
thoroughness or daring to carry out socialistic or collectivist maxims and theories of government and society—
maxims and theories which, at all events, are consistent,

---

[37] In June, 1890, the suburban municipality of Hawthorn petitioned the
Legislative Assembly to enact a 'really' compulsory Early Closing law.
1200 small shopkeepers had petitioned in favor of the Bill of 1885.

precise, and of logical obligation, if once we grant the socialist's premises. State Socialism in the Antipodes has therefore been a hybrid affair; the tentative experiment of men who hoped to do partly, and without committing themselves too far, what thoughtful socialists and collectivists tell us they can do completely, if we will only give them a free hand. Experiments in crypto-socialism, tried upon a society at base, free, commercial, modern, English, would long ago have broken down on the financial side had it not been that the legendary repute of those lands for natural wealth, such as gold, wool, fruitful soil and a fine climate, has tempted investors in Europe to fling their money at the heads of Australasian borrowers. Latterly, as the frightful cost and necessarily unproductive results of State Socialism became apparent to Colonial ministers, they have, to prevent a collapse of the whole thing, been driven to apply for ever-recurring loans in Europe—on false pretences. Sir Charles Dilke does not see the pretence, or is silent about it. The tone of his book, where State socialists and the despotic Colonial proletariat are in question, is one of deferential subserviency, seasoned with half-genuine admiration, recalling those third-rate fashionable novelists of fifty or sixty years ago, who affectionately described the births, deaths, mariages, and occasional foibles of our ancient aristocracy. As to the money lent or the credit extended by persons in this country to Australasian governments, financial institutions, and private traders, it may perhaps some day be worth the while of a 'Council of Colonial Bond-holders' to enquire into the nature of the 'securities' which now cover those investments. In one sense it is true that Britons have lent goods,

rather than cash, to Australasian colonists, always on the
implied understanding that the latter will send us back
exchangeable utilities in return—as soon as the reproduc-
tive public works become productive. Public works constructed on State socialistic principles, unfortunately,
never do become productive.[38] Australian colonists send to
the foreigner fewer and fewer goods or utilities each decade; instead, reams of promissory notes. Whether this
system of one-sided free trade be destined to last for a long
time or a short time, certain it is that it has already wrought
profound—but, I trust, not irreparable—injury to colonists themselves. Victorians of the new generation have,
seemingly, come to believe that the real source of wealth
is in Lombard Street, rather than in the soil and climate of
their superb fatherland. The subtle poison of State Socialism appears to be hurtful to workers born in the colony
especially. Their fathers roughly held that man, standing
face to face with reticent Nature, is duty-bound to ask
himself, 'How much is in me? how much in my opportunities?' and thenceforward to fight his very best to vanquish
difficulties, perhaps in the end wrenching fame, wealth,
and comfort from the circumstances surrounding him.
Such, as we know, was the old pioneer spirit which for a
while opened up a bright and noble destiny for the colony.
In that kind of struggle often the prize won was not so
good a thing as the lessons learnt in trying to win it. State

---

[38] I know that it is the private opinion of two of the most experienced
members of the late and present Victorian Ministries that the whole of the
money (some £1,000,000) already advanced by the State to local Irrigation
Trusts, under the vaunted State Irrigation scheme, must be ultimately
repudiated by the localities in question.

Socialism today in the Antipodes seems to me to preach to willing disciples the despicable gospel of shirking, laziness, mendicancy, and moral cowardice. The further consciousness among all classes there, that triumphant and popular State Socialism depends for its existence on absorbing money from abroad, without reasonable prospect of ever being able to repay it, seems to me bad also.

CHARLES FAIRFIELD

CHAPTER 5

THE DISCONTENT OF THE WORKING-CLASSES

EDMUND VINCENT

CHAPTER 5

THE DISCONTENT OF THE WORKING-CLASSES

Children in the nursery are chidden for discontent, but there is a discontent of grown men which has in it something of the divine element. If all men were able to satisfy conscience and ambition by doing their duty in that state of life into which it had pleased God to call them, civilization would advance with but tardy steps. It was no culpable discontent which induced George Stephenson to engage his mind upon things foreign to his duties in the Tyneside colliery, which led the first of the Herschels to prefer the study of the stars to service in the Hanoverian Guards. In truth, there are many species of discontent. There is that which is the spur of ambition, which leads men to strive for better things, which causes them to rise in the social scale; there is that which crushes them into dull and hopeless apathy; there is that which renders them prone to grumble at a fate which they do not attempt to improve by making themselves too good and too strong

for it, which makes them prone to jealousy of their neighbours, which renders them ready to suspect that the in-
feriority of their position and the degradation of their
surroundings are the results of injustice and of oppression.
In the discontent of the working-class all these elements
are present in varying proportions. The better and more
skilled workman strives to raise himself by cultivating his
skill; the unskilled labourer's discontent shows a larger
measure of jealousy, albeit he too has his honest ambitions.

The discontent of the unskilled labourer is the material
upon which the agitators, roughly described as socialists,
who have been largely responsible for recent disturbances
in the labour market, exercise an increasing influence, and
the object of this paper is to inquire in what sense of the
word these men are socialists. Then comes the question
whether the unskilled sections of working-classes follow
these men because they are socialists or simply because
they are useful in the struggle for higher wages, and
whether the working-class do or do not relish socialistic
legislation when it enters into their lives and sensibly
curtails their liberties as individuals. Last comes the question whether the methods adopted by the so-called socialists are of a character which can be tolerated in any
well-regulated community. And here let me say by way
of preface that the word socialist is used not in a scientific
sense, but to denote a class of men who call themselves
socialists, whom other people call socialists, whom the
writer, for his part, would much prefer to call professional
agitators.

The field of survey is conveniently narrow. London is
the centre of socialism in England; disputes between labour

and capital in and about London have been, to a certain
extent, but to an extent more limited than is commonly
supposed, used by the socialists for their own purposes;
and the London socialist leaders are but a few in number.
They are Messrs. Burns, Hyndman, Champion, Tillett, and
Mann, and, perhaps, Mr. Cunynghame Grahame. Of these
Mr. Burns is far and away the most influential, and, in a
paper which aims to be practical, his character and his
beliefs must be reserved for particular notice. Mr. Hyndman, sometime of Trinity College, Cambridge, law-
student, newspaper-correspondent, and author, is a more
cultivated man than Mr. Burns, and understands better
than he the theoretical principles of socialism. But Mr.
Hyndman is not a man of influence. Mr. Champion, once
an officer in the army, is a man of some education and of
considerable business ability—he was of great service during the Dock Strike in this respect—but he is no orator,
and suffers in the opinion of those whom he addresses, not
only here but in Australia, by reason of a suspicion, not
altogether ill-founded, that he is not of their class. Moreover, he has a habit of giving moderate counsel, which
rendered him unpopular at the end of the Dock Strike, and
during the Gas Strike, and has produced a similar effect
in Australia. Tillett is the comedian of the group, a man
with some capacity for organisation, a speaker who can
hold a popular audience. But he is lacking in education and
knowledge, and not a man of solid weight. Mann is a
ferocious orator, calling himself a socialist, whose occupation consist in stirring up class against class. Untiring
and energetic, ready for any quantity of work, careless as
to the results which his speeches may produce, he is the

most dangerous of them all. Both Mann and Tillett have recently, in the matter of the grain-porters' dispute, shown that, in extreme cases, they recognise the value of moderation. Mr. Grahame, who is nothing if he is not a socialist, has no following in the East End, and is not always welcomed by the leaders of agitation: for example, on a certain critical Saturday during the Dock Strike, when a manifesto, calling for a general cessation of labour had been issued and not withdrawn, Mr. Grahame shouted to the mob, 'Revolutions are not made with rose-water.' On that very evening he received from the headquarters of the strike committee an intimation that his services were no longer required. He was a nonentity; he was ordered to go away and to place himself out of reach of doing mischief. He went off like to a child which had been scolded. He had to learn early, as every man who engages in active socialism must learn sooner or later, the first lesson of slavish obedience. Two other working socialists, Dr. and Mrs. Aveling, may be mentioned. They are cultivated socialists of the revolutionary order, ready at any time to make speeches, to keep accounts, to frame placards and manifestoes for the agitators; but they are not persons of commanding influence. No apology is offered for these brief character sketches, for, if the writer's view be correct, the man's personality commands the following no less than the creed. Indeed, the rude socialism of the men who call themselves socialists is in itself somewhat chaotic, nor, until quite a recent date, has there been clear evidence to show how much influence was exerted by the men themselves, how little their socialistic views were accepted, how easily, when the simple and unsocialistic desire for an increase of wages desired free play, they and their crude socialism were thrown aside.

The prominent figure of the group is that of Mr. John Burns. He is the life and soul of that which, for the lack of a better name, may be called the practical socialism of London, the socialism of action as opposed to the socialism of the library. 'If ever I cease to be a Socialist,' he said in the course of the Dock Strike, 'I shall be a Conservative.' The probability is that he has never been a theoretical socialist at all; that he has never analysed his creed so as to discover whether one article of it is consistent with another. His views are not sufficiently defined nor capable of scientific definition, but for all that he is a notable and a powerful personage. It has been the fashion to describe John Burns as a charlatan; but no greater mistake, no more foolish blunder, has ever been made even by men who, living out of the world, presume to pass judgment upon the men who live in the world. Let men who, prone to pronounce impetuous judgments, and ready to impute mean motives, describe such a man as Burns by the words trickster and self-seeker, take their Carlyle to heart, reading particularly his dissertation upon Mahomet; let them remember that in the autumn of 1889, John Burns held 100,000 men at his beck and call; that when he speaks in Hyde Park thousands assemble round him while other orators are deserted, and they will refrain from charging with insincerity a man who has many faults and some virtues, a man who is before all things absolutely sincere. For our part, using the words of one who was in his time a keen and not over kindly judge of human character, 'We will leave it altogether, this impostor hypothesis, as not credible; not very tolerable even, worthy chiefly of dismissal by us.'

John Burns has all the faults which are natural to a man of implacable zeal, imperfect education, and undisciplined sympathies. His life has been passed among the working-classes; he knows the hardships of their life and the vices which they practise; he is quite as prone to dilate upon their sensuality as upon their grievances, to rebuke as to incite. The fault of the man is that he has read too much and yet too little; that he has been taken with the notion that he has a mission to fulfil; that he has gone to work without giving due thought to the methods of working, without sufficiently considering the results which his acts may bring about. Trained as a working engineer, imperfectly cultivated, but yet having a strong taste for culture, to which he is able to give spasmodic indulgence, he preaches a doctrine which is a curious mixture of Socialism, Communism, Collectivism and Trade Unionism. Ignoring the rule that men are by nature not equal but unequal, a rule of which he is a strong example, he believes in an essentially Socialistic Trade Unionism which aims to crush individuality and to equalise the earnings of strong and weak, wise and foolish. His object in life is mainly to improve the position of the working-classes, and the improvement at which he aims, justifying the means by the end, is a real improvement. He would like, and he rarely omits an opportunity for making his desires plain, to see his fellows more sober, more pure, more enlightened; we are all of the like opinion, but we are not all imbued, as he is, with a trust in humanity which is almost touching in its implicity. He believes that a working-class with more leisure would show a keen desire for self-improvement; he thinks that a working-class with higher wages would spend its surplus earnings in obtaining the means of education, in providing comforts for the home in which the wives and children have to live, and to be reared, would altogether tend to become more divinely human and less deplorably bestial. He does not know that the discipline which men undergo in winning these advantages for themselves is more valuable than the things gained, is the necessary guarantee that the advantages shall be properly used. Therefore he aims to raise wages generally, and to shorten hours of work by all and any means. At the same time he has no fear of bringing about the destruction of trade— it may be that he hardly understands how delicate a plant trade is, and his view may be summarised by saying that he thinks the masters to be perfectly capable of taking care of themselves. This is a quaint creed, unreasonable and illogical; a creed which the experience of men contradicts, since it is found that in times of prosperity the collier of the Midlands and his neighbour the potter buy champagne and bull-dogs in preference to the cheapest of literature; that the wives of gas-stokers have been heard to complain of the eight-hour shift, as opposed to the twelve-hour shift, on the ground that it gives the men more leisure for spending their earnings at the public-house, and leaves them less money for domestic purposes; and that, as a plain matter of fact, trade is easily driven away from a port, especially from a port such as London, which is not altogether conveniently situated. But the creed, chaotic as it is, is held by Mr. Burns with undeviating sincerity, and it explains his actions. In him we find, in these later days, a man who will support legislative interference with the hours of labour, and legislative regulation of the conditions and of the remuneration of toil; a man who will join in the direction of any and every labour movement or strike of which the avowed object is either to raise wages or to drive the labouring community within the limits of a militant Trade Unionism; a man who will join heartily and make his influence felt in promoting any and every movement, measure, or scheme, which appears to be likely to lead to an improvement of wages, to an amelioration of the conditions and to a diminution of the hours of toil. He is, in fact, a socialist with variations.

In the course of the recent labour movements—in which the agitation among the police is not included, since the police laughed at the efforts of the social democrats to interfere in affairs outside their scope—the writer has enjoyed abundant opportunities of seeing the so-called socialists at work. They were the life and soul of the Dock Strike; they were repulsed by the blind leaders of the blind during the Gas Works strike; they led the men at Silvertown to their ruin; they promoted and encouraged the miserable affair at Hay's Wharf; they had a considerable share in the organisation of the Eight-hour Demonstration in Hyde Park, and they attempted to thrust themselves upon the parties to the recent railway dispute at Cardiff. These movements are of importance, because the first of them was the beginning of a chapter in English History which is not yet closed, nay, has threatened of late to be written in terrible characters; because, through them all, and in spite of their differences in character, the so-called socialists pursued their aim with undeviating purpose.

The Dock Strike was, at the outset, a revolt against conditions of toil which were intolerable. In the year 1889 the Directors who were in nominal control of the mass of the London Docks found themselves, not by their own faults but through the mistaken policy of their predecessors, in a position of great difficulty. They were weighed down by a burden of debt from which no financial magic could relieve them; they were at the mercy of their creditors; the capital value of their property had been greatly reduced; they were in the position of a manufacturer who, having enlarged his buildings and increased his plant to meet a trade which was expected to grow, has found that the trade has diminished steadily. But this was not the worst feature of their position. The system upon which the work at the Docks was done was, and had been for many years, the worst conceivable. The permanent staff of labourers was small; the main part of the work at the Docks was systematically performed by casual labourers. There was little picking or choosing at the Dock gates; there was no inquiry into character as a preliminary to employment; and employment, at a small rate of pay, it is true, but still at some rate, was almost always to be obtained. Discharged servants, convicts released from prison, agricultural labourers thrown out of work, militiamen when their training was over, in brief all the men who, either from fault or misfortune, had no settled occupation, knew that at the Dock gates there was always a fair chance of obtaining something to do. The inevitable result followed. Year after year the stream of the reckless, the incapable, the unfortunate men, the men who had been failures, flowed steadily towards the East End of London, and the condition of their lives grew worse and worse. There were more men to work than before and, if anything, less work required to be done; the wage-fund was spread over an increasing number of mouths and bodies. Meanwhile the congestion of the population caused the rents of houses and of single rooms, however dilapidated, to rise rather than to fall. Sanitary considerations, never held in much respect by the poor, were utterly neglected. Overcrowding, squalor, poverty and immorality continued to increase without check. The wages, when they were obtained, were insignificant, but it is not here contended that they did not amount to an adequate remuneration for the work done. On the contrary, it is asserted that the work done by the average dock-labourer was barely worth fivepence, let alone six-pence, by the hour to the dock-owners who employed him. Those who accused the dock-owners of hardness of heart, because the labourers could not earn enough to support life adequately, forgot that it was the irregularity of the work rather than the inadequacy of pay for work done which caused the misery. In short, there was too little work and there were too many men to do it. The fault lay in the system which had encouraged a population of men who could not earn enough to support themselves in decency to assemble and to multiply in the East End.

The result was that in the summer of 1889, Burns, Mann and Tillett found in the waterside districts an undisciplined aggregation of individuals living from hand to mouth, accustomed to walk upon the verge of starvation, discontented with a lot which could not satisfy any man, passing an existence so miserable and squalid that they had nothing to lose. It was no very difficult matter to stir this population into rebellion, and the only troublesome part of the business was to organise the mass of individuals into one body. How the Dock-labourers Union was formed, how the stevedores and the lightermen, in other words the skilled labourers and the monopolists, made common cause with the 'dockers,' how, eventually, the members of the Joint Committee of the Docks were coerced into something near akin to total surrender, into making concessions which were larger than their responsibilities warranted—these and like matters are foreign to the present purpose. More interesting is it to observe that the leaders of the agitation, while they were careful never to advocate and never even mention legislative socialism, were nevertheless compelled, not only to teach, but also to enforce the first principle of communism, which may be taken to be that of equality, not natural but artificial. Trade Unionism of the new, that is to say of the militant species, succeeds by subordinating the individual to the class. The foundation upon which it rests is that the strong man shall earn no more than the weak; and to this principle the dock-labourers, as a class, offered no opposition. They objected vehemently to piece-work, to that payment by results which rewards the industrious and the sturdy workers, and leaves the idle and the weak to their fate: they cried out for one uniform rate for all workers. Later in time, as we shall note shortly, the 'dockers' practically repudiated all the socialism underlying this principle. But even here there is room for doubt whether the mass of the dock-labourers accepted the principle of equality upon its merits, since the contract system has one inseparable fault

in London and elsewhere. The foreman, gaffer, or head-
man of a gang, has always the opportunity of swindling his
subordinates. He rarely loses it.

The coercion which the members of the Union used
upon other labourers—and with a great deal more effect
than ought to have been permitted in a civilised community
—was essential to success. The idea underlying it was only
partially socialistic, but it was the natural outcome of
socialistic spirit. '*Ex hypothesi*,' the leaders would say,
'the Union represents the true interests of the workers.
Sequitur that it is the duty of every worker to be a member
of the Union. We will enforce that doctrine by preventing
non-Unionists from going to work.' The whole doctrine
and the manner in which it was carried out were but ampli-
fications of the principle that the individual must be
subordinated to the class; if he accepted his slavery willingly, so much the better for the class; if he rebelled against
it, so much the worse for him. Of intimidation, of the open
and physical kind, some instances were detected; but it
was an open secret, and a fact thoroughly understood by
both parties to the struggle, that much intimidation existed
in concealment. Men able and willing to work were op-
pressed with a vague and mysterious terror that, if they
worked, they would be made to rue the day. It may be
answered that there was no evidence to justify this terror.
The answer is that the working-men, who knew their own
class, felt it; that although willing to work and spurred by
hunger, fear stopped them from stepping into vacant
places.

It was no matter for surprise that speaker after speaker
should institute comparisons between the lot of the rich

and the poor. 'The rich man rolling in his chariot,' 'the popping of champagne corks at the Dock House'—*vide* the *Star*, erroneously, *passim*—were naturally brought into contrast with the lot of the starving dock-labourers. Such comparisons are the weapons with which the agitator fights; but the feeling to which these comparisons were addressed was nothing more than that vague discontent with existing conditions, that desire to become rich by acquiring the property of other people, that jealous feeling of injustice which is always to be found in the lowest scale of society. At ordinary times the ashes of this jealous discontent do but smoulder; but they are always there, and the agitator with his windy speech blows them to a white heat. It is a part of his regular business. Neither, if the thing be looked at dispassionately, is the permanence of this discontent a matter for wonder, nor the thing itself a mere silly feeling which can be argued away. The lot of him who is born in the lowest scale of society is hard; it is easier to persuade him that he has been defrauded of his opportunities, than to convince him that he has missed them; to those who would fain reason with him, speaking of 'Laws' of political economy, of supply and demand, and so forth, he answers that he knows no laws save those which man, who made them, can alter. The appalling ignorance of the people, the readiness with which they accept statements and arguments of glaring absurdity, renders them an easy prey to the agitator. The agitator cries out for education. He may be well-assured that in proportion to the knowledge of a man are his desire and determination to work out his own destinies, to argue rather than to fight, and that if culture ever does obtain a firm hold upon the working-classes of England, the result will be diminution in the number of strikes, increase and improvement of profit-sharing schemes, and the extinction of the agitator's craft. Among the better class of the working-men the agitator is even now a nonentity.

We have gone rather far from Mr. Burns, but it must be remembered that he had lieutenants who were more ignorant and less scrupulous than himself. In the matter of omission, however, he and his lieutenants were at one. Rarely, indeed, in those days did they allude to the possibility of legislative interference between labour and capital. Never did they suggest a limitation of the hours of labour. From time to time Mr. Burns would deliver himself of a fiery exhortation to the people, would allude, almost in the words of a recent preacher of note, to the 'carnal, low-lying marshes of sensuality' in which they lived, would speak to them hopefully of the millennium in which they would have more leisure for improvement of themselves so that they might be better husbands, better parents, better citizens. But Mr. Burns and his satellites were very well aware that the hope which buoyed up the people was that of obtaining more money, and that mere love of socialistic theories went for nothing; so Mr. Burns and his friends made a species of compromise, and salved their socialistic consciences by urging that the hours of work to be paid for at ordinary rates should be few, and the hours of work to be paid at extra rates should be many. Given a certain quantity of work to be done and a limited number of men to do it, in proportion to the shortness of ordinary hours and to the number of 'over-time' hours, will be the increase in the wages of the earner. With regard to other socialistic measures, projected and effected, it will be convenient to speak later; it will be enough to say here that, during the Dock Strike, it would have been in the last degree imprudent to enunciate the principles of an Eight-hours Bill. Your casual labourer at sixpence an hour would like the legitimate day to be as short as might be, and the overtime, at eight-pence, to be long; but the principle of the Eight-hour movement eliminates overtime altogether: to advocacy of that purely socialistic principle a mixed crowd in Hyde Park will listen; but the moment it is seriously threatened numerous sections of the working-classes, as the Trade Union Congress showed, are up in arms. A very recent incident in the history of the Dock Labourers' Union shows how little the dock labourers realise the principles of socialism. The socialists helped the dock labourers to victory in August of 1889. Twelve months later the socialist leaders, under compulsion from below, announced that for the future admittance to the Union would be rendered more difficult. In short, they attempted to create a monopoly of work in the London Docks for the 22,400 London members of the Union. This, of course, is not socialism, but its very opposite, selfishness.

The gas-workers affair, in which the London socialists were not allowed to play any part, was never a strike in any accurate sense of the word, for the simple reason that the would-be strikers were replaced without much difficulty. The energetic policy of Mr. George Livesey converted men who said they were out on strike into men who were out of employment, and all the talk of the necessity of arbitration or the possibility of it, all the well-meaning efforts of cardinals and ministers to interfere

in the matter, were entirely futile. There was nothing to ar-
bitrate about, no mediation was possible; the outgoing men
were men who had been gas-stokers, who knew how to
charge a retort or to stoke a furnace, and that was all. Their
best chance of becoming gas-stokers again was to seek employment elsewhere. It is necessary to impress this point,
although it is foreign to the immediate purpose of this paper, because Mr. Livesey has been much misrepresented.
He has been spoken of as a merciless man who would not
yield an iota, whereas in fact he was a merciful man,
albeit strong of purpose, who having at last accepted a
challenge to fight, took without a moment's delay such
measures that, while victory was certain, retreat was impossible. The world did not know at the time what the
series of provocations had been; it did not know that concession after concession had been followed by demand
after demand, that the men, acting upon the orders issued
by the executive of a Union, which was and is by the
confession of the secretary (see the January number of
Time) purely militant, had embarked upon a policy of
aggression; that they were asking for more than was reasonable. It has learned this now. It must also be well aware
that the objection of the leaders of the Union to the profit-
sharing scheme, which, on the face of it, was a scheme of
socialistic tendencies, in the best sense of the words, was
due not to any suspicion that it would be worked unfairly,
but to a knowledge that it must have the effect of checking
the policy of restless importunity upon which the existence
of the Union and their prosperity as leaders depended. But
it is said that Mr. Livesey openly stated his intention of
crushing the Union and of destroying the men's right of

combination. As a matter of fact, Mr. Livesey made no such statement, but there is not a particle of doubt that he did mean to take a course that would result incidentally, but none the less inevitably, in the destruction of the Union, and that from the public point of view he would have been entirely justified in aiming to crush the particular Union to which he was opposed. He saw, he must have seen, that this Gas-Workers' and General Labourers' Union was purely and undisguisedly a confiscatory engine in everything but name. The difference between it and the established Unions may be easily stated. The older Unions, presided over by men having some knowledge of political economy and of the conditions of trade, have a defined policy. They desire, when it is possible, to improve the position of the working-man; in times of commercial prosperity they will insist, using his obedience to them as a weapon, that he shall have what they consider his fair share of that prosperity; in times of commercial depression they will help him and, in effect, they perform many of the functions of a friendly society. Admission to such Unions is a privilege not lightly to be obtained. This policy is stigmatised as degenerate by the secretary of the new Union. His policy and that of his Union is that of the daughter of the horse-leech; it is a policy of continual importunity. The new Union cares not whether men are ill or well paid; it is ever ready with a fresh demand. Concession does but whet its appetite; it claims for labour the whole of the profits made by labour and capital combined; it aims to be the absolute dictator of the conditions of toil, to say who shall work and how much he shall receive. And this, be it observed, was the Union which grew from that which Burns, Tillett, and Mann created. Its development in the direction of greed shows how little the socialistic theory of life affected the dock-labourers and their fellow-unionists. This was the Union which Mr. Livesey aimed to crush, and it is here deliberately said that the endeavour so far as it succeeded—and it did succeed to the extent of setting the South Metropolitan Gas Company free—was entirely to be justified. The public were largely interested in the result of the conflict inasmuch as the position of the Gas Company was such that its shareholders could not entirely lose their money, until the increase in the cost of labour was such that men ceased to consume gas. Mr. Livesey therefore was a trustee, and the public were his *cestuis-que-trustent.* He had a duty towards his men, a duty to see that they were reasonably paid; but he was under an obligation no less paramount to see that the public was not imposed upon, as it would have been if a firm front had not been shown to the Union. The Union would have coerced him, if it had been able to do so, into complete neglect of the obligation to the public.

Enough has been written to prove that the New Unionism which has been at the bottom of all the recent troubles in London, adopts the confiscatory articles of the socialistic creed. Some of the founders are sincere and enthusiastic, if not well-informed, socialists; but the bulk of its followers only care to use the socialists as means to securing higher wages; others, it may well be, have personal objects in view; some, while they think they are sincere, do not mind combining the pursuit of their own interests with that of the principle which, more or less honestly, they believe to be just. That is not the point. It is more worthy of notice that the principle which underlies the militant Union is the principle of socialism. In the first place, the individual is subordinated to the class; in the second place, the class desires to obtain the whole of the profits which are derived from capital and labour combined. In other words it desires to confiscate capital.

Meanwhile, it is to be observed that, wherever the working classes are brought into contact with legislative socialism as an actual fact, they invariably rebel. The greater part of the socialistic statutes of recent times are simply hateful to the people whom they were intended to benefit. The enforcement of cleanliness, of sanitary regulations and such matters, is attended with the greatest difficulty as the promoters of 'model dwellings' have found to their cost, because there are no people in this world more sensitive than the working-classes of this country to encroachments, real or fancied, upon their liberty. The proverbial saying that the Englishman's house is his castle does but emphasize the fact that there is nothing more hateful to the average Englishman than interference. He loathes the inspector and the official, but the inspector and the official are the inseparable accidents of the socialistic community, and every socialistic measure which is passed into law brings into birth new officials and new inspectors not only of houses but of persons. It is idle for Parliament to enact that children shall be vaccinated, that children shall be educated, that children shall not be set to work while they are of tender age, to formulate rules supposed to prescribe the minimum number of cubic feet of air allowed to each person in a house, the minimum of sanitary conveniences and so forth, unless Parliament also sends somebody to see whether any attention is paid to its commands. Yet the people who are despatched upon these errands are universally detested; indeed, it is not more unpleasant to be a tax-collector than an inspector of nuisances. It is only after socialist measures become law, or when they threaten the interest of an intelligent class, that those whom they affect realise the position. Of this an excellent example has lately been afforded. The Bishop of Peterborough recently introduced a Bill affecting the liberty of the working-class with regard to the insurance of their children on the ground that in some instances the liberty was abused. His proposal received much support from the press and the sentimental public, but it created such a storm of indignation among the working-class that in all probability nothing more will be heard of the measure. Again, not many months have passed since a meeting in support of the Eight-Hours Movement attracted a huge crowd of more or less enthusiastic persons to Hyde Park. There need be no hesitation in saying that the measure contemplated by the promoters of that meeting would, if it ever became law, involve the greatest possible amount of interference with the liberty of the working-man and his freedom of contact. There are twenty-four hours in the day; it is proposed, to put the matter plainly, that no working-man should be allowed to sell to his employer more than eight hours of those twenty-four; that the remaining sixteen hours must be spent in compulsory idleness, or as the enthusiast would put it, in cultivated leisure. It is the firm opinion of the writer that if that measure ever became a part of the law, it would, within a year, be held so intolerable by the working-classes that Parliament would be compelled either to depart from the practice of centuries and eat its own words by an immediate Act of repeal, or to stand by and see its orders ignored. The textile trades have found this out, but great numbers of the people support this utterly despotic movement now and will, very likely, continue to support it until they find themselves writhing under the pressure of a law which they have themselves helped to create. For the present, they are reminded that the hours of toil are long; they are frightened with idle tales to the effect that their lives are shortened by excessive toil, whereas in truth the working-man's day is not nearly so long as that of the busy lawyer, or the journalist, the doctor, or the active clergyman. But they are not told, and all but the more intelligent omit to remember for themselves, that in a world which is hard and practical, a world in which buyers, whether of work or of things manufactured, will give that which the thing bought is worth to them and no more, a diminution of the hours of labour involves an inevitable diminution of the earnings of labour. Nor will they realise this until it comes home to them in the shape of bitter experience.

In conclusion upon this head let the opinions set forth in the foregoing words be summarised. The working-classes, especially the lowest among them, the men who have least to lose and most to gain, are not averse to the confiscatory side of socialism; nay, finding that socialism at the outset does tend to improve their position, they will honestly and in good faith proclaim themselves socialists. They would be glad to earn more and to work less. So would every man upon whom the curse of Adam has fallen: and the vision which is presented to them is that of a golden age, in which the least possible amount of work shall be rewarded with the greatest possible amount of pay. On the other hand, they bitterly resent all laws which are socialistic in their tendencies, that is to say, all laws which interfere with their individual liberties; but the pity of it is, that they rarely perceive the socialistic tendencies of a projected measure and the menace to their liberties which it involves until they feel its pressure. Then, and not before, they appreciate the fable of the Stork. Moreover, as soon as socialism has done its work of raising their wages, they desert it altogether.

With regard to the legality of the methods employed by the socialist leaders in the course of strikes there has been some question; concerning the facts there is none. Dock-labourers have been induced to threaten that they would not touch coal brought to Cardiff, for example, from collieries upon proscribed lines, and it has been announced that even if coal was placed on board vessels, the seamen and firemen would refuse to navigate the vessels. The same menaces, futile for the most part, but significant none the less, since they show the existence in outline of a vast and far-reaching conspiracy, have been held out in every one of the great disputes that have been mentioned. Mr. Wilson's threats during the Dock Strike, the nefarious manifesto issued during that strike, with the view either of causing or of terrifying the public with the apprehension of a general paralysis of trade; the threats of Mr. Wilson and of an Irish agitator, representing the coal-porters, during the gas-workers' affair; the abortive manifesto issued to the carmen of London by Mann and his allies during the strike at Hay's Wharf; and the incidents of the recent disturbance at Cardiff—all these are of such a nature that nobody, remembering them, can doubt the design which these men, call them socialists or not as you will, deliberately entertain. They divide mankind roughly and inaccurately into capitalists and workers, and they desire to so perfect the organisation of labour, that whenever there is a dispute between an employer and his men, the whole force of the labour of the kingdom shall be brought to bear on that dispute with a view to settling it in favour of the men.

Now of these menaces, it is contended, all are distinctly illegal, upon several grounds. Neither carman, nor coalporter, nor seaman, nor any man who is not engaged upon piecework, has a right to say to his employer, 'I will not touch these goods,' 'I will not navigate the ship in which they are conveyed,' unless he has entered into such a contract with his master as will save him from the consequences of his *prima facie* illegal refusal to perform the duty for which he was hired. In the absence of such a contract, he is liable to be prosecuted at the instance of his master. But it is here proposed to formulate, and that without much hesitation, a wider proposition, to wit that in the absence of such a contract the recusant men are liable to be prosecuted not only by their masters but by the aggrieved persons, and, in the presence of such a contract, not only men but masters are liable to be prosecuted by the aggrieved persons. Who are the aggrieved persons? They are the merchants and shippers who, by reason of what, for the present, shall be called an agreement, are prevented from having their goods carried in a lawful manner. Now all conspiracies are agreements; in fact, all agreements are conspiracies; and of agreements or conspiracies some are criminal and some are innocent. It happens, very fortunately, that the line between the criminal and the innocent conspiracy has been recently drawn by the Court of Appeal in a recent case, the result of which is that a conspiracy, even though it may tend to injure the property or the prospects of C, is innocent, as between A and B, if it is calculated to result in benefit to them. This doctrine has been questioned, and will be tested in the House of Lords, since it renders the denotation of the words 'innocent conspiracy or agreement' wider than it has ever been. It will certainly not be extended. The inevitable inference from it, whether it be correct or too wide matters not, is that a conspiracy between A (Coal-porters Union) and B (Seamen and Firemen's Union) to the injury of C (the South Metropolitan Gas Company) is criminal, even though it be entered into with the view of doing service to D (the gas-stokers). In short it is believed that the simple law of the matter is that, in the case of a strike, the Union which is a stranger to the dispute has, being an aggregation of individuals, a doubtful right to subscribe to the strike fund, but no right whatsoever to go out of its way to injure the employers concerned.

Let us away from technicalities and look at the morality of strikes. Small matters may be passed by. No human being in his senses really thinks that anybody has a right to intimidate, by word or deed, the man who offers to take work upon terms which the intimidator has refused. No reasonable man can think that the Unionist has a right to say to his master, 'You shall not employ a non-Unionist,' or to make things unpleasant for the non-Unionist if he is employed. Some things must be taken as postulates, and amongst them are the propositions that a man has a right to take such work as may be offered to him upon such terms as he can obtain, and that an employer has a right to offer terms of employment at his discretion. It may be that the employer may offer less than will support the man, whereas he could afford to support him and still make a profit. In such a case he is cruel, unjust, wicked; but in a world which becomes more and more practical, it is impossible to conceive a community the laws of which would refuse to recognise and support the right of free contract in relation to adult human labour, which would deprive the working man of freedom in the use of the only capital he possesses, his sturdy body and muscles; and it is needless to point out that, if there existed a law regulating wages, nothing would be more simple than to evade it. There have been such laws in the past; they were consistently evaded: there is neither rhyme nor reason in passing laws which cannot be enforced. If a law be passed to the effect that the writer shall not work more than so many hours per day, and shall not receive more than x nor less than y for his work, he will engage, given a demand for his services, to work precisely as long as he pleases, and to take on occasion xy or $\frac{x}{y}$.

It would be idle to deny the absolute right of the individual, or of the members of a given Union, to strike when they please. A strike, that is to say, a strike brought about by formal giving of notice, and not by sudden refusal to work, may be foolish, may even be wrong from the point of view of the wives and families whom the men are bound to support, but cannot in any advanced community be made punishable at law. We must allow men to take their own measures for the improvement of their own position so long as they do so without disturbing the public peace, and, if they are punished, it must be for disturbing the peace or for combining to disturb it, not for combining to further their own interests, whether wisely or foolishly.

This Union of Unions, indefensible as it is at law, is a thing which cannot long be tolerated in a civilised community. Let us examine this chronic conspiracy of which manifestoes and speeches from representatives of men not concerned in this or that dispute are the only sign. It is hardly an existing fact; it is something more than an idea. (Since these words were written the Federation of Labour, which is the Union of Unions, has made great strides to the front.) It represents in fact the determination of various men, not entirely without influence among the working-classes, that whenever employer and employed are at variance, the whole force of the employed in the kingdom, and for aught we know in the civilised world, is to be brought to bear upon the employer; that he is to be boycotted until he has been driven into submission; that other masters are to be coerced into helping in the process of boycotting. Now this determination comes, in the first place and manifestly, from a desire upon the part of agitators to use the most effectual weapon at their disposal, and it is based, since there is no other possible foundation for it, upon the idea that Labour and Capital are constantly at war with one another, that there is a distinct line and opposition of interests between the classes and the masses. It is unnecessary to show in detail the errors of this idea; to point out that without the aid of the mind which planned a railway, the men who found the money to lay it, and the directors who watched over its destinies afterwards, there would have been no room for engine-drivers, stokers, plate-layers, guards, brakesmen, signalmen, porters, and all the rest of them, and that the case of every industry is analogous.

Nor is war between capital and labour a real or a permanent thing. It may very safely be said, even in this era of agitation and strikes, that in spite of the endeavours of the Tilletts, the Wilsons, and the Manns to induce men to believe that they are being ill-treated, the men who are contented with their employment and with the rate of wages paid to them vastly outnumber the malcontents; but the last-named are, of course, the men who make the most noise. Strikes will come from time to time, and they are genuine fights to which men apply, sadly but with accuracy, the language of the battlefield. Men will not, by wilful blindness to the truth, by blind use of inappropriate terms, hasten the coming of those halcyon days when employer and employed shall have an equal interest in work done upon this or that profit-sharing principle, or when every dispute between man and master shall be settled by quiet discussion of a council table between representatives of either party. The intolerable incidents of the present state of warfare are bringing those days appreciably nearer to us. Numerous profit-sharing schemes have been established, and of these a few, notably those of Mr. George Livesey, are eminently successful. We hope to see more of such schemes in the future, and of designs, such as that which the Sliding Scale Committee embodies, designs calculated to render strikes impossible and founded upon principles capable of wide application.

In the meanwhile, although there is nothing in the nature of constant war between capital and labour, there are —and there is no sort of use in shutting one's eyes to the truth—frequent battles. It is urged in this connection that the ends of the State are best served when the field of those battles is most narrowly confined. If, to take a recent example, when the proprietors of Hay's Wharf are at daggers drawn with their men, all the carmen and all the dock-labourers, stevedores, lightermen, and coal-porters of London, make common cause with the men of Hay's Wharf, there can be but one result. Masters unite and working-men learn that their maxim 'Union is strength' is of universal application. If the working-men of the kingdom or of the world are to form themselves into one aggressive body, it is almost a matter of necessity that employers in their turn should be driven into united action for defensive purposes. The results of collision between bodies so large must be serious; even now strikes in which men are supported, not only by the money, but also by the threats of outsiders, in which masters are encouraged by men engaged in kindred enterprises to stiffen their backs, are carried to such a length as to be productive of incalculable loss and to strain public patience almost beyond endurance. In proportion to the increase of the strength of the Union of Unions, and to the corresponding development, in spite of diversities of interest, of the spirit of unity among masters, is our approach to that state of warfare between capital and labour in which industry and commerce must necessarily languish and the public peace must, almost inevitably, be broken more and more often. The writer, for his part, having no confidence in the medicinal art of the statesman, and having a due regard for the fact that parliamentary efforts to deal with questions involving the relations between capital and labour have failed almost without exception, ventures to think that out of all these evils good will, after much suffering and tribulation, surely come. Let anything approaching to a general struggle between capital and labour once be fought out, and the result will not be dissimilar to that of the Franco-German War. The loss and the pain to both sides will be so great, whole districts and provinces will be so impoverished, that without the sanction of Parliaments and without the help of Governments, men and masters will combine to establish institutions, calling them Tribunals, Boards, or Committees, and to provide for them such an efficient sanction as shall make their awards certain of effect and render impossible future conflicts of equal magnitude. In short, although there are clouds in the sky now, there is room for hope. There is no danger that the Armageddon of capital and labour will be fought; but there is almost a certain prospect of a sharp conflict all along the line. From it labour will emerge convinced that, on the whole, without capital, it is helpless, and capital with the knowledge, which indeed it possesses already, that labour is not to be trampled upon lightly. On anything approaching to confiscatory socialism there is no real danger, for two reasons. Man is not by nature socialistic. He will, as a plain matter of fact, continue to love himself better than his neighbour, to seek in the first place his own advantage. Moreover, those who have some of this world's wealth, and who are, or deem themselves, a little stronger, a little more skillful, a little more clever than the average of their fellows, are the greater number of mankind. To such men, to every man who has anything to lose, to him who feels the dignity of honest work, to him who loves freedom, to him who hopes to raise himself, the idea of socialism, as a practical thing, is altogether odious. Such men feel that to surrender their liberty of action, to resign themselves to living upon one dead level, to lay aside hope and ambition, would be to relinquish their humanity. They will not do so, and, if they would, they cannot; for a man can only rid himself of the individual spring of action, as he can relieve himself of his shadow, by going forth into outer darkness.

Edmund Vincent

CHAPTER 6

INVESTMENT

T. MACKAY

CHAPTER 6

INVESTMENT

It is a commonplace of the older political economists that capital is the result of abstinence from consumption. But an important process of civilisation does not so readily lend itself to definition in a brief sentence. Investment, that is the conversion of revenue into capital, is itself a form of consumption. It naturally implies abstinence from other and more obvious forms of consumption. Thus by means of the process of investment a man consumes a part of his revenue in acquiring, not food which is obviously perishable, but a machine or an improvement of his land, objects which are less obviously perishable. But the advantage thus acquired is by no means permanent, for a machine wears out and land loses its heart, and the usefulness of the expenditure, to which the name of capital has been given, disappears unless fresh doses of capital are from time to time administered. There is no such thing as permanence in human affairs; there are only degrees in the rapidity with which things are consumed.

These considerations, though familiar enough, are of importance in view of the socialist proposal for the nationalisation or socialisation of all forms of capital. We intend, therefore, to examine the operation of investment, or, as we may term it, the application of revenue to this less rapid form of consumption. The most enthusiastic socialist does not deny the usefulness of capital. His grievance is the *private* usefulness of capital. It is not disputed that capital makes labour a thousandfold more productive, that mere human labour is in itself weak, that it only becomes powerful when allied with the mechanism of the inventive arts. This alliance is effected by capital, and results in an accelerated and increased production of wealth. So far there is no difference of opinion. The socialist, however, argues that capital should belong to mankind at large, to the nation, to the municipality, to a public body or bodies, and not on any account to a private capitalist. We, on the other hand, argue that capital should belong to him who has earned it, that he alone can make the best use of it, and that he alone should suffer if it is allowed to disappear in ill-considered ventures, or to waste away more rapidly than is necessary for want of due reparation and care; further, that the right of bequest and inheritance is at once the most economical as well as the most equitable method for the devolution of property from one generation to another; and that the socialist ideal of the universal usefulness of capital, which is our ideal also, can be reached by an ever-widening extension of private ownership and by that means only.

The regime under which we live makes considerable experiment in both these theories of the tenure of capital.

There are tendencies working in both directions, and the question, as far as it is a practical one, is—To which side should a wise man lend his influence? Reasonable men in both camps are averse to revolutionary methods, and are agreed that change must be gradual.

An examination of the principles underlying these experiments in investment will afford matter for the consideration of those whose minds are still open to conviction.

I. There is a vast amount of capital invested and being invested under government and municipal control. The post-office, telegraphs, roads, sewers, and in many instances gas, water, docks, and a variety of other undertakings, are carried on by capital under State control.

II. Other enterprises are carried on by private capital under a State-granted monopoly: e.g. railways, canals, liquor traffic, gas and water, when supplied by a private company, electric lighting, telephones, and, if we include those industries which are more or less under Government regulation, such as shipping, insurance, banking, and joint-stock enterprise generally, we might very largely extend our list.

III. Capital is invested privately by private persons in private enterprise.

With regard to this last division, it is necessary to remark that even here freedom of action is much less than is generally supposed. It is impossible to draw the line with any precision between private capital controlled by the State and capital which is freely employed. Absolutely free employment of capital unencumbered by officious protection does not exist. Practically this statement may appear trivial, but from a philosophical point of view it has

an importance which warrants a passing remark in explanation of our meaning.

The enforcement of mercantile and other contract, the
Government enforcement of settlements of land and personal property, its protection of endowments, its support
of contracts lasting more than a generation, in some cases
for a whole century, all these, intended as they are for the
protection of property, act in restraint of the liberty of
each passing generation in this matter of investment. We
are not arguing in favour of a repudiation of contracts. On
the contrary, though it may appear paradoxical to say so,
we have a suspicion that contracts are observed with more
regularity when their observance is not a matter enforce-
able at law. Even in the present state of society it is not
difficult to adduce instances of this. Any one acquainted
with business knows that in every trade a vast amount of
business is done on terms which are not cognisable at law.

It is notorious that a large amount of property is held by
Roman Catholic trustees on secret trusts which the law
does not recognise. We have never heard that such trusts
are imperfectly carried out.

The mere pressure of necessity has been sufficient to
uphold the desert law of hospitality.

Again, there are probably no debts more regularly paid
than gambling debts, debts of honour as they are called,
and that by a class of men who are not abnormally sensitive to moral consideration. Indeed the 'plunger' has little
scruple in cheating his money-lender and his tradesman,
but as a rule he pays his bets.

Under the present system, inconvenience has without
doubt arisen from too indiscriminate an enforcement of

the so-called rights of property; from legislation which attempts to conserve to a man the administration of his fortune after his death; which permits a pious founder to stamp his educational ideals on future generations, or to endow the professional mendicant for all time; which enables a man to attach his personal debts to land which he has once owned, and so impede the exchangeability of property which is so essential to its value. We suffer also from the fact that dishonest men are able to defy and evade the law, and the injured, knowing the law's delay, feel helpless. These remarks are made with a view of showing that a superstitious respect for laws which guarantee to owners too extended an authority over their property is by no means a tenet in our creed. On the contrary, we believe that under a more open system human ingenuity could ultimately devise better guarantees for appropriate social conduct with regard to property than at present exist, for by the cumbrous procedure of the law-court only the minimum of right conduct can be enforced, and yet men presume on its guarantee and enter into contracts with men of inferior character, because they think that, if necessary, they can enforce their contract. We hardly appreciate how much our own honesty depends on the exercise of reasonable vigilance by our neighbours. Under an open system more circumspection would be necessary before making a contract; there would be room also for a fuller development of trade, arbitration, and protection societies, those equitable Judge Lynches of mercantile life, and as a result a very great commercial value would be added to a well-earned reputation for honourable character. All these considerations would play a part in creating a weight of custom and opinion sufficient to enforce the due observance of engagements. Such a force is, we believe, ready gradually to take the place of legal compulsion, if by general consent the mechanical responsibility of the law was allowed to become a diminishing quantity.

It cannot be denied that those who seek to uphold the rights of property are under some disadvantage, because of the difficulty of identifying the rights of property which are necessary and beneficial. The right of property in slaves is no longer recognised, the right of indefinite settlement is curtailed, copyright and patentright, forms of property peculiar to a modern phase of civilisation, are limited to an arbitrary term of years. Are we quite sure that the present legal definition of property and its rights is adequate and final? It is not reasonable to think so. The rights of property are those which the mutual forbearance of the members of society finds convenient and indispensable. It cannot be said that these can be unerringly identified by laws which are for the most part the result of class legislation. The complete rehabilitation of respect for the rights of property, which seem to some to be at present in danger, requires *voluntary* and *universal* recognition of the necessity of property, and it might seem logical to argue that this recognition will only be given when the principle of nonintervention by the State is much more widely accepted than it at present is in any existing organisation of society, and this indeed is the view of philosophical anarchists like Mr. Benjamin Tucker of Boston, U.S.A. But owners of property who after all are the majority of the nation, are not at all disposed to dispense all at once with the advantage of legal protection for their rights; and with the advantage, the value of which they perhaps exaggerate, they must also have the disadvantage. The disadvantage is that a certain suspicion is thrown on the whole institution of private property by reason of the officious protection given to it by the law, and because it has before now been detected in supporting rights which were contrary to public morality and public policy. This admission does not imply any doubt in our mind as to the justice and necessity of the institution of private property, but it seems to us to explain the plausible nature of the socialistic attack on a most useful and beneficent arrangement which, as far as experience at present goes, has never been dispensed with in any civilised community.

It is, however, only fair to admit that those who have a leaning towards the doctrine of a philosophic anarchy, but who, as opportunists and practical men of the world ask for slow and gradual advance, should not complain too loudly because private warfare by means of legislative enactment has succeeded to private warfare by force of arms, and because though the weapons are changed the spirit of war is still present. We may resist the attack, indeed it is our duty to do so. We can also look forward to the anarchical millennium when parliamentary obstruction and the organisation of harassed industries and rate-payers protection societies have rendered the legislative brigandage of party politics impossible. The necessity of mutual forbearance which has induced men to forego the practice of private warfare may some day induce them to forego the practice of legislative warfare. It is unwise of enthusiasts to insist too much on ideals which are apt to bring ridicule on their cause. In real life we are concerned with tendencies. These are coloured no doubt by the ideals which we allow ourselves to cherish, but it is sheer madness and contrary to the evolutionary theory on which our whole argument rests, to ask for a full and immediate application of principles which require centuries for their development.

We desire to see each generation enjoy to the full the whole resources of the country unfettered by the will of dead generations and by restrictions of the State placed on the free circulation of capital. Progress lies in that direction, for in an atmosphere of liberty human character has an adaptability which will prove equal to all occasions. And in a state of civilisation one aspect of this adaptation of character consists in what has been well called the socialisation of the will. The socialist looks for an automatic performance of social duties under the compulsion of a force *ab extra*. We, on the contrary, contend that individual wills which have not learnt the adaptations taught by self-control, will set such compulsion at defiance, and that the desired result can only come from the impulsion of a force *ab intra*. This consists in the character saturated with the motives of the free life, and in the conviction, realised by experience, sanctioned by free choice and made instinctive by custom, that the free interchange of mutual service and mutual forbearance is the beneficent and yet attainable principle on which the well-being of society depends. If we believe the improvement of human character to be the true line of progress, we cannot afford to neglect these considerations, for they contain some of the most potent factors which make for the endowment of appropriate social conduct.

To return from this digression to our subject—we may shortly sum up the forms of investment under three heads:

(1) State investment.

(2) Private investment under a State-given monopoly.

(3) Private investment which, subject to the foregoing remarks, may be popularly described as free.

We premise that the consumption or deterioration of capital may proceed from various causes. It may be in the nature of things. Thus the value of manure will be exhausted by lapse of time, a valuable machine will after a time wear out. An arbitrary alteration of fashion or demand will render some apparatus useless. Such a deterioration is a misfortune, out of which no form of investment can entirely contract itself.

Again, deterioration of capital is caused by new inventions. Thus capital invested in stage coaches has vanished away, because of the superior convenience of railway travelling; and every one in his own experience knows how machinery becomes antiquated, depreciated in value, and at length superseded by new machinery. Such process of improvement brings with it a distinct advantage to the community.

Now how is this question of deterioration affected by the nature of the tenure of capital? Let us take a variety of instances.

One of the most usual forms of a State investment of capital is in a war. Our judgment as to the wisdom or otherwise of such expenditure will depend on our view of the justice and necessity of the war, a point which, for our present purpose, we may leave out of sight. Obviously private enterprise could conduct a war for us. Whether the existence everywhere of bodies who are able to carry on war for us is an advantage or not is another question which we need not here consider. We accept under present circumstances the occasional necessity of war. Now expenditure on war can be provided out of current revenue; it is then consumed like our food supplies, and there is an end of the matter. If however the war takes dimensions too large to be paid for out of current revenue, a charge is made on the revenue of the future, and a loan is created. As a matter of fact our national debt is mainly due to our great wars. In the event of a successful war, additional national prestige is gained by means of an investment guaranteed by authority, but there are no tangible assets to represent the investment; it is just as much consumed, as if it had all been paid out of revenue. Now the loan is a permanent charge, as long as the nation exists or till it is paid off. It represents perhaps a reasonable expenditure, and we do not wish to criticise adversely the conduct of our forefathers in creating these loans. It is however necessary to compare this form of capitalisation with the capitalisation of a private man who can only derive interest and profit from his investment so long as it represents some present utility to his fellowmen. When this utility ceases, even the principal vanishes away. Pitt's wars, and shall we say the old service of mail coaches, were both necessary and useful in their day. Pitt's capitalisation was under the guarantee of Government, and we are still liable for it, principal and interest. Mail coaches, their owners and the capital and interest involved, have long since disappeared without injustice to anyone, and leaving no burden on the present generation.

As patriots we may not grudge the liability with which the heaven-sent minister has saddled us; but when we come to consider the application of private men's revenue, under the name of taxes, to payment of interest on State undertakings less important than the maintenance of our national existence, we are at liberty, without fear of being accused of want of patriotism, to look closely into the assets which represent our money. To do this we ought to have accurate and intelligible accounts. Of our imperial expenditure we know something mainly from commissions appointed from time to time to consider the inefficiency of our spending departments. But with regard to our local expenditure and indebtedness we have little or no information. It is stated in every elementary handbook on Local Government 'that there are difficulties amounting to impossibility in the way of accurately ascertaining from published returns the present total amounts of local taxation and expenditure.'[1] The same authority tells us that the returns are much in arrear or made up to different dates. Comparison is only conjectural, as the same local authorities perform different functions in different localities, and the overlapping of authorities is quite chaotic. Further, 'the capital expenditure on sewerage, on streets, on gas-works, and on water-supply, is not distinguished from the ordinary expenses of maintenance'; and again, 'imperial subventions appearing in the returns of any one year have

---

[1] 'Local Administration' by Messrs. Rathbone, Pell and Montague. Imperial Parliament Series, by S. Buxton, M. P.

been made in respect of the expenditure of the past year or years.' Chaos is a mild term for such a system of book-keeping.

Now this inability to value its assets is inherent in a monopoly. These monopolies represent absolute necessities of life, and whether the service be good or bad, the public has to put up with it. Competition is excluded, and the monopolist can value at any price he pleases. The service of the Post-Office, for instance, is alleged by Mr. Henniker Heaton to be inadequate. He conducts an agitation in Parliament; the monopolist yields to noise, reduces his terms, and charges the deficit to the community at large. The most perfect system of account-keeping by a State-trading monopoly can never be satisfactory, for, *ex hypothesi*, it has entered into a conspiracy to protect its capital from deterioration by prohibiting competition. In the open market, where there is no monopoly, there is a gradual deterioration of capital by reason of the improvements made by neighbours. A tradesman must replace his machinery by improved machinery or see his antiquated apparatus gradually become valueless. His attention is kept fixed to this point by the sight of custom going in other channels. No owner will agree to acknowledge the deteriorated value of his plant unless he is obliged to do so. Hence Government monopolies are very slow to adopt improvements. Each official is unwilling to admit the weaknesses of his own system, nor will he readily dis-endow his own knowledge and labour by accepting improvements which will oblige him to acquire fresh knowledge and which will render his present services antiquated. Competition compels private tradesmen to improve their ways. In a monopoly there is no such force making for progress, unless we so term the blind sentimental agitation which is now assailing the Post-Office in favour of an Anglo-Saxon penny post.

It is not easy to estimate the loss of the community through Government monopoly; at best it is only a calculation of what might have been, if private enterprise had not been stifled.

We can give one or two slight but suggestive instances. There are still Government offices where all letters are copied by hand and where none of the mechanical processes which give an exact facsimile of the letter copied are admitted. The rest of the clerical work of the establishment is presumably conducted in the same way. This does not of course prevent them from hiring a man in from the street to copy a confidential document as in the celebrated Foreign Office case.

Again, Mr. Stanley Jevons gives a curious instance of the slowness of Government to adopt improvement from the history of the Mint. In his treatise on Money, he states that the present Mint is quite inadequate for meeting the demands thrown upon it.[2] 'What should we think,' he asks, 'of a cotton-spinning company which should propose to use a mill and machinery originally constructed by Arkwright, or to drive a mill by engines turned out of the Soho works in the time of Boulton and Watt? Yet the nation still depends for its coinage upon the presses actu-

---

[2] 8th Edition, 1887, p. 120; the preface is dated 1875.

ally erected by Boulton and Watt, although much more convenient presses have since been invented and employed in foreign and colonial mints.'

In such a case one is able to detect the inadequacy by means of a comparison with other countries, but in the great majority of instances it is only possible to conjecture the loss sustained by the community by the absence of that competition which forces owners to increase the public utility of their property if they wish to maintain its value.

Nor does the State trader escape from the difficulties which best his career when he displays enterprise, as the rate-payer of such towns as Bristol and Preston might realise if they took any interest in the matter.

The Bristol Docks account shows that for the year ending April 30, 1890, the Corporation incurred 'a total loss on working Dock Estate and City Quays combined' of £18,911 4s. 5d.[3] This deficiency has to be made up by a rate in aid levied on the borough and city of Bristol, and accordingly £20,360 was last year taken from rate-payers. The result is that part of the expense of the shipping trade at Bristol is every year paid by the rate-payers, a large number of whom derive absolutely no benefit therefrom. We talk with some complacency of the folly of French sugar bounties and of McKinley tariffs, but the facts above given point to a state of affairs even more egregious and unjust. Either the shipping of Bristol is a decaying industry, and ought not to be bolstered up by subsidies from people living in the suburbs of Clifton, or (and this is the more probable alternative) a Corporation, even as respect-

---

[3] Published in the *Bristol Times and Mirror*, 15 July, 1890.

able as that of Bristol, is an unsuitable body to have charge of such enterprise. In any case the money of the rate-payers is being improperly applied.

The following particulars with regard to Preston are taken from an article in the *Pall Mall Gazette*, 18 April, 1890: Many years ago a company called the Ribble Navigation Company was formed; it paid no dividends, and its shares became worthless. An agitation was got up to make the town council buy up the company, improve the navigation, and make docks. The agitation succeeded, and 'it may be assumed that some of the active promoters were not wholly disinterested.' The expenditure was not to exceed £500,000; at the beginning of this year £751,000 had already been borrowed, and Parliament was asked to sanction further borrowing powers of £220,000. 'The eight miles of channel to the sea have yet to be provided for, and the cost may be anything from £300,000 to £1,000,000, as its course lies over shifting sand-banks fifteen to thirty feet deep. By the course pursued this money must be spent, or all that has been already sunk has been absolutely squandered. The friendly societies, who feel the effect of the abnormally high death rate (Preston, according to the Registrar General, is the unhealthiest town in England), have petitioned for better sanitary conditions, but where is the money to come from with such a burden on the back of the town?' At present the resources of the rate-payers 'are being squandered on a wild goose scheme to open out the river to sea-going vessels along a shifting channel in sixteen to seventeen miles of sand.' 'Certainly Preston has not been happy in its local rulers.' We should prefer to put it, that England had not been happy in allowing its municipalities to embark on such hazardous enterprises.

Again, a municipality lays down millions in a system of sewerage. Science is perpetually preaching to us that sewage can be utilised, yet our towns and houses are undermined by inaccessible drains, which are really little better than elongated cess-pools. Is it a wild conjecture to surmise that if the experimental energy of private enterprise had been allowed to enter the field, our practice would not lag so far behind scientific knowledge on this subject?

As it is, an enormous local debt has been created, and a very inadequate and unimproving service of sewerage has been obtained. Now if this matter had been dealt with by private enterprise (we do not say that it is possible, we are only using the case as an illustration) the capitalisation necessary for carrying out these works would have been made at the risk of private persons, who would have had to pay for their own failures. The community could have accepted each improvement without remorse and the deterioration of the earlier systems would have been constantly and gradually making room for improved methods. As it is, the ratepayers are saddled with an enormous debt, and being monopolists, served not by experts but by boards whose inefficiency is notorious, they hesitate at experiment, and there is no automatic pressure put on them to acknowledge the deterioration of their property or to incur fresh expense in its reparation or in the provision of a substitute.

George Stephenson's locomotive was preceded by that of Trevethick. Now our situation as regards sewage is as if the Government had bought up the invention of Trevethick and established a monopoly. The Peases would not have been allowed to employ Stephenson to make engines for the Darlington and Stockton Railway; and the Government, which had sunk its money in the comparatively worthless invention of Trevethick, would have effectually deprived mankind of the use of the locomotive engine.

It may be suggested that in the matter of sewage municipalities have by a happy inspiration adopted an adequate and absolutely efficient system. It is improbable; and we can make no better comment on the suggestion than to quote one or two passages from the Presidential address of Dr. G. V. Poore, M.D., F.R.C.P., delivered in August of this year (1890), to the Section of Preventive Medicine at the Sanitary Congress. Dr. Poore has had an abstract made of the chief outbreaks of typhoid fever in this country, which have been reported on by the medical officers of the Privy Council and the Local Government Board:

'One factor in common to all these outbreaks, viz., the mixing of excremental matters with water. . . . There is no doubt that whenever excrement is mixed with water we are in danger of typhoid. Typhoid was not recognised in this country until the water-closet became common. We doubtless manufactured typhoid in a retail fashion in old days, but with the invention of the water-closet we unconsciously embarked in a wholesale business. We had not been many years at this work before we recognised that the water-closet poisoned all sources of water. We have had to go far afield for drinking water, and the result has been that as we have left off consuming the springs which we have wilfully poisoned, the amount of typhoid fever has somewhat abated. When the more remote sources get poisoned in their turn—as with our increasing population and our methods of sanitation they inevitably must— the present comparative abatement must, one would fear, cease.'

Such is the criticism on our present system, passed by a gentleman chosen by the Council of the Sanitary Institute to preside over their meeting. Dr. Poore proposes his own remedy, namely, the treatment of sewage with earth and not water. We are not competent judges, and will not assume that Dr. Poore's panacea is final and adequate, but it is clearly a misfortune that as a nation we have embarked on costly systems of sewerage condemned by so competent an authority, and that the position of each member of the community is that he is a part owner of this inadequate service, and that his whole interest lies in patching up and not abolishing a system which in all probability is inherently bad. This impotence Dr. Poore refers to its proper source in the concluding paragraphs of his paper; he says:

'Parliament has compelled us to hand over our responsibilities to public authorities, with the consequence that the individual has lost his liberty and independence, and is drifting into a condition of sanitary imbecility.'

A rich man who can pay to have his house drains inspected yearly, and who can pay for remedying defects, can make the present system tolerable, but to the poor the expense attending such a course makes efficiency impossible.

We cannot therefore gauge the loss of the community arising from the perhaps necessary monopoly of sewage works in the hands of municipalities.

From another point of view monopoly has its inconvenience. It would, for instance, be an economical, and, under proper management, a profitable expenditure of money, to have subways under our principal streets for the passage of the various pipes and wires which traverse our towns.

No public body, burdened as they all are with the discredit of years of unprofitable and incompetent management, dare suggest such an enterprise to the rate-payers. It is a difficult matter, and could only be effected by first-class financial and engineering ability. Public bodies very properly feel that they cannot experiment with rate-payers' money, or even incur expense in setting great engineers to estimate the cost and practicability of such schemes.

We have no wish to depreciate the public spirit which undoubtedly animates many, nay perhaps all, of our municipal bodies. The discredit into which after a brief period of popularity they inevitably fall, is due, not to personal consideration, but to far deeper causes. The interests confided to them are too large; they are a standing obstruction to the subdivision of labour and investment which is at the root of the efficiency of the services of civilised life. It is true that private enterprise shows a disposition to organise itself on a large scale by means of trusts and other combinations, but this new departure has been preceded by a great specialisation and subdivision of energy, and forms no precedent for the establishment of a great monopoly *'per saltum.'*

Our most obvious and primitive wants had happily been to some extent arranged for before Government had been fully organised. Government has rarely interfered to help the governed in the distribution of food or in the victualling of great centres of population. Consider the marvellous world-wide interchange of service, both of labour and capital, which is involved in feeding London for a single day. This goes on day after day and year after year without any difficulty, and we are so accustomed to it that we rarely pause to admire. All this is done without the assistance of Government.

With advancing civilisation new wants became apparent; the community became anxious about sanitation, about education, about gas, water, electric light, and a variety of other interests, but by this time the State was fully organised. Men in a hurry refused to wait for the satisfaction of their wants by the system of private enterprise and competition, and they obliged the heavy hand of the State to interfere. Thus it comes that interests which in a civilised community are not inferior in importance to our food supplies, are left as monopolies in the hands of Government. To deal properly with the sanitation of a large town a vast subdivision of labour and management is perhaps necessary. Our public bodies are composed of very worthy persons, but they cannot discharge the functions which in a free state of enterprise would be performed by perhaps hundreds of separate purveyors of service, and notoriously the scientific officials of our municipalities are inadequately remunerated, and as a consequence the highest professional talent is not at their disposal. It is only by considerations such as these that we can estimate the loss which the public suffers from these monopolies. They and the bodies which administer them form a huge obstruction to beneficent applications of capital to the service of mankind. Capital is free to serve us in some of the most elementary needs of life. It cannot be dispensed with in more complicated matters, but it is tied about with endless restrictions and impediments; it is taken from us forcibly in taxation, not freely and experimentally adventured; it is spent timidly by a conscientious board, and recklessly by a corrupt board; if badly spent it still remains a debt upon us, and we are forced to make the best of the bad article supplied; we cannot accept the pressing offer of ingenious and scientific men who ask leave to try again at their own charge and risk to improve these most important services of civilised life.

The matter is not without difficulty, but the present solution—the solution of granting monopolies more or less complete in so many of the most important services of life —is unworthy of human ingenuity and cannot be considered final. This perpetual forestalling of a free-trade solution has weakened the power of private initiative; but if our superstitious reverence for Government can be shaken, we do not despair of retrieving again our steps and of giving to these higher services of civilised life the vigour and elasticity which belong to the humbler primitive services which supply us with our food and clothing.

Such, we believe, are the causes of the discredit into which local government bodies are constantly falling. It is not due to personal considerations. The members of municipalities and vestries represent very fairly the virtues and vices of their fellow-citizens. Many of them are persons of ability and position; some are retired tradesmen who, when they become too old to attend to their own business, are kind enough to occupy their declining years in the management of ours. Others are men still engaged in trades and professions. The employment given to them by their neighbours of free choice leaves them with some leisure on their hands, and, if they are public spirited, their services prove useful for the discharge of functions which, because of their importance, have been withdrawn from private enterprise and confided to municipal monopoly. Some, again, are well-to-do persons of good will who follow no calling. Their time hangs heavy on their hands, and they are sent out to get experience of life by assisting in the management of public business. To these of late years there has been added some admixture of first-class agitators. The whole is a fairly representative body rather above the average in respect of public spirit, but a good deal below the average in administrative ability.

It is, in our opinion, a tactical mistake on the part of those who have an instinctive distrust of public bodies to abuse the *personnel* of which they are composed. The constantly recurring scandals are due not so much to the incapacity of vestrydom as to the impossible duties for which it is held responsible.

Another Government enterprise which is not a monopoly has been undertaken professedly in the interest of the working-class. We shall be accused of temerity when we say that the institution we have in our mind—the Post-Office Savings Bank—has been a very doubtful benefit. A bank is an institution in which men place monies either on current account or on permanent deposit. A banker is an expert in investment; he uses a proportion of his customers' balances in financial operations and in investment. His customers obtain financial assistance such as their credit warrants, and a considerable portion of a banker's reserves are invested in the businesses of his customers and of the class to which his customers belong.

The working-class, however, is served by a bank which gives them no such assistance. The reserves of the Post-Office are placed in the hands of the Commissioners for the Reduction of the National Debt, who in turn invest them in Government stock, or lend them for financing the various spending departments of the State. It will be said that a workman has no credit which would enable a banker to employ capital in his service. This, however, is a great misconception. We refer the reader to the paper in this volume by Mr. Raffalovich, and to the suggestions which he there throws out for the use of savings banks' reserves for promoting the erection of working-class dwellings. It is moreover the business of a *bona fide* banker to devise forms of security by means of which he can give financial assistance to his customers.

Consider what an impulse to thrift and working-class investment would have been created, if the Post-Office Savings Bank had been debarred from investment in Government securities, and been obliged to invest workmen's savings in assisting schemes for their service. This is the function of the banker of the middle and upper classes. It is through the legitimate assistance of the banker and the insurance agency that the proletariate of this and other countries are to be encouraged to pass from the hand-to-mouth life of wage-earning into the greater security enjoyed by those who rely on investment as well as on labour for their maintenance.

This Post-Office Savings Bank is therefore, in this view of the matter, one of those 'short cuts' to prosperity of which the civilised world is very full. They are admirable in intention; they have also their advantages in practice, but they forestall and prevent the higher and more useful adjustments of mutual service. They are part of the bondage on the free development of character and energy which, more than anything else, impedes the true progress of the working-class.

It is satisfactory to know that the National Penny Bank, a legitimate private enterprise, is now beginning to make great progress, and to pay a dividend to its shareholders. It is to be hoped that its successful competition with the Post-Office is only the beginning of the rescue of this industry from the hands of Government. The sterilisation of working-class savings under the present system is a grave misfortune. If working-class banking was conducted by persons who had to conciliate the good-will of their customers, it would become more the practice to invest reserves in undertakings likely to benefit the working-class. It may even be possible that the working-class savings bank may one day be instrumental in promoting schemes of industrial partnership in well-established businesses. Co-operators are fond of talking of labour hiring capital, and of reversing the present plan of capital hiring labour. From whom could the co-operative labourer borrow with more fitness than from the savings bank of his own class? Loans of course cannot be obtained from a bank without undeniable security, and this he would have to provide, but the difficulty is superable, as M. Raffalovich has aptly shown, by a combination of insurance and loan. If a beginning were made in the simpler matter of house property, there can be little doubt that human ingenuity would soon extend the system to other matters, more especially to various forms of industrial and co-operative partnerships.

All attempts of this kind are impossible under the present system of Government banks, for Government can only invest in its own securities. Thus the author of the article on the Post-Office of the United States in the *Encyclopaedia Britannica* points out that the United States cannot have post-office savings banks, because the Americans are fast paying off their national debt. 'It is plain,' he says, 'although the difficulty does not seem to have occurred to many of the advocates in the United States of a savings bank system, that to be lasting it must be founded upon a Government debt, a condition which does not and is not likely to exist in that country.'

It is obvious that the same line of argument can be applied in a minor degree to the monopolies granted by the State to private capitalists. The risk of loss is undertaken by the private adventurer, but if a success is made the public is at the mercy of the monopolist, tempered only by the expensive and incomplete protection given by the State. The Board of Trade has recently held an elaborate enquiry upon Railway Rates. The expense of the enquiry has been great, and the rates which the Board proposes to fix must be to a large extent arbitrary; they have none of the cogency which rates fixed by free competition would have.

It would be rash to say that greater freedom of railway-making for the purpose of creating more competition is either possible or impossible. We need have no hesitation in saying that, if it were possible, it would solve a great many, at present insuperable, difficulties.

Our argument is that the public has been deprived of the full value of railway enterprise by the granting of monopolies. Railway companies have been able to hold on to inferior machinery and to pay fancy prices for the acquisition of land, and they are unable to give increased facilities to travellers, because they are too tender of share-holders' capital inflated beyond its value by causes such as the above.

If there was more freedom of trade in this matter there might well be ten times as much capital invested, and all of it represented by more efficient machinery. The experience of America in the matter of telephones and electric lighting shows that *the mere fear* of competition is sufficient to make monopolist companies reasonable.

Generally it may be said that we have much to learn from America in this matter of monopoly. It is there that a solution of a difficulty, which all admit, is to be looked for. Protection has made the United States a dear country to live in. But, as has been recently pointed out, it is in some respects not such a dear country as it was. This fact is attributed, probably with justice, to its cheap system of transport. A railway monopoly which results in high transport charges is tantamount to a form of protection. An American railway is built and worked very much more cheaply than an English railway, and the evils of monopoly are in this respect less apparent. In England we hear constant complaint of the difficulty of transporting fish, fruit, vegetables, and many other articles of which the first cost is low, because the rates of transport prevent their being brought within the reach of consumers on reasonable terms. An employer of labour in England and America writing to *The Times* of October 1, 1890, compares the English and American system, and asserts that we in England have done nothing since Stephenson to cheapen and improve our system of inland transport. The statement may be exaggerated but contains its grain of truth.

We hear numerous complaints of the congestion of population in great towns. Light railways are put forward as a panacea for the congested districts in Ireland. There are of course many causes which contribute to the growth of large towns, and undoubtedly the high price of transport is one of them. Human ingenuity cannot altogether abolish space, but, if price of transport is any criterion, it has brought America and India nearer to English ports than London is to Manchester. And why? mainly because sea transport is open to free competition, and land transport is a monopoly. If it were possible (it may be impossible, for some difficulties are insoluble), to reduce largely the cost of inland transport, there are many large industries which could just as well be carried on in the country as in the town, to the infinite advantage of our labouring population. It is noteworthy that the country factory is much more usual in America than with us. Our policy of protective monopoly requires very careful examination before we sit down meekly under our present disabilities.

Another curious point has arisen in the United States with regard to the railway monopoly. Trusts are arrangements projected by private enterprise for mitigating the evils of competition, for it is not here denied that there are evils in competition. Like every other human arrangement, trusts are liable to be abused, and it is alleged that some of the American Trusts have become oppressive, and that, in various trades, monopoly has been established to the detriment of the public at large. A leading working-class member has recently defended the attempt to make a Salt Trust in England, on the local and intelligible ground that it was an application of the principles of Trade Unionism to the affairs of the capitalist. Free combination, so long as it respects the freedom of the uncombined, is a necessary and legitimate method for overcoming certain social inconveniences, and as a rule the free community has its own remedy if the combination becomes oppressive. Given a fair field and no favour, an oppressive monopoly unsupported by force would not last for a week; it would at once be deserted and routed by indignant customers.

It is very noteworthy therefore, that the principal ground of complaint against the Trust in the United States is based on the allegation that Trusts have corrupted the railway monopoly, and have secured for themselves preferential rates and even induced the companies to charge extraordinary rates to outside competitors. The accusation is strenuously denied by the advocates of Trusts. The denial, however, appears to amount to this, that the preferential rates were secured by the corporation now forming various Trusts prior to their amalgamation in Trusts. It follows, therefore, that if to give preferential rates is corrupt on the part of a Railway Company, the corruption dates from a period before the era of Trusts. At any rate, it seems to be admitted by the more moderate opponents of the Trust system that, but for the Railway monopoly and preferential rates, an oppressive Trust would be an impossibility.[4]

Under the present system mechanical traction has been confined to unduly narrow limits. Its extension to the uses of private life ought not to be beyond the power of human ingenuity, and here there is room for vast applications of

---

[4] See Foreign Office Report on Trusts, No. 174, p. 72.

capital. M. Raffalovich has pointed out how closely the question of an increased and cheaper service of locomotion is connected with the solution of the difficulty of housing the working-class.

In the case of the electric light, Government has pursued its usual course. It grants a monopoly but couples it with conditions intended to prevent private capitalists reaping too large a profit. At first the conditions were too onerous, and the country was deprived of the use of the electric light. We have many other illuminants, and it is a question whether the public required any protection in this matter at all. The most obnoxious clauses of Mr. Chamberlain's legislation have now, at great expense and loss of capital, been repealed, and by degrees the electric light is coming into household use.

The only force which can curb the pretensions of trades-men, and yet at the same time act as an incentive to enter-prise, is freedom of competition. Government can limit the division of profits by regulations which astute financiers can easily evade. But the process is apt to degrade the morals of commerce, or to drive the more sensitive into other fields of labour, and in this way to injure the interest of the consumer, who in the last resort has to pay for all this hampering of industry.

But the most familiar instance of private capital doing business under the support of a State monopoly is the liquor traffic.

In the proper sense of the term a public house should be a *public* house, and as much a place of amusement as of re-freshment. The amount of capital employable in this trade is measured by the ability and willingness of the working-class to reward such investment. Paternal government has by creating a monopoly focussed *all* this capital on the sale of spirituous liquor. The workman still manages to pay for his drink, but his rational entertainment and his skittles can no longer be provided, because he has to pay perhaps eight or ten times its value for his glass of spirits or beer. This is not the act of the publican but of the Government, which attempts to improve the morals of workmen by putting a prohibitive price on their liquor. The result, as in most such cases, is the reverse of expectation. The taxes and the monopoly under which the poor man's caterers have to labour have been prohibitive not of liquor, but of rational amusement, and as a result the poor man is too much bound down to the one amusement which his protectors have left for him, namely the pleasures of strong drink. Can we wonder that under such a system drink has taken too large a share of a workman's spare time and spare cash?

Every class is entitled to spend a portion of its earnings on amusement. Those who are able to amuse us are at present as handsomely paid as any other servants of the public. The public entertainer of the poor has by the inordinate taxation of one necessary item been degraded to being the mere keeper of a drinking-shop, an enterprise from which many conscientious and enterprising tradesmen stand aloof. We do not assert that excessive drinking is *caused* by this monopoly. Excessive drinking and excessive eating are animal pleasures, which the civilised man soon outgrows if his opportunities of rational entertainment are not unduly curtailed. The poor man has suffered from this curtailment of the more refined methods of amusement, which would have weaned him from the coarser pleasures of appetite. The drinking habits of the richer classes, where drunkenness is now comparatively speaking rare, have passed through these same phases.

We may here, as conveniently as elsewhere, say a word on the philanthropic employment of capital. The employment of purely philanthropic capital to giving a supply of the necessaries of life to classes of the population at less than the market price is unsatisfactory. It keeps commercial capital out of the field, and attracts attention away from the cause of defective supply. In London there is a great deal of semiphilanthropic capital (for the most part it is now becoming distinctly commercial capital) employed in providing houses for working-people. It is not too much to say that its usefulness varies inversely to its philanthropy.

It is only a minority that can be housed on philanthropic terms. Commercial capital, which is plentiful but timid, is frightened away by philanthropic enterprise, and the majority have to remain inferior houses.

A very apposite illustration has been given to the writer by a friend who is partner in a large mill business in the North. Some thirty years ago his firm, being desirous of cultivating friendly relations with their work-people, built one or two streets of small houses. They were wealthy people, and they built a class of house rather in advance of the best artisan house of the day. The houses were readily let to their work-people, and for a time answered the purpose intended. At the present time, however, our informant states that he does not think any of his own work-people live in these houses, which still belong to his firm. His people have found that thirty years have brought great improvements in the art of house-building, and the men who formerly lived in the prize philanthropic house of thirty years ago have migrated to commercially built houses, where they get hot and cold water laid on, baths, and other modern improvements. Now if artisans' dwellings were widely supplied by philanthropic effort, or if, with a view of serving not only a minority but the whole of the working-class, philanthropic investment were made compulsory and the matter undertaken by the municipality, it is obvious that the gradual improvement above described could never have taken place. The bumbles of each generation would decide in what sort of houses each class should live. Stagnation and discontent on the one hand, or ruinous extravagance guided only by sentiment and without any economic principle to restrain it, and ending without doubt in a violent reaction, are the alternative horns of the dilemma which would of necessity arise in such a state of things.

The socialists argue that Government should arrange for a gratuitous use of capital to each successive generation. In other words, Government is to organise industry, and to give to each labourer his due; no charge is to be made for the use of capital; superintendence and reparation of plant must of course be paid for, but no one may derive any advantage from investment, but only from labour. Let us consider this proposition more closely. Each year's increment will be taken by the State; each labourer will receive his wage, and a portion will be retained by the State for the reparation of capital and for making that increase of machinery which is necessary for the support of an increasing population.

In fact it will be the duty of the State to capitalise a portion of each year's revenue. Now this superintendence of capital will have to be paid for. Inspectors and auditors will be required far beyond what is necessary under the present regime where most men are dealing with their own and not their neighbour's property. The use of capital therefore will not even here be given gratuitously. Further, it would give rise to a perpetual dispute as to the amount of capital to be subtracted from the due need of the labourer. The increment taken for capitalisation and for the cost of superintendence would be regarded as a tax, and would be paid as grudgingly. There would be a never-ending battle between the bureaucracy and the labourer. The former would naturally wish to increase the capital under their charge, and the labourer would resent all such deductions as a fraud on his claim. The fact is, that a gratuitous supply of capital is an absurd idea. Capitalisation or investment is essentially a form of consumption, and is in the main directed to the purpose of freeing the investor from the inconvenience of personal toil, in a word to labour-saving. If men or bodies of men labour assiduously and apply part of the revenue obtained from their exertion to this form of consumption, they only do so because they derive advantage therefrom. If that advantage is made to cease, this form of consumption will go out of fashion; if the control and resulting benefit of investment is taken away from individual men; if the benefit of capitalisation only reaches them after it has filtered through the hands of a bureaucracy—they will inevitably identify their interest with the labourers' share in the division, and they will embody this view in their mandate to the organising bureaucracy. Man's maintenance, therefore, will gradually return to a dependence on labour alone, and each day's revenue will be consumed by the labourer as he receives it, and application of revenue to investment will cease. Can one conceive a surer means of bringing about a return to barbarism?

We have now compared the value of private as against State investment, but we have considered it mainly from the side of the consumer. His wants, we have endeavoured to show, will be best and most economically met by a free system of investment wherever that is possible, and we believe that it is applicable to a much larger sphere than it at present covers.

This, however, is a small matter compared to the influence of investment as a factor in producing the appropriate social character in each individual investor, and to this aspect of the question we now turn. Human happiness depends very largely on two equally necessary qualities, namely, on the individual energy which is able to satisfy *reasonable* wants; secondly on the self-control which holds in check *unreasonable* ambitions. The operation of investment has an important influence in stimulating and informing these valuable social instincts.

There is a threefold activity involved in the full ideal of civilised life. Each man is a consumer and should be a labourer and an investor. It will be found that our social troubles are caused because this threefold function is imperfectly performed by large masses of the population. We are all of us of necessity consumers, and most of us have capacities for consumption far beyond what our means allow us to gratify.

The primitive means for gratifying consumption was labour; but with the first fashioning of Adam's spade it became clear that investment was a necessary complement of human labour. Without it labour was a poor and feeble thing. We are familiar with the principle of the subdivision of labour; we do not always remember that this subdivision of labour without a corresponding subdivision of the duty of investment has produced a one-sided civilisation and interfered with the threefold economic harmony above described.

The consumer who is labourer only and not investor has his potentialities for consumption checked. The burden of supplying the complement of capital necessary to an increasing population of labourers falls on investors who are, by the service thus rendered, enabled to subsist without labour. The direction of this production remains with the investor, for he is the only consumer whose consuming power is still effective. His capital and other men's labour are therefore employed in the manufacture of luxuries which he only can purchase, and this one-sided form of consumption gives employment to silversmiths, painters, sculptors and other purveyors of the arts and luxuries of life, while at the other end of the scale the labourer has barely sufficient to eat and drink. Rich men might give away their superfluity, and large benefactions are from time to time given to public purposes. But experience shows that rich men cannot get rid of their responsibility by a mere scattering of gifts. For gifts thus scattered too often prove mere narcotics dulling the energy of poorer men, and obscuring the truth that in a society not yet become socialistic, the duty of private investment is as paramount as the duty of personal labour. The desire to consume, if it be not debauched by public charity, should prompt an exercise of both functions by each member of society. It is only thus that a liberal interpretation can be given to the term 'reasonable,' when we said above that human happiness, materially at all events, depends on the ability of each man's energy to satisfy his reasonable wants. A larger performance of this duty of investment would lead, we argue, to a much larger consumption, and hence a much larger production brought about by an *ever-increasing* application of capital or labour-saving investment, and an *ever-decreasing* application of the less effective instrument, namely, human labour.

Let us turn to our second proposition, that happiness depends on self-control as much as on the gratification of even our most reasonable desires. There are ambitions which are antisocial, and there is nothing which ministers more to their repression than a knowledge that honest conduct, or what we have termed appropriate social action, is not impracticable, and in fact that it is easier than an opposite course. The desire to consume will prompt an infirm will to an attack on the rights of others. But a conviction of the necessity of mutual forbearance, acknowledging the justice of other men's defence of their own, renders the road of transgression practically narrow. The wonderful internexus of social life which preserves automatically by mutual forbearance each man's claim, has reversed for practical purposes the truth of the adage.

The social organisation which surrounds us gives an impetus towards right against which only despair can make us rebel. But here there is no ground for despair. Progress in a free atmosphere will inevitably lead men to an exercise of energy where such a course promises success, and to self-control where the conditions of difficulty are at the moment insurmountable. This double training of character in energy and self-control is the principle to which society owes all its nicest adjustments.

The labourer, therefore, who wishes to improve his position will be impelled to investment as the necessary complement of his labour; and, in turning to investment as a method of meeting some of the struggles of life, men's minds are opened to many salutary reflections.

Men realise that the power of labour, which from a point of view we may term man's only inalienable capital, is expended by mere effluxion of time, is rendered useless by sickness, and disappears at death and old age. Men, therefore, must, if they are wise, form a sinking fund by insurance or by savings to replace the yearly expenditure of their labour capital. This desire to make ends meet has important consequences. It limits the rate at which men create responsibilities; it promotes the application of revenue to the slower processes of consumption; it postpones the age of marriage, and has its influence on the birth-rate; it keeps the growth of population automatically proportionate to the growth of capital.

The first exercise of the investing instinct will be in matters which directly minister to the wants of the investor. Thus, the investments of the working-class are placed for the most part in their own institutions, such as Friendly

Societies, Trade Unions, Building Societies, Co-operative Societies. This is the earlier stage of investment, but the full subdivision and mutual service of investment is not complete till investment passes beyond this stage. *A* makes boots and exchanges his service for wages; then, buying a coat, he pays the wages of *B*, the tailor who made the coat, and the reward of *C*, the investor who supplied the capital necessary to the transaction; and, be it noted, *B* and *C* are possibly the same person. If *A* wishes to contribute his full share to the social machine, and to draw out of it something beyond his wages, he is bound to contribute to the service of investment as well as to that of labour. Nor is there any reason to limit the range of *A's* investment. The tailor is not bound to invest in a tailoring business. So long as his investment is serviceable to the rest of the community he will be entitled to draw a revenue from it, and with this revenue he can reward the investors whose capital ministers more directly to his wants. This is the full subdivision of investment which we affirm to be the necessary accompaniment of the subdivision of labour.

How, it may be asked, will this ideal affect the status and wages of labour?

First, we urge it is the only ideal which is compatible with Freedom. State regulation of labour, and State investment of capital may have charms for the speculative enthusiast. To those who have had any experience of it the regulation of bumbledom in all its grades is simply intolerable. Liberty is an essential in any elevated ideal of life.

Next, how would it affect wages, and how would it affect interest and profits?

In the first place, if there was a more general exercise

of investment, each man would have in his own pocket a potential strike-fund and his family and class would all, more or less, be in a position to help him. Wages must rule high, for the only limit on their rise would be the labourer's own interest as an investor. The investing labourer would not be indifferent to dividends, and the labouring investor would be a permanent influence in favour of liberal wages. The gradual acquisition of a small revenue from investment would do more to raise the economic position of the labourer than all the trade unions that ever existed, useful and beneficial as these have been.

Unfortunately for the country, the primitive instincts towards investment in our poorer classes have been so debauched by our socialistic poor-law, that vast arrears of work have to be overtaken in the quickening of motive and the building up of habit.

Nor do we think that the rate of interest and profit would fall. Skill and success in the application of investment would be more valuable functions than ever. The competition of capital for employment would be greater than ever, there would be therefore more demand for the service of the competent *entrepreneur*, and his wages, that is profit, would not fall. But while the competition of capital was keener, the field of investment would be vastly enlarged. First, because every man would be interested in reducing the demand on human toil, and as a consequence a powerful impulse would be given to the adoption of labour-saving apparatus. The life of a machine would be much shorter, for none but the most modern machinery would be used. An ingenious and anti-socialistic writer has argued that possibly interest will cease to be paid, and that on the contrary men would be willing to pay for the luxury of deferred consumption.[5] This view overlooks, we think, two important considerations. It overlooks the willingness of men to pay for a rapid succession of labour-saving inventions, and, secondly, it overlooks a still more important item, the increased potentialities of the consumer. If consumption of necessaries and luxuries was likely to stand still, there would be something to be said for this view. But all this investment and all the implied multiplication of the power of labour and production is with a view to consumption. If we look round we see everywhere restricted consumption because of the unperformed office of investment. With increased investment there will come increased consumption. There is, therefore, a vast field of profitable investment at our very doors, namely, in the application of capital to the uses of the poor, but it can only become profitable as the poor learn by degrees the valuable duty of investment.

We have attempted to show that the State cannot successfully perform the duty of investment for its members. State property is always ill-managed; it does not disappear automatically when it becomes effete; and its universality would deprive citizens of the school of experience where, more than anywhere else, their character acquires the due admixture of energy and self-control.

If there is to be any legislation conveying property from the haves to the have-nots, we sincerely trust that the conveyance will be complete and final, and that as far as possible nothing will be left in the unfruitful paralysing

---

[5] J. H. Levy, *The Outcome of Individualism.*

tenure of the State. We are against all confiscation, not because there is no precedent for it, or because existing titles to property are indisputable, but because it is utterly impossible amid the larger proportions of modern life to dress the injustice of earlier times without committing fresh acts of injustice on a much larger scale. But even if this consideration is disregarded it would be foolish as well as knavish to entrust any more property than we can help to a tenure at once demoralising and unprofitable.

T. MACKAY

CHAPTER 7

FREE EDUCATION

B. H. ALFORD

CHAPTER 7

FREE EDUCATION

As the subject allotted to me is one in which the point of view of the writer is a serious element for the consideration of the reader, it is well to state at the outset that I write as a Manager of some standing in charge of a so-called Church School. The position that many of the Managers of such Schools have taken up, is clearly enough stated in words spoken (according to the report in *The Times* of August 8th) by the Bishop of Bath and Wells. 'He said they must look at the question not merely in the light of their original opinion as to whether education was a good thing or not, but they must look at the position of it outside. If they succeeded in preventing Government from bringing forward their scheme, in which they proposed to safeguard the interests of Voluntary Schools, they might be perfectly certain that when a Government of a different political constitution came into power they would carry Free Schools without the safeguards.' This appears a very candid confession that the authorities of the Church of England (as far as one Bishop can pledge them) desire to avoid discussing the principle of Free Education, because, if they were forced to come to an adverse judgment, they might imperil the fortunes of a certain class of schools. But would it not be more patriotic to enquire into the advantages or disadvantages for the nation of Free Schools, and abide by the decision—rather than determine beforehand upon risking any national disadvantage, in order to maintain a form of education which might not finally be secured even at the price of such a surrender?

My purpose is to keep the vexed questions as between school and school, government and government, out of sight, and to consider:

Firstly: What can be urged in favour of Free Education on broad grounds? What answering arguments can be suggested?

Secondly: What radical objections may be taken to the whole proposal?

I. And, as a preliminary, it were well to ascertain what financial change would occur on the adoption of Free Education in England. I take the Balance Sheet of my own schools as a basis of calculation. They contain about 300 children, and last year (1888–1889) cost £600 to maintain —or £2 a head. This sum was raised in the following proportions: £250, or 16s. 8d. a head, reached us out of taxation in the form of Government grant; £150, or 10s. per head, were provided from voluntary sources; £200 or 13s. 4d. a head, came in the shape of pence from the parents. The proposal now is to throw this last item upon the locality, to be raised there in addition to any existing School Board rate. But the change will involve a further displacement: the item of voluntary aid, which at present meets one-fourth of the expense of our Schools, could not be relied upon to remain at that level. Even enthusiasts for denominational teaching will be pressed by the increased rates, and lessen their subscriptions; the lukewarm will probably drop them altogether; so that the alteration will not merely bring about the transfer to the rates of parents' payments: it will also bring about a loss of at least a third of the subscriptions, which will have to be made up out of rates. So that the probable Balance Sheet of the future, in a 'freed' Church School costing £600 to maintain, will run as follows—By Government grant, £250; from Voluntary sources, £100; by Rate, £250; or, in other words, the demand upon the pocket of the nation in respect of denominational schools alone will be doubled. This educational tax for 1888–1889 reached two millions: the addition to the School Board rate therefore threatens to reach another two millions, as soon as the schools are 'freed.'[1]

For this large increase of burden to be laid on the community the following are among the principal reasons urged:

(1) That Free Education is the logical sequence of the Act of 1870, and that, wherever there is compulsion, there ought to be payment in respect of the things required by the State.

The arguments which start from postulating certain unwritten rights of the citizen are highly effective in popular oratory; as when, for instance, Mr. Chamberlain asks, 'of

---

[1] Any other scheme which may be proposed laying the expense on the taxpayers rather than the ratepayers may serve to conceal the cost to the public; it will not diminish it.

the two chief obligations put on parents, why should vaccination be given, and education sold?' but such appeals have to face this historical fact, that the legislature has not recognised their *a priori* validity: each case is considered on its own merits: distinction is made between claim and claim; which would not be done, if the claims were all fundamentally and equally just. As a matter of practice, the cost of the community being secured against small-pox has been discharged by the State: but again, the cost of the community being secured against insanitary drains has not, for this is an obligation laid on the landlord. Mr. Forster provided power to establish certain Free Schools for the children of parents unable to pay fees—as a matter of expediency: it never occurred to him that education must be free wherever it was compulsory, as a matter of equity. And not only did it not occur to the author of the settlement of 1870, but one of the strongest supporters of compulsion, Mr. Fawcett, took issue with the Birmingham League on this very point, and protested against universal Free Schools. Was he the man to commit a logical injustice?

(2) But the same argument reappears in a form of lesser stringency—pleading that, if not unjust, it is at least inconsistent that parents should be forced to pay where they have no option as to incurring the debt.

It may be replied that, having borne that anomaly for twenty years, we might be content to let it abide as a tradition, side by side with many time-honoured absurdities which the Frenchman is more anxious to rectify than the Englishman. There might be some reason, however, why the matter is deemed more pressing now than at the outset of the new educational scheme: so the advocate of Free

Schools may be asked to show cause why he presses the matter *now*, and selects this above other apparent State anomalies as requiring to be altered. And he would probably answer that the difficulty of remitting the fees of impecunious parents has increased, and that to abolish all fees is a consequent necessity.

There is no doubt that it has been a crux from the beginning, how to provide a good machinery for determining cases of exemption from payment in School Board districts. For some time the Guardians acted—I believe in certain places they act still—but it was felt that parents incurred an unnecessary stigma in applying through the Relieving Officer. At present, in London at least, voluntary committees undertake the investigation and remit fees. A few years ago their methods were revised and put upon a basis which approved itself to the Chairman of the Board. Whence then the present outcry? I venture to think it does not come from parents—not even from hard-worked Committees, though they have an invidious task to perform—but mainly from the collectors of fees, the teachers, and officials of the schools. They find it difficult to get in the weekly pence, and they would gladly see them abolished. No doubt: but this is a very different plea from that of justice to parents, and must be met in a different way. When this is used as of force to bring about free schools, we are bound to point out that there is another outlet from the difficulty. We can improve the machinery; we can be firm, even generous with the officials. It would be cheaper to pay more for collection than to abandon a large source of revenue altogether in a fit of despair.

(3) There then occurs what is not so much an argument

addressed to the reasonable as an inducement put before the indolent. It is said, 'This must come: it is in the air: it is no use resisting it. Lord Salisbury has practically conceded Free Schools.' But every English Premier moves with the opinion of the country, and that opinion is neither so settled nor so pronounced as to require present action. Even if it were, the evil or good of any proceeding is not determined by the clamour for it. It is for those who believe there is mischief in the demand to demonstrate the mischief and see what resistance can effect. Nothing arises so soon, but nothing subsides so fast as a popular cry.

(4) But when the advocates of Free Education have exhausted their pleas, reasonable or specious, there is still an arrow left in the very phrase which describes their proposal: it is winged with the epithet 'free.' This is one of several deceptive words which fly about in these educational controversies. One class of schools is called 'National' when in truth it is distinctly representative of a religious body: the same class of schools is with equal infelicity still called 'Voluntary,' although compulsion applies to them (for better or for worse) as much as to any. We had begun to understand and make allowances for these fallacious epithets, and now we have a third unreality set before us in the prefix 'free.' It has great attraction for the easy-going: it is as if the master taught for nothing; or nobody was saddled with the cost of his teaching: therefore it must be excellent, and a thing to be voted for with both hands.

II. But let men who have minds and consciences pause a little: for the question admits of being looked at in another light, and may then possibly assume a very different complexion. I admit that my answers to the advocates of Free Education might be overruled, if there were nothing positive to be urged beside—no principle at issue, no social mischief underlying this attractive scheme.

It is proposed, in consideration of the poverty of some parents, to make all parents a present of the fees they have been accustomed to pay for their children in primary schools. This sounds a generous proposal: it is really a new and hazardous step: it does not mean the extension within its own sphere of a principle already at work: it means the intrusion of that principle into another and an alien sphere, to which, we contend, it is not applicable. For let us consider what the State has hitherto done in the way of tutelage. It has set itself to remedy—failures: children, for whom parents can make no provision at all, it has sent into work-house schools: children, over whom parents can exercise no control—these it has sent into industrial schools: children, for whom parents can make only part provision —finding food, but not education, these it has paid for in primary schools. Some consider that the State has gone too far in doing these things, but it cannot be questioned that the State has proceeded cautiously, has made investigations, even, in suitable cases, extracted pledges for repayment of the outlay incurred. Hitherto every care has been taken by the authorities to assume any parental function which the parents were able—morally and financially—to perform themselves. Now it is proposed to alter this; to make a fresh and insidious departure, concealing how much it means, and pretending that there is no rupture with the past. Now the State is to come forward and say to parents, capable as well as incapable, 'We will do for

your children, without reserve or enquiry, what hitherto
we have done, with reserve and after enquiry, only on
behalf of proved failures; for the future we will accept all
the children you send us, and teach them at the public cost.'
But this is an entire subversion of the principle which has
governed England hitherto. We have always impressed
upon parents that the children they had they must also
maintain until they could shift for themselves; that nutrition of mind was necessary as well as nutrition of body;
whereas now we are expected to turn round and say,
'nutrition of mind is exempted from your duties and converted into a State charge.' But is it possible to make a first
breach in parental responsibility which shall also be the
last? It becomes increasingly evident that nutrition of mind
is correlated to nutrition of body; that the payment of
school-fees is a farce for the unfed, and foolishness for the
half-clothed. The example will have been set that distinc-
tions as between the solvent and insolvent poor are either
impossible or invidious, and the State which begins to
teach gratuitously must—in the name of the consistency
invoked at the outset—end by establishing free meals and
free clothing for the behoof of all attending primary
schools. Nor do the socialists conceal that this is the object
aimed at by them, and their idea of the logical necessities
of the case. So our difference on this point from the State-
socialists is vital, and must be reasoned out. They see the
unequal distribution of this life's advantages; they perceive that superior education accounts for most of these
advantages; they fancy that by making education more
general they shall succeed in distributing these advantages,
and especially wealth, more equally. So they are for freeing

education at all cost. 'At all cost'—but have they really considered what the cost amounts to? They are thinking of it merely as a matter of £ *s. d.;* but is it only that? Can it be so limited? Do they not seek to be generous to the pockets of some men without being just to the nature of all men? Are they not worshipping the name of State, endowing it with unreal force, and fancying it can deal with the problems of life apart from the character of individuals, which, after all, is the main factor in solving the problem? For can the State be better than the persons composing the State? and can they be good without discipline? Now the discipline which has hitherto gone to the training of Englishmen has been of this nature. The child has been brought up as part of the small community called a home; there he has learnt what submission to authority means, through being subject to his parents; there he has learnt what co-operation means, through living with elder and with younger members of the family. Leaving home he has been thrown upon his own resources, and they have developed under pressure of the necessities of life: he has learnt to be prudent in foreseeing, versatile and courageous in meeting difficulties. Thus he is prepared in his turn to establish a home, to exert authority of his own, and to teach obedience to others. So by successive stages of often unconscious discipline a man becomes an orderly citizen; through submission, and independence, and the exercise of rule upon a small scale, he is fitted to combine with others trained after the like fashion in the great community of the State. But the present age is impatient; some of its hasty counsellors would dispense with preliminary training, and advise men that they can worthily take their places in a large society without having served any apprenticeship to the smaller. Acts of Parliament are henceforth to protect every citizen and labourer from many of the practical roughnesses which served to educate their forefathers; the State is asked to loosen some at least of the bonds which, as a child, attached him to his parents, and as a parent, bound him to his children. The Englishman is to become a good citizen *per saltum*, without having proved himself a good son, or a man of valour in the fight for existence. State socialism opposes science, and fancies it can improve the species physically by sparing us hardships, and morally by sparing us duties; whereas it is more likely to aid degeneration by encouraging the dependent character and discouraging the discipline of home.

Already among those classes of the metropolis which this proposal is intended to benefit, the parental tie is feeble; there is little sense of responsibility in having children; a weak control is exercised over them: there is considerable readiness to dispose of them to charitable institutions. The philanthropists who have most experience and who prefer radical to superficial improvement, are for appealing to family life and increasing the solidarity of home. Yet the proposals we are considering, if adopted, would inevitably thwart their efforts, and set the State to counterwork some of its wisest citizens. Mr. Fawcett, for instance, foresaw and deprecated this result of free schools as long ago as 1870, when the Birmingham League sought to make them universal. According to Mr. Leslie Stephen, in the biography he wrote of his friend, 'the fatal error, as he urged, was that the gratuitous system would diminish the sentiment of parental responsibility. To bring a child into the world was to incur a grave responsibility, and no action of the State should tend to obscure the fact. But to relieve a parent from the cost of his children's schooling would most emphatically diminish his motives for fore-thought.'

I might almost leave the controversy to stand or fall with this opinion of an educationalist so friendly to the working-classes and so fearless in counselling them; but there are two or three misconceptions as to the line of argument I have adopted which need notice. It is forcibly said in public, when this matter comes under discussion, that educated men have of long custom held exhibitions at school and the universities—have enjoyed in fact privi-leges which they now seek on principle to withhold from those of a lower class, who need them even more urgently. It is asked, 'has their discipline been injured by the advan-tages they enjoyed—or have the terrible things prophesied come to pass in their own homes?' And I can fancy students familiar with Mr. Fawcett's biography inclined to cry out against him when they read that, in selecting his college at the University, 'he chose Peterhouse deliberately on the ground that its fellowships were supposed to be of more than average value, and were tenable by laymen'; also that 'he won a Scholarship in the College Examination of May, 1854.' But I conceive there is a very complete defence for the Professor from any charge of inconsistency. I can imag-ine him answering that this personal argument ignored the difference between exceptional assisted and universal gratuitous education; that he was prepared to advocate the former for all classes, and deprecate the latter equally for all; that the advantages given to Exhibitioners and Scholars are on a level (not indeed in origin, but in effect) with the assistance given in every primary school to every parent who pays only thirteen or fourteen shillings a year out of a cost of forty. In either case there is a residue of duty left for the parent to discharge, and help does not supersede effort.

There are indeed some who are prepared to risk the deterioration of character threatened by those whom they think alarmists on account of the gain to be assured to education, as if every child were certain to come to school regularly as soon as there is nothing to pay. But does this expectation accord with our experience in such matters? Are gifts valued equally with things paid for? Are they not very much looked in the mouth, and criticised, and frequently rejected? In the case of children for whom we remit fees in our schools, a rule has had to be made that remission must depend on constant attendance; before this was done the irregularity was great. Let all fees be abolished and this resource fails. Other things being equal, regular attendance will certainly not improve but diminish with free schools. Nor do I imagine that compulsion will be found easier of enforcement than now, for it is not poverty which makes gaps in the school classes so much as mother's washing-day, and going on errands and attendance on the perambulator; which things, I presume, will continue much as before, being practically unavoidable. And illustrations come to us from countries where free schools are in force. Statements as to America have appeared in the public press, but perhaps the analogy of our own recent colonies is more in point. I have before me a letter from a lady who has long resided in New Zealand, and has paid careful attention to the working of its institutions, especially those which deal with the young. She writes—'Unless where compulsion is most rigidly carried out (a task of immense practical difficulty), the very children for whom a free education is provided do not attend the schools.' 'Free schools will not necessarily ensure the education of the lowest class; indeed we see a directly contrary effect; for the middle class gladly avail themselves of the advantages offered by primary schools, and send their children to them. Such children are a credit to the teachers, who naturally encourage this better class rather than the shifting, ill-mannered children of the poorest and the improvident.' I admit how pathetic all this is: how honourable is the purpose in a new country of improving on the methods of the old, and endeavouring that the sons should be better taught than their fathers were in England; but the failure constitutes a lesson that State machinery cannot bring about the improvement desired—indeed, stands in the way of it, because it impairs the one method of effecting slowly what it seeks vainly to effect hastily. For (again quoting from my correspondent) 'there is an increasing tendency on the part of the population of the colony to look to the Government for help, and such legislation in the name of progress shifts the centre of gravity in the moral world from the parent to the State—slowly but surely undermining the foundation of national life by the deterioration of the unit of the family.'

There will remain, I suppose, to the last a sentimental desire to give away whatever we prize as an infallible method of distributing it: there is also the general charm which socialistic schemes have for those who are in arms against the selfishness of the world, and believe that the true way of combating it lies in wide schemes of regulation. The two errors run up into one; and that one is a forgetfulness of the laws of virtue as laid down centuries ago in Athens and tested by long experience. There is no moral improvement possible without 'purpose': you cannot leave the will of the man himself out of question: what you bestow on him does not avail, unless it rouses his own determination to follow it up: wherein you coerce him for his own benefit, you do him no lasting benefit at all, as long as you retain the reins of restraint, and are unwilling or unable to trust him with them. It is the appetite for being taught which has to be created, and which must precede all machinery for satisfying it. But what creates appetite is not supply, it is exertion. There is no need to increase the difficulties of learning, but there is need of caution how they are diminished and education made too cheap and easy. The children cannot be separated from their parents in the estimate of school. What the young see the elder appreciate, they will appreciate, and the obligation which they find them ready to transfer to any who will undertake it, they will lightly esteem. Personal payment is a sign of value attached to the thing purchased: it may be reduced to a small sum quite out of proportion to the thing purchased, but as soon as it is abolished altogether, the whole matter of education falls to a lower level—the thing received becomes, like gas or water, an article laid on by the municipality, paid for out of the rates, and mental benefits assume a material complexion fatal to their majesty and worth.

In conclusion, let me reiterate that what moves me against Free Education is that it is a new departure; the application of an enervating doctrine to the roots of English discipline. The State would virtually say to thousands of parents, 'You have failed, and the ratepayers shall remove from you the last remnant of educational duties, and undertake to teach your children for you. Probably you will also be relieved of the cost of feeding and clothing them: but this is in suspense for a time, to see how you receive the earlier plan—whether you resent it as an indignity to learning and yourselves, or welcome it as an instalment due from the selfishness of the wealthy.'

I appeal to parents to suspect what the political parties vie with each other in thrusting upon them. Is it not a bribe? I appeal also to thinkers, who observe life and study character. Is there not a more excellent way? Can we not imagine and by determination realise an England which shall be pure without the supervision of a Vigilance Society, sober—even in the face of a thousand public-houses, open at all hours, and fond of knowledge, although—and even because—knowledge has to be won at the cost of self-denial, being the best inheritance a man can bequeath to his children as the fruit of the exertions of a lifetime.

B. H. Alford

Note—The writer has intentionally limited himself to criticism of the recent proposal to 'free' schools: he has declined to turn aside to discuss how far the school system in present use is satisfactory, either from the point of view of learning or the point of view of liberty. He has been content with the endeavour to show that any change in the way of gratuitous teaching would be a change for the worse.

CHAPTER 8

THE HOUSING
OF THE WORKING-CLASSES
AND OF THE POOR

ARTHUR RAFFALOVICH

CHAPTER 8

THE HOUSING OF THE WORKING-CLASSES AND OF THE POOR

It is a distinguishing feature of the end of this nineteenth century that human sentiment has become more than ever anxious about the condition of the working-classes, and has turned to a study of their position and to a search for ways and means of improving their lot.

Economists of the liberal school form no exception. They share in the universal solicitude which at the present time is assuming many forms. Some of these, whether their authors know it or not, are dangerous; some are actually harmful. Reasonable economists refuse to be drawn into accepting solutions too easily formulated. They know, thanks to an industrious study of economic and financial phenomena, what is the true effect of the incidence not only of taxes, but also of the incidence of legislation. They cannot forget, for example, the deplorable effects of the old Poor Law in England. They fear that the plans of the socialists, whether of the study, the senate, or the street,

349

the demands of sanitary reformers, the sentimentality of philanthropists, will infallibly lead to consequences diametrically opposed to the results aimed at.

By the side of the claims made in the name of the great mass of labourers, in the name of the industrial proletariate and of the poor, there has arisen during the last fifteen or twenty years a new danger. It has its origin in a false conception of the attributes and powers of the State. We refer to the claims made on behalf of a system of official and governmental hygiene, which pretends to abolish insanitary conditions of life, to make healthy dwellings and workshops, in a word, to take under control the private lives of the citizens. In the opinion of many people at the present day, the modern State should be called on to determine the rate of wages, the length of the working-day, the price of provisions and other necessaries of life; to divide profits among the different branches of native industry, by the aid of innumerable laws, by a protective tariff, and by means of an army of inspectors. The Sanitarians ('Hygienistes' in the French term), in their turn, set out a programme of requirements and dictate the conditions under which houses are to be built and inhabited, the nature of the materials to be used, and the number of the tenants.

Hygiene, as M. Leon Say declared at the meeting of the 28th June, 1890, at the Academy of Moral and Political Sciences, has become a science of much wider scope than formerly. It is not content to advise on matters concerning cleanliness, food, and the sanitation of the dwelling-house, but it claims to be able to prevent the spread of epidemics by carrying on an offensive warfare against the germs of disease.

Whether these pretensions are well founded or not, they have rendered sanitation popular. It has also created a group of Sanitarians who wish State protection to be introduced everywhere. M. Leon Say suggests a doubt whether people will be happier when the Sanitarians become master and succeed in regulating our lives to the minutest detail. In his opinion those who look at this matter from the scientific point of view should spare no effort to check this new protectionist movement. M. Leon Say has declared himself before all things a strong advocate of private initiative, all the more so because the limits of the rights of the State in the matter of hygiene cannot be determined.[1]

This conception of the State, as possessed of the attributes of omnipotence and providence, does not find favour with everyone. But even the select minority, which condemns all this absorption of economic activity, this reduction of labour to a state of pupilage, resists but feebly the pretensions of hygiene, and so it comes that we find in an essay by the Comte d'Haussonville the following phrase, which shows us how far the error which we are discussing has advanced:

---

[1] Hygiene has, in fact, become an official career. Those who fill the posts given by the State, seek to make themselves indispensable. One of the most distinguished of French doctors wrote to me recently that it will be necessary to make a new '89' against the tyranny of hygiene, and to risk a revolution in order to gain our liberty of eating and drinking, and to limit the busybodydom of Sanitarians in the concerns of our private life.

> The State, I mean by the term the power of the public which
> is exercised by the central or municipal authority, is primarily
> the guardian of the public health, of public and moral hygiene.
> As it is the duty of the State to take measures to prevent the
> birth of epidemics and to arrest their progress, so also it is its
> duty in a general way to see that the lives of its citizens are
> passed under conditions of good hygiene.[2]

The reader must not suppose from our protest against
the meddlesomeness of official hygienists that we are indifferent to the very great importance of good sanitary arrangements, but we believe that there are methods of
attaining our ends other and better than those put forward
by the prophets of universal interference.

Before embarking on the discussion of the Housing of
the Poor, we may here interpose a statement of the elaborate programme of the German socialists which will appear to contain the maximum of demand of this kind.

In 1873 the German socialists considered a petition intended for presentation to the Reichstag. It contained the
following points:

(1) Every commune ought to be compelled by legislation to provide lodging sufficient for those within its jurisdiction, and as far as possible in detached dwellings.

(2) Every commune shall be authorised to appropriate
lands not yet built on, whoever the proprietor may be, in
order to construct dwellings and school-houses; further, it
shall be at liberty to exercise this right of expropriation
even outside its own territory.

---

[2] Cte. de Haussonville *Socialisme d'État et Socialisme Chrétien, Revue des
Deux Mondes* du 15 Juin, 1890, p. 859.

(3) The State shall provide sufficient capital under the form of paper-money.

(4) This paper-money shall be secured as a charge on the lands and buildings. Each commune shall receive the necessary sums in the shape of an advance without interest, and with the obligation to repay after a long period.

(5) Whoever has claim to a dwelling will pay a suitable rent-premium and must himself inhabit the dwelling.

(6) The communes shall remain proprietors of the land and buildings. They may not however disturb any of their tenants in the enjoyment of their premises, so long as the conditions of tenancy are fulfilled. As a temporary measure every commune is obliged to provide shelter provisionally for those who have none until dwellings are made.

These propositions, and even the idea of petitioning, were strongly opposed. By a large majority it was declared that these propositions were reactionary and altogether too moderate; that their authors wished to deceive the people of Berlin, and that the meeting rejected all such rubbish. Workmen were invited to join themselves to the association of German workmen in order to solve the Social question by common action on the lines of Liberty.[3]

---

[3] M. Engels, the fellow-worker of Marx, and the philosopher of revolutionary socialism, has attacked what he calls the 'bourgeois' solution of making the workman the owner of his house. In Germany, according to him, the number of workmen in the small industries who own their houses and a little bit of garden, is very considerable; none of them, however, receive anything but a miserable wage. It is only a trick to enable the infamous capitalist to buy his labour cheaper in proportion to the extra production of the labourer and his family on their own land. As they cannot live by the trade of agriculture alone, they are content with very

To show what is asked for in France, we may state that an administrative commission was appointed, in 1883, by the Préfet of the Seine in order to study the question relative to the creation in Paris of cheap dwellings. A score of projects and petitions were examined by this commission, a labour which has not yet borne fruit. Nationalisation of the soil according to the gospel of Henry George, and schemes for lotteries were agreeably mixed. One councillor demanded in the interest of the town of Paris the confiscation of the soil within the circle of fortifications, and the compensation of landlords by means of communal bonds secured by mortgage and redeemable. M. Lerouge proposed the construction, by the town, of three-storied houses on the land adjoining the fortifications within the walls by means of capital raised (1) by a loan of 300 millions of francs, (2) by a tax of 2 francs per head on every one coming to Paris from a distance greater than twenty-five kilometres. The Federative Socialist Union of the Centre demands the application of the surplus of the forthcoming budget, to the construction by the town of Paris of workmen's dwellings, and the establishment of a tax of 20 per cent on dwellings remaining unoccupied for a month. We meet also many proposals for a lottery with a capital of a milliard of francs, for the purpose of making

---

small wages to make ends meet. This state of things has its influence on the town-workman, and contributes to keep the rate of his wages very low. In time past the ownership of his house was perhaps a benefit to the labourer; today it is a cause of bondage for himself and a misfortune for the entire working-class. According to M. Engels, the insanitary condition and dearness of dwellings are the necessary accompaniment of our present social organisation, and will only disappear with it.

dwellings for those members of the Parisian proletariate whose income does not exceed a certain figure.

In England the demand made on the State varies. At one time it is for the multiplication of inspectors of nuisances and an enlargement of their duties and powers; at another it adopts the language of the Social Democratic Federation, and insists on 'the compulsory construction of healthy artisans' and agricultural labourers' dwellings in proportion to the population.' The Glasgow municipality has already made some experiments in the building of artisans' dwellings, and the London County Council is proposing to build common lodging-houses.

To sum up the views of these reformers, some are in favour of a nationalisation of dwellings; others demand that the State or the local authority shall build for its own functionaries, for workmen and for the poor; others wish to combat the *usury* of the landlord, the excessive price sought for dwellings which are insanitary and too small.

Among the most important factors of development physical, moral, and intellectual, the Dwelling must be placed in the first rank; it is the sphere in which the life of the individual and of the family is passed. No one denies the inconveniences, physical and moral, of the insanitary dwellings inhabited by a portion of the working-class and by the poor. The miserable condition of their homes, the overcrowding which reigns there with its following of disease of all kinds, with its accompaniment of crime and vice, the permanent danger which results therefrom to public health and public order, all these have been oftentimes brought to light. We are not dealing with a curse purely local, for indeed it appears to be universal. Everywhere we meet the same melancholy phenomena, in France, in England, in the United States, in Germany, in Switzerland, in Austria, in Belgium, in Holland.

Attempts have been made to remedy this by legislation, by sanitary regulations, and by the assistance of charity. Progress has been made; but it has not been possible to transform the dwellings of the workmen and of the poor (I speak of the great mass of the wage-earning class) into proper and comfortable quarters; above all, it has not been possible, even by artificial means, to increase the resources and wages of the poor to any sufficient extent.

The knot of the difficulty is the poverty of those who live huddled up in infectious hovels, ignorant or indifferent to the requirements of hygiene, of modesty and decency. This may be the result of circumstances or may proceed from evil habits of intemperance and idleness, or from mere absence of desire, due to inexperience of better things.

All the harrowing descriptions which we have read, and which we have been able to verify, combine to make more pressing the solution of the problem—'How to improve the housing of the working-class and of the poor?' It is admitted that the present condition is deplorable as regards the health not only of the inhabitants themselves, but of the whole town, because these insanitary dwellings are the breeding place of infectious diseases. The misery which they endure in this respect makes workmen and the poor an easy prey for the propagation of revolutionary ideas; a social danger is thus added to the physical danger. The lodging of the poor is one of the most complicated subjects and most difficult of solution. It forms one of the branches of the entire social problem equally with questions of food and clothing. The same rules and the same principles, with certain restrictions obvious enough to common sense, apply to this whole combination of problems. The part of the State and of municipalities is clearly indicated—their mission is above all a mission of hygiene and of police—it is to make war on insanitary dwellings; but this action must be subordinated to some indispensable conditions.[4]

One cannot under any circumstances ask the State to supply dwellings or food gratuitously, or under cost price, without doing an injustice to those who do not share in these favours, and without risk of demoralising the poorer classes. Such food and dwelling at a cheap rate entail a loss on the State, which requires the imposition of a tax to meet it. This increase of taxation falls on the whole nation, and falls most heavily on the poor. Such State aid has moreover a further disadvantage. It discourages private enterprise and private industry. If the State constructs, or causes others to construct, houses to be let below cost price, it impedes private building and produces a result the very reverse of that hoped for.

Insanitary conditions proceed from the great crowding of human beings in buildings which were not made for the accommodation of so great a number of persons, from the entire neglect of sanitary rules, and from the accumulation of filth.

---

[4] We are aware of the English laws of 1875 and 1885 giving to the local authorities the power to improve, if necessary to demolish, insanitary areas in cases where the responsibility cannot be equitably fastened on an individual owner. These laws have been applied in London and Birmingham. In London there has been spent in this way some £1,841,176. The original estimates have always been exceeded, sometimes doubled, or even trebled. 33,000 persons can be lodged in the improved districts.

The causes of this overcrowding are the extreme poverty of the inhabitants which prevents their seeking for houses, healthier, larger, and in consequence dearer, and which forbids any great number of them living at a distance from the place where they earn their living; the increase of population due to natural causes and also to the constant immigration of workmen drawn from the country or provincial towns towards the capital; lastly, the demolition of quarters inhabited by workmen, which have disappeared to give place to new streets, railway stations, and markets, or which have been swept away for reasons connected with the health or embellishment of the town. For this extreme want there is no remedy. Poverty is incurable. For the cure of bad habits, in respect of cleanliness, we must arm ourselves with patience. This is a matter of education.

By the aid of an active and energetic watchfulness on the part of local authorities, we might, it will be said, prevent the existence of insanitary dwellings, force landlords to keep their property in a better state; we might exercise a closer inspection of the construction of new houses and require that they come up to a certain minimum of sanitation. But it must not be forgotten that in many countries laws and police regulations have not been wanting, that there has been no lack of weapons in the administrative arsenal. We must not lose sight of the fact that legislation against bad sanitation requires, in order to be effective, a complicated and costly staff of inspectors perpetually on the move; that the application of rules depends less on the officials and magistrates than it does on the inhabitants themselves, who are more disposed to evade than to conform to regulation. If the poorer classes inhabit garrets, cellars, holes and corners, without light or air in houses badly built and badly kept up, it is because they cannot find better at a price which they can pay, and they prefer to lodge in these hovels rather than not be lodged at all. So we are brought back to our problem the solution of which, to say the least, is very difficult—given a great town, to furnish the poor population which accumulates there, with lodging, suitable, spacious, airy, and provided with everything that is desirable.

Let us resolutely exclude heroic remedies, which can only be worse than the disease. We mean the remedies of socialistic formulas. There is no one formula or panacea. It is to the progress of comfort, moral education, of the practical instruction of the industrial classes, that we must look for the gradual amelioration of the hygienic conditions of populous centres. Public administrators can without doubt carry out useful works and improve the general state of sanitation by the construction of drains, and by procuring water at a reasonable rate; general rules also can be established for the safe guard of the public health, but it is wise to think twice before allowing authority to interfere in the domain of private life, on the plea of the public safety.

It cannot be forgotten that every infraction of the liberty of contract carries in itself the germs of retribution. Try to protect the workman against the extortion of his landlord by the intervention of the law and we all know the unfortunate consequences which result. It is useless to waste our time over projects of fixing a dwelling-house tariff by the local authority.

Among the most efficacious means of influencing the homes of the working-class, we must set the improvement of ways of communication and facility and cheapness of transport.

Satisfactory results have been obtained by private initiative by the construction of model mansions, of working-class cities. The portion of the working-class who are in the easiest circumstances, those who earn a regular wage, have to some extent obtained their requirements from this source, and in consequence there are so many the less to be brought into line with the others.

It is the business of private industry, of philanthropic enterprise, of associations of workmen themselves, to supply better dwellings. If the buildings set apart for the dwellings of workmen brought in a fair revenue their number would at once increase. But I repeat, it is only by reflex action that we can hope to reach those whom the English call the residuum, the dregs of destitution. The work must proceed step by step, stratum by stratum. First, we must offer houses relatively comfortable and healthy, with an option to the tenants to become owners. Here we shall be dealing with the *élite* of the working-class, and with small *employees* (these last are as interesting as the workman and have much more to complain of, for they are liable to more expense), but the indirect result of the improvement will be felt down to the very bottom of the scale.

I have insisted from the very beginning of this paper on what I might call the negative side of the problem, on the objections to every intervention of the local or national authority, and to State trading in dwellings. I have insisted on the great difficulty of the problem, on the poverty of those who inhabit crowded, unhealthy, and inconvenient rooms, and on the excessive price, in proportion to their resources, which they have to pay. The more modest the income, the more serious becomes the proportion of it absorbed by rent. In the workman's budget the fifth or the fourth part of his wages is devoted to rent.

I have hastened to arrive at positive results in order to come in view of the bright side of my subject, and, after having displayed its difficulties, to show what private initiative has been able to undertake. Progress must come from the *élite* of the governed acting for themselves. The weight of a sound and persistent public opinion is an essential factor, and we can all do something to keep it watchful and awake. We must try to prevent the return of those periods of apathy and indifference which follow the shock of a somewhat lively agitation, the revelations made by writers, or the close of an epidemic. But, even during these periods when attention wanders to other objects, philanthropists or economists, reformers or capitalists follow their voluntary mission, seek to educate the rich and comfortable classes, and to call them to a recognition of the social duties which they have to perform.

We may be permitted to pay a compliment to the Academy of the Moral and Political Sciences, which for the last forty-one years have devoted much serious attention to this grave problem. The Society of Social Economy, under the influence of MM. Picot and Cheysson, has devoted many sittings to the question, and, taking one step further, has by means of private initiative organised an enquiry and addressed an appeal to men of public spirit. It carries out, in its own organ *La Réforme Sociale*, the publication of the reports which it has collected.

The English parliamentary enquiries are well known, as is also the private enquiry made in Germany by the care of the *Verein für Sozialpolitik*.

During the Universal Exhibition of 1889, a Congress on cheap dwellings was held at Paris, which voted, among other resolutions, to recommend the formation of national societies. It should be the object of these bodies, by means of conferences, publications, collection of information, to encourage the industrial- and working-class in the construction of healthy and cheap houses, by the help of co-operation or local associations. It recommended also the formation of an International Society for the study of questions relating to the improvement, sanitation, and construction of cheap dwellings.

At the conclusion of a conference held on the 1st February, 1890, at Paris, the French *'Association des habitations à bon marché,'* was founded. It numbers more than 300 members, and has control of a considerable capital. It does not itself engage in building, but makes it its business to stimulate public opinion by lectures and by pamphlets, and to assist with advice and information, those directly interested (the wage-earning and working-class), as well as the capitalist class, in the construction of houses to be let at low rentals. Its action has already made itself felt in France. Here in truth is an example of private initiative worthy of imitation outside of France.

The collection of works dealing with the housing of the working-class and of the poor would already fill a library, and it increases every day.[5]

---

[5] A bibliography has been published by MM. Raffalovich and Rouillet, chez Rongier et Cie, Éditeurs. Paris.

Great successes have been achieved on a practical basis. They have been gained where the matter has been treated on a business footing, not as a matter of charity pure and simple. It is of the highest importance to prove that the capital engaged in the construction of sanitary dwellings is not lost, that it has obtained a fair remuneration, and that it has every chance of security. Proof of this is indispensable, if other capital is to be attracted. It has been proved to demonstration in England, in France, in the United States, in Belgium, in Denmark. The capitalists, who have either turned builders themselves or subscribed to joint-stock companies, or bought and repaired old houses, have, it is true, limited the remuneration of their capital to a sum lower than that which some owners derive from the purely commercial development of their real estate.

They content themselves with a return of 4 per cent in France, in England, and in Germany, and of 5 or 6 per cent in the United States. They have got rid of the charitable character of their enterprise, which is humiliating for those who profit by it. People do not appreciate a gratuitous benefit equally with that which they have gained for themselves at cost of personal exertion. To be complete we must add another category, namely philanthropists, like Peabody, Michel and Armand Heine, who have devoted large sums of capital to the inauguration of the work, leaving the rents to accumulate for the extension of the operation. The tenant in such cases enters into an ordinary contract, and, as far as he is concerned, the transaction is of a purely commercial nature.

If this supply of healthy and relatively cheap dwellings has not brought about a lower rate of rent it is because the supply is still limited. We know, however, of places where rent has decreased in the immediate neighbourhood of these more comfortable houses, notably at Lyons. Even when it is not possible to supply accommodation at a price appreciably lower than the market rate, it still remains that new dwellings, built in a spirit of progress and philanthropy, present conditions of health and convenience far superior to anything to be found by their side. In this way, the means of having a real home which will keep together the members of the family, and prevent them from seeking outside for unwholesome distractions, is placed within the reach of the working-class, particularly of the *élite* of that class.

Long ago the question of working-class dwellings has been solved, as far as concerns the part of the population which works in factories established outside of the towns. For the most part in the great mining and mineral industries, as well as in the country factories for spinning and weaving, etc., where a great number of workmen are regularly employed, the dwellings necessary for the workman and his family have been added as an *annexe*.

This creation of such villages as are to be seen in the industrial regions of the north, east, and west of France, forms part of the normal outlay of capital required from large employers of labour. The employers have an interest in attracting and retaining in the neighbourhood of their works the labourers whom they require, and in settling them there under conditions favourable to their health and to the moral and material welfare of their families. It is this clear understanding of the interest of industry which has created these groups of working-class dwellings, and which makes the extension of the system certain, especially where the nature and importance of the establishment render it possible.

For France we may quote the case of Anzin, le Creuzot, Commentry, Blanzy, Beaucourt, Noisiel. In the coal districts of the north in 1875 eighteen firms out of twenty-three had built 7000 houses, at a cost of eighteen million francs. The rent of these was very considerably lower than the ordinary rent of such houses. In England many instances of this kind can be quoted; the best known are the establishments of the Salts at Saltaire, Messrs. Hazell, Watson & Viney, printers, at Aylesbury, Messrs. Cadbury Bros., cocoa manufacturers, at Bourneville, Messrs. Unwin Bros., printers, Chilworth, Messrs. Courtauld & Co., crape manufacturers, Halstead, and the many colliery villages belonging to large-minded employers of labour like the Peases of Darlington. In America the industrial village is more familiar, and the best example is furnished by the American Watch Co. in the village of Waltham, which has now the largest watch factory in the world. In Prussia seventy industrial firms have built 529 houses, of which their workmen may become owners; 1141 have built 8751 houses for letting. Out of 4850 industrial firms 34 per cent have provided, directly or indirectly, for the lodging of their workmen (1878). In the coal basin of Saarbruck 3742 houses have been built. The miners' banks have contributed 2,062,000 marks, the State, the proprietor of the mines, has advanced 1,897,000 marks, of which, in 1874, 814,000 marks had been redeemed. At the Silesian mines, in 1872, 450 houses had already been built, containing house-room for 1800 families. The most important experiment was that of Krupp at Essen, where out of a staff of

65,776 persons, 18,698 in 1881 were living in houses belonging to M. Krupp.

These few figures show that it is in their own best interests that employers have been prompted to provide for the
housing of their workmen. In a certain number of cases
they have in addition given facility to their men to become
owners of their houses by payment of annual sums, calculated so that the purchase-money is met by payments
spread over a more or less extended period.

Very great importance rightly attaches to the possibility
of turning the workman or the petty *employee* into a
landed proprietor. It is the best means of encouraging the
spirit of order, of economy, and of inculcating the all-
valuable sentiment of personal responsibility.

Among the institutions which aim at the creation of
cheap dwellings we must distinguish the different objects
which each has in view.

(1) Those which aim at building small houses, with
facility given to the tenant to become owner by means of
annual instalments. Such building can be done by associations of working-men and small capitalists, by joint-stock
companies, or by individual capitalists.

(2) Those which aim at building large houses with accommodation for many tenants.

(3) Those which seek to improve old houses.

These objects are pursued by a variety of organisations,
viz.:

I. BUILDING SOCIETIES.   Those who attach a great value
to individual action, to self-help, and to the co-operation
of individual effort, will understand why we put Building

Societies in the first rank.[6] Their name of building societies indicates the primary object of these associations, but it no longer describes their present mode of operation. They no longer build (at most they finish the construction of houses left unfinished by borrowers). They are essentially loan societies, their capital comes from contributions paid as a rule month by month, but their advances are only made on the security of real estate, land or houses. The peculiarity of these advances is that they are repayable, capital and interest, by monthly payments. It follows that as these societies receive a portion of their capital at once they are able to make advances much larger in proportion to the actual value of the mortgaged property than an ordinary creditor. This mode of advance is very advantageous to persons of small fortune. The workman earning a good wage, the clerk, the small shopkeeper, although he has but a small disposable capital, is able to buy his house, and often becomes owner of it at the end of twelve or fourteen years, for a total sum of not much in excess of what he would have had to pay in rent alone.

In the United Kingdom, on Dec. 31, 1886, there were 2079 societies, of which 1992 were in England, 46 in Scotland, and 41 in Ireland. Their mortgage property amounts to £53,101,000. They owe 35-1/3 millions to their shareholders and £15,837,000 to other depositors.[7]

---

[6] According to the definition of the law of 1874, Building Societies are established for the collection of funds or capital in order to make advances to their members on real property by way of mortgage. Some also make advances on shares, but this is the exception.

[7] In Leeds, a town of 320,000 inhabitants, two societies account together

A building society often works in alliance with an estate or land society, which purchases at a low price large areas of land and re-sells them by lot with the extra profit which the building of a city gives.

The English co-operative societies have organised building departments, or have affiliated themselves to building societies.[8]

The number of co-operative building and loan associations spread throughout the great American republic may be fixed at between 3000 and 3500. The savings accumulated during forty years in the shape of houses and land and paid by the occupants and their families, must certainly exceed one hundred millions, reckoned in English money, and reaches perhaps one hundred and sixty millions. For the last twelve years in Philadelphia alone these accumulations of capital are reckoned at twenty millions sterling, and the yearly deposits at more than one million. At the present time the deposited savings amount to forty millions sterling for this town alone. In the whole country there are six times as many building societies as here.

In Philadelphia out of a population of 900,000 souls, 185,000 were workmen, and out of this number it is calculated that 40,000 to 50,000 workmen were owners of their own houses. It is true that at Philadelphia the land on which the town is built permits an unlimited extension,

---

for 11,000 members. In the last twenty years more than 18,000 houses have passed through the hands of the Leeds Permanent Building Society. The average value of a house is £166. In 1886, 9400 were mortgaged, of which 3000 belonged to workmen. In Newcastle, Birmingham, and Bristol, we find the same facts as at Leeds.

[8] Sixty societies have spent more than £500,000 in the building of cottages.

and each year the city surrounds itself with a new ring of neat little houses of red brick, each of which forms the home of a single family. The public health is better at Philadelphia than at New York. From the point of view of poor-law and charitable relief the comparison is equally favourable, for with its 900,000 inhabitants Philadelphia hardly spends more than Boston, which has a population of 360,000. Workmen are not afraid to go for lodging to the suburbs and to make a railway journey of an hour or three-quarters of an hour twice a day. The system of street railways is nowhere so fully developed as at Philadelphia. In New York building societies have made great and sudden progress. From January to September, 1888, more than 15,000 persons became members.

We may congratulate ourselves on this rapid development; we have here the proof that, with the aid of suitable associations, persons earning two shillings per day can create a capital and can lend it to others. At the same time it is not necessary to deny the dangers which may result from ignorance of the most elementary rules of finance and account-keeping, and from a tendency to speculate among those who lead and form the membership of these societies.

The system of building societies is certainly one of the best contrivances to give birth to a spirit of economy among persons who have but a very small income to spend. It offers a great attraction to those who pay rent for house or boarding-house accommodation and who wish to free themselves from it. Borrowing, which so easily demoralises a workman, becomes in this case a stimulant to thrift and wise household economy.

Outside of the Anglo-Saxon countries we meet with associations for building in Denmark. At Copenhagen an association has been founded, in 1865, by the workmen of the firm of Burmeister and Wain. It numbered, in 1884, 13,500 members; it has aided in the construction of 562 houses to the value of five and a-half million francs, and inhabited by 4381 persons. A quarter of the sums advanced has been repaid, and 200 new houses are being built. Similar societies exist in many Danish towns; in Switzerland (notably at Bâle); in Germany under the influence of Schulze-Delitzsch, the great promoter of the co-operative movement in Germany, great importance has always been attached to the co-operation of small capitalists for the purpose of combined action in the construction and purchase of houses; but it does not seem that this movement, which has produced such remarkable results in England and the United States, has been equally fruitful on the other side of the Rhine. Instances are to be found at Insterburg, Halle, Flensburg. In 1886 a society of this kind was formed at Berlin (Berliner Baugenossenschaft). The system adopted is that of a weekly deposit, giving a right to a share of 250 francs. When anyone has been a member for six months and owns at least one share, he may lay claim to a house when its building is finished. If there are several candidates, lots are drawn.

We shall speak later of the permanent society of Orleans. At Reims, the real estate union (L'Union Foncière) was founded, in 1870, by the *employees* and workmen of the town. It is a co-operative society for the construction of working-class dwellings, and commenced its operations in 1873. Members of the society are required to pay an entrance fee, which is not returnable and to contribute an annual deposit of twenty-five francs at the least, bearing interest at five per cent. The society possessed some years ago forty-eight houses, each of which had cost from 4500 to 6000 francs. The yearly instalment to be paid by those who mean to become proprietors in twenty years varies from 250 to 450 francs.

At the risk of seeming to lack method, we must here interpose a word in passing on the co-operation of Savings Banks, fed as they are by the thrift of the poorer classes. In Italy and in the United States they employ a part of their funds for mortgage loans, to facilitate the construction of cheap houses. Men whose opinion is entitled to respect have urged the same duty on the Savings Banks of France. Thanks to M. Aynard of Lyons and to M. Rostand of Marseilles, a first step has been taken in this direction.[9]

II. We come next to the Joint-Stock Company (Société anonyme), whose business it is to build cheap houses and to sell them by means of yearly instalments to workmen. The list is happily a very long one, and we cannot pretend to set it out in any completeness.

In the first rank, on the continent, we must mention '*La Société des Cités Ouvrières*' of Mulhouse. With a capital of some hundred thousand francs, to which are added loans guaranteed by the Society, 1200 working-class houses have been built in the space of thirty years; a thousand of these houses have been paid for by purchasers by means of a deduction from their wages, the amount of which has

---

[9] See *Les Questions d'Économie sociale dans une grande ville populaire,* par Eugène Rostand.

not been much in excess of the ordinary rents paid in other parts of the town.[10] At Paris we find *'La Société anonyme*

---

[10] At Mulhouse, the number of houses built on 30 June, 1888, was 1124, against 948 on 30 June, 1887. There have been, therefore, 176 houses built in ten years, costing on an average 3160 marks (3950 francs). The total sum paid by the purchasers is 3,539,495 marks. They remain debtors for 367,681 marks. Turning to the cost price, which is 2,788,220, this shows a profit of 1,118,956 marks to meet taxes, interest, charges of transfer for this period of thirty-five years, say about 50 per cent. In the return for 1877, the sum due was 604,041 marks; it has been reduced to 236,360 marks. The sum paid by workmen in these eleven years has reached 983,663 marks.

In 1877, the house with a story was sold for 3400 marks; houses with a ground-floor only, were sold for 2600 marks. The prices have today risen to 4480 and 2760 marks. The price of the storied house had thus risen 32 per cent and that of the single storied house only 6 per cent; and the rise represents the rise in the price of labour, and in the value of the land. This one-storied house has not been built since 1886; workmen prefer the storied house, and it has been found necessary to enlarge the dimensions. This in part explains the advance in price which is due to the increased value of the ground, the expense of building, and to the improvements added to the original plans.

M. de Lacroix, in a report on the Institutions of Public Utility in La Haute Alsace from 1878 to 1888, asks if this house of 4480 francs, which has now taken the place of that valued at 2760 francs, and which up to this date had been generally built, was not too dear for a working-class family whose income has not increased in the same proportion.

'It appears that it is not so, and the cause is not that which we could have wished. The ground-floor cottage with its kitchen and two little rooms could only with difficulty be made to serve for more than one family. It was not in fact built for this purpose, and it would have been desirable that it should never be diverted from its original use. The laws of hygiene would have been better observed. But the purchasers in their anxiety to discharge their debt sought too often to create a source of revenue by letting a room or even a small tenement; and it is this cause which has given rise to all the irregular gable ends and additions, which the Society cannot prevent, and which gives to the parts of the towns occupied by one-storied dwellings an aspect so odd and unseemly. Once embarked on this road the workman sees that the storied house lends itself better to this trade, and his demand is therefore for that class

des habitations ouvrières de Passy-Auteuil' founded with a capital of 200,000 francs. This society has limited the maximum interest payable on its capital to 4 per cent per

---

of house. The Society supplies his demand, and it is thus that the new storied house of 1887 appeared. But what happens? the owner makes three tenements of his house. One on the ground-floor, one on the first floor, and another in the attics. He occupies one himself, generally the ground or first floor, and lets the two others—one at ten or twelve marks per month, the other at four marks; and in this way he gets nearly five per cent. interest on the purchase-money remaining due after his first deposit of 240 marks has been made. But at the price of how much inconvenience? This house, which is intended to shelter one family of five persons, shelters three families of perhaps ten or twelve persons—and all the rules of hygiene are set at defiance. Too often these houses, without the possibility of objection on the part of the Society, and without, in many instances, its knowledge, pass into the hands of speculators who do not inhabit them, and who have no other object in view but to crowd them as much as possible in order to derive a larger revenue from them.

M. de Lacroix adds, sadly, that the great idea dreamt of by the founders of the Permanent City of Mulhouse, has not yet borne all its fruit. 'If on the one hand we have succeeded in awakening in some the instinct of thrift and family life, our success in solving the problem of healthy and cheap dwellings is still very imperfect. It is true that the Society could have succeeded completely in this second part of its task if it had retained ownership and merely let its houses. This is done in the country, and in many foreign centres of industry. But the arrangement is not without its difficulties. How is a society to be financed which never realises? What substitute can be found for the moralising stimulus of thrift which takes possession of every man who possesses a corner of land or a morsel of stone?'

We have felt obliged to make this less encouraging quotation. It shows how difficult is the task of improving the dwellings of the poor. Things would not go better if the houses were built at a loss by the State or by the municipality. There are in this matter difficulties which are inherent in all human affairs. English societies have had the same experience; at Shaftesbury Park particularly, I understand. There, attempt has been made to repurchase the houses from the owners in order to prevent the abuses described. It is on this account that some well-informed persons recommend building for lease and not for sale.

annum. It has thus been able to fix the rent of its houses between 438 and 480 francs (all instalments of purchase-money included), in addition to a sum of 500 to 1000 francs payable on entrance.

At Lille *'La Compagnie immobilière de Lille,'* founded in 1867, with a capital of 100,000 francs, which was increased by a gratuitous subvention given by Napoléon III, has built 301 houses, of which 201 are sold to their occupiers. The price of each of these is about 3000 francs; one-tenth is payable in advance along with the cost of registration, the balance by instalments, monthly or fortnightly, during a period of fifteen years as a maximum, with power to pay at an earlier date. Since the origin of the society the annual interest of 5 per cent has been regularly paid to its shareholders.

At Saint-Quentin *'La Société anonyme Saint-Quentinoise'* has its home (price of a house 2500 francs). At Amiens *'La Société anonyme des maisons Ouvrières,'* founded in 1865, with a capital of 300,000 francs, has created a new quarter, built eighty-five houses, sold at a price below the usual price of the neighbourhood (price of houses 3523 and 2762 francs, payable by monthly instalments of 20 francs in fifteen years). Nine-tenths of the capital has actually been repaid; interest at 5 per cent has throughout been earned for the shareholders, and there remains 170,000 francs profit, which is to be used for the establishment of a school of domestic economy and apprenticeship.[11] We have spoken above of the Union fon-

---

[11] See *Les Maisons ouvrières d'Amiens,* par Élie Fleury.

cière of Reims. At Nancy *La Société immobilière*, with a capital of 200,000 francs, has built fifty-seven houses, costing from 4500 to 7000 francs, all sold to workmen. It has always paid 5 per cent to its shareholders until 1884, since then 2-1/2 per cent, and is now in liquidation. At Havre a company, '*La Société Havraise des Cités Ouvrières*,' was formed in 1871 with a capital of 200,000 francs under the direct influence of the Mulhouse association. It has built 117 houses representing an expenditure of over 500,000 francs. In 1884 it had sold already fifty-six houses, of which thirty-eight were entirely paid for; conditions of sale—first deposit 300 francs, complete purchase in fifteen years by monthly payments of 24 francs, in twenty years by monthly payments of 20 francs. The interest is limited to 5 per cent. At Bolbec there is a *Société des Cités Ouvrières* with a capital of 100,000 francs.

At Orleans, in 1870, two workmen resolved to create the '*Société immobilière*,' whose object it is to develop the spirit of thrift by giving facilities for the acquisition of property. It has built 220 houses in 1887, all of which had found buyers who are paying off the purchase-price in periods of twenty-five years.

In Belgium we may mention '*La Société Verviétoise*' (of Verviers) for the construction of working-class dwellings; '*La Société Liégeoise des maisons Ouvrières*,' with 425 houses, of which 237 are sold.

In England, we know the Artisans, Labourers, and General Dwellings Company, whose object is to supply at a very low price a house for each family; it was instituted as a reaction against the system of barracks.

Not being able to build in London itself, it has gone into the country to seek for large areas. Up to 1881 it endeavoured to encourage workmen to become proprietors. But at the present time the company is buying back the houses in order to avoid the evils of sub-letting and overcrowding. The company has created regular little towns, 6000 houses. Its capital is about £1,250,000; the dividend is 5 per cent.

III. We now come to our third category, to those institutions whose object it is to build houses for a large number of tenants, but with good sanitary arrangements and a higher degree of comfort. In this class we must put the various societies and foundations which exist in London. These have spent nearly four millions, and house 70,000 persons. We can only name the Metropolitan Association, the Peabody Gift, the Improved Industrial Dwelling Company, the Society for Improving the Condition of the Labouring Classes.[12] The capital employed is remunerated at the rate of 3 to 5 per cent. In the case of the Peabody legacy there are no shareholders, and the revenue is employed to extend the work. An interesting enterprise, which is less known, is that of the Surrey Lodge Estate, founded under the auspices of Miss Cons, who lives in the midst of her tenants, and pays 4 per cent to her shareholders.

In Paris, thanks to the munificence of the Messieurs Heine, '*La Société philanthropique*' has built its first block of dwellings, Rue Jeanne d'Arc, in the middle of the XIIIth

---

[12] According to a table prepared by Mr. Gatliffe, during the last forty years up to 1886, 26,643 families, or 146,809 persons have profited from the improved dwelling movement in London.

arrondissement. The building contains seventy-seven rooms divided among thirty-five tenancies.[13] Two other blocks are to be erected in different parts of Paris, in quarters where healthy dwellings are most rare. A dwelling with forty-five tenements has been begun in the boulevard de Grenelle.

At Rouen (December, 1885), 500,000 francs have been raised, and six separate houses built containing ninety-five tenements.

At Lyons, in June 1887, tenants took possession of the first group of houses built by MM. Aynard, Mangini, Gillet. These gentlemen have contributed from their own pocket 200,000 francs, and to this has been added a loan of 150,000 francs from the reserves of the Savings Bank. The remuneration of the capital is guaranteed at 4 per cent. The promoters of the enterprise at Lyons having thus obtained a solid base of operations and these definite results, founded a company with a capital of a million; 200,000 francs deposited by themselves, 300,000 francs to be raised in shares, 500,000 francs advanced from the reserves of the Savings Bank. They then bought 7500 metres for the building of twenty houses. At Marseilles, thanks to the efforts of M. Rostand, the Savings Bank of the town has been authorised to give assistance to a similar

---

[13] M. Picot delivered an eloquent address on the occasion of the opening of these dwellings, 18 June, 1888. 'It is a social triumph, for it shows to the irresolute the possibility of action. If the *"Société philanthropique"* earns 4 per cent on the capital employed, it refutes the wild notions of the Socialists who expect everything from the State, and who demand that the Communes should employ municipal resources, and that the State should use the budget of France for the construction of houses for the proletariate.'

enterprise. It is only just to make the savings of poor people flow in this direction. Since 1882, the Savings Bank of Strasbourg undertook to devote 392,000 francs from its reserve to the construction of working-class houses. In Italy, the funds of Savings Banks and of the Sociétés de secours mutuels, are employed in the building of small houses.

At Brooklyn, we find the Improved Dwellings Company, founded by Mr. White, which pays a dividend of 6 per cent. At New York there is the Improved Dwellings Association, which divides 6 per cent, and a more recent enterprise, The Tenement House Building Company, which limits its dividend to 4 per cent.

To Miss Octavia Hill belongs the merit of inventing a system of her own, of which we cannot speak with too much respect. Her aim is the improvement of the housing of the poor by the purchase of insanitary houses, which are then put into a good state of repair, and managed economically in such fashion as to obtain a fair return upon capital, and all this without a suspicion of charity or socialism. In place of a dole, time and personal service is given, and the beneficial influence of intercourse between the tenants and their landlords or rent-collectors, who are all actuated by a spirit of well-considered philanthropy. In 1885, Miss Octavia Hill and her imitators were owners of fifty-seven buildings of the value of £311,767, and affording accommodation for 11,582 persons.

Miss Octavia Hill has founded a school not only in London but even in the United States, notably at New York and Boston, in Germany, at Darmstadt, and at Leipsic. At Berlin a company has been formed; its council numbers

M. Gneist among its members. It purchases houses, repairs them, lets or sells them, and seeks to develop in them habits of order. The authorised capital is one million marks, of which 348,000 marks are subscribed.

We must here ask permission to refer to the scheme of 'tenant thrift' (*épargne locative*), which M. Coste has explained in his admirable work *Les questions sociales contemporaines*, 1886, p. 430. It consists in a plan for the gradual acquisition of mortgage bonds which confer a right of lease and a contract for sale of the house occupied by the tenant, with a gradual reduction of the amount of rent. Would it not be possible for insurance companies to make advances to workmen for the purpose of helping them to become owners of their houses? Workmen desirous of owning their own home could easily take out a policy from a life insurance company sufficient to give a reasonable security for the required advance. There could be no investment more secure than the loan to a workman on the security of the house in which he lives. We suggest the following procedure. The workman must accumulate his savings in a bank, until the sum collected amounts to a guarantee for the loan which he wishes to obtain. He then withdraws his deposit from the bank; at the same time he takes out a policy from the assurance company with which he also makes his deposit and obtains a loan. In this way, if he dies tomorrow, it is certain that by means of the policy of insurance the debt will be extinguished.[14]

---

[14] I have received from the kindness of M. Cheysson the following note. Let us take for our example the head of a family, aged 35, and a cottage, value 6000 francs. The Society let it with a contract for sale by instalments, payable in twenty years with interest at 4 per cent.

I have now arrived at the close of my survey, and it may be interesting to set down the resolutions proposed by me, and adopted by the International Congress held at Paris during the Universal Exhibition, 1889:

(1) The problem of the supply of healthy and cheap houses, owing to the complexity of influences at work, does not admit of an universal and absolute solution.

(2) It is for individual enterprise or for private combination to find the appropriate solution in each case.

The direct interference of the State or of the local authority with the market, for the purpose of competing with private enterprise, or fixing the rate of rent, ought to be excluded from consideration. It is only admissible when the matter in hand deals with means of communication, sanitary police, and the equalisation of rates.

(3) The development of the construction of cheap

Rent .... 240 francs.
Instalment of purchase-money 201   "

Total yearly payment 441   "

The Society contracts with an Insurance Company a policy stipulating that, if the workman dies before twenty years, the assurance company instead of his heirs, will pay the instalments still due. The annual premium for such a policy would be

88.20 francs.
Add to this the rent 441   "

Total 529.20   "

Under these conditions the head of the family does not leave debt behind him if he dies. The house is free on the day of his death, and becomes the property of his heirs. This premium is equal to 1.5 per cent of the price of the house. If instead of availing himself of this additional security for purchase, the father of the family devoted this sum to the more rapid extinction of his debt, he would be able to complete his purchase in fifteen instead of twenty years. Which is best for him, to complete his purchase, if he lives, in fifteen or twenty years, or free himself from all fear of an interruption by death of the process of purchase?

houses in the outlying parts and suburbs of towns is closely connected with a service of frequent and economical transport (that is, reduced tariff on railways, workmen's trains, means of access into towns, tramways, steamboats, etc.).

(4) Among the resources to which appeal can be made, it is fit to mention the reserves of savings banks.

The intervention of savings banks in the development of the housing of the poor is legitimate and useful under conditions of reasonable precaution. The legislature can and ought to favour such intervention, by giving more liberty of investment for the deposits and trust funds of savings banks, and by reducing the burden of taxation.

(5) In order to reconcile the liberty of the purchaser with the obligations by which he binds himself in the contract for the purchase of a house, and in order to lighten, in case of death, the liability which falls on his heirs, it is worth while to consider carefully various combinations, e.g. clauses for the cancelling of contract and for the repayment of instalments, life insurances, mortgages, etc.

To the above I add the resolutions passed at the same Congress on the motion of M. Picot, Member of the Institute:

(1) Wherever the economic conditions permit of it, separate dwellings with little gardens should be preferred in the interest of the workman and his family.

(2) If the dearness of the ground or some other cause makes it necessary to build in the centre of the towns houses in which many families are accommodated under one roof, all the conditions of independence ought to be carefully preserved in order to minimise the contact between them.

(3) The plans should be conceived with a view of avoid-

ing all occasion of meeting between the tenants. The stair landings and the staircases should be well lighted, and ought to be considered as a prolongation of the public road. Corridors and passages of all kinds should be carefully avoided.

Each tenement should have inside a w. c., receiving its light from outside and provided with water.

(4) For families with children of different sexes a division into three rooms is indispensable, in order to permit separation of the sexes.

(5) Every restriction by which injury might be done to the complete independence of the tenant and his family ought to be prohibited.

I think this rapid survey of facts justifies our contention that although the difficulty is very great, rapid progress is being made in its solution, that the main obstacles to be removed are:

(1) The doubt that investment in working-class houses may not prove remunerative.

(2) The oftentimes destructive habits of poor tenants.

(3) An inconvenient system of land tenure prohibitive of free trade and enterprise in building operations.

(4) The uncertainty caused by the threatening attitude of municipal socialism.

The first three of these we have shown to be superable; the last can only be cured by a healthier tone of public opinion, and by a fuller appreciation of the success which has attended private initiative.

Arthur Raffalovich

CHAPTER 9

THE EVILS OF STATE TRADING
AS ILLUSTRATED BY THE
POST OFFICE

FREDERICK MILLAR

CHAPTER 9

THE EVILS OF STATE TRADING AS ILLUSTRATED BY THE POST OFFICE

O ut of the multiplicity of affairs with which the State busies itself, not one can be instanced in which it has been thoroughly successful. The reason of this is not far to seek. Years ago Mr. Herbert Spencer pointed out the positive and negative evils consequent upon the State frittering away its time and energies in schemes with which it should have no concern. Admittedly the main duty of the State is the defence of citizens against aggression; it is manifest that this duty must be ill-discharged if the State undertakes other functions. 'It is in the very nature of things that an agency employed for two purposes must fulfil both imperfectly; partly because while fulfilling the one it cannot be fulfilling the other, and partly because its adaptation to both ends implies incomplete fitness to either.'[1] It is therefore quite natural to find that when the State undertakes to

---

[1] Essay on 'Over-legislation.'

do those things which it ought not to do, it does them badly; and that its conduct of affairs which are foreign, as well as those which are germane, to the discharge of its primary duty, is characterised by bungling, extravagance, and inefficiency.

Although most people admit the superiority of private enterprise and administration to State-ownership and control, an exception is generally made in favour of one particular department in which it is contended the State has succeeded as a trader. That department is the Post Office, and socialists, who advocate State-ownership and control of everything, instance that department as showing what the State can do when it takes the place of private enterprise, and they contend that it could undertake the distribution of goods, clothing, food, etc., just as well as it undertakes the distribution of correspondence. Mrs. Besant's advice to 'anyone who thinks such distribution impossible' is to 'study the postal system now existing.'[2] From the Individualist point of view nothing could be better. If people would make themselves acquainted with the facts connected with the general working of this socialist ideal, the Post Office, the socialist bubble would soon burst. To afford them an opportunity of acting upon Mrs. Besant's advice is the object of the present essay, the writer being persuaded that the best refutation of the specious theories of Socialism lies in the fact of their utter and disastrous failure whenever and wherever they have been put into practice.

---

[2] *Modern Socialism*, pp. 29–30.

If the State had originated and developed the present postal system one could readily understand the unlimited praise which is frequently bestowed upon it by the average member of the community, who looks merely at the surface of things, and who, when he contemplates this colossal concern, with its facilities for the collection, distribution, and delivery of letters and telegrams and parcels, is filled with wondering awe. But when we consider that not one of the many benefits connected with the system originated with the State, but that all have been forced upon it from without, and generally after long years of agitation and pressure, and that even now the most important part of the work, that of conveying the mails, is done by private enterprise, there is no apparent reason why we should feel indebted to the State for whatever advantages we happen to enjoy. Indeed, we have reason to complain that in consequence of State monopoly we have not a more perfect system than the one in existence. Over two hundred years ago private enterprise had established a penny post in London. 'To facilitate correspondence between one part of London and another,' says Macaulay, 'was not originally one of the objects of the Post Office. But in the reign of Charles the Second, an enterprising citizen of London, William Dockwray, set up, at great expense, a penny post, which delivered letters and parcels six or eight times a day in the busy and crowded streets near the Exchange, and four times a day in the outskirts of the capital. The improvement was, as usual, strenuously resisted. . . . The utility of the enterprise was, however, so great and obvious that all opposition proved fruitless. As soon as it became clear that the speculation would be lucrative, the Duke of

York complained of it as an infraction of his monopoly,[3] and the courts of law decided in his favour.'[4] Mr. Herbert Spencer, commenting upon this fact, says that if we judge by what has happened in other cases with private enterprises that had small beginnings, we may infer that the system thus commenced would have developed throughout the kingdom as fast as the needs pressed and the possibilities allowed.[5]

The very monopoly enjoyed by the State in the carrying of letters is in itself a tacit acknowledgment of its inability to contend with private enterprise. By the Act 1 Vic. cap. 33, the Post Office acquired the exclusive privilege of conveying from one place to another all letters, and of performing all the incidental services of receiving, collecting, sending, despatching, and delivering the same. Certain exemptions from this exclusive privilege are made. For instance, a person may send a letter by one private friend to another, or by a messenger on purpose, concerning the private affairs of the sender or receiver thereof; letters of merchants, etc., may be sent out by vessels of merchandise; or letters concerning goods or merchandise, sent by common known carriers to be delivered with the goods which such letters concern, may be sent, provided neither hire, nor reward, nor other profit, nor advantage be received for

---

[3] At the Restoration the proceeds of the Post Office ('a rude and imperfect establishment of posts for the conveyance of letters' set up by Charles I, swept away by the Civil War, and resumed under the Commonwealth), after all expenses had been paid, were settled on the Duke of York.

[4] *History of England,* vol. i. pp. 385–6, 7th edition.

[5] Essay on 'Specialised Administration.'

receiving and delivering such letters. Excepting these exemptions from the exclusive privilege of the Post Office, it was enacted by 1 Vic. cap. 36, that—

> Every person who shall convey otherwise than by the post a letter . . . shall for every letter forfeit £5, and every person who shall be in the practice of so conveying letters . . . shall for every week during which the practice shall be continued forfeit £100; and every person who shall perform otherwise than by the post any services incidental to conveying letters from place to place, whether by receiving or by taking up or by collecting or by ordering or by despatching or by carrying or by re-carrying or by delivery, a letter . . . shall forfeit for every letter £5, and every person who shall be in the practice of so performing any such incidental services shall for every week during which the practice shall be continued forfeit £100; and every person who shall send a letter . . . otherwise than by the post, or shall cause a letter . . . to be sent or conveyed otherwise than by the post, or shall either tender or deliver a letter in order to be sent otherwise than by the post shall forfeit for every letter £5; and every person who shall be in the practice of committing any of the acts last mentioned shall for every week during which the practice shall be continued forfeit £100; and every person who shall make a collection of exempted letters for the purpose of conveying them or sending them otherwise than by the post, or by the post, shall forfeit for every letter £5; and every person who shall be in the practice of making a collection of exempted letters for either of these purposes shall forfeit for every week during which such practice shall be continued £100; . . . and the above penalties shall be incurred whether the letter shall be sent singly or with anything else, or such incidental service shall be performed in respect to a letter either sent, or to be sent, singly or together with some other letter or thing; and in any prosecution by action or otherwise for the recovery of any such penalty the onus shall lie upon the party prosecuted to prove that the act in respect of which the penalty is alleged to have been incurred was done in conformity of the Post Office laws.

It will be seen that under such restrictions and prohi-
bitions any attempt on the part of private enterprise to
compete with the State in the carrying and delivery of
letters is out of the question. Some time ago the Postmaster-General discovered that certain of the public, dissatisfied with the facilities offered by the Post Office, were
forwarding letters as parcels by the various railway companies. Many small provincial newspapers, whose proprietors could not afford to pay for press telegrams, were
receiving 'copy' from their London correspondents and
agents in this way. Immediately the matter came to the
knowledge of the Postmaster-General he addressed a letter,
dated April 1st, 1887, to the various railway companies,
pointing out to them that they were infringing upon his
exclusive privilege, and requesting them to discontinue the
practice, which, he stated, was imperilling 'the privileges
conferred upon him by law for the benefit of the public,'
and endangering the public revenue.

It is difficult to get people to realise that a thing which
for the most part only costs a penny is yet much dearer
than it need be. But such is undoubtedly the fact. It was
calculated by Sir Rowland Hill that the cost of conveying a
letter from one point in the United Kingdom to any other
was 1/36 of a penny. Suppose, then, we assume that the
cost of collecting, stamping, conveying, and delivering a
letter posted in London and addressed to Glasgow to be
one-sixth of a penny, it will be seen that an enterprising
postal agency would be able to carry a letter for which we
now pay the State a penny for a halfpenny, and even for a
farthing, and realise a handsome profit. We do not argue
that a penny postage is a colossal grievance, for many

people have been heard to exclaim that a reduction of the rate of postage and a consequent increase of correspondence are a prospect which they cannot regard with equanimity. This of course is the reason of the long-suffering of the public in this matter. But our object is to point out that a Government monopoly charges at least double what would be charged under an open system, and to ask the reader to believe that the effect of enlarging the sphere of Government monopoly would be to double the cost of living all along the line. As to our foreign and colonial letters, Mr. Henniker Heaton, M.P., has shown that, assuming one-sixth of a penny to represent the cost of conveying an ordinary letter from London to Southampton, the total cost of conveying a letter from London to New Zealand would be a farthing, one-twelfth of a penny being allowed to cover the cost of carrying from Southampton to destination, which is more than twelve times the highest rate for the most precious goods. Yet for this service, which could be performed at a handsome profit at a penny per letter, the State has all along been charging sixpence; and it was only during the last session of Parliament that the Government, in response to a strong and indignant feeling in the country aroused by the member for Canterbury, whose exposures of Post Office extravagance, bungling, and inefficiency have attracted so much attention, virtually confessed that the public had been overcharged all along, and that henceforth a uniform rate of two-pence-halfpenny for letters would be instituted between England and her colonies. The average citizen will doubtless bless the Post Office for the reduction, unconscious of the fact that he has been overcharged throughout the past, and that the overcharge will continue at the rate of three-halfpence per letter until the postage is reduced to a penny. Merchants, newspaper proprietors, and others who have been aware of this, have evaded payment by posting their letters in France or Germany, whence the rate to nearly all parts of the world is 100 per cent cheaper than it is from England; and it has been stated that one London firm alone saves £1300 per annum by posting its letters in France for India and China, where the rate is twopence-halfpenny as against fivepence charged in England. When it is considered that a letter posted in New York for Singapore, and carried there *via* England, *in one of our mail steamers,* costs twopence-halfpenny, whereas a letter posted in England for Singapore is charged fivepence; that the cost of letters from England to Shanghai, if sent through the French or German Post Office there is twopence-halfpenny, but if through the English Post Office at the same place the charge is fivepence per letter, and that the same is the case in Zanzibar and other places; that millions of samples of English merchandise are still being sent from London to be posted in Belgium back to every town in England at half the rates which are charged if posted in England;[6] and that these and other facts stated above are merely samples, taken at random, of the multitudinous anomalies of our State postal system, some idea may be formed of the enormous saving to the community, especially the commercial section, to whom this matter is of serious consideration, were the present State monopoly abolished and replaced by private enterprise.

---

[6] Mr. Henniker Heaton's *Postal Reform,* and his letter in *The Times,* Sept. 11th, 1889.

We do not share Mr. Henniker Heaton's opinion that the Post Office will ever prove an efficient machine while under State management. The Postmaster-General, however, has confessed to the justice of his complaint, and has yielded to criticism in Parliament a reduction of rates which would long ago have reached the public under a system of private enterprise.

What a public misfortune it would be if we were dependent for all reductions of price in articles of daily consumption on the successful badgering by private members of the minister in charge. The present plan seems to be to put up the rate of postage and lower the rate of telegrams quite irrespective of cost price, and merely according to the whim of some hard-pressed Postmaster-General.

The principles upon which this State monopoly is conducted are of anything but a business character, and are such as if adopted by any private firm or company would result in speedy ruin. Its periodical accounts, says Mr. Henniker Heaton, are of such a nature that no one can find out what the gross receipts and net profits are within three-quarters of a million of money; and it has been stated that they are never properly audited. Its revenue is hundreds of thousands more than is represented in the estimates, the amounts being paid away in contracts with foreign Governments which have never been submitted to or sanctioned by the House of Commons. For the use of the Brindisi route it has been frequently pointed out that it ought not to pay more than £31,200, yet it actually pays £84,000, or £52,800 more than is fair and necessary. Its stationery contract with Messrs. De la Rue and Co. lost the country from £60,000 to £70,000 a year, making a total loss to the British public of £500,000 on the ten years' contract; yet the Postmaster-General repeatedly stated in answer to questions in the House of Commons that 'the contract was a positive boon to England.' In a letter published in the *Times* on September 11th, 1889, Mr. Henniker Heaton says:

> The extraordinary method is pursued of paying out of the current revenue of the Post Office the cost of land and buildings required for Post Office purposes, and through this means the Postmaster-General owns already land to the value of more than two and a quarter millions in London alone. No business man in the world would conduct his affairs in this manner— taking no account of the money he expends in landed property and buildings. Yet this very department, that trifles with hundreds of thousands of pounds, refuses to allow a local postmaster in my constituency to expend 1s. 6d. in mending a lock of a door, but insists on despatching an officer from the Board of Works to the scene at a cost of £3 10s. This I proved before the Select Committee.

From what other cause than a systematic looseness in appointing its officials is it due that the abstraction of postal orders is of almost daily occurrence? During the year 1887 the Postmaster-General stated that the abstraction of these orders 'reached portentous dimensions.' During 1889, 325 dishonest letter-carriers were found guilty and dismissed for irregularities, and on an average more than three officials per week were convicted and sentenced to long terms of imprisonment for stealing letters, and a large number cautioned for suspicious conduct or carelessness.[7]

Who has not suffered under the discourtesy of the offi-

---

[7] Mr. Henniker Heaton's *Postal Reform*, p. 14.

cials, both male and female, employed by the Post Office to attend to the wants of its customers? Who, residing in a suburb in which the Post Office is inside an ordinary baker's, grocer's, or chemist's shop, has not been annoyed when the shopkeeper, after blandly asking them what they required, and being told it was a penny stamp, abruptly turned to wait upon their own customers first, keeping the State's customers waiting until they had time to serve them? During the middle of the present year (1890) the relations between the young ladies of the Ludgate Circus Post Office and the general public became so strained that the Postmaster-General was compelled to remove the whole staff and replace it by one of males. One does not find such a state of affairs existing in any private establishment. A customer enters a draper's, tailor's, or other shop, and meets with courtesy and pleasantness, and is served with promptitude. A spirit of discourtesy in such places would drive customers away. But in the Post Office it is different: the customer has no remedy; he cannot go elsewhere to get his postal wants supplied. The officials know this, hence their attitude towards the helpless public. Let the shopping public contemplate what shopping would be under socialism, when every article would have to be purchased in establishments conducted in the same discourteous manner as the Post Office, and their bias will be anything but socialist.

The arbitrary and frequently impudent manner in which the Post Office treats its customers forms the subject of hundreds of letters which annually appear in the public press. The victims of what Mr. Herbert Spencer calls 'the stupidity, the slowness, the perversity, the dishonesty of officialism' in the Post Office, finding they have no remedy for the wrongs that they have been subjected to, give vent to their well-founded indignation in the columns of *The Times* and other papers. Thus we read of a firm of merchants in Edinburgh complaining that through the admitted carelessness of a Post Office telegraphist a telegram addressed to them was never delivered, and they sustained a loss of £100. When they sent in a claim to the postal authorities they were told that 'the department is not legally responsible for the delay complained of,' but that it would refund to them the sum of 7-1/2d., being the amount paid for the transmission of the telegram! Commercial men and others lose thousands of pounds every year by delay and wrong delivery of letters and telegrams. Valuable goods are damaged, lost, or stolen when sent through the parcels post, and the complaining owners receive nothing but a stereotyped expression of regret from the officials, and a disclaimer of all responsibility. In the case of the parcels post the public have only themselves to blame. If parcels sent by private carriers—who, as will be presently shown, carry them quicker and cheaper than does the State—are damaged, lost, or stolen, or even delayed, the owner receives full satisfaction for any loss sustained. So that if people are foolish enough to 'slight the good and faithful servant, and promote the unprofitable one,' they must put up with the consequences. We find other victims complaining that while the Post Office imposes a fine in the event of the face of a postcard bearing any words in addition to the address, it almost invariably disregards its own part of the contract and defaces the letter on the back of a postcard by affixing its official stamp upon it. During last August, the writer, whilst staying in a little town on the Norfolk coast, received four postcards in three days, and each card was defaced in the manner described, several words in two of them being completely obliterated. A protest against this breach of contract elicited from the Secretary the consoling reply that he regretted the cause of complaint, and that the special attention of the postal officials at C—— had been called to the matter. If a private firm repudiated responsibility for its blunders and carelessness, we should regard the fact as disentitling it to our custom. Can the systematic repudiation by the State be regarded in any other light? Again, others write to protest against what they justly term 'the contemptible trick,' 'a breach of trust and confidence'—the opening of letters by the Post Office. What could be more contemptible than the trick recently performed by the Post Office upon the Postmen's Union. At eleven o'clock on the morning of Saturday, August 16th, 1890, one of the officials of the Union posted in the Finsbury district several postcards addressed to clubs in the immediate neighbourhood, asking them to get volunteers to carry collection-boxes on the following day (Sunday) at the dockers' demonstration, on behalf of the postmen dismissed during the recent postmen's strike. These postcards should have been delivered before 6 P.M. on the same day at the latest, but they were kept back by the Post Office officials and not delivered till the Monday, too late for the purpose they were intended for.

With regard to the recent strikes among the postmen, it would be well that the working classes to whom the spe-

cious doctrines of socialism are being preached should
realise the change for the worse that would take place in
their position as workers in the event of the present industrial system being replaced by one of a socialist character.
With the 'New Unionism' which seeks to enslave the
labourer under a new form of tyranny, we have no sympathy whatever. At the same time it must be borne in mind
that the right of voluntary combination for the legitimate
purpose of mitigating by lawful means some of the evils
of competition is one of the most cherished privileges of
the English working class. It is true that in asking its
servants to forego this privilege the Post Office offers pen-
sions and other advantages which to some might seem an
adequate substitute. This, however, rightly or wrongly, is
not the view of many Post Office servants. And even
though it may be reasonable to ask the labourers in one
or two industries to contract themselves out of their right
of combination, it is quite unreasonable to propose that
the whole of the working class should abdicate their liberty
of action in the way required by the Post Office officials.
But this is really the proposal of the socialists. It is very
probable that Mrs. Besant is right in thinking that the
Post Office officials have a comfortable berth, but the fact
does not reconcile them to the restraints imposed upon
their liberty, and we are not disposed to blame them. The
socialist organisers of the strike spared no effort of rhetoric
in enlarging on the servile condition, as they termed it, of
the State servants, and the secretary of the Union described
the Postmaster-General 'as a task-master worse than the
vilest East End sweater.' Yet this is the institution which
Mrs. Besant quite correctly puts forward as the most nearly

successful example of State socialism which the world has ever seen.

We pronounce no judgment on the merits of the quarrel between the Postmaster-General and his servants. We point out, however, the anomaly that when a labourer takes service in a State monopoly he is called on to surrender his right of combination with his fellows. There is, of course, justice in this: the Post Office has prevented competition, and is bound to protect the public against a cessation of the letter-carrying service. This it can only do by introducing a species of military law, a condition characteristic of all socialist institutions, which workmen should bear in mind.

Attention will now be called to a few facts in connection with certain attempts on the part of the Post Office to compete with private enterprise.

The Parcel Post. This department of the Post Office was established a few years ago with the object of the State becoming exclusive carrier of small parcels. This attempt to compete with railway companies and other common carriers has been financially a signal failure. In the matter of rates we find those charged by the railway companies and carriers about 50 per cent less than those charged by the Post Office, the former collecting and delivering the parcels within ordinary limits without additional charge. Instead of a person carrying his parcels to a Post Office, where he has to wait and get them weighed, and where he is compelled to prepay the carriage before they are received, a railway company collects them without charge, and it is optional whether the carriage is paid by the sender or the consignee. If parcels are handed over to the Post Office they are sent by certain trains only during the day, whereas if handed to a railway company they are despatched by the first passenger-train after receipt. The Post Office receives parcels up to a limited time only, whereas the railway companies receive and despatch them by the latest transit, including midnight service, thus ensuring a very speedy delivery next morning without any extra expense. In the case of parcels handed to a railway or carrying company being damaged or lost the owner is entitled to full compensation without having to pay any charge beyond the ordinary carriage, whereas if they are handed to the Post Office 'The Postmaster-General will (not in consequence of any legal liability, but voluntarily and as an act of grace) . . . give compensation for loss and damage of *inland* parcels' not exceeding £1 where no extra fee is paid, not exceeding £5 where an insurance fee of a penny is paid, and not exceeding £10 where an insurance fee of twopence is paid. 'In no case will a larger amount of compensation than £10 be paid.'[8]

Savings Bank. The Post Office Savings Bank was established for the encouragement of thrift among the working classes. With its abundant facilities for the receipt and payment of money one would imagine that the Post Office would be certain to meet all the banking requirements of the working classes, and make it almost impossible for private enterprise to compete with it in this particular field of industry. Such, however, is not the case. Not only does the Post Office fail to meet those requirements, but its business as working-class banker is conducted with that

---

[8] *Postal Guide.*

lack of enterprise which is characteristic of all Government departments, and in point of convenience and advantage to customers it compares very unfavourably with working-class banks conducted by private enterprise.

The Post Office Savings Bank receives deposits of one shilling, or any number of shillings, but a person is not allowed to deposit more than £30 in one year, or £150 in all, exclusive of the interest of 2 ½ per cent per annum for each complete pound. The hours during which offices are open for the receipt and payment of money are the very hours during which the working classes are engaged at their work, and during which the Post Office clerks are busily engaged in discharging their ordinary duties. There are, however, certain offices open on Friday and Saturday evenings till 7 P.M. or 8 P.M., but only for receiving deposits. When a depositor wishes to make a withdrawal from his account he is compelled to call at a Post Office and obtain a notice of withdrawal form, which he must fill up and post to the office of the Savings Bank Department, from which he will in the course of a day or two receive a warrant from his local Post Office to pay him the sum required. He has then to pay another visit to the Post Office, and after presenting his pass-book and signing his name to the warrant in the presence of the postmaster or other Post Office official and satisfying the said postmaster or other official that he is really and truly the person in whose favour it is made, he succeeds in obtaining a withdrawal from his account. If a depositor is sick or abroad, or by any cause prevented from presenting the warrant in person, payment is made to 'the bearer of an order under his hand, signed in the presence of any officer of the Post Office other than the paying officer, a minister of any religious denomination, a justice of the peace, a commissioner to administer oaths, or, in case of sickness, the medical attendant. If the depositor be resident abroad, the signature must be verified by some constituted authority of the place in which he resides, or a notary public."[9]

It is obvious that these absurd regulations are most inconvenient to working-class depositors, and a source of considerable annoyance and irritation. Many accounts have been wholly withdrawn, or transferred elsewhere in consequence.

If we compare the general working of the Post Office Savings Bank with that of a banking business conducted by private enterprise, the comparison will be very unfavourable to the latter. Take the National Penny Bank for example. This was established in 1875, having for its objects to promote thrift by affording facilities for the exercise of thrift, to establish a permanent Penny Bank, *open every evening,* and to make such Penny Bank absolutely safe, self-supporting, and on a commercial basis. It has a head office at Westminster, a city office, and branch offices in various parts of the metropolis and the London suburbs. These offices are open during each evening to receive deposits from one penny upwards *to any amount, and to pay withdrawals on demand.* Interest is paid at the rate of 3 per cent per annum on complete pounds left in the Bank for complete calendar months. Depositors may *withdraw money by post* by simply sending a written application accompanied by pass-book, and, if the depositor so desires, an amount will be sent by cheque to any person named by

[9] *Post Office Guide,* p. 390.

him. The Bank also advances money to working men to enable them to purchase their own houses, charging interest at 5 per cent per annum.

The growth of this National Penny Bank is most encouraging, and its success depends on the facilities which it offers to its customers. We could wish that the directors could find it possible to overcome the obvious difficulty of expense, and to imitate the collecting insurance companies, so that these advantages and opportunities for saving could be brought to the door of every working man. The Bank is now paying a dividend, and has proved that working-class banking can be made a profitable industry. There can be little doubt that banks of this sort will soon supersede the Post Office.

Insurance Department. The above is no mere assumption: for in the allied industry of insurance the business done by private enterprise far surpasses that done by the Post Office, aided though it is by its ubiquity and the undeniable nature of its security. The following table will give an apt comparison of the business of the Post Office, as against the business of one company, viz. the Prudential Assurance Company as shown by the latest returns:

	No. of Contracts in Existence		Premium Revenue		
Post Office	Insurance Deferred Annuities	6,210 1,015	Insurance Annuities	£ 14,121 19,625	Increase in the 10 years 1879–88
		7,225		33,746	£3,694
Prudential (Industrial)	8,518,619		£3,336,742		£1,849,202
Prudential (Ordinary)	177,208		£904,915		£611,313

Telegraphs. When the possibility of conveying intelligence instantaneously for long distances was demonstrated, and when Cooke and Wheatstone patented their magnetic needle telegraph in 1837, the State did not avail itself of the invention, but remained satisfied with the old semaphore. The new invention was worked by private enterprise for thirty-three years, and 'during this period,' said Sir Charles Bright in his address to the Society of Telegraph Engineers and Electricians in 1887, 'those engaged in the undertaking had provided the capital, incurred all the risk, and developed the telegraphic system into a highly lucrative business, from which the profits were steadily increasing, so much so that the net earnings of the two largest companies ranged from 14 to 18 per cent per annum.' When the State realised that the business was a financial success, it took steps to acquire all the telegraphic undertakings in the kingdom, and in 1868 an Act was passed entitling it to do this, and in the following year a further Act was passed which gave to the Post Office the monopoly of telegraphic communication. From that time till now the telegraphs in the hands of the State, while they have remained very stationary in respect of public utility, have been a financial failure, the annual deficit frequently exceeding half a million, as was the case in 1886–87, when the deficit for the year was £540,527. Yet the Submarine Telegraph Company has been conducting the communication between England and the continent under the Channel with great efficiency, and at moderate rates, and has deservedly been reaping a profit for its usefulness, and paying a dividend of 15-1/2 per cent. The telegraphs' deficit is made up of various items, the principal representing interest on capital, the outcome of the bad bargain the State, with characteristic stupidity and shortsightedness, made at the outset with the private companies, and the rest representing unprofitable management of the business, and squandering of money in large salaries to useless officials. If a private company conducted its business in such a loose manner it would be classed as a dead failure, and would speedily terminate its existence in bankruptcy proceedings. But as the business is a State monopoly the taxpayers are compelled to give it a whitewashing to the tune of half a million per annum, and to allow it to pursue its career of wasteful inefficiency.

For the purpose of comparison it may be stated that the various railway companies in the kingdom annually receive, transmit, and deliver over their own respective systems hundreds of thousands of their own private telegrams at a cost of a mere fraction of a penny per telegram; while the State experiences a loss upon every telegram that passes through its hands, although the minimum charge for sending a telegram is sixpence. The following figures, published during January, 1887, speak for themselves. The Post Office within an area of twelve miles from the General Post Office sends a weekly average of 290,027 telegraphic messages over its wires at an average cost of eightpence per message. The United (now the National) Telephone Company, within area of five miles from the same centre, in one week of December, 1886, transmitted 449,696 telephonic messages at an average cost of three farthings each. It may be added that while the Post Office has an annual deficit of about half a million, the National Telephone Company at its meeting in July last declared a dividend of 6 per cent, and reported an increase in the gross revenue, a decrease in the working expenses, and a large addition to the reserve fund.

The only branch of the postal service which is a financial success is that of letter-carrying. As already shown, the actual cost of an ordinary inland letter is 1/36 of a penny: all the rest is clear profit. The heavy losses sustained in every other branch of the postal service have to be covered by the profits realised by the penny post. It will perhaps be as well to hear what the Postmaster-General has to say in reference to these matters. Replying to a deputation from the Wolverhampton Chamber of Commerce, which waited upon him on January 27th, 1888, to call attention to several anomalies connected with the postal and telegraph regulations, and to complain that orders, invoices, shipping instructions, bills of lading, etc. post were charged letter-rate if any note was added, and to request that documents of a commercial character— orders, invoices, shipping instructions, bills of lading, &c. —should go through the halfpenny post, and to seek some reduction in the charges for sending telegrams from Post Offices through the telephone to their destination, and to point out that private firms were producing and selling postcards at 6 ½ d. per dozen, while the Post Office charged 8d. per dozen, the Postmaster-General said,

> That to make arrangements for matter not enclosed to be carried for 1/2d. instead of 1d. could not be done. It would have an effect upon the revenue which could not be contemplated without horror. The penny postage earned an income which had to be expended on other branches of the service. Telegraphs were a losing business, and the deficiency was paid by

the penny postage. The carriage of newspapers also involved considerable loss, and the halfpenny post was rather a losing than a paying concern. Anything which largely shifted correspondence from the penny to the halfpenny rate might actually disturb the equilibrium of the revenue; therefore anything that struck at the penny post could not be entertained. . . . As to postcards, when they were sold at 8*d*. per dozen and private firms could produce them for 6-1/2*d*. there must be some unsatisfactory practice. He had information on that subject which he hoped to utilize for the public benefit.[10] Respecting telephones *it was unsatisfactory that the Government had to compete with private firms*, and before long the system must be taken up by the Government and telephones placed on the same footing as telegraphs, and be controlled altogether by the Government.[11]

Socialists will agree with their friend, the Postmaster-General, that it *is* unsatisfactory that the State has to compete with private enterprise. If the State could suppress private enterprise, if it could eliminate the factors of human progress, commercial success, and national greatness, it would enable socialism to take the place of civilisation; but while private enterprise enjoys its present freedom, which will be as long as men value liberty, socialism has no chance of success.

---

[10] The manner in which the Postmaster-General has utilised his 'information' 'for the public benefit' is worthy of notice. He has caused the Post Office to issue postcards of a similar quality to those hitherto produced and sold at a profit by private firms for 6-1/2*d*. per dozen at 6*d*. for ten, and in order to prevent private firms selling at a lower rate than the Post Office he has increased the rate for stamping private postcards from 1*s*. 6*d*. to 2*s*. 6*d*. per quire, thus imposing a fee of 200 per cent above the price at which any printer would execute the work! See Mr. Henniker Heaton's *Postal Reform*, pp. 12, 13.

[11] *St. James's Gazette*, June 27th, 1888.

Whether or not it is the intention of the State to take over the telephone, it should not be forgotten that it did its best to obstruct its introduction, and prevent the use of that ingenious and novel invention in this country. Although the telephone was not invented and brought to this country till 1877, it was found to be embraced by the wide-meaning terms of the Telegraphs Act of 1869. The Post Office declined to use it or to allow private enterprise to do so. The State having become a trader in the conveyance of intelligence electrically, was afraid that by allowing private enterprise to use the telephone the telegraph monopoly would be seriously interfered with. But this dog-in-the-manger policy was of short duration. The public, fully alive to the advantages to be derived by such a cheap and handy means of communication as the telephone would afford, demanded that some concession should be made by the Post Office. This was eventually done, the telephone companies being permitted to establish communication in certain places, provided they handed over to the Post Office *one-tenth of their gross receipts*. Thus the National Telephone Company supplies a customer with a telephone for the use of which it charges £20 per annum, £2 of this going to the Post Office, 'simply as blackmail,' says Sir Frederick Bramwell, and the public are kept out of the use of this important means of communication unless they submit to this monstrous tax.

It is, indeed, sad to reflect that in this England of ours, which boasts of its freedom, a Government department should be permitted to restrain and hamper the development of this cheap means of communication, which has really become one of the necessities of commercial life. The fact that we have the present limited means of telephonic communication (the number of instruments under rental in England being 99,000, while in America at the beginning of the present year there were 222,430, being an increase of 16,675 over the number in 1889) is due entirely to the bulldog pertinacity, the watchful care, and the courageous energy of the telephone companies in resisting the Post Office in its endeavours to uphold its retrograde position.

Upon the occasion referred to above, the Postmaster-General said that he 'should be glad of any suggestions which would assist in placing the whole system of telephoning in this country on a satisfactory basis.' But there is really one way in which the State could assist in doing this, and that is, by removing all the restrictions which it has placed upon the development and extension of telephonic communication in this country, in order that the public may enjoy the full benefit of the telephone, which has been well referred to as one of the most ingenious inventions that ever was made.

Notwithstanding the very profitable nature of the letter-carrying monopoly, it cannot be said that, at times of great press of business, the public is served with that absence of fuss and effort which ought to characterise a great and wealthy corporation. At Christmas-time the Post Office is completely disorganised. Its customers are pitifully implored not to pay exclusive regard to their own convenience, and to despatch their packages and letters according to a timetable drawn up by the Post Office to suit its own convenience. But despite these precautions, the deliveries turn out irregular or break down altogether;

and although the same disorganisation reappears each succeeding year, just as if the stress of business which causes
the breakdown had never occurred before and was quite
outside the field of human prevision. This disorganisation
and breakdown commences a week or ten days in advance
of Christmas, and even on the 15th of December the block
and muddle have been so well developed that it has taken
a letter two days to travel between the S.W. and E.C. districts; a book posted in London for Paris has occupied four
days in transit; and within the metropolitan district telegrams have laboured along at the rate of one mile in
twenty minutes. For a few days previous to Christmas the
first delivery of letters falls two hours in arrear, and by the
24th it has been known to break down altogether. It may
be said that private trading companies sometimes break
down under a foreseen stress of business, and that the railway companies at Christmas allow their train-system to
get disorganised. This, no doubt, is true; but we are searching (in vain it may be) for some point in which the State
monopoly shows its superiority. It may, however, be
pointed out that private carriers do not cry to be let off,
but rise to the requirements of the occasion, provide additional facilities, and all the time by prodigal advertisement
solicit rather than deprecate the patronage of the public. It
should, moreover, be borne in mind that the services most
liable to break down at times of pressure partake more or
less of the nature of monopolies. The Post Office and the
railway system are liable to break down, but the ordinary
services which are bought and sold in the open market do
not break down. The moral is obvious. Let us have no more
monopolies than are absolutely necessary. Let human in-

genuity do its best to make free exchange of service everywhere the rule. It is difficult to see why this rule should not apply to the Post Office.

Again, the cessation of postal deliveries during the recent strike among the postmen furnishes a lesson to the commercial world which should act as a warning to the public not to encourage a State monopoly in the means of carrying everything. Today, with the various private carriers and railway companies, a strike among the servants of any particular company is fraught with comparatively small inconvenience to the public. All our large commercial and industrial centres are supplied by several distinct railways, each competing with the others for public favour and patronage. So that in the event of a strike taking place among the servants of one railway company running between Manchester and London, goods and passengers would simply be carried by the others. But if all the means of communication were in the hands of the State, and its underpaid and overworked servants came out on strike, the trade and commerce of the country would be paralysed, and wholesale disaster and ruin would ensue before the stupidity and wooden-headedness of State officialism could be brought to realise the situation and devise a remedy.

It is not in the Post Office alone that State-trading stands self-condemned. Evils, direct and indirect, must result from the State undertaking functions which can only be properly performed under ever-varying conditions by a free initiative, whose very existence depends on its ability to provide constant and adequate satisfaction of public wants. And if those persons who demand the municipalisation of this industry, and the nationalisation of that, would only direct their attention to the State monopolies with which we are pestered at present, they would have demonstrated to them the inherent rottenness of the principles which they so loudly advocate, and would discover that after all private enterprise, stimulated by the necessity and advantage of mutual service, was the principle which alone could make for improvement, success, and progress, to all of which State-trading is essentially prohibitive.

FREDERICK MILLAR

CHAPTER 10

FREE LIBRARIES

M. D. O'BRIEN

CHAPTER 10

FREE LIBRARIES

A Free Library may be defined as the socialists' continuation school. While State education is manufacturing readers for books, State-supported libraries are providing books for readers. The two functions are logically related. If you may take your education out of your neighbour's earnings, surely you may get your literature in the same manner. Literary dependency has the same justification as educational dependency; and, no doubt, habituation to the one helps to develop a strong desire for the other. A portion of our population has by legislation acquired the right to supply itself with necessaries and luxuries at the cost of the rates. The art of earning such things for themselves has been rendered superfluous. Progress therefore halts because this all-important instinct has fallen into disuse. At a point the rates will bear no more, and those who depend on them for their pleasures are doomed to disappointment. They are entitled to our pity for the helpless condition into which the system contracts their faculties and their character. Those who have been compelled to accept a semi-gratuitous education, which is not, in all probability, the sort of education they would have chosen for themselves, but which is intended to create a taste for reading, can hardly be expected to relish paying the market value for their books and newspapers. They have been taught to read at other people's expense, and why should they not be provided with books in the same easy way? It is not at present proposed to supply them with foolscap, etc., in order that they may 'keep up' their writing proficiency, but no doubt this is a luxury reserved for the near future. No doubt this 'cheap' way of getting literature helps to throw light on the fact that so many public books are injured by bad usage, and defaced by marginal notes. That which is got for nothing is valued at nothing. Possibly the advocates of literary pauperism will see little force in the argument that if readers were left to pay for their own books, not only would books be more valued, but the moral discipline involved in the small personal sacrifice incurred by saving for such a purpose, would do infinitely more good than any amount of culture obtained at other people's expense. It is true the Free Library party strongly repudiate the charge of dishonesty; but it is difficult to see any real difference between the man who goes boldly into his neighbour's house and carries off his neighbour's books, and the man who joins with a majority, and on the authority of the ballot-box, sends the tax-gatherer round to carry off the value of those books.

We insist most strongly on the injury done to the pauperised recipients of these favours. Want is the spring of human effort. Self-discipline, self-control, self-reliance, are the habits which grow in men who are allowed to act for themselves. The meddlesome forestalling of individual effort, which is being carried into mischievous excess, is going far to bind our poorer classes for another century of dependence.

Let us run, as rapidly as possible, through a few of the pleas set up by the advocates of this form of municipal socialism. Good books, it is said, are out of the reach of the working man. Even if this were true, it is no reason for persuading him to tax his neighbour for them. If the working man cannot come by his books honestly, let him wait until he can. But a glance down the lists of some of our publishers will show anyone that the statement is not true —is the very reverse of truth. When books like 'Pilgrim's Progress,' 'The Vicar of Wakefield,' 'Rasselas,' 'Paul and Virginia,' Byron's 'Childe Harold,' 'Lady of the Lake,' 'Marmion,' and others, can be purchased from Messrs. Dicks at twopence each; when all Scott's novels can be obtained from the same publishers for threepence per story; when, from the same source, any of Shakespere's plays can be got for a penny each, it will not do to say that the best kind of literature is unpurchasable by a class that spends millions a year on alcohol, as well as thousands on tobacco and other luxuries. Three or four pence, which even comparatively poor people think nothing now-a-days of spending on an ounce of tobacco or a pipe, will buy enough of the best literature to last an ordinary reader at least a week or a fortnight. And when the book is read, there is the pleasure to be derived from lending or giving

it to a friend, and of accepting the loan or gift of his in
return; a custom that largely obtains in country districts
where no socialistic collection of unjustly gotten books
exists to hinder the development of personal thrift, or
poison the springs of spontaneous generosity. Lying on
the table where this is written is a list of the works published in Cassell's National Library. How some of the old
book-lovers who are gone—who lived in the days when
the purchase of a good book involved some personal sacrifice—would have appreciated this valuable library! Here
are 208 of the world's best books, each one of which contains some 200 pages of clear readable type. The published
price is threepence each; but a discount of twenty-five
per cent is allowed when four or five or more are purchased. It would be a waste of space to give the entire list;
but a few typical examples may be taken. Here are the
Essays of Lord Macaulay; here are works by Plutarch,
Herodotus, Plato, Xenophon, Lucian, Fénelon, Voltaire,
Boccaccio, Goethe, and Lessing—in English, of course.
Here is Walton's 'Complete Angler,' Goldsmith's 'Plays,'
Bacon's 'Wisdom of the Ancients' and 'Essays.' Here are
works by Burke, Swift, Steele and Addison, Milton, John-
son, Pope, Sydney Smith, Coleridge, Dickens, Landor,
Fielding, Keats, Shelley, Defoe, Dryden, Carlyle, Locke,
Bolingbroke, Shakespere, and many others. All Shakespere's plays are here complete, and each play is accompanied by the poem, story, or previous play on which it is
founded. Here, for example, is the last of the series as yet
published, 'All's Well that Ends Well'; it contains a trans-
lation of the story of Giletta of Narbona from Painter's

'Palace of Pleasure': it is worth threepence to a student, if only for showing the difference between raw material and finished product. Hundreds of new novels, including some of those of Thackeray, Kingsley, Dickens, Lytton, and other well-known authors, are to be obtained in most places for 4-1/2*d.*, and their second-hand price is less still. Considering the marvellous cheapness of good books, it is difficult to understand how anyone can either blackmail his neighbour for them, or encourage working-men to do so. If a man will not deduct a few coppers now and then from his outlay in other luxuries to purchase literature, he cannot want literature very badly; if he does not value books sufficiently well to buy them with his own earnings he does not deserve to have them bought for him with other people's earnings. That poor women and others, who are often the sole support of a large family of children, should have their hard earnings confiscated to maintain readers—many of them well-to-do—in gratuitous literature, is an injustice not to be palliated by all the hollow cant about culture and education so freely indulged in at the present time. Some time ago there was a discussion on 'the sacrifice of education to examination.' There is another question quite as serious—the sacrifice of justice to so-called education.

But, we are told, the educational value of Free Libraries is so great as to outweigh all other considerations. Some estimate will shortly be given of this value, but just now it is not out of place to inquire what is meant by this misleading term, education. What is it to be educated? I am a farmer, let us say, and my fathers have been farmers for

generations back. Heredity has done something to fit me
for a farm life, as it has fitted the Red Indian for his
hunting grounds. But I have a son whose tastes are similar
to my own. I was bred up on the farm, and accustomed
to rural work from infancy. I have thus acquired a practical knowledge which life-long experience alone can give.
Naturally I decide to give my son the same education. No,
no, says the State, you must send your children to this
school for some five or six of the best hours of every day;
we cannot allow you to bring them up in ignorance. Now
what does this mean? It means that just at the time when a
child is beginning to form his tastes, just at the period
when the daily habituation to the simple duties of farm
life would lay the foundation, both of sound health and
practical knowledge, he is taken out of the parent's control, and subjected to a mind-destroying, cramming process, which excludes practical knowledge and creates a
dislike for all serious study—for force is *always* the negation of love. And this, forsooth, is education! This is fitting
men and women for the practical duties of a world in which
the largest proportion of the work requires no book learning to do it! The pulpit and the press, the guides of popular
opinion, have put it about that there is nothing like books,
the shoemaker has been heard to make the same remark
about leather, and our School Board mill does its best to
turn out the article 'clerk' for a uniform pattern. When
shall we learn that the only useful education for nineteen
out of every twenty is one which develops a quick ear, a
sharp eye, a strong well-knit and muscular frame, and that
it is not to be got by repeating lessons, but by continual
contact with the facts of everyday life; for thus only can

children acquire a practical knowledge of the world in which their future life has got to be lived.

It is hardly necessary for us to say that we have no objection, either for ourselves or for our neighbours, to novel-reading. On the contrary, we regard it as a legitimate form of recreation. All we argue is that it is not a luxury which should be paid for out of the rates. Now, to listen to the advocates of Free Libraries one would imagine that these institutions were only frequented by students, and that the books borrowed were for the most part of a profound and scholarly character. But the very reverse of this is the case. The committee of the Blackpool Free Library, in their Report for the year 1887–8, say: 'Works of fiction and light literature enjoy the greatest degree of popularity, each book circulating eleven times in the year, while *the more instructive books in the other classes circulate only once during the same period.*' The following table, taken from page 5 of the Blackpool Report, shows 'the number of works in the Library in each class, the number of issues in each class, the average number of times each work in each class has been issued, and the daily average issue in each class':

Classification of Works	Number of Works	Number of Issues	Average No. of Times Each Work Has Circulated During the Year	Daily Average Issue
Class A—Theology, Philosophy, &c.	359	199	0.5	0.7
" B—History, Biography, Travels	1,416	2,700	1.9	9.0
" C—Law, Commerce, &c	144	100	0.7	0.3
" D—Science, Art	496	990	2.0	3.4
" E—Fiction and Poetry, and General Literature	3,785	41,199	11.0	137.0
Total	6,200	45,188	8.5	150.2

No wonder is it, after such results as this, that the Committee should express the opinion 'that the rich stores of biography, history, travels, and works of science and art which have been added in recent years are deserving of greater attention than has hitherto been given to them.'

It will be seen that in the above table, novels, poetry and general literature are all lumped together. The usual and more satisfactory custom is to classify fiction by itself. The following tables, taken from page 7 of the Report of the Cambridge Free Libraries for 1888–9, show the work done there during something over thirty years (See Table A). A similar return is given (in Table B) for the Norwich Free Library.

The aggregate yearly issue of course varies in different towns. We print a table taken from page 18 of the eighth annual Report of the Newcastle-upon-Tyne Free Library (See Table C).

We give also a balance-sheet which will serve to show the kind of expenses attendant on these institutions (Table D).

Of course the cost of a Free Library varies with the amount realised by the rate which is levied on the assessed rentals of householders. Subjoined are two tables, taken from the second and third annual Reports of the Yarmouth Free Library, which show both the amount paid and the work done for it in a number of boroughs in different parts of the country (Table E).

The rate is limited by law to a penny in the pound. There are, however, various devices by which it may be raised. The most usual is to smuggle a clause into a 'Local Im-

TABLE A
Classification of Books Issued from the Reference Library

Opened 1855 Issue from	Theology and Philosophy	History	Biography	Law, Politics, and Commerce	Science and Art	Natural History	Poetry	Fiction	*Periodical Literature	Miscellaneous Literature	Total Issue
1855–88	1,343	15,025	2,974	1,264	6,034	2,146	4,514	34,803	96,426	4,330	168,859
1888–89	32	802	34	37	1,044	68	972	130	7,238	80	10,437
Total	1,375	15,827	3,008	1,301	7,078	2,214	5,486	134,933	103,664	4,410	179,296

Classification of Books Issued from the Lending Libraries

Opened 1858 Issue from	Theology and Philosophy	History	Biography	Juvenile Books	Law, Politics, and Commerce	Science and Art	Natural History	Poetry	Fiction	Periodical Literature	Miscellaneous Literature	Total Issue
1858–88	25,701	90,972	33,616	68,345	8,634	33,207	18,931	29,311	1,009,230	139,432	39,370	1,496,749
1888–89	1,143	3,368	1,715	5,577	385	1,985	809	1,155	54,329	5,697	1,476	77,635
Barnwell Branch	44	822	114	1,082	19	283	62	104	10,025	4,068	198	16,821
Total	26,888	95,162	35,445	75,004	9,038	35,475	19,802	30,570	1,073,584	149,197	41,044	1,591,209

* It is worthy of note that periodical literature is largely made up of fiction in the shape of long and short stories, and is much read for this reason.

TABLE B

A Classified Register of Issues of Books in the Norwich Free Library from 1878 to 1887-8*

Year	Days Open	Art, Science and Political Economy	Biography and Correspondence	Poetry and Drama	Fiction	History and Travel	Magazines, Reviews, and Miscellaneous**	Law and Theology	Natural History	Yearly Issues	Average Daily Issues
1878	267	978	1,132	595	18,485	1,814	2,779	270	255	26,308	99
1879	291	843	964	353	21,300	1,828	3,443	560	911	30,202	104
1880	290	1,141	1,697	639	19,733	3,030	5,119	339	336	32,034	110
1881	231	907	1,903	501	18,881	2,749	7,323	295	277	32,836	142
1882	196	921	1,311	318	19,318	2,577	5,736	211	500	30,892	158
1883	244	1,437	1,148	566	32,586	3,033	9,512	202	422	48,906	200
1884	242	1,547	1,315	550	41,233	3,217	9,396	192	356	57,806	239
1885	238	1,751	1,742	552	47,326	2,891	10,755	282	704	66,003	277
1886	239	1,779	1,734	510	55,318	3,433	11,251	317	774	75,116	314
†1887	60	434	379	124	15,042	687	3,037	95	113	19,911	332
1887-8	242	1,713	1,271	763	57,440	2,342	12,728	293	700	77,250	319
Totals	2,540	13,451	14,596	5,471	346,662	27,601	81,078	3,056	5,348	497,264	196

* Taken from p. 12 of the 1887-8 Report.
** Largely read for the sake of the fiction they contain.
† In 1887 the Library year commenced March 26th instead of January 1st.

TABLE C

Work Accomplished in the Lending Departments of Twelve Public Libraries in England, as Compared with Newcastle-upon-Tyne*

No.	Name of City or Town	Date of Establishment	Population of Municipal Borough according to Census return for 1881	Number of Lending Libraries	Number of Readers' Tickets in use	Total Number of Volumes in Stock	Total Issue	Turn Over	Stock of Volumes in Prose Fiction	Issue in Prose Fiction	Turn-over of Prose Fiction as Compared with Stock	Percentage of Issue in Prose Fiction as Compared with Gross Issue
1	Liverpool	1852	552,508	2	9,035	47,283	427,532	9.04	17,408	328,240	18.85	76.77
2	Birmingham	1861	400,774	5	20,111	58,658	542,901	9.25	21,779	347,334	15.94	63.97
3	Manchester	1852	341,414	6	42,695	102,696	775,000	7.54	28,039	545,844	19.46	70.43
4	Leeds	1870	309,126	27	21,259	115,695	739,618	6.39	46,090	421,832	9.15	57.03
5	Sheffield	1855	284,410	5	13,639	77,224	208,862	2.70	18,490	135,743	7.34	64.99
6	Bristol	1876	206,503	6	18,654	72,600	642,432	8.84	17,571	371,548	21.14	57.83
7	Newcastle-upon-Tyne	1880	145,228	1	11,968	31,498	259,462	8.23	7,827	126,806	16.20	48.87
8	Leicester	1870	122,376	2	6,408	20,588	126,391	8.56	7,974	106,528	13.36	60.41
9	Sunderland	1860	116,542	1	2,628	13,567	109,953	8.10	4,967	94,012	18.93	85.51
10	Preston	1879	96,532	1	13,990	15,637	104,000	6.93	3,396	71,297	20.99	68.55
11	Norwich	1857	87,842	1	3,660	11,966	81,065	6.77	3,543	60,849	17.17	75.06
12	Wolverhampton	1869	75,766	1	2,000	25,000	62,901	2.51	7,234	44,253	6.11	70.35
13	Rochdale	1872	68,865	1	6,500	29,170	145,770	4.99	11,583**	118,033**	10.19	80.97

* It will thus be seen that Newcastle-upon-Tyne is seventh in population, seventh in number of readers' tickets in use, fifth in stock, fifth in turnover, seventh in libraries.

** Includes juvenile literature.

TABLE D

NEWCASTLE-UPON-TYNE PUBLIC LIBRARY BALANCE SHEET, 1888–9

PUBLIC LIBRARIES CAPITAL ACCOUNT

Dr.	£ s. d.	Cr.	£ s. d.
1889.		1889.	
March 25. To Balance from last year	0 6 9	March 25th. By Balance to next year	0 6 9
	£0 6 9		£0 6 9

LOANS

Outstanding 25th March, 1889 .... £23386 0 0

PUBLIC LIBRARIES RATE ACCOUNT

Dr.	£ s. d.	£ s. d.	Cr.	£ s. d.	£ s. d.
1889.			1889.		
March 25. To Balance from last year		2120 8 10	March 25. By Interest on Money Borrowed, Dividends on Stock, and Redemption of Loans ..		877 1 5
" Amount of Rate received, less Poundage		3027 13 1	" Salaries	818 17 11	
" Catalogues sold	3 16 0		" Books, Magazines 638 14 2		
" New Supplementary Catalogues sold	15 10 0		" Binding Books, and Carriage . 120 2 9		
" Juvenile Catalogues sold ...	5 5 6			758 16 11	
" Vouchers sold	19 15 7		" Librarian's Disbursement, etc.	23 9 4	
" Fines and Damages	159 6 6		" Printing, Stationery, etc. ..	91 2 7	
" Sundries	5 8 1		" Rent, Gas, Insurance, Water, Coals, etc.	210 2 2	
		209 1 8	" Repairs to Buildings, Fittings, etc.	127 13 0	
			" Fire—Renewal of Books ...	9 1 6	
					2039 3 5
CLASSES			CLASSES		
" Hire of Rooms for Examination	2 2 0		" Grants and Fees to Teachers, etc.	62 16 1	
" Fees	0 10 0		" Gas, Printing, Examination Papers, etc.	21 16 6	
		2 12 0			84 12 7
					3000 17 5
			" Balance to next year		2358 18 2
		£5359 15 7			£5359 15 7

J. J. PACE, *City Treasurer.*

TABLE E

	Name of City or Town	Established	Population	Contribution from Rates £	Total Borrowers	Total Vols. in Lending Library	Annual Issue	Daily Average	Prose Fiction Issues	Percentage of Issues in Fiction
	Barrow-in-Furness ...	1881	50,000	810	2,072	11,116	77,565	262	37,868	48.82
	Bolton ...	1852	105,414	1,500	9,109	26,067	83,081	271	67,697	81.48
	Cheltenham ...	1884	43,972	1,037	4,070	7,384	102,305	355	66,733	65.22
	Rochdale ...	1872	68,866	940	6,000	28,208	138,360	477	108,800	78.63
Comparative Statistics of Ten Free Libraries for 1887–8	St. Helens ...	1877	57,403	800	1,528	11,430	97,060	313	78,083	80.34
	Smethwick ...	1877	25,076	340	3,685	5,697	54,510	225	31,492	57.77
	Wandsworth ...	1885	210,434	800	1,290	6,721	91,878	378	60,208	65.53
	Wednesbury ...	1878	24,564	260	......	7,008	68,595	287	36,565	53.15
	West Bromwich ...	1874	56,295	613	......	10,508	65,909	260	39,231	59.37
	Wigan ...	1887	50,000	620	......	9,397	64,849	222	52,463	80.89
	Aston ...	1878	58,650	670	2,700	6,918	91,761	301	54,002	58.85
	Cambridge ...	1855	41,000	746	2,688	25,206	92,453	...	63,392	58.57
	Chester ...	1877	40,500	636	1,257	13,052	50,555	167	44,497	88.02
	Halifax ...	1882	77,000	1,100	7,834	28,086	103,812	355	64,113	61.75
	Hanley ...	1887	50,000	620	3,231	4,407	87,745	283	69,838	79.59
Comparative Statistics of Thirteen Free Libraries for 1888–9	Middlesborough ...	1871	56,000	912	3,437	14,429	86,079	...	46,309	53.80
	Norwich ...	1857	91,000	1,045	3,550	11,534	82,636	341	57,440	69.51
	*Preston ...	1880	95,000	1,190	13,990	15,637	85,020	360	71,297	83.86
	Stockport ...	1875	60,000	921	......	13,299	79,427	269	63,593	79.81
	South Shields ...	1873	57,000	850	9,594	11,341	85,869	291	48,689	56.70
	Walsall ...	1859	60,000	520	10,103	13,022	73,554	...	53,135	72.25
	Wolverhampton ...	1869	80,000	1,013	......	24,328	62,901	256	44,253	70.34
	Yarmouth ...	1886	50,000	650	3,085	6,870	110,438	380	88,611	80.33

* Closed seventy-two days.

provement Act' or 'Omnibus Bill.' The following letters
were received in reply to an inquiry on this point:

WIGAN FREE PUBLIC LIBRARY,
February 11th, 1890

Dear Sir,   The clause we have obtained for increasing the
rate to 2*d*. was contained in a local Act (or omnibus Bill), which
included as well many other matters relating to other departments of the Corporation. The Mayor of Wigan took the chair
at a public meeting of the ratepayers, and the Bill was approved
by a majority of those present. No poll was taken or asked for.
Very few libraries are rated at less than 1*d*. in the £. I do not
believe they could work at all successfully on less except in the
case of very large centres, producing a large return. I do not
know of individual cases of libraries on less than a 1*d*. rate.

I am, yours truly,

M. D. O'BRIEN   H. T. FOLKARD

TOWN HALL, PRESTON,
February 11th, 1890

There was no poll on the Bill which contained the power to
increase the Free Library rate to 1-1/2*d*.

H. HAMER,

M. D. O'BRIEN   Town Clerk

OLDHAM,
February 12th, 1890

Sir,   The Council of this borough obtained power to levy a
higher rate than 1*d*. in the £ through an Improvement Bill,
which, I believe, passed the House of Commons in 1865.

Yours faithfully,

THOS. W. HAND,

M. D. O'BRIEN   Chief Librarian

FREE LIBRARY, NOTTINGHAM,
February 11th, 1890

Dear Sir,   Our library rate is only 1*d*. in the £, though we
get a separate allowance from the Council of £1500 per year for

support of nine or ten reading-rooms in different parts of the borough.

Yours truly,

Thomas Dent

M. D. O'Brien

Leicester Free Public Library,

February 11th, 1890

Dear Sir,   A poll was not taken when the library rate was increased to 2*d*. in the £.[1] The present levy is 1½*d*., which is allotted by the Council to three committees, Free Library, Museum, and Art Gallery. When the rate was increased a clause was inserted in the local Act.

Yours faithfully,

C. Kirby

M. D. O'Brien

Reference Library, Birmingham,

February 20th, 1890

Dear Sir,   The Free Libraries' rate in Birmingham for last year (1889) was 1.27*d*. in the £.

Yours truly,

J. D. Mullins

M. D. O'Brien

But although the nominal and frequently exceeded limit is now one penny in the pound, there is no knowing how soon it may be raised. Already the Library Association of the United Kingdom, a body composed of librarians whose bureaucratic instincts naturally impel them to push their business by all possible means, has awarded a prize of ten guineas for a draft Library Bill, which, among other things, permits a twopenny instead of a penny rate. 'But,' says

---

[1] When the article on Libraries in the present edition of the *Encyclopaedia Britannica* was written the Leicester rate was 1/2*d*. in the £. It is a common argument of the Free Library agitators to tell the ratepayers that the library rate will only be 1/2*d*. in the £. This was done at Hastings, where the Acts were recently rejected by a majority of more than three to one.

the *Daily News* of Oct. 4th, 1889, 'the feeling appeared to be unanimous that it would be *unwise* to put this forward as a part of the Association's programme, as it would enormously increase the opposition to the adoption of the Act in new localities.' No regard for the ratepayers' pockets holds them back; but only a fear of injuring business by frightening the bird whose feathers are to be plucked. Were it not for this the Bill would be pushed forward, and those ratepayers who have voted for the adoption of the Act in the belief that no more than one penny can be levied, would have the rate suddenly doubled over their heads without knowing it. Perhaps, after all, it would serve them right.[2]

The enormous amount of light reading indulged in by the frequenters of Free Libraries leads us to expect that these places are largely used by well-to-do and other

---

[2] *Free Life* of 10th Oct., 1890, illustrates the greediness of officialism for power in the following:

'The *Pall Mall Gazette* reported (September 20) that, at the Library Association at Reading, Mr. MacAlister proposed, "that in the opinion of this association the time has come when the essential necessity of public libraries as an extension of the compulsory national education being recognised, the question of establishing libraries be no longer left to a plebiscite, and that the establishment of a suitable library in every district as defined under the Acts be *compulsory*." He expected that the resolution would be lost, as on other occasions, but he should move it year after year till it was carried. Mr. Tedber said they would be laughed at if they passed such a resolution just now. Mr. MacAlister said he was aware of the objections and the dreadful things that would be said if they passed the resolution, but it seemed to him absurd that libraries should be the only institutions whose establishment depended on a popular vote. It seemed to him a reproach to civilisation and to the latter end of the nineteenth century that such should be the case. If he had moved such a resolution before compulsory education was adopted he could understand that the arguments against it would have been strong indeed; but we compelled people

idlers. And this is exactly what we find. Free Libraries are perfect 'god-sends' to the town loafer, who finds himself housed and amused at the public expense, and may lounge away his time among the intellectual luxuries which his neighbours are taxed to provide for him. Says Mr. Mullins, the Birmingham librarian, 'No delicacy seemed to deter the poor tramp from using, not only the news-room, but the best seats in the reference library *for a snooze.* Already the Committee had to complain of the use of the room for *betting,* and for the transaction of various businesses, and the exhibition of samples, writing out of orders, and other pursuits more suited to the commercial room of an hotel.' And referring to another Free Library, the same authority continues: 'In the Picton Room of the Liverpool Library, alcoves were once provided with small tables, on which were pens, ink, etc., but it was found that pupils were received in them by tutors, and much private letter-writing

---

to read, some of whom did not want to, and he considered it a cruel thing to create a want the country was not prepared to supply. He held that to make it compulsory to establish free libraries was the logical outcome of the Education Act. *The resolution was negatived by four votes—33 to 29.* A few more MacAlisters scattered about the country, and people will begin to see what a weapon taxation is to put into the hands of logical fanatics, starting from a false premise. In some parts of the world there is a law obliging a man who has a vote to record it; perhaps Mr. MacAlister will propose presently that we should be obliged to read the books in his libraries.

'What is interesting to observe in all these matters is that the compulsion-fanatics have given up the idea of the people choosing for themselves what is good for them. That pretence is worn out and thrown on one side, and whatever the busy-bodies think good for body or soul, that is to be established forthwith. How ludicrous this reign of busy-bodydom would be, if it were not for the rather dismal fact that so few people take the trouble to fight the busy-bodies resolutely.'

was done therein; so that when a respectable thief took away £20 worth of books they were closed.'[3]

After the cant usually indulged in by the officials of literary pauperism such candour as this is positively refreshing. It is seldom the high priest allows us to look behind the curtain in this fashion. As a rule, the admission is much less direct, and can only be gathered from a careful analysis of the statistics. According to the Bristol Report for last year, there were 416,418 borrowers during the twelve months preceding December 31, 1889: of these 148,992 are described as having 'no occupation.' The Report of the Atkinson Free Library of Southport informs us that out of the 1283 new borrowers who joined the library last year, 536 are written down as of 'no occupation.' At the same town, in the years 1887–8, there were 641 who, according to the report, were without any occupation, out of a total of 1481. According to the annual Report of the Leamington Free Public Library for 1888–9, 187 made a return 'no occupation,' out of a total of 282 applicants. In the Yarmouth Report for the same year, out of a total of 3085 new borrowers, 1044 are described as of 'no occupation'; the report for the previous year states the proportion as follows: Total of borrowers, 2813; 'no occupation,' 1078; in the year before that the total was—3401; 'no occupation,' 1368.

Some reports give a fuller analysis of the different classes of people who use the libraries to which they refer. In the Wigan Report for last year we are told that 13,336

---

[3] Report of a Conference in Birmingham of the Library Association of the United Kingdom, published in the *British and Colonial Stationer*, 6th Oct., 1887.

people made use of the reference library in that town during 1888–9. The largest items of this amount are given as follows: Solicitors, 1214; clergy, 903; clerks and book-keepers, 1521; colliers, 961; schoolmasters and teachers, 801; architects and surveyors, 418; engineers, 490; engine-men, 438. At Newcastle-on-Tyne, last year, there were 11,620 persons used the reference library, and only 3949 of these were of 'no occupation.' Yet, notwithstanding the numerical weakness of the letter, they managed to consult nearly half the books that were consulted during that year. The total number consulted was 36,100; and 16,800 were used by people who had 'no occupation.' And this is legislation for the Working Classes!

There is little doubt that at least forty-nine out of every fifty working-men have no interest whatever in these institutions. For one penny they can buy their favourite newspaper, which can be carried in the pocket and read at any time; whereas if they wanted to see a paper at a Free Library they would generally have to wait half an hour or an hour in a stuffy room, without being allowed to speak during the time. The following sensible remarks are from the pen of one who has risen to an honourable position from a very humble beginning without the aid of Free Libraries or Board Schools:

> Not long ago a conference of working men was held at Salford to consider the question of rational amusement, when, in reply to a series of questions, it was stated that Free Libraries were not the places for poor, hard-working men, who had social wants which such libraries could not gratify. It was argued that people who went to work from six in the morning till six at night did not want to travel a mile or so to a Free Library.

Music, gymnastics, smoking and conversation rooms, and other things were suggested, but in summing up the majority of replies, it appeared that amusement rather than intellectual improvement, or even reading, was what was most wanted by men after a hard day's toil. This appears to have been realised in the erection, according to Mr. Besant's conception, of the Palace of Delight in the east end of London.

The truth is that a Free Library favours one special section of the community—the book-readers—at the expense of all the rest. The injustice of such an institution is conspicuously apparent when it is remembered that temperaments and tastes are as various as faces. If one man may have his hobby paid for by his neighbours, why not all? Are theatre-goers, lovers of cricket, bicyclists, amateurs of music, and others to have their earnings confiscated, and their capacities for indulging in their own special hobbies curtailed, merely to satisfy gluttons of gratuitous novel-reading? A love of books is a great source of pleasure to many, but it is a crazy fancy to suppose that it should be so to all. If logic had anything to do with the matter we might expect to hear proposals for compelling the attendance of working men at the Free Library. But surely in this nineteenth century, men might be trusted to choose their own amusements, and might mutually refrain from charging the cost thereof to their neighbours' account. This pandering to selfishness is bad for all parties, and doubly so to the class it is specially intended to benefit.

The following imaginary dialogue will perhaps serve to show the inherent injustice of literary socialism.

A and *B* earn 1s. each by carrying luggage. Says *A* to *B*: 'I am in favour of circulating books by means of a subscription library; from this 1s. I therefore propose to deduct 1d. in order to compass my desire. There is my friend C, who is of the same opinion as myself, and he is willing to subscribe his quota to the scheme. We hope you will be willing to subscribe your mite, but if not, we intend to force you to do so, for, as you know, all private interests must give way to the public good.'

'Perhaps so,' replies B, 'but then, you see, I have my own opinions on the subject, and I do not believe that your method of supplying literature is the best method. Of course I may be wrong, but then I am logically entitled to the same freedom of thought and action as you yourself are. If you are entitled to have your views about a "Free" Library and to act upon them, I am equally entitled to the same liberty, so long as I don't interfere with you. I don't compel you to pay for my church, my theatre, or my club; why should you compel me to pay for your library? For my own part I don't want other people to keep me in literature, and I don't want to keep other people. I refuse therefore to pay the subscription.'

'Very well,' rejoins A, 'if that is the case I shall proceed to make you pay; and as I happen to represent a numerical majority the task will be an easy one.'

'But are we not man and man,' says B, 'and have not I the same right to spend my earnings in my own way as you have to spend yours in your way? Why should I be compelled to spend as you spend? Don't you see that you are claiming more for yourself than you are allowing to me, and are supplementing your own liberty by robbing me of mine? Is this the way you promote the public good? Is this your boasted free library? I tell you it is founded upon theft and upon the violation of the most sacred thing in this world—the liberty of your fellow man. It is the embodiment of a gross injustice, and only realises the selfish purpose of a cowardly and dishonest majority.'

'We have heard all this before,' replies *A*, 'but such considerations must all give way before the public good. We are stronger than you are, and we have decided once and for all that you shall pay for a "Free" Library; don't make unnecessary resistance, or we shall have to proceed to extremities.'

And, after all, the so-called Free Library is not really free—only so in name. If the penny or twopenny rate gave even the shabbiest accommodation to anything like a fair proportion of its compulsory subscribers, there would not be standing room, and the ordinary subscription libraries would disappear. According to Mr. Thos. Greenwood, who in his book on 'Free Libraries' has given a table of the daily average number of visitors at the different Free Libraries distributed up and down the country, there is only one per cent, on an average, of visitors per day of the population of the town to which the library belongs accommodated for a rate of one penny in the pound, sometimes more, sometimes less; but the general proportion is about one per cent. Now what do these facts mean? If it costs one penny in the pound to accommodate so few, what would it cost for a fair proportion to receive anything like a share that would be worth having? Even now it is a frequent occurrence for a reader to wait for months before he can get the novel he wants.[4] Says Mr. George Easter,

---

[4] This is not mere theory. I have before me a letter from a friend in which

the Norwich librarian: 'Novels most read are those by Ainsworth, *Ballantyne, Besant, Braddon, Collins, Craik,* Dickens, Fenn, Grant, *Haggard, Henty,* C. *Kingsley, Kingston, Edna Lyall,* Macdonald, Marryat, Oliphant, Payn, Reade, Reid, Verne, Warner, *Wood, Worboise,* and *Young;* of those underlined (in italics) the works are nearly out.'[5] The fact is, the Free Library means that the many shall work and pay and the few lounge and enjoy; theoretically it is free to all, but practically it can only be used by a few.

While there is such a run on novels, solid works are at a discount. At Newcastle-on-Tyne during 1880–81 we find that 2100 volumes of Miss Braddon's novels were issued (of course some would be issued many times over, as the whole set comprised only thirty-six volumes), while Bain's 'Mental and Moral Science' was lent out only twelve times in the year. There were 1320 volumes issued of Grant's novels, and fifteen issues of Butler's 'Analogy of Religion';

---

he says he has ceased to borrow books from the Sheffield Library because 'if you wanted any popular fiction you had a great difficulty in getting it, and often, if you did get it, the books were in such a dirty condition as to detract from the pleasure of reading them.' On one occasion when the Sheffield Central Library was opened after a holiday, the books having all been called in for inspection, there were about half a dozen people at the door ready to rush in and get the latest popular novels before the rest of the public could secure them. The difficulty of getting any particular novel is so great.

[5] A few years ago the authorities had to take strong measures in the interests of students against the novel-reading users of the British Museum. It was found that vast numbers of people used the library only to get at the newly published novels, which in many cases are issued at 31s. 6d. the set of three volumes. And it must be admitted that there is something very arbitrary in taxing the general public for a library, and then preventing them from seeing the only books they care to read.

4056 volumes of Lever's novels were issued, while Kant's 'Critique of Pure Reason' circulated four times; 4901 volumes of Lytton's novels were issued, while Locke 'On the Understanding' went eight times. Mill's 'Logic' stands at fourteen issues as against Scott's novels, 3300; Spencer's 'Synthetic Philosophy' (8 vols.) had forty-three issues of separate volumes; Dickens' novels had 6810; Macaulay's 'History of England' (10 vols.) had sixty-four issues of separate volumes. Ouida's novels had 1020; Darwin's 'Origin of Species' (2 vols.) had thirty-six issues; Wood's novels, 1481. Mill's 'Political Economy' had eleven issues; Worboise's novels, 1964. Smith's 'Wealth of Nations' (2 vols.) had fourteen issues; Collins' novels, 1368.

'No worse than in other libraries,' it may be said; 'knowledge is at a discount: sensation at a premium everywhere!' Perfectly true; but are people to be taxed to give facilities for this? Novel reading in moderation is good: the endowment of novel reading by the rates is bad—that is our contention. And when it is remembered that any book requiring serious study cannot be galloped through, like a novel, in the week or fourteen days allowed for use, it becomes at once evident that this gratuitous lending system is only adapted for the circulation of sensation, and not for the acquirement of real knowledge. It would be interesting to know what portion of a book like Kant's 'Critique of Pure Reason,' or like Smith's 'Wealth of Nations,' was studied, or even read, during the year! And this is the sort of thing people allow themselves to be rated and taxed for! This is progressive legislation, and its opponents are backward and illiberal!

Free Libraries are typical examples of the compulsory

co-operation everywhere gaining ground in this country. Like all State socialism they are the negation of that liberty which is the goal of human progress. Every successful opposition to them is therefore a stroke for human advancement. This mendacious appeal to the numerical majority to force a demoralising and pauperising institution upon the minority, is an attempt to revive, in municipal legislation, a form of coercion we have outgrown in religious matters. At the present time there is a majority of Protestants in this country who, if they wished, could use their numerical strength to compel forced subscriptions from a minority of Catholics, for the support of those religious institutions which are regarded by their advocates as of quite equal importance to a Free Library. Yet this is not done; and why? Because in matters of religion we have learnt that liberty is better than force. In political and social questions this terrible lesson has yet to be learned. We deceive ourselves when we imagine that the struggle for personal liberty is over—probably the fiercest part has yet to arise. The tyranny of the few over the many is past, that of the many over the few is to come. The temptation for power—whether of one man or a million men—to take the short cut, and attempt by recourse to a forcing process to produce that which can only come as the result of the slow and steady growth of ages of free action, is so great that probably centuries will elapse before experience will have made men proof against it. But, however long the conflict, the ultimate issue cannot be doubted. That indispensable condition of all human progress—liberty—cannot be permanently suppressed by the arbitrary dictates of majorities, however potent. When the socialistic legislation of today has been tried, it will be found, in the bitter experience of the future, that for a few temporary, often imaginary, advantages we have sacrificed that personal freedom and initiative without which even the longest life is but a stale and empty mockery.

M. D. O'Brien

CHAPTER 11

THE STATE AND ELECTRICAL DISTRIBUTION

F. W. BEAUCHAMP GORDON

CHAPTER 11

THE STATE AND ELECTRICAL DISTRIBUTION

On the third of April, 1882, the House of Commons ordered to be printed a Bill 'to facilitate and regulate the Supply of Electricity for Lighting and other purposes in Great Britain and Ireland.' This was the Electric Lighting Act, 1882, in embryo; the first attempt at legislative control, by a general Act of Parliament, of an industry that had begun to loom large in the public mind.

Some of the provisions of this Act, and of subsequent enactments affecting electrical undertakings, constitute what is admittedly a new departure in industrial legislation. Yet the provisions themselves and their tendency, particular and relative, may be said to be almost entirely unappreciated and unknown, except by those immediately affected—sometimes even by them. Ohms and volts and amperes, and other so-called 'electrical jargon,' have apparently frightened men away from the whole subject. It is hoped, therefore, that a short review of the evolution of the provisions and enactments above referred to, and an examination of some of the more important of the questions involved, by one who has been concerned in the business of electric supply from its first inception in this country, who has given much thought to the subject, and who engages to severely ignore anything like technical jargon, may prove both interesting and useful.

The history of parliamentary connection with the subject of electrical distribution dated from the Session of 1879, when several Bills were promoted by local authorities and others praying for powers to supply electric light. This was the year of the Paris Electrical Exhibition. Multitudes of people then realised for the first time the beauty of the new illuminant, and especially its immediate availability, in the form of the glow lamp, for domestic no less than for public use. A laboratory toy, to the lay mind, had been suddenly metamorphosed into something practical, something that you could 'turn on in your house like gas,' and a good deal more. And the gas companies, in their first startled recognition of the appearance of a dangerous rival, swooped down upon it with a claim to a monopoly of the streets for lighting purposes. The whole subject was referred to a Select Committee of the House of Commons. In the Report subsequently presented to the House, the Committee, after brushing aside contemptuously the monopolist claims of the gas companies, (*a*) recommended that every facility should be given to local authorities to carry out, or to procure the carrying out, of experimental electric lighting, but (*b*) expressed the opinion that the time was not yet ripe for any general legislation upon the subject. Consequent upon that recommendation, seven private Acts of Parliament were granted, for a term of five years (ten years in the case of Hull), to as many local bodies, authorising them to raise limited sums of money (generally £5000, but in the case of Hull and of Liverpool £50,000) for the purpose of experimenting in the supply of electric light.

During the three following years huge strides were made, at any rate in the popularization of the idea of an early distribution of electricity from large centres. Everybody knows, many but too well, the history of that short and disastrous interregnum, the harvest of the patentee and the company-promoter. Every difficulty was said to have been overcome, and electric light as 'the light of the future' became a commonplace. The House of Commons, on assembling for the Session of 1882, found itself inundated with Electric Lighting Bills. Patent-owning electric companies, gas companies, gas-owning corporations, and corporations unencumbered with that dubious property, jostled each other in the eager race for statutory powers to supply electric energy. But if the new industry was to assume any more important *role* than that of setting up a show-light on a town parade, if it was seriously to contest, as it was trumpeted to be about to do, the whole field occupied by the gas companies, some recognition was essential of the duties and responsibilities no less than the privileges incident to such a position. No such recognition, it must be confessed, or only a very inadequate one, was discoverable in either of the Bills before the House of Commons. The Electric Light Companies sought a kind of roving commission, to open streets, to erect posts, and to contract with local authorities for the supply of electricity, in any part of the kingdom. Provisions were of course inserted guarding against wanton interference with gas and water mains and telegraphic wires, but the promoters were before all things owners of patent rights in dynamo machines and lamps, for which they were eager to find a market, the more extensive the better. The gas companies proposed simply to extend to electric supply the provisions of the Gas Acts; and the corporations, gas-owning and other, were also generally content with the incorporation in their Bills of legislative enactments already in force. The Bills differed widely in their details, but there was a common want of appreciation of the necessities of the case. The general legislation deferred in 1879, had now become, if not absolutely necessary, at any rate very desirable. So much is conceded; the interests of public and the best interests of the electrical industry itself alike required it.

But legislation of what sort, within what limits? It is here that we arrive at the parting of the ways. Regulations guarding against misuse of the streets; regulations protecting the public, as far as possible, from the danger of a careless distribution of electric energy, and penal clauses enforcing those regulations; these were no doubt required. Provisions ensuring an impartial and efficient supply of light at a maximum price were perhaps also necessary, though not so obviously so, at least at the first, in face of the inevitable competition with gas. But these things being premised, the electric light would seem to have had special claims to indulgent treatment. (*a*) It was known to differ in its very essence from all other forms of artificial light, simply glowing in vacuum, consuming no oxygen, and creating no noxious fumes. Its use in home life would thus make for healthfulness as well as for beauty. (*b*) Its supply would provide a much-needed outlet for private enterprise and the energy that had long drooped under the depression of trade and commerce. (*c*) It would have to be begun and continued, in competition with an illuminant which, however inferior as an illuminant, was cheaper, and might be still further cheapened, and which had the nine-point advantage of possession. For these among other reasons the legislature might have been expected to look with encouraging face upon the new candidate for statutory powers.

But without insisting upon these claims to a 'most-favoured' treatment, any Electric Lighting Act intended really to 'facilitate' the supply of electric light had, on the face of it, one would say, to recognise three essential features.

(1) It should embody full powers to enable the undertaker to generate his electricity, and to distribute it along or under the streets to his customers, and it must make the acquisition of those powers as easy as possible.

(2) While strictly guarding the safety and the rights both of the public and of previously existing and interested bodies, it should not enforce conditions impossible or injurious to the economical working out of the problem of electrical distribution.

(3) It should (therefore) give security of tenure sufficient to attract the investor and to ensure the full development of the industry; and in this connection special regard should be had to any inherent difficulties in the way of such development.

The Bill referred to at the beginning of this paper was on the 17th April, 1882, read a second time in the House of Commons, and committed to a Select Committee. Let us see what sort of recognition it proposed to give to the principles just enunciated.

Full statutory powers to supply electricity for any public or private purposes might be obtained:

(1) By license; to be granted by the Board of Trade to any local authority, company, or person, with the consent of the local authority having jurisdiction within the area to be supplied. This license was to be for any period not exceeding five years, to be renewable at its expiration, with the renewed consent of the local authority interested.

Simple and inexpensive as the acquisition of powers under this form of tenure would be, it was obviously open to the objection that the persons seeking them would be entirely in the hands of the local authority. And it was admitted even by the Board of Trade that, from simple inertness, or from an endeavour to impose unfair terms, or from an indisposition to introduce a competing illuminant, where the local authorities themselves supplied gas, the indispensable consent might be unreasonably refused. The period, too, was so limited, and its renewal so uncertain, nobody could seriously contend that this met the necessities of the case. Another form of tenure was therefore provided, which would, *inter alia,* be virtually an appeal from the local authority to the Board of Trade and to Parliament. This was to be obtained:

(2) By provisional order; to be granted by the Board of Trade, without requiring such consents as were required to the grant of a license, and for such period, whether limited or unlimited, as the Board of Trade might think proper. Of

another (at least implied) form of tenure, that by Special Act, nothing need be said.

It will be shown presently how far the Board of Trade afterwards fell away from this state of grace; but, keeping in mind the avowed object of the Bill, the clause just summarised was, one would say, precisely what it should have been.

The same remarks, with slight modification, may be made relative to the provisions contained in the Bill for the regulation and control of the operations incidental to a system of supply.

But the crucial feature of the Bill was contained in a sub-section to the clause authorising the grant of provisional orders.

This sub-section provided that at the expiration of *seven years* from the date of the legal commencement of a provisional order, or of any subsequent period of *five years*, any company or person supplying electricity within any area should be compelled, on requisition, to sell their undertaking to the local authority, and to sell it at the then market value of the works and plant suitable to the carrying on of the undertaking; all other considerations that usually attach to the sale of a business (goodwill, profits, compensation for compulsory sale, etc.) being expressly excluded.

Does it not read almost like an exquisite bit of irony, the description of such a measure as 'a Bill to facilitate . . . the supply of electricity'? It must, however, be stated, in fairness to the framers of this clause, that in introducing the Bill to the Select Committee the question 'whether seven years was the proper figure or not,' was announced as a question for the consideration of the Committee. But the *terms* of compulsory purchase were regarded as an essential feature of the Bill, and the clause as it stood indicated very plainly the spirit in which the Government proposed to deal with the latest industrial application of scientific discovery.

A large number of witnesses appeared before the Committee to give evidence relating to the provisions of this Bill —witnesses on behalf of the Corporations and of the Electric Light Companies. Having heard all these witnesses, the Committee, towards the end of May, formulated certain resolutions, which were subsequently embodied in a fresh Bill.

In this Bill the tenure of supply by private undertakers was extended to *fifteen* years. Certain other amendments, and a few new clauses, one of which will demand some attention by and by, were added before the Committee rose, and then the Bill was reported to the House of Commons. Before the close of the Session it had passed through a Lords' Committee, and had become the Electric Lighting Act, 1882.

With the Act at length before us we have the materials for a discussion of the 'facilities' it gives to the supply of electricity, we can mark the advance it records in the direction of industrial socialistic legislation. Its provisions were to apply 'to every local authority, company, or person who might by this Act or any license or provisional order granted under this Act, or by any special Act to be hereafter passed, be authorised to supply electricity within any area, and to every undertaking so authorised, except so far as may be expressly provided by any such special Act' . . .

(Section 2). The Act assumes as a postulate the principle that every local authority is within its own area the lighting authority. It is in truth a Corporations' Act, with clauses, partly permissive, partly prohibitive, for outsiders. It will be best therefore to consider first its provisions as applying to local authorities.

The acquisition by them of powers to supply electricity for any public or private purposes within their own area, whether by license or provisional order, was, in accordance with the spirit of the Act, a simple matter of procedure, the provisions for which need not be detailed. For powers to supply *outside* their own district (as they then sometimes supplied gas, and might reasonably propose to supply electricity) the consent had to be obtained, in the case of a license, of the Local Board having jurisdiction over such area. As in the Bill previously analysed, and applicable equally to local authorities and to private undertakers, the license was to run only for a limited term, extended in the Act to *seven* years; the difference in favour of the Corporations being that, of course, no consent, other than that of the Board of Trade, was necessary to its renewal. The term of the provisional order might be of unlimited duration.

Under either of these forms of tenure ample powers were given to them, partly by fresh enactments, partly by the incorporation of certain sections of the Land Clauses Acts and the Gasworks Clauses Acts, (*a*) to levy rates for the purpose of defraying any expenses incurred either in promoting a license or provisional order themselves, or in opposing one promoted by any other person; (*b*) to borrow money on security of the rates for the purposes of electric supply; (*c*) to acquire lands (by agreement, not compulsorily) and patent rights, etc., and to construct works, or to contract with any company or person for the construction and maintenance of such works, or for the supply of electricity; to break up the streets (their power to do this without being subject to indictment for creating a nuisance had hitherto been something more than questionable), and, generally, 'to do all such acts and things as may be necessary and incidental to such supply' (Sections 7, 8, 10, 11, 12).

If to shape a perfectly clear course for the immediate creation of electrical undertakings by local authorities had been the same thing as to 'facilitate the supply of electricity,' then the Electric Lighting Act, 1882, would have been an unqualified success. But it also claimed to be an enabling Act for the furtherance of private enterprise; this in fact was ostensibly its very *raison d'être*. Let us see by what provisions it proposed to justify the claim.

As by the Bill so by the Act, powers to supply electricity were to be acquired by license or by provisional order; the conditions on which they might be obtained were also, with mere verbal elaborations, unchanged. The objections to a tenure by license have already been sufficiently stated. It was a mere tentative system, avowedly for the purpose of promoting experiments which no sane responsible capitalist would be at all likely to undertake. It has been relegated, by common consent, to the limbo of the inoperative. The conditions regulating the grant of provisional orders are contained in Section 4, Sub-sections 1, 2, 3. The local consent to the application was, as it has been shown, unnecessary. Any initial obstruction, for either of the reasons before indicated, by an intractable Corporation was thus rendered impossible. But ample notice had to be given by the promoter of his intention to apply for an order; the order when granted was subject to confirmation by Parliament, and, like any private Bill, might be opposed and, if valid reasons were shown, defeated by the Corporation or by any person interested. Such procedure seems to me to have been entirely fair to everybody concerned. So far, then, the Act was favourable to private enterprise; it satisfactorily provided for the easy acquisition of statutory powers.

In the exercise of those powers the undertakers were not to prescribe the use of any particular form of lamp or burner, nor to show any undue preference either as to the supply of or the charges for electricity; and they were to be subject to any regulations and conditions that might be inserted in their order, or that the Board of Trade might at any time subsequently think it desirable to issue, (*d*) for defining 'the limits within which and the conditions under which a regular and efficient supply of electricity was to be compulsory or permissive,' (*e*) 'for securing the safety of the public from personal injury or from fire or otherwise,' (*f*) for 'authorising inspection and inquiry by the Board of Trade and the local authority,' (*g*) 'for the enforcement of the due performance of their duties, and for the revocation of their powers, in the event of their failing to properly carry them out' (Sections 6, 18, 19, 20).

It may be said generally that the Board of Trade have freely exercised the rights and obligations conferred upon them by the Act. The provisions of the 'model order' issued in 1889, and the subsequent rules and regulations made for the protection of existing interests and of the persons and property of the public—all these are stringent, no doubt, and very properly so, but they cannot fairly be said, except perhaps in some recent attempts by the Postmaster General, to be obstructionist; they impose no burden that cannot well be borne. Except where from their position as the local governing body, they were obviously exempted, these regulations apply equally to local authorities. And with this general statement this part of the subject may be finally dismissed.

There remains the very pith and marrow of the Act—its provision for 'security of tenure sufficient to attract the investor and to insure the full development of the industry.' This, as we have already seen, was considered by the framers of the Bill to have been adequately provided for by the grant of a tenure of fifteen years, to be terminated in the manner and on the conditions summarised in a previous page. The House of Commons tacitly acquiesced; and it was reserved for the Lords to make a further extension of the period to twenty-one years. Seven years, fifteen years, twenty-one years—such is the grudging gradation in the history of this facilitating Act. As (assuming the continuance of the present tendency of legislation) the application of the terms of this compulsory purchase clause will in all probability be indefinitely extended in the future, it will perhaps be well to give the essential part of the clause *in extenso*. Section 27, then, reads as follows:

Where any undertakers are authorised by a provisional order or special Act to supply electricity within any area, any local authority within whose jurisdiction such area or any part thereof is situated may, within six months after the expiration of a period of twenty-one years, or such shorter period as is specified in that behalf in the application for the provisional order or in the special Act, from the date of the passing of the Act confirming such provisional order, or of such special Act, and within six months after the expiration of every subsequent period of seven years, or such shorter period as is specified in that behalf in the application for the provisional order or in the special Act, by notice in writing require such undertakers to sell, and thereupon such undertakers shall sell to them their undertaking, or so much of the same as is within such jurisdiction, upon terms of paying the then value of all lands, buildings, works, materials, and plant of such undertakers suitable to and used by them for the purposes of their undertaking within such jurisdiction, such value to be in case of difference determined by arbitration: Provided that the value of such lands, buildings, works, materials and plant shall be deemed to be their fair market value at the time of the purchase, due regard being had to the nature and then condition of such buildings, works, materials and plant, and to the state of repair thereof, and the suitability of the same to the purpose of the undertaking, and, where a part only of the undertaking is purchased, to any loss occasioned by the severance; but without any addition in respect of compulsory purchase or of goodwill or of any profits which may or might have been or be made from the undertaking, or of any similar considerations.

Read with such provisions as these, the Act says in effect, 'Get capital, build your electric lighting stations, put down your electric conductors, get customers and pay dividends if you can. If you fail, all the worse for you; if you succeed, all the better for the local authorities. In other words, "heads they win, tails you lose." '

Had there been any precedent for such legislation affecting any similar industry? Yes, the Corporations said, the Tramways Act of 1870. And, in fact the forty-third section of that Act is substantially in the same terms as this section. But were the conditions attending the initiation and

the working of the two undertakings in any way analogous? Compare them. The laying of a tramway in any
street practically means the suspension for the time being
of the traffic of that street; and when laid the rails occupy
a large portion of the *surface* of the street, to the great
detriment, and permanently so, of all other traffic. Electric
conductors, on the other hand, would be laid in narrow
trenches under or near the footways, involving no interference with the traffic of the streets, and little with that of
the pavements, immediate or prospective. The Tramway
Company would enjoy during their twenty-one years'
tenure an unquestioned monopoly; the Electric Company
would have to reckon with possible competitors. Again,
the Tramway Company on making their road and running
their cars, might reasonably hope for an immediately remunerative business; no educating process is needed to
induce a man to try a penny ride on a tram-car. Widely different would be the conditions attending the successful
introduction of electric lighting. The prejudice of habit, the
fear of 'shock,' of fire, of failure in the supply, the great
initial expense and inconvenience of 'installing' the necessary wires and lamps, to bring into the house a light which,
beautiful and pure as it might be, would after all cost more
than the light already in possession—all these difficulties
would have to be slowly and painfully overcome, and
would necessarily postpone to a distant date anything like
a general use of the new illuminant. If this be so, it follows
that even with an indefinite tenure the profits on the necessarily large capital of an Electric Supply Company would
certainly be represented during, say, the first two years,
by zero, and during a further two or three years, at least, by

a very modest figure indeed. But a tenure of only twenty-one years, terminable by the purchase of the undertaking at its mere structural value, would seriously endanger the company's capacity to earn any dividend at all. This point will be best illustrated by a quotation from a recent article in *The Times*—

> The amount that would be refunded to the company by the sale of their undertaking must of necessity represent but an infinitesimal part of the total capital that would have been spent in the building up of the business. This deficiency must be provided for somehow. A sinking fund, large in proportion to the shortness of the tenure, must be set aside out of income for the reduction of capital. The larger the sinking fund the higher must the charge be for electricity, the more disadvantageously must electric light compete with its cheaper rival, gas, and the more restricted, in consequence, must be the area of possible supply. . . . The injury would extend to the ratepayer whose 'interests' are to be so jealously guarded. He would suffer, too, by paying an unnecessarily high price for the electricity he would consume.[1]

But the damaging effect of legislation of this character upon the development of electrical enterprise does not stop here. To quote again from *The Times*' article—

> There is another consideration and a very important one. Nobody supposes that the last word has been said upon the question of dynamic machinery. Electrical science will probably stride onward, to discovery, to improvement. Can it be expected that a company which, on arriving at mere maturity has to look only for extinction; can it be expected that such a company would be eager, especially during the last few years of its life, to adopt improved methods of supply? Who would supply the

---

[1] *The Middleman in Electric Lighting.*

capital for the purpose? It may be answered that an arbitrator
would be bound to take into his consideration, in awarding the
price of the undertaking, the greater suitability of the new
methods for the purpose of the undertaking. Possibly; but
would he award anything at all for the old and discarded
machinery—machinery, it must be remembered, which would
still have served to earn dividends? Here would be a dead loss.
Thus a short tenure would have also a tendency to discourage
invention.

With such obvious differences in the conditions incident
to the development of the two industries, the legislation
affecting tramway enterprise was still referred to again
and again by representatives of local authorities before the
Committee upon the Bill, as a precedent that ought to be
followed in dealing with the subject of electrical distribution. It *was* followed, as we have seen. But it was followed,
with a difference of the highest importance, to which attention has not yet been drawn. Section 19 of the Tramways
Act expressly provided that notwithstanding the statutory
right of the local authority to make, or to compulsorily
purchase, a tramway, 'nothing in this Act contained shall
authorise any local authority to run carriages upon such
tramway, and to demand and take tolls and charges in respect of the use of such carriages.' They might devote it to
gratuitous use of the townsfolk, they might lease it to a
company or an individual, but they could not themselves
work it for profit. It is more than doubtful whether they
have power to purchase the rolling-stock at all. So that, as
Sir Frederick Bramwell remarked to the Committee, 'There
would be nothing to prevent the company who had enjoyed
the tramway up to the time of the compulsory purchase,
from being the persons to offer themselves as lessees, with

the very reasonable prospect that they would be taken, knowing more about it, and having everything ready,'— and this, although the tramway might have been a very profitable concern.

Thus it will be plainly seen that the Electric Lighting Act inaugurated a new principle in industrial legislation. It gave to municipal bodies, for the first time (and with every incentive to exercise it), the right to confiscate for the general profit, without compensation, a business created and developed by private enterprise.

Four years after, in 1886, three Bills proposing 'to amend the Electric Lighting Act, 1882,' were introduced into the House of Lords. No. 1 (Lord Rayleigh's Bill) proposed 'to place electric lighting undertakings in the same position as gas undertakings, but as regards privileges and obligations'; thus abandoning frankly the very principle— the confiscating principle, as it may fairly be called—of the previous Act. By this Bill a standard price for the supply of electricity, and a standard dividend, were to be fixed; these were to be subject to variation on the well-known principle of the sliding scale, as now applied to the prices and dividends of gas companies. Any increase of capital beyond that set forth as the company's authorised capital in the provisional order, was to be offered for public tender. The undertaking could be purchased only on such terms as might be agreed upon between the supplying company and the local authority. No. 2 (Lord Ashford's Bill), while retaining for local authorities the compulsory purchase power, extended the tenure to forty-one years, and provided for the sale of the undertaking as a *going concern.* Of these two Bills the first, as placing electric companies on an equal footing with gas companies, was the fairest, both to the new industry and to the public, and the most consistent with all previous legislation affecting similar undertakings. Finally, No. 3 (the Government Bill) proposed simply to extend to thirty years, or perhaps longer, the tenure authorised by the previous Act; the terms of purchase, compulsory and confiscatory, being retained unaltered. The three Bills were committed to a Select Committee of the House of Lords, before whom a whole crowd of witnesses again appeared, to support or to oppose, as their views and interests might direct, the various proposals to amend the Act of 1882.

One thing was clear and indisputable; that Act had failed, utterly failed, as we have seen it was bound to do, to facilitate the supply of electricity. Of the fifty-five provisional orders granted to over-sanguine Electric Light Companies in 1883, only one (the Birmingham Order, under which nothing had been done) remained in force. Having legislated with the sole idea of preventing a possible future evil, Parliament had fully succeeded in making impossible the attainment of any present good. But the Corporations to whom such facilities had been granted by Parliament, who had some of them also obtained provisional orders and private Acts, and for whom confiscatory purchase clauses did not exist, what had they done to help on the development of electric supply? Nothing. Why *should* they pull the chestnuts out of the fire, when the private capitalist had been ordained to do it for them? Theirs was naturally enough a policy of masterly inactivity. So it was that in 1886 the only central electric supply stations to be found in the whole kingdom (those at East-bourne, at Brighton—of very limited proportions—and at the Grosvenor Gallery, in London) distributed their electricity by means of overhead conductors, and without statutory powers of any sort. To explain this fact the Corporation representatives talked vaguely, and—may it be said?—ignorantly, of the 'engineering difficulties' which, along with the reaction from the wild speculation in electrical securities, had stopped the growth of the industry. To this speculation and its disastrous effect, reference has already been made in a previous part of this paper. It probably would have acted prejudicially upon the investing public though only for a short time; investors soon recover their equanimity in presence of even a reasonably good opening for the profitable employment of their capital. But they are largely influenced by the opinions of their financial advisers; and these gentlemen said unanimously, 'Don't touch anything electrical under the Act of 1882; it won't work.' The 'engineering difficulty' question was all moonshine. On the continent and in America, where electrical distribution was no better understood than in England, almost every large town had, as a matter of course, its central distributing station. If there, why not here? Sir Frederick Bramwell, Professor George Forbes, and Mr. Preece, all gave evidence to this effect. They also gave evidence upon another point of the greatest importance in this connexion. It was this. In neither of the countries referred to had the legislature made any attempt to restrict the free action of private enterprise. The municipal bodies prescribed regulations for the placing of electric conductors, etc.; they in no case proposed at any time to confiscate to their own use the business that might be created. Who could gainsay the practical illustration thus afforded of the paralysing effect of the new legislation?

Well, the Act must be amended. But, again, in what direction? The financial witnesses—Sir John Lubbock, Mr. Hucks Gibbs, the late Mr. Lionel Cohen, and others—strongly urged the abandonment of the confiscatory nature of the purchase provisions. Only Bill No. 1 or No. 2, they said, would attract capital; a mere extension of tenure on the old lines would be futile. The principle was a vicious one, and would fail again, as it had already failed. The Corporations vehemently opposed this; any amendment to the Act of 1882 should, they said, continue to recognise both the right of compulsory purchase, and the sale of the business at the market value of the plant.

When, in 1888, the comparative cessation of the hubbub over the General Election and the Irish question again permitted attention to electrical interests, it was found that the Electric Lighting Act, 1888, did, in fact, amend the previous Act in the direction clamoured for by the Corporations. Section 2 extended the tenure to forty-two years, and the optional period thereafter to ten years; the purchasing conditions, with one apparently trifling exception, remaining unaltered. This exception consisted in the insertion of a provision that, in valuing the buildings, works, etc., 'due regard' shall be had 'to the circumstance that they are in such a position as to be ready for immediate working.' This is certainly in favour of the seller; to what extent it is so, time and occasion alone can show. Section 3 provided that the Board of Trade might, if they thought fit, vary the terms upon which an undertaker might be required to sell, 'in such manner as may have been agreed upon between such local authority and the undertakers.' But to balance the concession made by Section 2 to that marauder the private capitalist (without whom it seemed that after all electrical distribution would never come to be an accomplished fact), it was provided by Section 1, that no provisional order should be granted by the Board of Trade, except with the consent of the local authority interested, unless the Board of Trade should be of opinion that, having regard to all the circumstances of the case, such consent ought to be dispensed with, in which case they might dispense with it accordingly.

These provisions have been in force for two years. It is somewhat early perhaps to discuss the effect they may ultimately have, primarily upon the development of the ever-broadening industry to which they apply, and, by reflex action, upon individual enterprise generally in this country. Tendencies may be noted, however, and especially we may record already ascertained results. In London, provisional orders for the full statutory period have been granted to various companies in respect of by far the greater number of important parishes—important, that is, from an electric lighting point of view. Capital, more or less (in some cases, the majority, in fact, very much less) adequate to the requirements of the districts, has been subscribed, and electric conductors have been and are being laid and houses lighted in every direction. Here there are no gas-owning local authorities. In the provinces, speaking by comparison, scarcely a start has been made. Yet during the last Session more than one hundred provisional orders were applied for. A large number of those applications were no doubt of a sufficiently dubious character to court

and to deserve refusal; a great many more, however, were
honestly made by companies prepared to properly discharge the duties and responsibilities they sought. In by
far the greater number of instances, doubtful and good
were alike refused; the local body rarely taking the trouble
to inquire into the status of the applicant. The local authority 'objected to any interference with their streets';
and this in face of the provisions in the model order enabling them to break up the streets and to lay the mains
themselves, at the cost of the undertaker; they 'intended
to apply for an order themselves'; they 'owned the gas supply, and feared the danger to their securities involved in
the introduction of a competing light.' These are actual
summaries of some of the reasons urged against the grant
of provisional orders. In one case well known to me, that
of Barrow-in-Furness, the Corporation opposed the grant
of an order, solely on the ground that there was not a demand in Barrow for electric light. They are of course a gas-
owning Corporation. The applying company satisfied
themselves by a canvass of the town, that a demand did
exist sufficiently to justify them in investing their money
in a supply station; but the Corporation's objection was
held by the Board of Trade to be a valid one, and the order
was refused. There is no need to multiply examples; it is
sufficient to say that in no single instance during last Session was an order granted, without the production of the
written consent of the local governing body. The condi-
tional veto granted to Corporations by the Act of 1888
has in practice become absolute. It would thus seem that
the whole future of electrical distribution outside London
rests entirely with local authorities, a large proportion of

whom, from their position as owners of gas undertakings (upon the security of which vast sums of money have been borrowed), have the strongest possible motives for delaying, and, if it may be, for preventing altogether the development of the industry.

This aspect of the affair has been emphasised by a fresh concession to local authorities made by the Board of Trade at the beginning of last Session. Reference was made in a previous page to one of a few new clauses added by the House of Commons' Select Committee to the Bill which afterwards became the Act of 1882. That clause (Section 11 in the Act), after giving power to local authorities holding provisional orders to contract for the construction of works or for the supply of electricity, concluded in these words: 'but no local authority, company, or person shall by any contract or assignment transfer to any other company or person, or divest themselves of any legal powers given to them, or any legal liabilities imposed upon them by this Act, or by any license, order, or special Act (without the consent of the Board of Trade).' The part within parentheses was added by the Lords' Committee; as the Bill left the House of Commons, the prohibition was absolute and unqualified.

In deference to representations made by the Association of Municipal Corporations, the Board of Trade decided a few months ago to remove that prohibition altogether, so far, that is, and only so far, as it affected the interests of Corporations. A new clause was thereupon agreed to between the Association and the Board of Trade, and was subsequently inserted in all orders granted to local authorities, providing that the local authority might at any time by deed, to be approved by the Board of Trade, transfer to any company or person, for such consideration as might be agreed upon, the whole or any part of the area included in their order, with all the duties and responsibilities incident thereto.

The importance of such a concession may not be immediately evident to the lay reader. It means this. A Corporation—a gas-supplying body, let us say, or one whose interests are largely controlled by directors and shareholders in a local gas company—may obtain a provisional order, without having the slightest intention to supply electric energy. They will thus shut out effectually any inconveniently enterprising individual or company. This order they have the power to transfer for a consideration, to farm out on such terms as they may think fit to dictate. They would stand in fact in the position of middlemen. Would they be likely to offer such terms as would facilitate the supply of electricity? Why, as with exquisite *naiveté* they have asked, should they cut their own throats? Without for one moment imputing deliberate *mala fides*, it is fairly open to a Philistine to doubt whether human nature becomes so impeccable in a councilman that he may not by accident mistake self-interests for public interests. The sound has indeed a familiar ring, as if such a thing had already happened. Of course there is another side to the question. There are honest and well-intentioned Corporations desirous of a supply of electric light, who, while fearful to trade with the ratepayers' money in a comparatively untried business, are yet unwilling to assent to the grant to a company of powers in their towns underived from themselves. In this case the new clause *may* work well. Its general tendency, however, seems to be in a retrograde direction, as giving to interested bodies wide powers to impose terms which under the Act of 1882 had proved prohibitory of electrical development.

The situation, then, created by the Electric Lighting Acts, and emphasised in their administration by the Board of Trade, may be thus summarised. Local authorities have a preferential right to undertake the supply of electricity themselves; they may obtain statutory powers, with the right to farm them out for their own profit; they may assent to the grant of such powers directly to private capitalists taking all the risks incident to the business of electric supply, while they reserve to themselves, at the expiration of forty-two years, or of such shorter time as they may succeed in bargaining for as the price of their consent, the comfortable option of purchasing the undertaking, if it should be a successful one, at something like an 'old metal' valuation, or of declining to purchase an unsuccessful one at any price. And this comfortable option they may exercise every ten years thereafter.

It will be obvious from the foregoing analysis that the tendency, if not the intention, of such legislation is to discourage the supply of electricity by private enterprise, and thus either to arrest the development of the industry altogether, or to throw it into the hands of the local authorities. But are trading municipalities such unmixed blessings that we can afford to bind down the agent that has made us the foremost industrial nation of the world? Or, to narrow the issue to the special subject of this paper, is electrical distribution one of those industries that ought to be in such hands?

The present writer holds anything but pessimistic views as to the future of electricity; still it must not be forgotten that the business of electric supply is as yet a speculative one. There is no accumulated experience to guide us. Continental and American companies do not count. Gas is generally much cheaper there, and in a large number of cases their electric conductors have been run on poles overhead and cheaply. Nobody working under the statutory provisions and restrictions which now obtain in this country has done so at a profit. Dividend-paying data can of course be furnished, and are furnished, in every case; their verification has yet to be accomplished. Ought rates to be raised for speculative purposes? Again, three or four different systems are employed in London by different companies to distribute electric current. We have high tension and low tension, alternating currents and continuous currents, supply with the agency of accumulators, and supply without them. The fittest of these will survive, if either survives —for already Mr. Edison is said to have announced his confident hope 'to obtain electricity direct, without the aid of steam-engines, or of any other motor power.' Which is the fittest? And are municipal bodies the proper people to determine such a question? Resolve them into their constituent elements, and Mr. Smith the bootmaker shall confidentially ask you whether 'volt' or 'ohm' is really the scientific name for a dynamo machine, and Mr. Jones the wine merchant shall make a virtue of the confession that he can't for the life of him make out how electricity can be got out of coals. Every electrical engineer who has been brought into contact with such bodies has met with many Smiths and Joneses. And these are the men, such are the electrical qualifications of the men (aggregated to the dignity of a local authority, of course), who are to determine upon the adoption of a system of distribution, 'to levy rates' (upon the rich and the poor alike, upon those that will and those that will not use the light for many years to come), 'and to construct works,' etc. for the supply of electricity.

Not only so. They are to be the managing directors of the undertaking. It may fairly enough be objected that they both can and naturally will engage the services of the most competent engineers available. No doubt. And a cockney with confused ideas as to the distinction between a harrow and a threshing-machine, may take a farm and engage a head man to manage it. But, although he will have the all-powerful gain-motive which the councilman has not, will his farming operations be likely to be as well or as economically conducted as they would be if he had been born a farmer? It is possible, certainly, to lay too much stress upon this point. Public spirit is also a powerful factor; but a controlling uninformed public spirit, whose servant the engineer will be, may make a pretty mess, with the very best intentions, of an undertaking so complex as the one we are discussing. Jobbery, or anything of the nature of jobbery, could not, of course, be respectfully predicted of an English municipality, the 'scandals' of Salford, and the Metropolitan Board of Works, and the jerry-built school-houses of the London School Board, *et hoc genus omne,* notwithstanding. But the Acts apply equally to Ireland, and Englishmen have a prescriptive right to say many things of the Irish. Who does not see what nice little 'jobs,' under the Electric Lighting Acts, will infallibly be perpetrated, in favour of certain well-known 'friends of the ratepayers,' at Curraghmacree?

Another consideration is the unlikelihood of the employment by local authorities of the necessary 'commercial traveller' element in the business. Our young giant requires to be dressed out to the best advantage, to be introduced and praised, to be *pushed* into public favour. In other words, electric energy, in the form of light or of power, is at present expensive. It has advantages that some people think more than compensate for its costliness, but they have to be made known and repeated. Why should the officials or the members of a municipality do this? It would be no advantage to anybody in particular. An example will be eloquent. At the beginning of last year the Corporation of Bolton, in Lancashire, were asked for their consent to any application by a Company for a provisional order. They refused to give it, intimating that they intended, if there were a sufficient demand for the light, to undertake the supply themselves. And they issued a circular to ascertain whether such a demand did in fact exist. The following is a fair summary of this precious circular: 'We proposed to charge 10*d.* per Board of Trade unit for the current we supply. This will be at least double the price of gas; would you like to have it at the price, and for how many years will you undertake to continue the use of the light?' With such advocacy as this, an invention had need be born into the world with an aureola. With such sponsors, what would have been the fate, not merely of electric light, but of nine-tenths of the inventions which, in private hands, have transformed society?

It is one of the boasted advantages of the conduct of

electrical undertakings by local authorities, that, while a joint-stock company must pay a dividend of 7 or 8 or even 10 per cent upon its capital, they can borrow money at 3-1/2 per cent; the difference representing so much profit to the ratepayer. But, apart from the preceding considerations, tending to disbelief in their capacity to work the undertaking as successfully or as economically as the profit-coveting capitalist would do, the extensive exercise of such cheap borrowing power, this competition of the public purse with the private purse, what effect will it have? Will it not drive the investor, who is not content with 3-1/2 per cent, to seek more remunerative channels for his money elsewhere? Capital will go out of the country, to promote the success of industries which compete with our industries at home.

But another principle underlies this question, larger and more vital still. It may be expressed and illustrated in this way. The greatest obstructionists to the advance of electric lighting have been and are the gas-owning Corporations. Not because they are Corporations, but because they have committed themselves, to the extent of very many millions of money, to the supply of one particular form of light, which might be superseded by the introduction of a competing illuminant. In the nature of things it must be so. Municipalities after all are but an aggregation of mortal men and ratepayers. Now, the creation of electric supply stations will involve the borrowing of one is afraid to say how many more millions of money. Well, the world will not stand still to guard those millions, any more than it has done in the case of gas. Imagine—and for the purposes of the argument it is perfectly immaterial whether the supply be undertaken and the millions borrowed tomorrow or in forty years' time—imagine the discovery of a new form of artificial light, as superior to electric light as that is to gas, will not the same battle have to be fought over again? We are creating a standing obstruction to progress, so many lions in the path.

These, shortly stated, are some of the reasons that seem to tell forcibly *against* the policy of placing the supply of electric energy in the hands of local authorities, and in *favour* of leaving it, with proper safeguards of the public interests, to the care of private enterprise.

The Electric Lighting Acts exist, however, and a precedent threatening to the old form of enterprise generally has been established. It is conceded, of course, that by Parliament this business of supplying light was looked upon as a special one, calling for exceptional treatment. But such special precedents are apt to develop into general ones; and having seen how far the legislature has already gone in fettering individual effort to encourage the supply 'by the people for the people' of one particular article (which after all is not so great a necessity as bread, and no greater a necessity, at any rate, than boots), we may pretty confidently hope, or dread, according to our views upon such matters, for an almost indefinite extension in the same direction. Municipal bakehouses, municipal boot factories, every form of industrial operation developed into everybody's business in general and nobody's in particular —to what Utopian prosperity and happiness may we not yet attain!

F. W. Beauchamp Gordon

CHAPTER 12

THE TRUE LINE OF DELIVERANCE

AUBERON HERBERT

CHAPTER 12

THE TRUE LINE OF DELIVERANCE

Most of the evils, even those which in the end may destroy, have a remedial character in the earlier stages. They are the useful, though often unpleasant, instruments of bringing us back into the true path, if we have left it, or of stimulating us to new endeavours' in seeking for it. Amongst these scourges, disagreeable for the moment, but useful as regards the future, the New Unionism, with its crude doctrines of sheer force, constraint of anybody and everybody who stand in the way of the immediate end, limitation of numbers and excessive prices built up on monopoly, ingenious dovetailing of political action into unionist action, universal federation with rigid centralisation and strict dependence of all parts on the centre, must take its place. Few people of clear insight are ready to suppose that good of the truest kind is likely to come to the workmen enrolled under these principles. Centralisation, coercion and monopoly, always have been the advance guard of eventual failure and suffering, and always

475

will be; though indirect good, by way of experience and healthy reaction, may come from them. No man raises, in a country that is not in decadence, the banner of retrogression, without influencing others to raise the banner of advance. Evil, it is true, provokes evil, but it also provokes good; and perhaps the New Unionism has its own special service to perform by leading workmen to reconsider the whole question of trades-unions, their relation to capital, and to that better future on which we all fasten our eyes. The old Trades-Unionism, like many another movement, has been useful in its day to the workmen, even though founded on shaky principles. It came into existence in a bitter time, when probably no truer system could have lived; it was to the men a first lesson in association, developing powers of administration and responsibility; it has done much in the way of benefit services; it gave a spirit of independence, and yet was an anti-revolutionary force; and it has taught capital the sharp lesson which was needed, at all events during one period of its history, that unless the fair claims of the men were respected, Trades-Unionism could throw the whole thing out of gear, and make a general mess for everybody concerned. But having said so much, it must be confessed that the old Trades-Unionism—with its many excellent points—has been, as regards great results, a failure, and that the New Unionism comes to help to make that failure evident. Let us see exactly what is happening now. The old Trades-Unionism, so far as it was restrictive, represented a dam. On the one side of it was skilled labour, organised and well paid; on the other side unskilled labour, unorganised and badly paid. As long as that state of things lasted, Trades-

Unionism was in a sort of way a success—for the trades unionist. He was, as was sometimes reproachfully said, the privileged class, the aristocracy of labour; and of course the more a union could restrict the admission of members into the trade by limiting the number of apprentices, or in other ways, the more it could for the moment (for there are always reactions in these things) keep up or raise its rate of wages. But the time was sure to come when the effort would be made to raise the waters on the other side of the dam, and then how would it be with the dam? If the unskilled labour could be organised and its price raised, that would mean (employers' profits remaining the same, as they are likely to do, being dependent on causes very hard to fight against, and adjusted in each trade by what obtains in other trades) that the skilled unionist labour would get a lower reward, so far as his wage depended not upon his higher skill, but on trade-union action. The effect of all restriction is to diminish production and raise prices. The trade which previously had a dam, when other trades had not, was at an advantage; for it was exchanging its restricted production against the unrestricted production of other trades—a state of things, which was good for it, but bad for all others. It was taking more and giving less. For this reason, as the New Unionists restrict production, the old trades will suffer. To give an example—the effect of the Dockers' monopoly is to lessen for all other trades the advantages of free-trade. Imported articles will be dearer in price, and the labour of other trades will exchange for less.

Today the New Unionists are bettering the teaching of the Old Unionists; and much as my sympathies go with the

sober part of the Old Unionists, I should be obliged to confess that the New Unionists would be right, if the underlying principles of Unionism itself were right. Let us see
what the New Unionists appear to be aiming at. All trades
are to be unionised—the unions being sufficiently strong
to disregard and coerce, when necessary, the outside labour, and yet not too large so as to depress the price of
labour in the trade itself. Those whom it is desirable to
bring into the union will be brought in by summary methods; those whom it is desirable to leave outside will be left
outside. But as these outsiders are always a menace to the
unionist, measures will be taken to provide at least for a
part of them. Of course it is obvious that the common rule
of a minimum wage acts harshly both on old labour and on
second-class labour; since both these classes lose all employment where the minimum can be universally enforced.
It is then at this point that the action of the State is rather
cleverly brought in to make good the gap which Unionism
fails to cover. Workshops are to be provided by municipalities and County Councils for the inefficient labour,
which, left in the employers' hands, would only drag the
union price down. What is to be done with the product of
such labour, which would be produced irrespective of demand, and independently of market price, is a problem
which, as far as I know, is not yet solved. At the same time
the State is to be made to serve another purpose. Municipalities and County Councils are to pay union price in all
their contracts, thus giving the key-note of wage. An ordinary employer might not be screwed up to the true pitch.
He or his customers might decline the article at the union
price; but the municipality or Council which has once been

captured, can be made to undertake certain work, and in doing it to strike almost any key-note that is desired. The body which spends public funds is independent of the market rate, and is therefore admirably suited for forcing the pace.

The crown of the system is the federation of the unions. When once federated, the power of all will be lent to one; and the area of subscription being made co-terminous with the whole country, and the boycott being duly systematised, both the non-conforming employer and the non-conforming workman will be satisfactorily reduced to submission.

The dream goes still further. What is to be done in one country is to be done in all countries; and just as the trades of a country are to be linked together as a whole, so are the countries themselves to be linked together. When that is done, then and there begins the millennium of labour.

Now it is a great advantage, in criticising separate measures, when we are able to see before us the perfect whole, into which the separate measures are some day to be combined. For example, we should never judge our socialistic future rightly, if we persisted in scanning each measure, that leads towards it, separately by itself. It is the same with the details of Unionism. We must not simply look to the detached struggles of today between labour and capital, as expressing what Unionism is, but also to the system in its triumph, as it will be when, complete in all its parts, it governs the world.

Having said so much, before reviewing what perfect Unionism would mean, let us try and solve the simpler problem by seeing what Unionism means in the detached and unconsolidated form in which it exists today. Before doing so we may all start on the same road. Unionist or non-unionist, we are agreed that labour has to win for itself a different and a better future. The smooth places of the world are not permanently reserved for some of us, and the rough places for others. Enormous is the amount of insincere speech that flows from the lips and pens of today upon this subject. The subject is a profitable one in the political market of our time, and therefore, as we may be sure, receives its full homage from politicians and professional philanthropists; but still no amount of insincerity can alter the great truth, written in the destinies of the world, that for everybody's sake the labourer has to climb not only to competence and comfort, but to the knowledge, refinement and higher civilisation, which at present are so much more easily reached by those who do not labour with their hands. That is the work we have to accomplish; the only question is, 'in what manner?'

There are two roads, and only two roads, which offer themselves to us. One is the road of restriction, regulation, monopoly, and absolute power entrusted to the hands which have to win the successive positions, and defend them when won; the other is the road of free action, unlimited competition, and voluntary association. Now I want to contrast these methods, because I believe it only wants time and full discussion to convince the greater number of our workmen, with their strong instincts in favour of liberty, that all the methods of restriction, whether perfect or imperfect, whether new or old, are wrong and will only end in disappointment after a grievous loss of effort and time. I believe that the weight of argument is strongly on the side of liberty of action and unrestricted competition, and that we lovers of liberty can win the battle, into which we are entering, if we only plead our cause efficiently. The coercionists of every kind can offer the bribe of immediate results; but we have in our hands the appeal to the truer reason and the higher motives, and the battle must at last make for us, if we know how to use our weapons.

Before comparing the two methods, one word as regards the Unionism of the past. I have already said how much I think we owe to it, and personally it is pleasant to me to recall my friendship in former years with some of the old leaders, Mr. Guile, Mr. Allan, Mr. Applegarth, Mr. Howell, Mr. Broadhurst and others, whom it was my privilege to know, and of whom I shall always think and speak with kindness; but in forming a deliberate judgment upon the subject, I can only say that the past is not the present, and the circumstances that once made Unionism, in the old depressed days of labour, of use to the workmen, are so wholly changed, that the time has come when it is right to preach a reformation in the unions themselves, and a change in the direction of the efforts and hopes of the workmen.

The question to face is, can Unionism, as we know it, achieve the new future of the workmen? I answer no, because, speaking of it as a whole, it is founded on distinctly wrong principles. If we examine ordinary Unionism and the full development of the new Unionism as we have sketched it, we shall find the same principles running through both. Unionism essentially means the sacrifice of one section of the labourers to another section—it means this in more than one sense; it means the setting aside of the desires and the judgment of the individual for the sake of a common end; it means temptations to coerce; it means regulation, restriction, and centralisation, with all the evils that flow from these fatal methods.

Let us take the simplest example. 100,000 workmen in a trade are negotiating with their employers. Is there any reason why the workmen should not act in a body as regards their wages? Every lover of fair play would be inclined to say, certainly not; and if the negotiation were really for the whole body, all the units of which were quite voluntarily acting together, one serious part at least of the present mischief of Unionism would disappear. But the unionist only bargains for a part of the 100,000. A union is formed with a certain subscription in preparation for emergencies; and from that moment, although certain common interests continue to exist, there begins to be a divergence of certain other interests between those who are in the union and those outside the union. The union, intent on raising wages, finds it must fix a minimum of pay below which its members must not go. But either this minimum is so low that it is of no service, or else it cuts off from employment the old worker and the second-class worker. These men are naturally below the minimum. Then, as a minimum tends always to be a maximum, it cuts off the best worker, who naturally looks for a larger return from his skill and industry. These three classes, however, are not so important from the unionist point of view as the class of ordinary workman who for many different reasons prefers to be outside the union. He is a real danger to the unionist, as when any quarrel occurs, he may take his place. He therefore must be brought in, until the number outside the union is sufficiently reduced so as not to be dangerous. Here begins the temptation to coerce. The quickest way of securing this end is to make life uncomfortable for the outsider who works in the same shop with unionists; finally, unless he joins the union, tools may be thrown down, and the employer have to choose between standing by a few men on principle or finding himself involved in a strike. But whilst it is necessary for the stability of the union to bring a certain proportion of the ordinary outsiders into the union, an artificial rate of wages cannot be maintained, if labour flows freely in the trade. Therefore the inflow into the trade must be restricted—it must be borne in mind that what I am saying applies only to certain trades, and that it would be an unfair description of many other trades—and this can be done by declaring that only he who has served his apprenticeship, or worked for a certain number of years successively in the trade, can be admitted, whilst at the same time the number of apprentices in a shop is limited.[1] Here—as so often happens with restrictions—there arises a difficulty, not easily got over. If only those who have served their apprenticeship or worked so many years are admitted into the union, the man who has not done so, remains a thorn in the side of the unionist; if he who has not fulfilled such conditions is admitted, the unionist has lost one important means of controlling the entrance. That the New Unionism has other means we see by the action of the dockers, who

---

[1] Mr. Howell—always, I think, a fair and just writer—in his interesting book (The Conflicts of Capital and Labour, p. 274) states that about 10 per cent of Trade Unionists have served their apprenticeship.

simply, after limiting their own numbers, refused to allow any man to work who did not possess the union ticket.

But then what does this control of the entrance mean? It means war on other kinds of labour. Just as the union means a kind of war upon those in the same trade whom it is important to bring in and yet themselves do not wish to be admitted, so it also means war on outside labour. It means that the labourers in other less well paid trades cannot find free access to the better paid trades, that the dam is preventing the true level being found, and that those inside the dam are profiting by keeping others out. Now that is a bad arrangement for all concerned. It is certain that artificial privilege works badly in the end for those who possess it, and carries in itself the seed of its own decay; but this arrangement works badly not only remotely but also immediately and directly. In a restricted trade a parent may be unable to introduce his own child into the shop where he works.[2] The thing which of all others he would most wish to do, to have his boy near him, under his eye, learning his trade, is the thing that is made difficult to him, where a system of restriction exists—a restriction that is increased at present by the stupid interference of our education laws. Never was a heavier price paid for a possible improvement of wage than this sacrifice of this most natural and healthy arrangement. But so it

---

[2] Mr. Howell states that many existing restrictions about apprentices are not enforced. Though partially enforced in some large trades, they are generally confined to smaller trades, and in these cases favoured by the masters (who can be just as restrictive as the men). In many trades only trade-skill, health, etc., are insisted upon as conditions of membership, which in view of the benefits to be paid is quite reasonable.

always is. The restriction we forge against others is always to our own grievous hurt. What I want to press upon those Trade Unionists, whose minds are open in this great matter, is that all systems of restriction hurt more than they advantage; that even the better forms of Unionism are always lending themselves to a certain amount of restriction, if they are to be effective for raising wages. We see that Unionism may mean interference and coercion as regards certain outside labour in the same trade; that it tends to cut off from itself the most pushing and the best men; that in some cases it dams back the labour that would flow into the more highly paid trades from less highly paid occupations; that it puts difficulties in the way of the instruction by the father of his son in his own trade; but besides these there are many other forms of restriction which are apt to spring up whenever men begin regulating for each other the conditions of their labour. The close delimitations of the labour of each trade, the rigid boundaries between mason, bricklayer, plasterer, and carpenter, often leading to much inconvenience and expense— such as we see in the case of the carpenter, who was fined because he was seen enlarging the holes in the wall in which his joists were to be placed; the rule, that existed in one part of England, that bricks laid in a district should be made in the same district, a rule that has stopped work for want of bricks, though bricks in abundance were to be had close by; the rule that stone dressed in the quarry must be dressed only on one side; that stone already dressed must be defaced and dressed over again by the men employed at the works; the rule that an employer building in another town must take half the men from his own town, even if he cannot get them; rules regulating what the bricklayer's assistant may do, and forbidding his rise, however competent, into the rank above him; the rules forbidding piece work; the rules forbidding certain methods of work and payment, which are not the authorised method, even if those in the factory or shop prefer the method in question and are earning more money under it; the rules enforcing a rigid uniformity in the method of doing work; the rules that a man is not to run or to sweat himself in his employer's time; rules against besting his fellows—all these are examples of how thick and fast restriction is apt to grow when once men begin to employ it as their instrument. It is only what we ought to expect. Restriction will always breed restriction, both because the first restriction is found to be incomplete without the second, and the second without the third; and because men who once lend themselves to restriction acquire the temper of betaking themselves to restriction in face of every difficulty.

A list of such union sins—and let it be well understood that they only apply to certain trades, and some at least, I hope, are growing obsolete—is to be found in Mr. Thornton's interesting book on Labour (p. 326). He himself considers that all such restrictions are not of the essence of Unionism. That may be true in the sense, that they are principally found in unions which have something of the nature of a monopoly. In trades, such as the cotton trade, where there is keen foreign competition and intelligent appreciation of the position amongst the workers, such restrictions are likely to be at a minimum; but the moment you have entered the path of restriction, you may be sure that whatever further restrictions are necessary to make your first restrictions efficient, will presently be employed. That is the danger of all restriction; there are so many steps waiting to succeed to the first.

Let us look quickly at some other faults of Trades Unions. It not only surrounds a man with restrictions, which every frank person will admit to be an evil, even if an evil accompanied with good, but it does much harm by disregarding natural variety, by tending to throw men into one class, and treating them as if they were all alike. Men are not alike in strength, endurance, or character; and it is much happier and better for them when these differences find their true expression. There are some men who prefer long hours and slow work; some who prefer few hours and sharp work; some who prefer long hours and sharp work, receiving for it higher reward; and it is a wrong and cruel system which ignores all these differences and dictates the same uniform work and same uniform pay to all men. If the life of labour is to be a happy life, one of the principal things to be done is to give every opportunity that is possible to the worker to follow his own manner and hours of work. At the British Association this year Professor A. Hadley mentioned an interesting fact. In America he found that in one factory, where the hours were longer, less work was done than in another factory where the hours were shorter. Why? Because the slower workers could not live the pace of the quicker workers, and preferred to work longer hours at the pace that suited them. Thus a natural sifting took place, which adjusted the work of the men according to their own likings. This is what the workers have to aim at. Not rigid uniformity, not an established number of hours, or one orthodox method, but infinite variety, meeting the varying wants of different natures.

Let it be remembered that there is no living man who can measure the full result of restrictions. They are always clumsy things, and though some of their results can be foreseen, they always produce some startling and unexpected results. In the case of Trades Unions they interfere rudely with the motives that influence a man's desire to do his best. Where piece-work is forbidden, the better worker, as we have seen, has to adjust himself to the pace of the slower man, he has to think whether or not he will do more than his comrades consider right. Most of us are more or less familiar with examples where difficulties with unions have checked attempts on the part of enterprising manufacturers to take a special branch of trade out of the hands of competing foreign countries by impeding adaptations that were necessary for the purpose; they are apt to lead to centralised management—one of the greatest curses in the world—placing the arrangements of the men in a particular shop with the employer at the mercy of some established system and the officers who enforce it; they sometimes hang like a thundercloud over the head of the best employers who desire to try new paths; and they are apt to destroy the possibility of a close alliance and partnership growing up between such employers and their men, and thus to prevent the energies of the country being freely given to production.

I am not bringing these charges, which for the most part are very old, because I think in labour disputes the men are wrong and the employers right. I only bring them because these evils seem to me the necessary result of restrictive methods. I think all restriction—wherever and by whomsoever employed—works out badly; and I feel sure that the workmen will never gain the inheritance waiting for them, as long as they seek to advance along that line.

Ahead a still graver evil lurks in these restrictions. As I have already said, no person who once enters the road of restriction ever stands still. Either, conquering all former scruples, he goes on supplementing the old restrictions with new restrictions in order to make them efficient, or, disgusted with the odiousness of compelling men to act against their own wishes and of reducing them to cyphers by regulation, he throws up the whole attempt and retraces his steps. We are now reaching a point where unionists must make their choice. If they are to persevere in the path of restriction, they must be prepared to put themselves and their brother-workmen under a system in which their own individual wish, and even the wish of their own particular trade, can count for almost nothing. You cannot form the 1/100th or 1/500th part of a huge fighting system, and keep any real control over yourself. The necessities of the system as a whole will govern your action, and you will be carried forward with the general movement, whether you approve or disapprove. I ask unionists to judge present Unionism, not simply by what we see today, not simply by the restrictions and coercions which they are occasionally tempted to employ towards their fellow-workmen either at the moment of a strike or when it is thought necessary to force men into union, but by the threatened development of Trade Unionism—all trades being federated into one body and negotiating with all employers,

federated into another body. I ask them if they are willing
to help forward such an organisation of society into these
two hostile camps. I ask them to think of the tremendous
power that must be lodged in a few hands; of all the
countless struggles and intrigues to obtain that power; of
the worthless men who will succeed in obtaining it; of
the fatal mistakes that will be made even by good and
true men, holding this power in their hands; and of the
harsh unscrupulous use that will be made of this power to
destroy all individual resistance that is inconvenient. I ask
them if this is an ideal to which they are ready to devote
such part of their lives and energies as still remain to them,
to organise society into two great armies, always watching
each other, and always preparing for bitter struggle; and
I ask them, even if, after the struggle, labour prove successful, if employers and capitalists were thoroughly
worsted and obliged to take such terms as might be dic-
tated to them, would such a defeat be good for labour
itself, would it make for its progress and its happiness?
Does not the sense of absolute power in the end wreck all
those who possess it; are there any amongst us who are
not destined to be corrupted by it, more surely than by any
defeat or reverse that can happen to us?

Now let me turn to the economical side. Can a system of
restrictions really better the men's position? can it better
wages? can it take from the employers and give to the men?
I venture to say that the mass of evidence is distinctly
against any true and permanent bettering of the men's
position by such means. Certain things may be conceded
at once. I think it was Mr. Mill who summed up the power
of trades unions in altering wages, by saying that they

could bring about the rise of wage quicker, and delay the fall somewhat longer; and a Midland manufacturer has lately (Free Life, 24 May) pointed out their equalising and averaging effect. Under their influence small masters on the one side, and some of the men on the other, do not grasp at every little turn of the market that takes place in their favour. Grant also, as Mr. Thornton points out, that if tremendous battles have been lost by the men, still they have led to after-concessions on the part of the masters in order to avoid a recurrence of such struggles; and that there has been this good effect in certain strikes, that they have allowed over-large stocks to be decreased. Grant also that where a trade is in the nature of a monopoly, as in the case of the London Dockers, or in a less degree the building trades, that wages may be pushed up *for a time* considerably higher than they would have gone, or than they can healthily go, as regards the trade itself; grant all this, yet is this a sufficient compensation for the state of war that is established between men of the same trade, between different trades, and between employer and employed; for all the individual inconvenience and restriction, and the loss of individual free action; for all the arbitrary things done by those in power, and the temptations towards coercing others; for all the sums that go daily and hourly in war-subscriptions, for such sums as the £427,000 of wages lost in the great Preston strike, or the £325,000 of the London building labourers in 1869, or, as the Economist reckons it, the millions that have been lost, all things counted, in the late Australian strike; for all the time and energy of the men spent on the unions; and, last of all, for the coming perfection of Unionism, when society will be split into two sections, living, like France and Germany, in the highest state of tension towards each other? If it can be shown that Unionism cannot permanently alter the wage of labour, and that economical injury constantly results from its action, would it not be wise and right for every unionist to reconsider the whole matter, and ask himself if he cannot spend the very limited amount of time and energy, that each man possesses, to serve the cause of labour in some other fashion?

It has been often said by economists that, as wages are paid out of that part of capital called the wage-fund, the true method of increasing wages is to increase the whole body of capital. This doctrine has been bitterly attacked, but it has never been substantially shaken. It is true that some part of wages may be deferred, and not paid until the product of labour has been realised, but that only means that the wages fund at a given moment may be looked on as consisting in part of new capital as well as old capital; it is also true that some products of labour may become capital in a few days or weeks; it is also true that at certain moments the capital that has been produced may be increased from what has already gone into consumption, as if everybody who had three coats determined to put one of them into the market; but the all-important fact— which in reality is a mere truism—remains, that only as the methods of production are improved and more is produced at less cost, can more be divided between employer and employed. Let it be clearly seen how the worker is benefited by increasing production, and by better and cheaper methods of production. Wages may remain the same; employers' profits may remain the same; and yet the labourer's condition be wholly changed by better production. Suppose that the employer and workman divide the product in the proportion of three to seven, three to the employer and seven to the workman, and suppose that the day's work today produces four, where yesterday it produced one. Then both the employer and workman get the advantage of seven and three multiplied by four instead of one. It is only necessary for this improvement in production to affect all articles used by the workman, and then as regards all such articles, his wages remaining the same, he is better off as four to one.[3] A clear perception of this method by which labour is benefited, shows us several great truths; how fatal is all protection; how unfair to the rest of labour are any forms of restriction and monopoly in certain trades, inasmuch as these trades take more and give less in the general exchange; and how un-

---

[3] As Professor Cairnes pointed out, whilst all improvements in manufactures help the workman, what tells against him is that his special article of consumption, food, gets dearer, as population increases, and lower-class soils are called into requisition. Against this, however, a good deal has to be set off. We have probably nearly as much room left for new knowledge and improvement in method, as regards the growth of food, and the use and preparation of food, as there is in other directions. We have only to think of unsettled questions, as regards sewage, the possibilities of certain plants storing up nitrogen from the air, and the growth of vegetarianism as a diet, to realise what changes the food question may undergo. Moreover, the workmen's wants are now extending in so many directions. Clothing, literature of all kinds, implements, better house accommodation, materials of culture and amusement, locomotion from railways to bicycles, and many other things, now begin to form a regular part of his budget; and as regards all these articles, he takes his enlarged share that results from improved production. The effect of modern years has been to call into existence an increasing number of articles, which are of increasing importance to him.

Professor Cairnes also laid stress upon another point adverse to the

wise are the struggles over the ratio or proportion in which the product is divided, when the matter of prime importance is to improve production, and thus increase the share falling both to employer and employed.

The question will however be asked, in face of modern industrial improvements, Why then are not our labourers better off? Amongst other reasons, the first and foremost reason must be that capital is not produced fast enough, or economically enough, which itself arises from various reasons—for instance, because of the stupid struggles between labour and capital; of the far too great luxury on the part of many of the rich, and their lavish expenditure on perishable articles, which when destroyed leave the world no richer—an expenditure, which, as they do not perceive, employs but wastes labour (if every rich person would religiously invest in industrial concerns £1 for every

---

workman. A large quantity of capital in a manufacturing country tends to take a fixed form, to be invested in machinery and buildings; and such fixed capital represents the profits of employers, and a permanent tax, therefore, that has to be paid to them. It is true; and for that reason I so earnestly desire to see a regular organised movement amongst workmen for investment, so that they might gradually become the part-owners of this fixed capital. Every workman should religiously invest something, if only 2*d.* a week, for this object; and every workman should belong to a Union that would make the investment for him. One other point, however, of an opposite tendency should be considered. As capital flows plentifully into a trade, bringing with it better machinery and better buildings, at first the owner of such better equipment obtains a higher profit than the owner of second-rate working material. He is like the owner of a better soil, and gets the difference of profit that exists between the two soils. But presently in manufacture the second-rate man tends to be eliminated, and the competition is then between men, who once were the best men in the trade, but after a few years only represent the average—having yielded the first place to later comers, who in their turn bring in later improvements. The consequence of this is that production is improved, the whole

£4 spent on himself, the change would be enormous in our prosperity); of imperfect systems of saving amongst the workmen; of imperfect free-trade in several directions, especially in the matter of land; of the restrictions and jealousies of trades unions; of the imperfect direction of joint-stock enterprise, which is as yet only young in the world; of considerable quantities of badly trained labour —our reformers not paying enough attention to offering facilities for third-class men to improve themselves; of the present fashion of sanitary reforms, applied officially and compulsorily, and the neglect of the individual intelligence of the people, on which far more depends; of the imperfect development of our moral qualities in every class which leads to bad and untrue work of every description and to waste; of the meddling and muddling of big and little Governments, which sends capital abroad, hinders

---

product is increased, and all concerned—except the manufacturer, who has fallen from the first to the second place—get a larger quantity as their share. The workman's share of the product is not increased in proportion (as regards the employer), but it is increased in actual quantity, because the product itself is increased. In this way fixed capital is on the side of the workman; as a tax, it is always tending to disappear; always tending to drive inferior and old-fashioned industrial apparatus out of existence, and thus to lessen the cost of production, and to give larger amounts of the product both to the employer and the employed, though the proportions that go to them respectively are unchanged. Here lies the whole gist of the matter. The workman has simply to care about the increase of the product, leaving the market to arrange the proportions that come to him. They will be increasingly in his favour. It is indeed to the workman more than to any other person that free-trade is of vital importance. The man who wants to be protected is the second-rate employer, with backward methods, who feels that he is being squeezed out by the better methods. One can only be very sorry for his position, which is often a hard one; but to protect him is to sacrifice general prosperity.

the workmen learning how to associate for their own purposes, wastes an enormous amount of energy in political
struggles, and weakens the productive machinery of the
nation, on which everything depends; and, lastly—
though many other reasons might be given—that many
of our ablest men do not go into trade, which is one of the
best and noblest occupations, partly because we have
foolish superstitions in favour of the professions, partly
because Government exactions and restrictions, joined to
labour troubles, not only lessen the reward of the employer, which is naturally but small in an old country and
age of sharp competition, but tends to deprive the trade
life of its enjoyable character.

Is it therefore worth while, I would ask of all open-
minded trade unionists, to be quarrelling about the proportion in which the product is to be divided, when the
great aim must be to make the course of production easier
and smoother, get more brains and invention devoted to
the work, and everywhere increase the points of concord
and lessen the points of fiction? Universal Unionism would
not help matters; for successful production depends upon
the willingness and, so to speak, good temper of capital—
its readiness to run risks and try new methods—and the
theory of universal Unionism—if candidly stated—is to
get capital into a corner, and make a mere labour's drudge
of it. Partial Unionism—even if effective—is only the momentary (not the permanent) bettering of certain trades at
the expense of other trades. Of course a trade unionist
might reply that the advance of wage may be taken, without raising prices, from the profits of the employers. But
that is in itself unlikely to happen, and not even perma-

nently profitable to the men if it does happen. The profits
of one trade are in strict relation to the profits of another
trade—capital, just as labour, always trading to an equality, and every trade expanding by the inflow of capital
when profits rise above the ordinary level.[4] It may be replied that this is true, allowing for some lapse of time, but
that the profits of the employer begin to rise the moment
that some turn in the market favours a special trade. That
also is true; but let us see what happens, first, if no trade
union interferes; and secondly, if it does interfere. Let us
suppose that the price of pig iron advances, that trade becomes brisker, and more iron is manufactured. The first
result of this is that unemployed men are brought in, and
half-time becomes full time for the employed men. Good
for the men in either case, even though for the moment
there is no rise in wages. But increased production means
lower prices, and though these lower prices check the employers' desire to produce, they also enlarge the demand
of purchasers, so that we may suppose that the trade still
goes on expanding. But this second expansion must result
in higher wages. The unfilled cisterns have now been filled,
and there must be an overflow. The unemployed have been
brought in, and the competition amongst the masters for
the men must carry the wage up. And notice in this instance that the rise has come about in a perfectly healthy
natural manner. There have been no disputes; contracts
have come in and been accepted; the trade has expanded
and contracted according to natural requirements; whilst

---

[4] This does not mean that the same percentage of profit exists in all trades,
but that the higher percentage is always balanced by disadvantages of
various kinds.

in the case of the men the unemployed have first been brought in, and then wages have moved slowly but surely up with the expanding trade.[5] Suppose also that the men have not at first secured the whole rise that ought to come to them. Are they injured? No. For if the profit of the masters is at all in excess it produces the very thing that is most in the interest of the men. They borrow capital and enlarge their turn-out, whilst, if the upward movement seems likely to last, new employers begin to enter the trade.

Now, take the other example. The same favourable movement of trade has taken place; but this time the union, on the alert, has insisted on a rise of wages. This rise of wages, perhaps slightly in excess of what the rise in prices justifies, may check the enterprise of the employer. Deprived of a part of the extra profit, he is less inclined to enlarge his business; he is puzzled about the future action of the men as regards the contracts which are offered him; at the same time the rise in prices following upon both the original movement in the trade and the subsequent rise in wages, is checking consumption and therefore checking the expanding condition of the trade, although so far as it exceeds the rise in wages it is tempting the employer to enlarge his operations.

Now I think it is hardly possible to review the two processes, remembering how all strain between employers and employed checks production, remembering the unwise things that will be done on both sides, the mistakes made on both sides, the waste of time and energy on both sides,

---

[5] Of course the two movements have been taking place together, but in an unregulated condition the employment of the unemployed would tend to be the first movement.

in offensive and defensive preparations, and the fatal effect of a fight at the moment when trade is becoming favourable, without believing that the workman would actually gain more in wages (I do not speak of a trade where there is a monopoly, which stands on a different footing) if his union abstains from all interference in the matter. The union is so liable to make mistakes; the market, left to itself, will not make mistakes. I suspect the union often acts like a fisherman, who snatches the bait out of the fish's mouth, in his hurry to secure his prize, instead of waiting for the fish to pouch it. The first rise in a trade is the bait to the employer to enlarge his business, put on more hands, and accept contracts. When he has once taken those steps, the wage must rise; even if the workman's share in the profit does not come to him quite as quickly as, strictly speaking, it ought, he has no occasion to repent it. It is probably the very best investment that he could have made. It is ground-bait, and with moderate patience will bring far more to his basket than what he loses at the moment.

But it may be urged that all this danger may be prevented by the sliding scale. The sliding scale has many virtues, as it removes to a great extent that uncertainty from the mind of the employer which is so fatal to successful production. But the sliding scale has special difficulties of its own, as, for example, where different elements are concerned in the price, so that a higher price may not mean a higher profit to the employer.

Of course, trades unions have a power to raise wages for a time in trades which are a monopoly, as in the Dockers' Union, or in trades which are partly a monopoly, as the building trades. But this power is both hurtful to others and limited in its own extent. In the first place, such extra wage is taken from the pockets of their fellow-labourers. It is in fact nothing but war against labour. Taking advantage of their position, these monopolists accept the labour of their fellow-workmen at a lower price, whilst they charge a higher price for their own. And does it profit them? The trade is pinched and starved by the high prices; there is perpetual war between employers and employed, wasting the extra gains of labour; capital arms itself at all points, and retaliates; quick brains begin to devise new methods of circumventing the monopoly and working through other trades or through other channels; whilst the men succumb to the universal fate which overtakes all those, poor or rich, who are artificially protected, and begin to deteriorate in their own character. There is also another consideration. The men not only hurt themselves as consumers, by restricting their own trade, but they may throw out of gear other allied trades, and by depressing the production of these other trades still further, hurt both themselves and all other workmen by reducing the general product. Under a free-trade system, it is impossible to measure the amount of disturbance that may be caused by even one dam being thrown across the supply of some particular labour. It is the interest of all other trades, as well as of the public, to discourage all such dams, and to make the free-trade footing universal for all. I do not mean that *A* and *B* should accept work on any terms other than those that they themselves approve; but that they should throw no dam round their labour by preventing *C* from taking a share in their work or from accepting terms which they decline. That is the true labour principle, universal individual choice, and no pressure exerted upon others.

Mr. Thornton (On Labour, p. 281) has supposed that in several cases the pressure of trades unions can permanently raise wages. Whilst I respect much that he has written, I do not think he has thought any of these cases thoroughly out. Excluding a monopoly or half-monopoly, and taking the case of expanding trade, or of an increased product, it can be shown that under a free system the extra profit must eventually come to the men, whilst the restriction or the pressure, employed to gain that profit, is likely in the end to destroy the extra profit by lessening the vigour and expansion of the trade. In the case of a universal rise of wage, he argues that capital would have no choice, no power of helping itself; but a universal rise in wage, without a universal rise in price—which latter rise would benefit nobody, but leave us all, with some momentary exceptions, as we were—is very unlikely to take place. The fact that capital goes so largely abroad shows that, as things are, we are near the margin of profit; and a slight unfriendly pressure exercised upon capital, a slight discouragement to its investment, would probably do far more in reducing wages by reducing the amount of capital employed, than in raising wages by raising the proportion of the product which comes to the labourer. Independently of this, the truth is, that the greater becomes the pressure of trade unions, the greater tends to be the rate of profit demanded by capital, in order to recoup risks and inconveniences, just as the existence of usury laws drives up instead of lowering the rate of interest; whilst the less the pressure and interference of the unions, the lower tends

to sink the rate of profit. Lastly, Mr. Thornton instances
the case of much capital invested in buildings and plant,
which could be nipped safely by the union because it could
not be withdrawn without great loss. But that is profit for
the moment at the cost of sacrificing the profit for the future. 'Once bit, twice shy.' The capital which is so treated
avoids the trade in question, like a plague-infested district,
and the trade suffers grievously instead of profiting by
such folly. Nor is it right to say a trades union could permanently raise wages in the case of increased product. If
such increase were general over the whole field of production, all the labourers would profit, with or without trade
unions, for there would be a larger product-fund to be
divided amongst them, and each man's labour would exchange for more. It should however be remarked that an
increased product in one trade, other trades remaining un-
developed and inactive, would not directly benefit the labourers of that trade—except so far as they consumed
their own product—since they would receive only small
quantities of the products of other trades in exchange for
their own larger product. It would, however, benefit them
indirectly, for it would imply that their trade was in a
vigorous and expanding condition, and was probably in
the hands of a higher and more efficient class of employer.
Mr. Thornton also says (276) that if in an expanding trade
with rising prices, the employers were to raise wages, then
there would be no need for capital to come in (and thus
reduce prices and presently wages, by restoring the balance of supply and demand); but that the employer would
go on receiving only normal profits, whilst the trade remained stationary. He forgets, however, that the labourer,

having got the whole rise, is at once placed in an abnormal position, and that other labourers would be attracted to his trade. The consequence would be that the labourer with the extra profit must either dam back by some artifice the inflowing labour, or lose his extra profit. He therefore would not be profited except at the expense of other labour.

Moreover, at the same time Mr. Thornton ignores the meaning of the rise in price. The rise in price almost always indicates greater demand, in some form, and as all large works pay better when fully employed, the production would be at once increased and new capital be necessarily brought in. Each employer would know that another employer would begin to run full time; and if he did not, it would be at the expense of the whole public, who would run short of their supply, and pay higher prices than they need pay.

Perhaps here it is right to say one word about high wages. They may be the truest sign of national health and vigour; or they may be just the reverse. If they are the result of monopoly, because in some special field labour has cornered capital, and by violence has driven other labour out of competition, or the result of the high prices existing under a protective tariff, they only indicate unhealth of the body economical, and are sure to be accompanied or followed by disturbances of various kinds; if they are the result of perfectly free competition existing everywhere, then they are the truest sign of health, for they show that capital is abundant; that being safe and unharassed, it is content with a small reward; that the labour itself is of high quality and therefore rightly commands a high reward, and that the product which is being turned out is sufficient to give this high reward to the labourer. Blessed would be such a country; for one could safely say of it, that the good sense, the self-restraint, the friendliness between classes, and the intelligence of its people were as fully expressed in those high wages as its adherence to that perfect free-trade and perfect competition which are the only equitable conditions for all.

Here however it might be urged, as it would be by some economists, that all this is true, demonstrably true, that it is only a truism to say that the labour of the country never can obtain for itself, except at the expense of other labour, more than the free and open market will yield, but that such a regulation of wages belongs to a state of perfect competition; that competition is still very far from perfect; that the labourer cannot take his labour to the best market and make the best price of it; that often ignorance on his part and other difficulties stand in his way; that there is amongst employers that 'tacit combination' of which Adam Smith spoke; and therefore that the Union of the workman is the necessary answer to the imperfections of the market.[6] Granted, if you like; granted, that competi-

---

[6] As regards combinations of masters, it must not be forgotten that it is in the interest of masters in some trades to preserve a state of restriction and monopoly; since, partly owing to the restricted numbers of the men, trade secrets, etc., they are able to make it difficult for new capital to enter such trades. It is in these cases that combinations of masters for settling wages are likely to be successfully carried out. In open trades the new employer is unlikely to enter into any such combination. He brings with him the advantage of all new improvements, probably has considerable capital behind him, and is determined to get good labour, even if he pays a slightly higher price than the market price. If the men would resolutely determine in their own general interest to discountenance a close or restricted trade

tion is not perfect, that there are many obstacles in the way of the labourer obtaining the perfectly just rate—*just* as declared by competition—in the open market, yet what is the true course to follow? To turn our backs on the method which must be pronounced to be the true one, because it is still imperfect, and plunge into an interminable morass of restriction and regulation, through which we can only make our way by guess-work and reckless adventure; or, instead of this, press steadily on in what we know is the true direction, and gradually remove the obstacles in our way? What we have to fear is not competition, but imperfect competition. No man, whether he is street-sweeper or writer of the highest philosophy, can reasonably claim more than what his work is worth to his fellow-men. Suppose that every man's work could be put up at a national auction, and sold with the whole nation as bidder, could any man reasonably complain of the result? He would have obtained the highest that his fellow-countrymen were willing to give; he has no title to more; and if by any device he succeeds in extracting more, he is behaving with something that is very near to dishonesty, since he is forcing this higher price at the expense of others.

Now let us see how far such perfect competition as I have sketched, a competition, under which men could realise the true value of their labour according to the wants

---

anywhere, they might depend, under the circumstances of today, upon the influx of new capital for making any combination of masters in the long run untenable. Should such combination be maintained, no better field could be found for a co-operative association, or a joint-stock company, run by the men.

of their fellow-men, is possible. *In old days it was not possible.* When villages and country towns lay cut off from each other, and ignorant of each other's doings, there could only be local not general competition. Now all is changed. Now-a-days we have both publicity and mobility. The spread of the press, the post that penetrates everywhere, the railways that link us together, all these are making it more and more possible for men to know the value of their labour and to offer it in the best market. Of course there are still left many restrictions and impediments, and many things still left to do to perfect the free labour mart—that outcome of a very high civilisation. Amongst these restrictions are the restrictions of trades unions, at which I have already glanced, which may limit the numbers engaged in a trade, which may disallow the non-unionist working with the unionist, and prevent a man acquiring a trade at any moment of his life. Till these restrictions are done away with, there can be no true labour mart. To get rid of these restrictions must be the work of a reforming party within the unions themselves; whilst the employers go on steadily with their present policy of opening registers of what is called 'free-labour,' and then of organising the free-labour men into unions for their own protection. To be weak is miserable indeed, and the non-union men will only take their proper place by acting together. But when these restrictions are removed, there is a good deal to be done. Every place should weekly report the state and the wants of its labour market—one statement being made by employers, one by the men; the Gazette of the Unions might contain notice of every shop and the number of men employed in it, with notes both by the men and the employer as to wages offered and the class of labour wanted. Unions might also probably do something in the way of owning and letting lodgings for their own members in search of work; and different trades could be combined for the same purpose. Once the great mass of our workmen recognise that the true and fair policy for all is making the labour-market as free of access as possible to all, of diffusing the widest information, and leaving every class of labour in the same trade to accept its own rate of pay and work its own number of hours, much can be done to help this object. The needful thing is to get effort into the right direction. To make it clear, let me sketch what would be the attitude of the men under the new state of things, and the part which their unions would play. They would stand on this ground. They would leave every man free to settle his own price of labour, just as every shopkeeper settles his own prices, though all prices would be published and some might be recommended. They would let every man follow his own inclination as to the number of hours he worked, or the character of his work—the result of which would be that a natural differentiation would take place, some workshops running longer, some shorter hours; some containing the pick of the workers, some the second-class and some the third-class men. They would break down every fence that prevented a man acquiring a trade for which he had an aptitude, and there would be nothing to prevent clever men, as happens even now in a limited way, following different trades at different times. There would be no minimum of wage, except such as each man chose to fix for himself, and there would be no strikes, such as exist to-day. In the case of a serious disagreement between an

employer and his men, the union would remove all such
men as wished to leave, giving them an allowance for so
many weeks whilst they were finding new employment.
But there would be no effort to prevent the employer obtaining new hands. All that had happened would be stated
in the Union Gazette, and it would be left for those who
chose to engage themselves at the vacant shop, to do so.
There would be no strike, no picketing, no coercion of
other men, no stigmatising another fellow-workman as
'scab,' or 'knobstick,' or 'blackleg,' because he was ready
to take a lower wage—all this would be left perfectly free
for each man to do according to what was right in his own
judgment. If the employer had behaved badly, the true
penalty would fall upon him; those who wished to leave
his service would do so; and the facts of the case would be
published. That would be at once the true penalty and the
true remedy. Further than that in labour disputes has no
man a right to go. He can throw up his own work, but he
has no right to prevent others accepting that work.

Under this system there would be no unions of exactly
the present type, but there would be far more association
amongst the men. The probability is that almost every man
would belong to some form of union. Information would
be the first great purpose. Information would not only be
supplied about labour and the state of the market, but about
the character of the shops. The employers would state their
terms and the quality of the labour they required. Publicity
would be an important agent of improvement; those workshops in which the comfort and health of the worker were
specially cared for would be described, and the effect of
their good example would be to bring others slowly up

from their lower level. At the same time the men, now that they had ceased to pile up great funds which might at any time be dissipated in war, would invest far more in remunerative undertakings. The union being no longer a war-machine would serve many great purposes. One great object that lies before every workman is to have two sources of revenue; his labour earnings, and his return from industrial investments. If all the money wasted in labour-war had been invested in industrial concerns, wages would be higher than they are now, and the men would be part owners of a considerable amount of the industrial machinery of the country, having gained the increased wealth, the business knowledge, and the influence, which would follow from such part ownership. Investment for their members will be a leading function of the new unions. By means of the weekly subscriptions they will be always buying shares in the industries of the district, in water, gas, omnibus, tramcar, dock and railway companies, in the great industrial concerns where their members work, and then passing these shares on to the individual members, as the small weekly payment comes up to the required amount. So also with land and houses. The unions would act as house-building societies, building or purchasing houses, and then passing them on in return for small monthly payments to their members. Those members who did not wish to purchase would hire direct from the union, which would itself become a larger owner of house property for this purpose, of a better and more convenient character than those houses in which workmen now live. More than this, every union of town-workers would have its farm in the country—held in good fee-simple, and not under any imperfect land-nationalisation tenure—which would provide pleasant and healthful change for its members in turn. Members would erect their own wooden rooms for the summer; there would be a sanatorium, and possibly certain articles, like fresh eggs and milk, would be regularly supplied to those who cared to make such an arrangement. The union would also offer certain training advantages. When work was slack and men were unemployed, workshops would be open where men would acquire a facility in the use of certain tools, and the power of taking up other kinds of work. It is hardly too much to say that every man would be more independent in life if he were up to a certain point a carpenter. At times of depression there are many simple things for his own domestic use that each man might make; and just as so many Norwegian farmers work in silver or make boats during the long winter evenings, so should the great bulk of English workmen have other occupations to fall back upon in times of non-employment. Besides the workshops, there would be educational opportunities, so that no unemployed man would let his time be wasted, as so cruelly happens at present. The New Union, like some of the London workmen's clubs, would have many different funds— each purpose, at which I have glanced, having its own fund, to which each member would subscribe or not as he chose; the out-of-employment fund, the benefit fund, the intelligence fund, the investing fund, the house-owning fund, the land-owning fund, the educational or workshop fund, and such other funds as were found desirable. Those who had chosen to subscribe to the educational fund, might in a serious time of depression be altogether withdrawn for some months from the labour-market—a voluntary levy of the other workers being added to their own fund.

I cannot follow any further, as I should like to do, the useful operations which the New Union would perform for the men. Once relieved from the miserable duty of fighting the employer, its energies would be called out in many directions, which are scarcely in the region of imagination at present. There is no want, intellectual or physical, which they would not strive to supply, often in competition with the open market—as can be seen today from what the best of the London clubs are beginning to do for the men. Sometimes, perhaps often, they would be beaten by what the trader offered, sometimes they would beat the trader; but the outcome would be for the ever-increasing advantage of the men. That is the true use of co-operation, to act as another competitive force, and thus to improve, not to replace, the competitive forces that are already in existence, whilst it is itself continually improved by them.

Such would be a part of the result of the abandonment by the men of their war-organisations. The whole result I cannot sketch here; I can only lay stress upon the vast effect of transferring the energy and intelligence that are spent today upon war-purposes to the direct purpose of reconstructing the circumstances of the workman's life. Now let us look in another direction—at the effect upon capital of substituting peace for war. Capital relieved of all attacks and of all misgivings would become intensely active. The same wise spirit in the men which had led them to abandon all attacks upon it through their organisations, would also lead them to put a sharp curb upon the mis-

chievous activities of the politician, and to prevent his
happy-go-lucky interference with it. Capital would thus
have that sense of complete security, which is beyond all
value to it. It would know that under all circumstances it
would receive its full market reward, however small it
might be. The consequences would be that this country
would become the home and storehouse of capital. Capital,
which now so largely drifts abroad into very speculative
enterprises, because in so many matters it feels uncertain
about the future, would prefer to develop new home enterprises; and not only would wages rise, but many useful
commercial undertakings would be carried out on behalf
of the workmen which now are left undone. In two senses
the workmen, if they so choose it, may become the masters
of capital. They may encourage capital to such an extent,
that the competition of capitalists will drive the reward of
labour up to the highest point, and the reward of capital
down to the lowest point; and secondly, being the largest
body of consumers, they may have capital at their feet,
trying to find out and discover their every will and pleasure. We have had lately a significant example of this new
disposition of capital in railway travelling. The third-class
passenger is found to be of more importance to the railway
company than any other passenger; henceforth his convenience and his pleasure will be more and more appreciated, whilst the first and second-class passenger will sink
in the scale of consideration. Then the ready inflow of
capital does so much to keep all trades in a healthy and
vigorous condition, and thus to raise the general product,
and thus to raise wages. With capital come in new brains,
new methods, new machinery. The old, cramped and per-

haps unwholesome factory, with its obsolete machinery, cannot live alongside of its new rival, and is gradually weeded out. The second-class employer and unthrifty manager is removed in the same way. Thus both efficiency is always obtaining, where capital flows freely in, and the product is always tending to increase. Let it be said again and again that upon the increase of this product depends the prosperity of the workmen, as a body. If this product is small, no earthly ingenuity, no organisation, no government systems, no grants in aid, no form of protection, can make the general condition of the labourers good. It is altogether past praying for. If, on the other hand, this product is large, and goes on steadily increasing beyond the increase of population, whilst all industrial processes are being improved in themselves, nothing can prevent the material prosperity of the workmen. Of course, as happens with every class, we may through mental and moral deficiencies throw away a large part of such prosperity; but with time will come the development of the qualities that are still lacking. One thing however—before alluded to— is worth repeating. A special trade may be working on free-trade principles and producing largely, and yet its members may not be better off than the members of other trades. They are not better off, just because other trades are cramped and restricted, are repelling capital, are not doing their duty in the general work of production. The first trade adds bountifully to the general wealth, but receives in poor proportion from the others; these others profit by its large production, whilst it itself suffers from their restricted production. It is the workmen's interest therefore that no trade-monopoly should exist anywhere, that every trade should be free from restrictions, should be attracting capital, should be producing largely and efficiently, so that in every direction where each man exchanges the product of his own labour, he should receive much in return. Moreover, the efficient direction of labour and the efficient production which take place where capital flows in freely help the workman in another manner. The middleman tends to be eliminated, and then there is more to be divided. He can only be safely eliminated by natural processes. Sometimes he is of real use and helps production; sometimes he is not; but this cannot be decided by a blind strike, but only by allowing the forces of competition to act upon him.

The point then that I urge upon Trade Unionists and all workmen is the same point I should urge upon nations. Seek to get rid of war. Seek to get rid of the war-organisation, which is a terrible hindrance to all developments of a higher kind. Give up attacking capital. Leave capital to reduce its own reward, which it will do far more effectually than you can do, by competition with itself. Create for it the most favourable atmosphere. Cultivate with all the better employers friendly personal relations. Disregard stories of excessive profits. Here and there some men, possessing powers of a very high order, and excelling in commercial judgment and aptitude for organisation, may build up great fortunes. Don't grudge such man a single penny of their wealth. They are the true servants and helpers of all. Remember that all ordinary profits are tending to fall. Indeed some economists go so far as to believe that in the future money will cease to pay interest. Be this true or not, let us suppose for a moment that by giving up trade union war the workmen should see, if it were only for a time, a large profit left in the hands of capitalists, whilst no rise took place in their own wages; would that be an unmixed evil for them? The answer must be 'No.' Because not only, as we have seen, would such trade be increasingly prosperous, but because the high profit is the very stimulus that is wanted to develop the workmen's co-operative and joint-stock association. The difficulty that now stands in the way of these associations is that small trade profits are not easily made, large trade profits with difficulty. If a large profit could be made easily in any trade, workmen's combinations could at once come into existence. Thus, looked at in every way, the workman has the ball at his feet, if only he will not kick it away from him. As the wealth of the country increases, larger and larger shares of it must come to him. He has only to let the natural processes go on, to resist all temptation to fight, or to rely upon artificial protection for his labour, and thus to shield himself from the stimulus which we all want to keep our good qualities free from rust, whilst he turns his spare energies in the direction of carrying out the things which most affect his comfort and happiness, and puts all his spare cash religiously into industrial investments, to become, as he is probably entitled to be, the true owner of this world and all that therein is—with a few spare corners perhaps left for the rest of us idlers. Honestly, happily, with no hurt and no oppression of others, he can obtain all that the State-socialist vainly promises at the end of useless crime and revolution—for crime and revolution will not bring it; they are instruments that defeat themselves —and far more, for he can obtain it, whilst he preserves that priceless gift of remaining the master of his own actions, and not being under the regulation of other men.[7]

A few last words. Of course this abandonment of industrial war on the part of the workmen would be nearly in vain, if the politician is still allowed to play his usual high antics upon his own stage, if capital is to be harassed by ill-considered laws, its reward filched from it, and thus the growing inclination to invest is to be checked, if land is to be rated in such fashion, that the tenth part or the fifth part, or more, is taken of its yearly value, if it is to be tied up in a new form of settlement by such stupidities as compulsory Compensation for improvement Acts, if everybody who climbs to power is to indulge his fancies and speculations at the expense of other people, if public departments are to spend without any real control from the public, if every new interest is to have its own department

---

[7] It might be well to summarise here the two things which seem of paramount importance to the workmen. First, the carrying out of a reform within the Unions, in the direction of giving to each man a much wider choice as regards his own conduct. For example, no central authority should override the terms which any shop chooses to make with the employer and only those who individually wish to strike should do so. Secondly, the abandonment of struggles with capital over wages. It must be remembered that everything turns upon the willing temper of capital. Capital stands on this vantage ground, that to set production going, or to increase it, it must be attracted, eager, and filled with confidence. We have therefore to insist upon these general truths—that all war between capital and labour is fatal to the general good; that it cannot permanently increase wages, seeing that higher wages can only permanently come from larger and cheaper production, and that capital must be coaxed, not bullied, into the perfect performance of its true service; that capital should be thoroughly secure and at ease, so that on account of this ease it should be content with a lower reward, itself by competition with itself reducing that reward; that no violence or threat of violence from any quarter should be offered it; that employers should be constantly tempted to invest their

and its own minister, with the special office of securing to it a share of the public doles that are going, if the number of officials is to mount higher every year, and the area of regimentation is to grow larger, if municipalities and county councils are to be encouraged to undertake trade on their own account, and to be the instruments of preserving monopolies for certain favoured bodies of workmen, if local debts are steadily to increase, with little or nothing to show of permanent value in return, if splendid salaries are to be the politician's dazzling reward, if huge showy reforms, affecting only the outside of things, are to be encouraged, and all the healthy conditions for personal improvement to be made light of by the lawmakers, if free arrangements between employers and employed are to be prevented, and schemes like Employers' Liability (with all the mischief of uniformity about them) are to be forced on

---

profits in their business, thus enlarging their operations and increasing the fund that gives employment; that a certain part of the capital that now goes abroad should by this increased sense of security be kept at home; that the fullest encouragement should be given to employers to introduce improved processes and improved machinery, no employer being afraid to invest the largest sums of money permanently in his business; that by such improved processes all articles should be manufactured at the lowest possible price, thus ensuring to the workman the highest return from his wages, and thus favouring this country as regards the exportation of articles; that in no trade should there be any restriction or monopoly, seeing that the higher prices derived from such restriction and monopoly are obtained at the expense of other workmen, who only receive free trade prices for their labour, whilst themselves paying to such monopolists protective prices; that all labour should be free to move in such channels as best suited it, and that efforts should be directed to perfect the competition of the open market, as offering both the truest and justest return for the labour of each—such return being measured by the wants of the public; that workmen should be more and more induced to invest in industrial concerns, thus becoming the owners of the fixed capital of the

the whole nation, if lawyers and doctors are to enjoy
monopolies, with all the vices and few of the apologies of
trades unions about them, if every blessed occupation in
turn, including accountants, teachers, journalists, and I
presume at last street-sweepers, are to ask for charters
and are to regulate their own numbers, under the flimsy
plea of saving the public from incompetence, if the workmen's thoughts and energies are all to be given to these
worthless political methods and to the barren struggle for
power over each other, if the lies, self-seeking and hypocrisy of party warfare are to reign supreme in our hearts—
then the immense gain which would come from a cessation
of industrial war will be neutralised both by other forms of
monopoly and by the continuance of political war. Both
forms are equally mischievous. Both in due time will destroy the nations that give themselves up to them, for both
are opposed to the great principle on which alone happy
and progressive society can be founded—the unflinching
respect for every man's will about his own actions.

AUBERON HERBERT

---

country, and thus possessing a second source of income in addition to
wages; that investing unions should be formed for this purpose; that no
foolish legislative steps should be taken to restrict or impede joint-stock
enterprise, and thus to throw fresh difficulties in the path of the workman
becoming possessed of capital; and that the politician should not be allowed either to come between the employer and the employed, in the
arrangement of their affairs, or to interfere with the profits of the employer, upon which the whole fabric of production rests, and with it the
prosperity of the workmen.

INDEX

INDEX

COLOPHON

The Palatino typeface used in this volume is the work of Hermann Zapf, the noted European type designer and master calligrapher. Palatino is basically an "old style" letterform, yet strongly endowed with the Zapf distinction of exquisiteness. With concern not solely for the individual letter but also the working visual relationship in a page of text, Zapf's edged pen has given this type a brisk, natural motion.

Book Design by JMH Corporation, Indianapolis, Indiana
Typography by Typoservice Corporation, Indianapolis, Indiana
Printed and bound by Worzalla Publishing Company,
Stevens Point, Wisconsin